LOVED BACK TO LIFE SERIES

BECOMING PEARL
An Autobiography of Love
By Pearl Sunshine

SCP - Shepherds Care Publishing

© 2020 BY SCPUBLISHING / MICHAEL E. CHALBERG

SCPublishing / Shepherds Care Counseling Ministries

2473 S. Higley Road - Suite 104 PMB 210

Gilbert, Arizona 85295

Loved Back to Life Series

Becoming Pearl

An Autobiography of Love

By Pearl Sunshine

Editorial Supervision: Michael E. Chalberg

Paperback Edition – ISBN 978-0-9746464-8-0

Ebook Edition – ISBN 978-1-7349703-2-6

© Shepherds Care Counseling Ministries is a nonprofit 501c3 org. All rights reserved. No part of this publication may be reproduced or Transmitted in any form or by any means without written permission Of the author.

Unless otherwise indicated, Bible quotations are taken from the New Open Bible, Study Edition, Copyright © 1990 by Thomas Nelson Inc.

Order:	scpublishing@shepherdscareministries.org
Email:	Pearl.Sunshine@scpublishing.org
Web:	www.shepherdscareministries.org
Editor:	shepherd2001@yahoo.com

TABLE OF CONTENTS

Forward - SCPublishing v

Introduction: "Pearl" by Jesus vii

Preface – Pearl Sunshine viii

Chapters

1. Becoming Pearl 1
2. A Big Adventure 15
3. Fire and Ice 18
4. Arthur 24
5. Daddy 27
6. The Twelve 41
7. Rainbows and Bubbles 49
8. What's in a Name 63
9. An Ending 68
10. The Forest of Difficulty 79
11. Putting the Pieces Together 93
12. The Truth will Set You Free 107
13. The Fountain 119
14. Removing the Marks 134
15. It's off to Work We Go 148
16. An End and A Beginning 157
17. Battles 165
18. The Land of Rest 179
19. Suffering and Hope 192
20. The Festival of the Crow 202
21. Choosing Life 210
22. Soaking in His Presence 220
23. The Hill of Change 232
24. Steps of Faith 245
25. The Procession 259
26. To the Gates 266
    End Notes 274

Forward by SCPublishing

Our new collections of autobiographies entitled: **_Loved Back to Life Series_**, are being presented to all who have lost hope in the power of God's unconditional love...to heal and redeem His purposes for our lives. We live in both the physical realm and the larger spiritual realm simultaneously, yet it is the physical experience which often defines our understanding of spiritual realities. So, we seek to find meaning to these realities, when we encounter suffering and pain, rejection and condemnation in our relationships with others...who are supposed to love, nurture, provide for our needs and teach us the truth about why our Heavenly Father created us to have an eternal relationship with Him.

When this relationship is broken by evil's influence, through control of those around and over us...we lose hope and trust in the power of God's love to overcome this evil and we cry out to the Lord, *"You would have been kinder to never have created me...just let me die."* This is often our primary mistake in seeking answers to why it seems that God isn't answering our prayers and we feel abandoned by Him as though our condition means we are unworthy of His love and presence in our lives. We are afraid to trust in and hope for, the fulfillment of God's promises and purpose for us in Christ Jesus. This is why this first autobiographical set by Pearl Sunshine is given in her own words, changing only names of those involved, without holding back any reality of abuses by evil controlling her life. The drawings given of the actual events from early childhood, depicting clearly the actions of others... family and Satanic cults can be triggering of painful memories for readers who are themselves survivors of such abuses. We ask that the readers have the strength and courage to continue reading when possible, to discover the joys as well of being drawn into God's heart. Her purpose here is not to convince anyone of the truth of evil in our lives, or her strength in continuing to follow the path that Jesus has set for her, to trust God's love again.

Her purpose, and ours, is to challenge our readers to understand more fully why Jesus is calling to us to trust in Him, and His love to heal and redeem us...to do for us what we can't do for ourselves...without Him. If we can believe in the promises that; **"I will never leave nor forsake you"**, **"I will come to you in the darkest depths and overcome the evil to set you free"**, **"I will love you back to life... eternal life with me"** and **"In this world you will have tribulations, but rejoice for I have overcome this world,"** then we can know the truth of who Jesus is in this life, and trust again in the plans and purposes of our Father God's unconditional love in action... right now... right here, where you are at. If these autobiographies, and the ones to follow in this series, help you to seek a renewed relationship of trust in Him...then the suffering you read about followed by their free will choices to continue on the journey, will have been worth it to each author. The introduction of Pearl by Jesus can challenge us all about what He means by saying, **"My grace is sufficient for you, for my power is made perfect in weakness."** This is the power of God's love freely given to us to survive this world with Him until we go home.

Ultimately these books and the others that will follow in this series, are about the personal commitment that God makes to each one of us to bring healing, as revealed in these private journals of one group of people with Dissociative Identity Disorder (DID) or Multiple Personality Disorder (MPD), who accepted God's call to receive His promise of healing for 'wholeness' in Him... living as one person with Him.

Our first series of books, **Shattered People: Journeys to Joy - Love**, focused on specific issues of people with DID and their struggle to receive healing later in life so they could be 'acceptable' to be loved by family and relationships in their closest circumstances. I offer commentary and counseling in this series as pastor, friend and counselor for them to promote treatment methods and dialogue about trauma and abuse survival, especially about our common questions to God on suffering, survival and how we all can know God through relationships within community and in our one on one time with Him. .

This series however, **Loved Back to Life**, looks at the individual searching for meaning and purpose directly from God in conversation with Him, expecting answers from no one else... not counseling or outside help for most of their lives. They seek meaning for a lifetime of feeling alone in darkness... evil that defined who they were, before discovering they were never alone. How they and Pearl come to trust in Jesus' love placed very deep in their soul long ago was as hard to believe for them, as the memories of suffering being revealed as true by those who had endured them... and the healing Jesus gives to both. These books allow you the reader to learn from their struggle to know God... to trust Jesus... to accept the Holy Spirit and their will for her life and how receiving God's love is the purpose of her life... a purpose she now wishes to share with all who suffer... to risk allowing Jesus in with His answers for healing.

Editor & Fellow Servant – Pastor Mike

- Dr. Joe Johnson, pastoral counselor. D.Min - Fuller Seminary 4/2020

"Pearl's miraculous story of redemption, healing, recovery and freedom from unspeakable suffering is a witness to what most people would say is impossible when they read these books. God brings Pastor Mike alongside of Pearl to share his love of Jesus to witness in confidence the power of Jesus to redeem and minister healing to Pearl, including each one of her dissociative parts (*alters*) more than I have ever known. Pearl opens her heart wide to the readers to the many ways she is healing and recovering from incredible abuses physically, emotionally and spiritually. I have learned that the biggest factor in healing trauma is to personally know that we are not alone... this is the cry of attachment pain, "Is anyone with me... am I alone?" Jesus never gives up on reaching her as Mike didn't, as He does with us, and I believe she'll never give up on them trusting they will be there for her."

Book One P1 – *Out of the Darkness: An Autobiography of Love: Part One*
Book One P2 – *Out of the Darkness: An Autobiography of Love: Part Two*
Book Two - *Becoming Pearl: An Autobiography of Love*
Book Three - *The City of Hope: An Autobiography of Love*
Book Four – A journey still being written.

Pearl by Jesus

My little one you are my Pearl of great price. I have brought you out of the darkness and out of great suffering to be my jewel, my precious and beloved child. That is who you are and will always be. You will show others what it means to be a child of the king my little one. You will show them how loved and precious they are to me no matter what this world has taught them about who they are. You will show them the truth. I will take all of your pain my little one and all of your tears and I will use them to bring hope and joy to those who need it the most.

I will send you out my little one to those who are lost in the darkness, to my hidden children who do not know what it is to be loved or wanted. Your story will give them hope and through you they will see and understand that they too are loved and wanted. You will show the world who I am through the things that I have shown you my little one and through the person that you are. You will show them the truth about what it means to be a child, a true child of God. My little one you will know what it is to love and be loved. I will give you a heart that is open and free. Free to love those I give to you and free to be loved also.

You will teach others how to reach out to those who have been hurt like yourself my little one, not only in your words but also in your actions. You will be a light for me in places where few other lights shine. I will give you a joy that will shine out to those around you bringing hope and life to those who have not known either. My little one you will be my blessing and my gift to this world, a jewel in my crown. You know what it is to suffer my little one, but you will also know what it is to dance with joy. You will love me with all of your heart and follow wherever I will lead you and when all is said and done and I take you home to be where I am, you will be glad that you lived the life I had for you my little one. Though the cost is very high you will say that it was worth it. All this and more will be true of you my little one, because you are my Pearl... and this is who I have made you to be.

Preface by Pearl

I wrote these books because Jesus asked me to . He asked me to because he wants to show you who he is and how much he loves his children. It will be difficult to read sometimes, the things I talk about are real and painful. They are the truth of what happened to me, but it isn't the darkness he wants you to see so much as the light that shines in the darkness. I didn't hold back or hide what happened or my own pain and brokenness, because it's only when you see the darkness for what it is, it's impact and the difficulty of recovering from it that you can see the miracle of what Jesus has done in his healing of my heart. He wants you to see through my story what he is willing to do to bring his children out of the darkness into the light of his love. Whether you have been hurt like me or not, we all need Jesus to go into the broken places and bring his light and his healing. We all need to know that we are loved and safe, always.

I hope that you will continue to read even when it is difficult and painful, because it is in those places we meet Jesus and see him most clearly for who he is. Don't be afraid because he is right there with you as you are reading, ready to bring life and hope and healing to your heart just like he did for me. His love for you isn't any less, his truth is the same for you as it is for me. He is with you and loves you just as you are, and he knows who you can be, who he made you to be, which is more than you can imagine right now. He is faithful to walk alongside you and lead you forward as you say yes to him, even if your yes is very small to begin with, he will take it and work through it to draw you closer to him.

My story may seem extraordinary to you and parts of it are hard to believe or understand... but see it as the beginning of a journey to discovering more of who Jesus is. Allow yourself to question and to wonder. Give yourself time to ponder on his words which aren't just for me but are his gift to all of us. He is with us on our journey drawing us forward towards his heart of love for us. This is just another step, one that I hope you will be willing to take.

Chapter 1

Becoming Pearl

I was a new person. Again. I had blended with Blossom and now I was the one on the outside living Jennifer's life. It had all happened very fast, but I think Jesus had waited a long time before he let us see that I was there. I think that was so that we would both be ready for the blending to come very fast, and he made it happen so fast, because he was being kind to us both, but especially Blossom. It was very hard for her to accept this new truth, that it was Jesus' plan for her to be part of who I am.

If I told you the whole truth all at once do you think it would help you?
I think it would be better because then I wouldn't have to go through all this stuff of thinking you lied, and you don't love me and I can't trust you, and there is no hope and you make me do this over and over, and I can't do it any more... I can't...Crying
What are you holding on to my little one?
You... Crying
And have I changed my little one. Am I different in any way?
You don't seem different... Crying
Because I am not my little one. I remain the same always. My love for you is unending and unchanging my little one. You are my beautiful Blossom child and will always be so. I have rescued you out of great darkness. I am healing and restoring you and giving you a new life where you can love me and serve me for all of your days. None of that has changed my little one. It is just the same.
I just don't understand why you don't tell me.
So that you can learn to trust me my little one.
It isn't working Jesus.
My little one there will be many times when I do not tell you the whole of my plans for you. That does not mean that I am lying my little one or that you have got it wrong only that I have told you in part. I do this for many reasons my little one all of which are to help you and not to bring you pain.
I think it is too hard for me... Crying
No my little one. What it requires is trust my little one. Trust in who I am and not in your own understanding of the things I have said or done.
That is a very hard thing... Crying
Yes my little one I know but it is not too hard my little one. It is not too hard. It is for your good that I am leading you this way so that you can learn to trust me no matter what happens, no matter what you see or don't see. Even if the things I do are not what you expected, you will know that they are good my little one and that who I am and my love for you has not changed.
But if you aren't ever going to tell me...then why tell me anything. I get so confused and afraid Jesus and I am afraid you don't love me or want me and that it has all been a lie...Crying.
I know my little one I know but it is in these times that lies are broken and truth takes hold at a deeper level. It is in these times that I can draw you close because your need is so very great. I know that you do not understand why it has to be this way my little one, but a faith that is deep and strong does not come without pain or without testing.
Doesn't it?
No my little one it doesn't. There is not one of my servants who has not discovered this truth. The way is not easy my little one but it is worth it, always.
But why are you bothering so much with me, when it is Pearl...or someone else maybe who will need these things.

Because my little one everything you are will be given to her. I know my dearest one that you do not fully understand this either, but she is learning as you are learning. She is becoming as you are becoming. As you grow stronger, she grows stronger. It matters my little one because you matter.
Do I? Crying....
Yes my little one you do.
I have gotten lost Jesus. I am confused and afraid and I don't know who I am. I don't want to be here in his life. It doesn't matter if I am Blossom or Pearl not here and you won't make it stop... Crying.
Yes my little one I will. Hold on to me my little one. I am your strength. I will not let you go.
There is no escape... Crying.
My little one do not look to escape but look to me. I am all that you need.
But what is it all for Jesus? I don't want to be here... Crying
I know my little one but my purpose in you is being revealed. I know you do not see this my little one but in the life that is being given to you will bring many to me. That is your purpose my little one. That is who you are in this world. You are my light to a lost and broken people who have no hope apart from me. You are learning what this means my little one in so many different ways. Hold on and do not let go. My timing is perfect my little one and my love for you is unchanging. There is hope my little one.

I felt very sorry for Blossum. It was confusing for both of us, but Jesus did help us to understand a lot of things that we never had before. We hadn't really understood that blending is temporary for this life, and that in heaven we will all be separate again. We hadn't understood that we are all together, all wanted and needed to be one and whole in Jesus, to do what he has called us to do in this life. We hadn't understood that for Jesus, all of the alters are still themselves...he still sees each one even now. Blending doesn't change who we are, not for him.

Once I had blended with Blossum and it was just me on the outside, it was easier to see who I was because I wasn't getting mixed up with her. I wasn't very interested in finding out about me though. When Aj and Blossum had first been on the outside they were excited to discover what was different about them, what made them who they were, but for me this was the third time I was learning I was someone else. I wasn't convinced when Jesus said it was the last time, and that I was at the center and there was no one else hidden away. I was expecting to find out I wasn't Pearl at all and have to do it all over again. I didn't like having to replace people like Aj and Blossum, I was worried that people would be sad about losing the person I was replacing and wouldn't want me.

I do feel a bit sad Jesus and a bit worried about what I will say to people who know her.
Tell them the truth my little one that is all you must do. My dearest one they will understand even if they are sad for a time.
Maybe. But what you are doing looks crazy. Why would you want me on the outside? It doesn't sense Jesus.
Maybe not to you my little one but to me it makes perfect sense, because I know who you are. You are not defined by your age my little one or your ability, but only by who I say you are.
And who do you say I am Jesus?
You are my Pearl my beloved one and in me you can do everything that I have planned for you my little one, no matter how it looks to the outside world.

It didn't make any sense to me that Jesus would make me the outside person, that he would leave a nine-year-old in charge of the body of a middle-aged woman and ask her to live as that middle-aged woman indefinitely having to do all the things an adult does, and not be able to be the child he said I was. Blossum hadn't understood that either. To me it has seemed a bit like Gideon's men in the bible, where Jesus sends Gideon into battle, but keeps on sending more and more of his army away. We had started off with Jennifer a capable adult, then it was Aj who was sixteen, then Blossom who was eleven and now me...a nine-year-old.

It was hard to have to relearn who I was again, but it was a little bit easier than the first two times. This time I understood better that no matter what my name or my age or anything else about me that kept changing, I was always Jesus child. That didn't change. Jesus was helping me to learn that my identity is found in him and not in anything or anyone else. Not in the things I have done or not done, not in the things that have happened to me, not in the things I know, not in who other people say I am, but only and always who he says I am. When I asked the question, who am I? ...which I have a lot, he always answered first that I am his child. That has never changed. I am always loved and wanted and safe. That doesn't change. That made it easier, but I didn't like it. There was more for me to understand though, about why he had led me the way he had.

Who am I Jesus? I know you have called me Pearl and you say I am nine and I belong to you, but I don't know. I suppose this Pearl is a lot of people joined together and even though it is all me somehow, it is more than me...and that is ok but kind of weird. Like I can do and be so much more than me somehow. And I know I am in the mix somewhere. I don't understand it.

My little one everything that you see in yourself is you. It is true my little one that you have blended with many others but they are all a part of who you are. They are not separate my little one. They do not think or act independently of you. They are in you and part of you.

No... but if me in heaven is me without all of them, then the real Pearl... is the one without them. Is that right?

Yes and no my little one. In heaven you will not be joined with them as you are now. Each of you will be your own person, separate and distinct, but neither will you be the Pearl that you would be now without them my little one, for in heaven you will be made whole and complete and perfect in me.

So, the true Pearl...I won't see her until I am in heaven and that would be true even if I wasn't blended with others.

Yes my little one that is so.

I know I don't need to worry about it Jesus. I am who you want me to be here in this life...you made me with a purpose and maybe that's why I am so many in one. I don't know...I suppose so, but I am still not sure what it means to be Pearl in this world and I am not even sure what I mean by that really. Maybe I am trying to feel safe in who I am and put limits on who I can be and I don't think you want me to do that. You want me to...I don't know...live without limits because I am in you and you are in me and you don't have limits.

Yes my little one that is so. In trying to define yourself and saying I am this and I am not that, you are giving yourself limits and boundaries that I have not given you my little one. You can be whoever you are called to be. You are who I say that you are my little one in any given situation. It does not matter if you think you can't or you are not, in me you can be anyone my little one as I enable you.

But even so...I am me.

Yes my little one you are and even though you can be anyone I call you to be the person that I will call you to be is you my little one, but not your idea of who you are but mine.

Which is a lot bigger.

Yes my little one it is.

I think it would be hard to feel safe in that if I didn't trust you Jesus.

Yes my little one it would but I am helping you to trust me my little one so that you can be all things just as I enable you to be.

Maybe that is why you keep on changing who I am, or who I think I am so I don't get stuck in thinking this is what I am and what I can do. I have to say I don't know and maybe I can be that and maybe I can do that, because how can I know? I have to trust what you know about me, not what I know about me.

Yes my little one you do and what I know about you will always exceed what you know about yourself.

That is true Jesus. So, when you say to me that you want me to do something and I think I can't...well I am wrong because you know, and I don't.

Yes my little one exactly so and I will often ask you to do things you are not aware that you can do or be, but I know my little one. I know everything you are capable of not in your own strength my little one but mine.

So I don't need to be anxious about anything you ask me to do, because you know I can do it and you aren't ever wrong.

Yes my little one.

I suppose I still might not want to though Jesus, but mostly what gets in the way is fear...but I don't need to be afraid.

No my little one you don't. Not ever.

Because you know who I am, and I don't.

Yes my little one.

So I am Pearl but only you know what that means.

Yes my little one I do but you will also learn what it means my little one just not in the way that you have been thinking.

A different way to see myself.

Yes my little one, not defined as the world defines you but as I define you.

Which is very different.

Yes my little one very different.

And I suppose even though I am not living as Pearl age 9 with my story... somehow, I am more than that. I mean that doesn't really say who I am does it. Maybe I have been thinking it does, but it doesn't. Maybe it says something about me I don't know, but it doesn't say who I am and if I think living as that Pearl is living as me, then I am wrong and all that time Blossom spent wanting to do just that...it wouldn't have helped her discover who she really is would it.

No little one it wouldn't. In many ways it would have limited who she could be.

So by helping me learn that...that I am not the person the world will see me as...if it ever does see me... if I can learn now to see myself like you do then I won't be limited by that and I won't see myself in that way. I can be more and the person you see and not have those limits on me that say I am this or that and not other things.

Yes my little one.

So, it is a good thing I can't be that me because you have something bigger and better and more complete in mind.

Yes my little one I do. My little one you are not defined by your past. That is not who you are. Nor are you defined by your age. You are only defined by me my little one. I say who you are.

And maybe that has been too scary before Jesus. It is still a bit scary...like being free, being free is a bit scary, like being surrounded by empty space...but I'm held by you. If I'm flying, I am flying with you and so I don't need to be afraid.

No my little one you can walk forward into who you are and the full freedom I have for you confidently and without fear, because I am with you and I will never leave you.

That is kind of wow Jesus. And exciting because it means that anything is possible.

Yes my little one it does.

And even though life feels the same and kind of boxing me in all the time, maybe we have needed that. Maybe if all that was changing while we were changing...I was changing...it would have been too much and I wouldn't have been able to see this or to learn about who I am.

No my little one you wouldn't.

So, all the things we have complained and cried about most are the things you have, I mean they are the things that have been helping me to discover the truth about who I am and who you are.

Yes my little one.

And I so need to know those things before everything around me changes and people see me for being pearl and start telling me who I am and who I'm not.

Yes my little one.

Am I finally seeing and understanding Jesus?

Yes my little one you are. Everything I have been doing, everything I have asked of you and of Blossum and Aj and Jennifer before her, has been for your good my little one...because of my great love for you and my desire for you to see and understand who you truly are. To prepare you for what lies ahead so that you are not swept away by the thoughts and opinions of others, and so that you can fulfil the purpose I have for you my little one. Just as I have said.

You have said Jesus. Over and over and we just didn't see it or understand. It helps Jesus. It does...but keep showing me because I might forget and stop seeing and I don't want to. I want you to put these things deep in my heart and mind, so I don't have to keep on fighting the same battles. There are new battles to be fought Jesus...I don't want to have to keep on fighting the old ones over and over.

I will help you my little one. You are making great progress. Hold on to me my dearest one. We are going on a great and wonderful adventure together. There is nothing to fear from this for everything is in my hands and you are held and you are safe and you are loved. You are my pearl, my beloved one and together we will do many great and wonderful things.

That was such a big and important thing for me to see. That all the things he had been asking of us, all the things we hated most and struggled with and complained and cried about. All the things that were the most difficult and painful about the life we were living, were the very things Jesus was working through to do all the things he needed to, so that the promise could come and we would be ready when it did. I have needed reminding about this a lot of times. But it did get better for me once I saw this, because I had understood in my heart that there was a purpose in all of it. Just like he always said there was.

I still didn't really see it made much of a difference who I was, if I was pretending to be Jennifer. Why did it matter who I was? I didn't really want to spend time finding out about me, but Jesus seemed to think it was important. I was finding that life on the outside was much faster than life on the inside. Even though in a lot of ways it was the same because I had seen and experienced most of the outside life through Blossom, somehow it was different. I couldn't seem to keep up. Like I had to run while everyone else was walking. It was exhausting. I was getting used to being me and making all the choices and decisions that went with being the outside person, but I was still aware of the inside and the alters. I was still sad and in pain from the past.

That was a lot of things all at once. A lot of things to feel and a lot of things to try and get hold of and all the while living the outside life. And I was trying to understand where I fit in Jesus plan and if it was different now somehow.

I have been thinking...I know you know... and wondering about your plans and if I want to do them. I mean...I don't know what I think about them really. I feel like...I need to say yes to them, and I am not sure I have. Help me...I am not sure what I am saying.

My little one before you knew that you were you, you could not truly make your own choice about these things, but now you know that you are Pearl and you have chosen me for yourself and understand better your part in my plans for all of you,

choosing to say yes to those plans is important my little one. You will need to give yourself over to my will for you without reservation, if you are to accomplish everything I have for you.

I don't think I want to say no Jesus. But somehow, I am not sure I have said yes with all of me and I am not sure why, cos it's not any different just cos it's me now.

But now it is your choice to make my little one and that is the difference.

My own choice. That is a strange thing Jesus. To make my own choice. What will Pearl choose…about anything. I don't know the answers yet.

No my little one but I do.

I am scared about leaving here Jesus. I don't want to be here, but I am scared about leaving and going to America if that is what you will ask me to do.

Yes my little one it is when the time is right.

And I need to do that to do what you want me to.

Yes, my little one you do. You cannot do it here.

And what do you want me to do?

I want you to tell your story my little one and let people see who I am in and through your life. I want you to love the lonely and the broken and to show them that there is hope for them, that they are loved and wanted just as they are.

And can I do it Jesus?

Yes my little one you can.

I think being seen and known as Pearl will be so strange Jesus and I can't imagine what it will be like. Good and bad maybe. Telling my story will be hard…our story it is of course, but I am the one who gets to tell it. Is that right?

Yes my little one it is.

Did you give me special story telling powers Jesus?

I have given you the ability to tell your story so that it will touch the hearts of those who need to hear it my little one.

And loving people can be very hard Jesus. They aren't always nice, and we get scared even when they are. I don't know how good I will be at that.

I will be with you helping you my little one.

And it won't be like this Jennifer life?

No my little one it will be altogether different.

That is good Jesus but a bit scary too. But good. Will you hold my hand?

Yes my little one always.

And we do it all together.

Yes my little one everything we do will be done together. You cannot do it without me my little one.

No. I don't want to Jesus. I wouldn't like that. And will I like it?

Much of it will be a joy to you my little one even when it is difficult and painful as often it will be. Some things you will not like so much my little one, but they are still things that need to be done and I will help you to do them.

And will I like being Pearl?

Yes my little one you will. You will be happy to be who you are my little one.

That is good Jesus. That is very good. And will I have friends and get to do some fun things?

Yes my little one you will have many friends and there will be times of fun and laughter my little one. You will not be alone anymore.

That will be strange too. Maybe a bit difficult.

You will soon adapt to your new surroundings my little one and your new way of life. It will be difficult at first my little one just because it is so different, but you will be loved and held by me, and my servant will help you and love you also my little one as will many others. You will not be alone anymore.

Maybe I will have to learn about that Jesus because I don't think I know about it. I know you are with me and always will be and that is so good, but I am always alone really, except maybe with Mr. Mike because he sees me. It is kind of different with him.
Yes my little one it is for now. But that will change my little one as you are seen and known for who you are.
I don't know why we are talking about really Jesus, except I need to choose to keep on this path, don't I?
Yes my little one you do.
I do choose Jesus. It is a big adventure you have planned, and I suppose I won't like all of it but it is our adventure and I don't want to miss it.
Yes my little one that is good. It is very good.

Jesus said that making my own choices was part of becoming who I am, but I often found it hard because I couldn't see that it mattered what I wanted. Why should it matter if I have a choice, if I have to choose what others want anyway? There were lots of choices that I had to make now. They seemed a lot more difficult because it was often more about what other people wanted me to choose and I got afraid. I was afraid of not doing what they wanted, but often what they wanted me to do made me even more afraid. It was a huge pressure and like Blossum, it made me want to disappear. Cheryl was wanting me to go for routine medical scans. It terrified me and I knew I couldn't do it, but I couldn't explain my fear either and it just made me feel like I was bad. It helped a lot to talk to Jesus about these things. There wasn't anyone I felt I could really talk to about these things because I was afraid, they would tell me I should do it. I couldn't even talk to Mr. Mike about it, because it was embarrassing.

I wish it was all different Jesus.
I know my little one.
I am glad you love me and know and understand who I am Jesus. I am not sure anyone else ever will not even me. It seems so mixed up. Am I bad Jesus if I don't do the medical things?
No my little one you are not bad. Healing comes slowly my little one and I understand that those things are difficult for you. I will help you and hold you and heal you my little one. You are my child and I am the one who is taking care of you.
Sometimes I forget that and it seems like I have to look after myself Jesus.
I know my little one but you are my beloved one and I know the things that are hard for you to do. I will help you to do everything that is necessary my little one, but that does not mean that you need to do everything that others might want you to.
And I'm not bad if I don't?
No my little one you are not bad.
I wish I had said it better to Cheryl, but I got afraid I suppose. Will you help me if it happens again? I know I just have to lie to mum, but I don't have to lie to Cheryl.
My little one you do not have to lie to anyone.
No, but just saying I am choosing not to do it. I am not brave enough for that Jesus and I can't give reasons...it is too difficult. It is this sort of thing that made Blossum wish she wasn't her. I don't think I am any different Jesus. I wish I wasn't having to do these things and make these choices.
I know my little one. I know that it is difficult but I have not told you to do them my little one. It is only that you feel you must in order to please those around you so that they do not get angry with you or try to make you do something you can't or don't want to.
Yes, but that is a big thing for me Jesus.
Why my little one?
Because...I don't want them to be upset with me...it scares me and makes me feel like I am bad and have to do what they want and I can't, and that makes me want to run away or not be. It isn't good Jesus and I don't know how to do it so it is ok. I don't know how to feel like

my choices are mine. They only feel like mine if others agree with them. I suppose I don't think I can make choices because they are what I want.

No my little one you don't. But that is not what I have said.

What have you said Jesus?

That you have free choice my little one. I will help you and guide you but the choice is always yours and whatever choice you make, I will continue to love you and hold you and I will never leave you.

But if I make bad choices...not what you want...I don't want to do that Jesus because your way is better.

Yes my little one it is but that is not always true of other people. Their way is not always better than yours my little one.

I don't know. I suppose... I don't know. I know sometimes I know I can't do what they want because I can't, but otherwise I suppose I do what they want. Jesus, I don't think I know about free choice. I don't think I am free a lot of the time. I don't like that, but is it true?

Yes my little one you are still controlled to some extent by fear, but I am healing you my little one and setting you free. It will not come all at once my little one but over time as you learn to walk in the freedom you are given. You are doing this all the time my little one but breaking free from fear takes strength and courage.

It does Jesus. I don't know if I can do it or how I am doing but I know you want me to...but I am afraid...maybe I am afraid even to have those choices. I don't know. Will you show me what it means to be free Jesus?

Yes my little one I will show you but remember my dearest one that not doing what others want you to does not make you bad. Making your own choices does not make you bad. Sometimes you may make a bad choice my little one...but that does not make you bad either. Mistakes do not make you bad and choices that are made when there is no freedom to choose to...do not mean that you are bad my little one.

Free choices were difficult for me. Sometimes I didn't even realize that the choice I was making was controlled by fear or something else, usually hidden in the past. I didn't have too much time to think about who I was or the future or the choices I had to make anyway. There was too much going on. I was feeling very stressed. I missed Blossom but it was more than that. Being me meant remembering the things that had happened to me, new memories that we hadn't had before. Things that Jesus wanted to heal of course. I wanted to learn about what had happened to me...just me and what it was that needed healing now I have been 'discovered'.

Why am I so stressed Jesus? It's horrid.

My little one there are many things that are making you feel anxious. Some of these are coming from the inside my little one for there is much that is happening there. The enemy is not happy at the changes and the healing that has come my little one and he will make it difficult for all of you if he can.

What is happening there Jesus?

Many of those who are healing are being attacked my little one. They are being reminded of the past and told that they are not safe where they are. That I will not care for them as I have promised.

But they have you Jesus and they have others there who will help them.

Yes my little one they do, but the attacks are making them afraid, nevertheless.

And that is part of what I am feeling?

Yes my little one for you are connected to them all.

Is that why I have been feeling like...I mean I have been remembering the bad things and kind of feeling like I am being sucked back into the past. What is that?

That is part of what is happening my little one, for the enemy does not want you to feel safe or to be able to take hold of the outside life. He is trying to take you back also my little one so that you feel afraid and vulnerable.

So, are they my memories?

Some of them are my little one but they also belong to others. As the enemy stirs up the things of the past you will experience both my little one but there is nothing to fear. I am always with you and will help you. All of this will be used for your healing my little one and for those inside also for it is all connected.
I was wondering about...the past. We always understood Blossum was never really on the outside but got hurt by the bad things because she was close and because of the connections I suppose.
Yes my little one that is so.
But you seem to be saying something different about me Jesus. Tell me.
You have spent time on the outside my little one when you were small. Those are the memories that you have with grandad and with others.
So not like Blossum?
No my little one not like her. After a time you were hidden away just as she was so that you could survive my little one, but unlike Blossum you experienced the bad things directly. You were the one on the outside my little one and not anyone else.
But there were lots of us back then Jesus. Sharing.
Yes my little one there were. Not one of you could have done it alone my little one.
So...is that stuff healing Jesus? I don't feel like it is.
Not completely my little one. I have been healing you as I have healed Blossum and others, but you still need your own healing my little one. It will come when you are ready to receive it.
Jesus, I don't even know anything about me and now I have to live this outside life with all of this stuff going on inside and outside. How will I do it?
In my strength my little one.

Jesus took me inside to see the changes that were happening there. He told me that the blending with Blossum had brought healing inside too and that new areas had opened up. The enemy was very angry about it, which was why they were attacking us but what was happening was good. What I saw inside was that there were many openings in the ground of the second land that Jesus told me led to caves where alters were hidden, waiting to be rescued. It was amazing to me that my blending with Blossum affected the inside world making it possible for those being held prisoner to be rescued. It makes me think about how we don't always see what will happen because we choose to trust and follow Jesus, but it is always more worth it...more than we think. But first it was time for me to spend some time healing and get stronger.

Rest in my arms my little one and do not be afraid. I am holding you. You are safe and you are loved. There is nothing to fear.
I don't like seeing and feeling those things.
I know my little one but my desire is to take them from you so that you don't have to see them or feel them anymore.
Ok. Well I will glad about that Jesus.
Come then my little one

So, I snuggled with him and I saw bad things. First was grandad and he had me across his knee and I had a bare bottom and he was hitting me with his belt. I don't know why. Then he picked me up by one leg and carried me upside down and he dropped me down on the table and did it to me. I cried and held on to Jesus. And he kissed my hair and told me he loved me and that I was safe. And then I was looking out of the window in the lounge. I was looking out into the garden. I must have been small because I was only just big enough to see out. That seemed to be a bad thing to do, cos grandad dragged me away and took me to the sofa and made me do bad things with him. And I cried and held on to Jesus and he said that was enough. Grandad was a bad man wasn't he.

I wonder sometimes if he was a bad man, or if like me, he was someone who had all his choices taken away. I don't suppose I will ever know the truth of why he was so very cruel. I know that Jesus knows and that is ok. I don't feel like I need to know or understand it all. Jennifer would get very tied up in all of that sometimes. I think that is because she was afraid it wasn't true and if she could only understand all the hows and whys she would be able to accept that it was true. But I know it is true. I don't want it to be. I still cry because it is. But it is and I know I won't ever understand the whole of it. I don't need to. Understanding it won't change it for me. Maybe it might make forgiveness easier, but I am not sure. I don't think choosing to forgive someone has anything to do with why they did what they did. It is only about surrendering them to Jesus and letting him be the judge. That is his job not mine. I don't want it. It is too heavy a burden for me to carry.

There were other memories like this that Jesus spent time healing just like he had with the others...but he was also healing me in different ways, showing me who I am to him.

> **Tell me about your picture.**
> Well I was hoping you would tell me about it Jesus. I am like a dancer and you are my partner and we are surrounded by light and I got my clothes on that you gave me, but I expect it says a lot more than I know.
> **Yes my little one it does. Look again. What do you see?**
> You are standing behind me holding my hands, like you are holding me and supporting me and protecting me and directing me to, like you are in charge of the dance.
> **Yes my little one that is so and what do you think the dance is?**
> I am not sure.... I suppose it is us moving together... um dancing is about expressing something isn't it... and so people will watch... sometimes but not always but we seem to be in a spotlight, so I suppose it is for people to watch.
> **Yes my little one it is.**
> So people will watch our dance Jesus and I suppose, maybe it is telling a story cos dances do that don't they, especially ballet though I never really saw one.
> **And what story are we telling my little one?**
> Our story Jesus, all of us and you.
> **Yes my little one and what do you notice about the dance?**
> Well, we look happy Jesus, we don't look like it is a sad dance and I am dressed in happy clothes so I think it is a good and happy dance that will make people... feel better.
> **Yes my little one and who do you think they will see when they look at the dance.**
> Me and you Jesus. Together. Cos I'm not dancing on my own.
> **No my little one you aren't. Do you think you know the dance we are going to dance together my little one or are you still learning?**
> I am still learning Jesus. I don't really know how to dance yet. I don't exactly know what it means except it is about our story and letting people see it in lots of ways but ... Maybe it is more about following you and learning how to do that than knowing a dance cos I suppose ...it might change depending on who we are telling it to or when or how.
> **Yes my little one as you learn how to follow me in the dance you will be learning how to tell your story as I desire. So that people can see me my little one and not just you dancing.**
> Well yes cos me dancing isn't anything. The dance is about you Jesus, mostly anyway cos it is your dance.
> **Yes my little one so what does it tell you about you and how I see you?**
> It tells me that we are together Jesus and I am safe and protected. It tells me you are in charge and all I have to do is follow. It tells me it is a beautiful and lovely dance to show all that you are, that I am a dancer and I was made to dance with you and not anyone else. That is who I am.
> **Yes my little one it is. What else do you notice about you?**
> Well, I have my crown Jesus. Is it a crown of suffering?
> **Yes my little one it is.**
> What does that mean?

It means my little one that you have suffered greatly. But that suffering has not overcome you instead it has become something beautiful and powerful. Something to be worn with joy my little one because of all that I will do through it.

I have a dancing dress Jesus that has pearls on it and little heart shaped rosebuds, that is from Blossom and dolly four... and is about your love and about life and becoming and growing. And there are my dancing shoes not like Blossom's shoes, but they have gold speckles on them. Because I dance with hope I suppose.

Yes my little one and you are dressed in white because I have made you pure and clean and your hair is golden because it reflects my glory.

What does that mean Jesus?

It is like a crown my little one, one which is given to you so that you can show people who I am.

So, showing people who you are is a gift Jesus.

Yes my little one it is.

And that is how you see me Jesus.

Yes my little one. You are my pearl. That is how I see you.

Jesus kept on showing me who I was. I was learning to see myself as Pearl and not anyone else but not knowing who that was. On the outside people saw me as Jennifer and I was still struggling with the way that people had seen me in the past. Someone who had no worth or purpose except to be used in the way they wanted. Learning to see myself as Jesus does was difficult but I was also having to live with the way others saw me. One of the most difficult things for me was being seen as a parent and all the expectations that went with that. Like Aj and Blossom before me I found it overwhelming and didn't know how to do it. Even though Sophie and Richard were adults now sometimes that didn't make it any easier.

Jesus, Sophie and Richard are both needing something I can't give them, and I feel like I am bad for that, but I can't help who I am. Maybe there is more I can do I don't know but I don't know how to be a good parent. I don't even want to be a parent. It feels like it is too much and too heavy for me and I am scared. I am scared because I think I am bad and I am scared because I think they are suffering because I am bad and I don't want that, but I don't know what to do Jesus or how to make it better and I am afraid you will ask me to be a good parent, when it is such a hard and scary thing for me and I don't know what it is even and Mr. Mike thinks I am bad and a coward and I expect he is right. Help me.

My little one that is not what he thinks. He understands that it is hard for you to think of yourself as a parent and to be a good parent is even harder. He does not think you are bad my little one.

Do you think I'm bad Jesus?

No my little one I don't but you do not need to be afraid of anything I will ask you to do.

You put me here Jesus, so I suppose you are asking me to be their mummy whether I feel like I am or if I want to or not.

Yes my little one that is so but I do not ask you to do it by yourself nor am I asking you to do or be all the things you think.

I don't know what I think Jesus. I suppose...I don't know...I just let them do what they want partly because I don't always have the strength and I am scared and partly because I think they are grown adults and should be responsible for their own choices. I don't know what a mummy is meant to do when the children are grown up, even if I was a normal one which I'm not. How do I know Jesus? ...Crying

My little one I will help you. Will you trust me to help you my little one?

Yes.

My dearest one there is a time for everything. There is a time for truth my little one. Do you believe this?

Yes, like there was for us.

Yes my little one and so it is for them. Both of them need the truth just as you did. It is a good thing my little one but must come at the right time and in the right way if it is to help them.

Yes. But I am not sure what this truth is.

It is the truth about themselves and it is the truth about you my little one. They are not separate for many of the things they struggle with are because of what has happened in the past.

They didn't have...the kind of life we wanted them to Jesus. They weren't loved and guided and corrected like they should have been. I think we did our best always to love them and help them, but I don't think it was good enough Jesus. And their dad has been useless... but how can I make up for all that? I can't...Crying

No my little one you can't and I am not asking you to. Others have played their part in their lives and now it your time my little one. What has gone before was not your fault or your responsibility but now the task has passed to you my little one. Will you accept it with my help knowing that I will not ask more of you than you can do?

I know you know best Jesus. I know you have a plan. I want to do what you want. I don't want to hide away in shame and fear. I have nothing to be ashamed of Jesus. I am doing my best it's just I don't know what to do or how to do it ...Crying.

I know my little one but I will lead you by the hand step by step in this as in everything. Will you follow me and trust me my little one? I know everything that they need and not all of it will come from you my little one but there are things that you can do and be and say that will help them to become more of who they were made to be. And that is a good thing my little one.

It is Jesus and why should I not love them enough to do that. I do love them enough, but I have no clue about any of it and I am afraid.

But I am your strength and your courage my little one and I will help you with this. It is not too hard my little one. You have overcome many things to reach this point. This is not too much for you.

Have I Jesus? I don't know what I have done and not done. I don't know.

No my little one but I do. I know the battles you have fought my little one and all the choices you have made even when you were not aware of it. All of those things have brought you here to this place in your journey with me and now you continue as pearl my little one. Being aware of who you are and the choices you are making may seem strange and frightening but my dearest one you are safe and you're loved and I am helping you with everything.

Yes. I don't need to be afraid Jesus. But I want to be sure as I can that I am doing and saying what you want because I have no idea how to be a mummy. I don't think of myself like that I forget that's who I am to them. I know I don't want to be a mummy because it's not who I am, is it? I don't know Jesus.

I have given you a place of influence in their lives my little one. A unique place that no one else has. This can be a great blessing my little one both to you and to them but it is also difficult. I know my dearest one that you do not see yourself as a parent for you understand that you are a child and you feel and act as a child when you are free to do so and being a parent is not something a child should need to do but this is the place you are in my little one. And you are able because I am with you and I make you able. I know who you are my little one and even though you are not any of the things you think you should be you are many of the things you need to be.
I just don't know Jesus. Of all the things I need to do and be this is the hardest. I don't know if it would be easier if they were little because I would kind of know what I am supposed to be doing but I just don't. And I think even if I tried to, it wouldn't help them, and it would make this harder and I don't know Jesus…Crying.
I know my little one. I know that you don't but I am asking you to follow me and let me help you. And I am not asking you to have all the answers or to make anything happen my little one. You are right in that they are adults and responsible for the choices they make but you have something precious to give to them my little one, that is yourself and the wisdom I will give to you. And you have love my little one so much love to give to them.
But I don't know how Jesus. It is all messed up.
I know my little one.
So, what do you want me to do?
I want you to trust me my little one. Trust me to lead you and guide you and give you the words you need to say. Do not be afraid my little one. I know it is hard for you but I will give you all the strength that you need.
I need to stop being afraid that they will be angry with me and not like me.
Yes my little one you do. Their opinion of you does not change who you are my little one. You are not bad. You are my pearl. You are my child and you are lovely to me.
I have to stop being afraid of what people think of me Jesus. It is especially hard with them I think but knowing I am safe and loved and not bad. When I know that properly I will be able to bear it better.
Yes my little one you will.
And one day I suppose they will know the truth about me and that will take a lot of courage and strength Jesus, so I have to get ready for that. And this will help me I know I need to trust you Jesus.
Yes my little one you do. I will help you my little one. Do not run away or try to hide from this. Do not let fear control what you do and say my little one. You are mine. You are my Pearl and I am with you always. There is nothing to fear.
Yes. I am so glad you love me Jesus …Crying
I will never stop loving you my little one. Never.
I think I am turning into Blossom with all this crying.
But you are not my little one. Blossom is in you and is part of who you are but you are you my little one. You are stronger and more able. You can follow me my little one wherever I will lead you.
Yes, help me then Jesus cos most of all I need to be brave. It is people that I am afraid of not really other things. I know that. I understand it I think, but please help me so I'm not. I don't want to be afraid.
You are safe my little one and you are loved. Whether people accept you or not that does not change.
Then help me learn a different way Jesus. Your way.
Yes my little one I will.

For you created my inmost being; you knit me together in my mother's womb. I praise you because I am fearfully and wonderfully made; your works are wonderful, I know that full well. My frame was not hidden from you when I was made in the secret place, when I was woven together in the depths of the earth. Your eyes saw my unformed body; all the days ordained for me were written in your book before one of them came to be. How precious to me are your thoughts, God! How vast is the sum of them! Were I to count them, they would outnumber the grains of sand.

Psalm 139:13-18 NIV

Chapter 2

A Big Adventure

Now I was preparing for my first big outside adventure- the half marathon. I had been training hard even in the middle of all the blending and healing that was happening. It felt like a big thing I was about to do, and I wasn't very sure I could do it, but I knew that Jesus would be with me. The race was being held in London and I was planning to stay the night before with Sophie who was living there at the time. That hadn't worked out and I booked into a hotel instead. I was upset that Sophie didn't seem to want to support me, but I decided I was going to have an adventure with Jesus anyway.

Hello Mr. Mike. So, I thought I would write you something. It is the story of my weekend. I know I told you some of it but not all and I want to tell you what I learned and what I'm thinking and what it might mean and what has maybe changed. I want to squeeze every last drop of goodness out of it and anyway if I write you about all the horrid stuff why wouldn't I write you about the nice stuff? So here it is.

Pearl and Jesus - Excellent Adventure
It started on Friday like I told you. It started then because that is when it changed. Sophie was texting me and saying how she didn't know how it was going to work and she couldn't find anywhere to stay, and she wanted to go out with her friends and come in drunk at 4am and she didn't want to wake me up and so on. So, I didn't know what to do about any of that, but I didn't get upset like I had at the beginning of the week. I just thought enough! I am not going to spend the weekend feeling stressed and like I'm a giant inconvenience. That wasn't the idea, the whole point was to spend some time with Sophie and for her to share in my adventure but it wasn't seeming like she wanted to and I thought she probably isn't even going to come at all so I'm just going to do my own thing. I remembered the race organizers had sent an email saying that there was a hotel giving discounts to people running in the race so I said to Jesus I'm going to check it out and if I can do it I'm going to because I don't want to stay at Sophie's. He seemed to think that was a good idea, so I rang the hotel and booked the room. That was kind of amazing all by itself. We have never booked a hotel that I remember, and I didn't know how to do it but I did. I can't afford it Mr. Mike but it was so worth it! And now because the hotel was where the race was it meant I didn't have to worry about how to get to the start line first thing in the morning and I was getting breakfast and I could shower afterwards.... maybe, because the checkout time was 12 and I didn't know what time I would finish. I felt so much better and much calmer like I could relax now and just enjoy the race. It wasn't just about the race it was a lot more than that. It was like a celebration of what Jesus has done because there has had to be so much healing to make me able to do it...I mean I am pearl and I was going on my own to London to run in a big race and do a half marathon! All of those things are too big for me. So even though I wasn't very happy with Sophie I said to Jesus that it was good we got to spend the time together just him and me and we would run together like we always do and it would be a big adventure and I was happy about it. And he said yes.

So, on Saturday I got the trains to London and that was all good and ok. We have done a lot of train travel, so I wasn't worried about that really. Sophie met me at the station, and she took me to a pizza place where she bought us a meal as a Mother's Day treat, and it was very nice and everything was ok. Then she took me to the tube station where I got on the underground train to go to the hotel. I was a bit scared to be alone in London at nighttime not knowing where I was going but Jesus was there with me and he held my hand and it was ok. Kate rang me with a good luck message. I thought that was so sweet of her and later I got an email from Mary joy saying how they were cheering me on and praying for me. I didn't feel alone. So, I came out of the underground station but no idea where the hotel was. On the website it said it was a five-minute walk so I was kind of expecting to see it but I didn't. So, I walked down the road a bit and there were shops and things and some people, and I thought I could ask them but somehow, I didn't and I started to feel a bit lost and scared wandering about in the dark on my own. I asked Jesus please help me...so I walked back towards the station and looked at a map, but it didn't help and then I saw a line of taxis and I thought aha! The taxi people will know where it is. So, I went to ask but the taxi man who was very nice told me to get in. I thought it was too close for a ride, but I thought oh well and got in anyway. I didn't have any better ideas. It turned out to be quite a long ride. When I walked back the next day it was about 15 minutes not five, maybe you could do it in five if you ran! So they lied. Why do they do that it doesn't help anyone. Anyway, so the taxi took me and I walked into the biggest poshest hotel I've ever been in, we've ever been in. We have never stayed in a hotel on our own, so I wasn't very sure what to do but I knew I had to check in. The lady was very nice. She had to repeat everything twice I think because I was a bit overwhelmed and not taking anything in really. I had no idea what I was doing. But I took the card she gave me and tried to look like I knew where I was going which I didn't, but I found the lifts...and I found my room. I was asking Jesus for help all the time of course. When I got in my room, I couldn't work out how to turn the light on. Nothing I pressed seemed to work. Lots of helps. Then I saw a little slot that said key card on it so I put it in there and all the lights came on. Well I didn't know! When I went in, I just stood and looked for ages because it was so lovely and then I ran around taking photos before I made it messy. There was a giant bed in a big room and a big telly and a little fridge and lots of other things. And the bathroom was twice as big as mine at home and the light worked. It took me ages to work out how to make things work like the telly and the bath and how to turn the lights off now I turned them on...I realized that at home I seem to cope very well and know what I am doing but that only cos I've done it all a thousand times. But me in a new place and it is very different, and I am pearl who is 9 and doesn't know how to do stuff. I turned on an air conditioning fan somehow, it took me ages to realize that's what it was and even longer to turn it off. But I sat and watched the telly and had a lovely bath and used the shampoos and stuff and it was a giant big soft white towel that I loved a lot. Yes, I had a good time.

I didn't sleep so good though even though the bed was very comfy. There was too much to think about. I got up at 6.30 and got dressed and went to breakfast. That was a bit easier because there was lots of people to follow. I talked to some of them, they were all running in the race. I don't suppose anyone else wanted to be up so early. So, I had a nice but light breakfast and noticed that the race was starting right outside the hotel. I had been thinking I would have to follow someone to find it, but it was right there! I was happy about that. When I checked in the lady said I would have to check out of my room, but I could use the gym to have a shower after the race. That wasn't what I was hoping for. I wanted to be able to relax and enjoy the room some more...but I was glad I could have a shower. But when I went to check out the man said I could have to room until 2 if I wanted which was brilliant and I said yes please! So I think Jesus fixed that for me. Then I went outside to where the race was. I was feeling scared. I am not sure why, but I didn't feel alone or sad because nobody was there with me. I sent messages to Cheryl and to mum to tell them I was there, and everything was good and then I went and joined the biggest queue I have ever seen for the toilet. There were a lot of them though, so it wasn't too bad...it was very cold though. I got freezing but the weather was perfect for running. Couldn't have been better. Thankyou Jesus. Then it was time to go stand ready to start the race. They put us in groups depending on how long we thought it would take us with the fastest runners at the front, so I was quite a long way back. It was very exciting standing there in the middle of all of those people waiting to run a half marathon. I got so excited I nearly cried because I thought how wonderful it was that I was even there at all. I heard the starting horn, but it was a long way off...and it took another twenty minutes for us to get to the start line because of how many people there were but then we were off. I found out straight away that they lied about the hills... they said there was only one slight incline near the beginning. Lies. There were loads of hills and two very big ones near the end. It wasn't just me thinking that, cos I did talk to some other runners. I did pretty good the first half and I did run up all the hills...then I started to get tired. I know from training I always get very tired around 7 or 8 miles and I just need to keep going and it gets better. So, I had a toilet stop which was much needed and a nice big energy drink and felt much better. I was pleased with how I ran, and I did enjoy the whole thing. People were coming out of their houses and cheering and taking photos... the runners were cheering each other on and there was music and drums in different places that I liked very much. The sun came out towards the end which was nice. I spent a lot of time wiping my eyes and my nose at the start because of the cold. But I was warm by now anyway because of all the running. When we got to the top of the last big hill... because there were hills...I could see Wembley stadium and that was a very good sight and then I passed the twelve-mile marker and that was even better. That last mile was pretty long though...but I kept saying to Jesus look what we are doing look where we are, and he just laughed and said yes I know. And when I was tired, he said come on you can do it and he did this little running on the spot thing making his knees go really high which made me laugh but cross at the same time because he wasn't tired at all!

There was a lot of walking happening by now, what with the hills and everything. I was breaking it up into run a bit and walk a bit because that was helping me keep going. It wasn't just me, everyone was the same. When I got to the stadium, I rang Cheryl and said I'm nearly there and she was cheering and then when I got into the stadium proper the noise was so loud with the music and drums and people cheering. Couldn't hear her at all. But I ran and did my pose for all the cameras at the finish line and I thought wow I did it... then I took a selfie in the stadium which I'm sending you... cos I still look kind of ok, I think. Then I went into the tunnel and got my goody bag and t-shirt and there was a band playing there too which was very good. Then when I came out again to where the hotel was on the other side Sophie was waiting for me. She hadn't seen any of it of course but she was there at just the right time and seemed very pleased and proud. Then we went to the hotel and I had a bath and then we went and had a meal at the train station. I had spaghetti and meatballs and it was very nice. Then I got my train home and that was the end of my adventure. It was a very good adventure and everything worked out perfect. Did you know that it was the first day of spring on Sunday? I don't know if it is the same for you. But that is how it feels. Like it has been a long dark winter but now it is spring, and the sun is out, and things are starting to grow. I think Blossum would be afraid to think that but I'm not. It feels like a turning point. I hope so. I am ready for more adventures and Jesus looked after me vey good and even though I had nobody there with me really, I didn't feel alone, and I had such a good time. I felt very loved by you and by my American friends and by mum and Arthur and Cheryl and that was kind of strange but lovely and not scary like maybe it would have been once. I think it is lovely that so many people cared and maybe got some joy out of what I did, like Arthur who was so happy he cried. Mum and Arthur sent me a congratulations card today, they have been so excited about it all and Cheryl said she was proud and that she couldn't have done it... Not the running but all the other stuff. So it is all good and even though I am tired I am still happy. I can't really believe I did all that, but I did. It makes me know that there is more that is possible for me. That dreams can come true and adventures can happen. And I have only been here for a month maybe, on the outside being me I mean. That is amazing isn't it. I think so. Jesus has done good! The End.

That was a very big event for me, and I still look back and think what a wonderful time it was. It seemed like a fresh start somehow and it gave me a lot of hope for the future and helped me feel more secure I think knowing that Jesus had been with me and had worked everything out perfectly even though I was totally out of my depth. Those were things I would need to know in the next few months because it was only the first of many adventures.

Chapter 3

Fire and Ice

I was getting used to being me. It was better because I didn't cry so much, I seemed steadier and stronger and life seemed easier. I didn't feel as anxious, I was more confident in who Jesus was. This was all good. It had been very sudden but I seemed to have settled into outside life very quickly, maybe because I'd done it before and knew that I could because Jesus would help me or maybe because I was stronger and more healed than before, or both.

It was only a few days after the race that I noticed another alter called Marie who was at the surface with me. I hadn't met her before and I didn't know why she was there.

Who is she Jesus?
She is my servant my little one. Her name is Marie and she is here to help you.
Why?
Because my little one there are many things that are about to happen that will mean that you will need her help.
That sounds scary Jesus and I have you for help why do I need her as well?
Because my little one it is better that it should be so for many reasons. There is nothing to fear my little one. I will be with you and will help you as I always do.
What do you want me to do Jesus?
Get to know her a little my dearest one allow her to write to my servant Mike for she has much to share with him as well as with you.
About inside stuff?
Yes my little one about the many changes that are happening and are about to happen.
Why don't you tell him Jesus?
My little one I am speaking to him constantly about many things but that does not mean I will not speak through others also my little one. You all have a part to play in my plans for you.
Is she going to do outside stuff?
Not for the moment my little one. For the moment you are able to keep on being the outside person.
Why would that change Jesus are you going to put her on the outside?
No my little one but she is going to share with you and help you as you need it.
In the future?
In the near future my little one.
I don't really understand Jesus but whatever you want that is ok.

I spent a bit of time talking to her. I wasn't sure I wanted her there really. I was only just getting used to being the one on the outside and I didn't see why I needed help really. It was a bit worrying that Jesus thought I would. What was going to happen?

A lot of things were going to happen. The first thing that happened was a huge rescue of alters from the caves that had opened up inside after me and Blossum had blended. I knew that there was still a lot of healing to be done. I knew that there were a lot of rescues to be done. The second land was opening up now that me and Blossum had blended and Jesus said that it was time to begin.

It was Easter Saturday and Jesus took me inside to the second land where the holes had opened up. There wasn't anyone else about except the angels that were with us. We climbed down one of the holes and walked down a dark tunnel. He told me the enemy had hidden these alters away and that they had all been hurt in the cult rituals, which had taken place at Easter, many Easters. I was feeling anxious, not just my own but from those who were hidden away and from those in the dell who were waiting to help. I didn't like being underground either, not one bit. It was hot, very hot as we got deeper. Jesus told me what to expect when we got to the cave and what to do...more or less.

So I went through a little hole that I had to crawl through. I went into a fairly big cave and I could see shapes laying on the floor and some that were two or three children tied together. It was horrible but I could see the door Jesus told me would be there. It was a strange thing to see in that place. It was a wood door but a metal round handle. When I touched it the metal was burning hot. The whole place was hot and some places in the cave were glowing red hot. I gave the torch to an angel who was with me and used my dress to help me turn the handle. I was wearing like a long wool tunic not my dancing dress. I opened the door and went in. Inside I could see one bundle on the floor in the middle of the room that I knew was the little one I was to rescue. I was expecting to see the enemy but they weren't there. But she was guarded. She was surrounded by a ring of fire. The fire came out of a kind of ditch and shot up in the air in big flames with no gaps between. To reach her I had to jump the ditch and through the flames. I wasn't too keen but I did it anyway. It is a strange thing because I knew it was hot and I got burned and it hurt, but I didn't feel it on the outside. I'm glad about that. The little girl was curled up on the ground. She was very dirty and covered in burn blisters. It was horrible to see her there and I wasn't sure what to do. She looked like she was about six or seven and smaller than me, but she didn't move and I knew I would have to carry her. I didn't want her to get more burned so I took off my dress and wrapped her in it, but that meant I got more burned of course. Anyhow so I picked her up and jumped through and carried her to Jesus who was in the big cave now.

What now Jesus?
Now my little one the battle will begin. Here take your dress my little one. I will hold her close to me.
Around the edges of the cave I could see dark shapes moving.
I see them Jesus.
Yes my little one but there is nothing to fear.
While I watched, the enemy came out of their hiding places, but then the Angels, there seemed to be a lot of them, attacked. They moved so fast they looked like streaks of lightening. I just stood with Jesus who held the little girl. Eventually it was quiet and the enemy and the Angels were gone...kind of through the walls.
It is done my little one and though they will try to return they cannot enter here. Come now. Let us help those who have been held captive for so long. Let us begin with this little one.
Who is she Jesus?
She is the one they put in the place of my accuser my little one. They made her take the place of the enemy in the ceremonies and rituals. She did not have a choice my little one but she came to believe that she was evil and that all those here suffered because of that. She believed she deserved to be in that place my little one.
Does she have a name?
She was called the dark one my little one. But I will give to her a new name. I will call her Beloved because that is what she is.
She looks terrified Jesus.
Because she does not yet understand my little one....Will you hold her?
Yes of course.
Little one you are no longer held by darkness and fire. I have come to rescue you and all those who were held here. Do not be afraid. I will not hurt you. You were not to blame for all the hurt and pain that was done to these little ones. You did not deserve the punishment that you have endured. I will show you the truth of this for I know the truth of all things. Will you allow me to show you my little one?
Oh Jesus how will she overcome all of that?....Crying
I will help her my little one. I am able. You can help her my little one if you are willing.

Crying…What are you going to ask me Jesus?...Crying
You know already my little one.
But...how can she choose Jesus?
Look at her my little one. She clings to you.
It's not the same.
No my little one but why don't you ask her?
Crying….Would you come and be with me and we will do this together you and I? And I will help you and show you that you are Beloved and not the dark one.
She looked at me and clung to me but she didn't speak.
That is a yes my little one. If you are willing.
So much pain Jesus….Crying
Yes my little one I know.
Crying…Crying…Ok. I know it is the quickest way to help her.
Yes my little one it is and it will help you also.
Will I remember?
Yes my little one you will.
Crying…Crying…Ok
So Jesus blended us right there and I cried and cried because there was so much pain. ..on the outside I mean.

While I was crying on the outside Jesus was helping the other children. When I went back they were gathered around him. He asked me to lead some of them back to the surface, helped by the angels and then bring back help from the dell. I cried the whole time because I was in so much pain, but I led them out and took a group from the dell back down with me. I don't know who any of them were. I was crying too much and then I was back on the outside.

Later on that day Jesus told me that fifty-six had been rescued. I thought that was such a lot and couldn't imagine how those in the dell would cope with so many hurting children, but Jesus wasn't finished yet. Later on that day we went down another tunnel to where a group of older girls were. It took a little while to persuade them to follow me but they did and they met Jesus. They had been told lies about him that made them afraid but when they met him somehow they understood that he was safe. I left them all in the dell. Later still we rescued a group of children that were together in a pit. The angels drove off the enemy that were guarding them and these too were taken to the dell.

The next day was Easter Sunday. I was so tired after all those rescues but Jesus said to be awake early, that it would be worth it. After a night of fear dreams I was awake at 6.30am.

I looked at the land in front of me that had been like a wasteland with the holes and caves in that had opened up when me and Blossum blended. Now it looked like a round flat dish. It reminded me of a Lilly pad but made of mud. As I watched the ground started to move and make different shapes...little hills and ridges and then it turned green with lovely grass and flowers and there was butterflies and sunshine all still in a circle.

That was weird Jesus...It is very beautiful now Jesus not like before.
It is a special place for all of the children my little one. Come I will show you.
So we went over to it and I could see that it was full of ridges and grooves that you could climb on. There were swings and grass slides down the slopes. Places made of something that looked like slate with chalks for drawing and little sheltered places that were kind of safe places to hide or feel safe without being like dark holes. While we watched it filled up with children from the dell. Me and Jesus played on the swings for a while
Oh wow Jesus. It is brilliant. They can just come here and play and be safe.
Yes my little one they can and look behind you my little one.
So I looked behind me at the dell and saw that the huts around the edge had changed. It was like they had been given another storey but the top one was bigger than the bottom one.

The huts have grown. They look kind of strange.. They remind me of treehouses
Would you like to see my little one?
Ok.
I saw that there were ladders going up to the top storey. I suppose that was for the children. They looked fun and lovely.
I suppose this is for all the extra people.
Yes my little one.
How is everyone?
Some are doing well as you have seen. Some still need a lot of love and care my little one.

He showed me that the land beyond was still bare and icy, and he said that there were more alters waiting to be rescued and that there would be a time of warfare, because it was the last stronghold of the enemy in the land. But it wasn't time for that yet he said, because changes on the outside were coming and I needed to be stronger.

I thought how lovely he was, that he had done all of that over Easter...like a little picture of what he did on that first Easter. He led the captives to freedom and brought new life. I am supposing he is doing that all the time because it is who he is. He is the resurrection and the life. He sets the captives free.

> ***The Spirit of the Sovereign Lord is upon me,***
> ***Because the Lord has anointed me to preach good news***
> ***to the poor. He has sent me to bind up the brokenhearted,***
> ***to proclaim freedom for the captives and release***
> ***from darkness for the prisoners... Isaiah 60:1***

Jesus showed me the land that had joined, that had once been over the bridge. It looked cold and bare and icy. There were angels all around the rim of the playground guarding it because Jesus said that the enemy was still present in this icy land. There were still rescues to be done but time was needed for those in the dell to heal first and for me to be stronger.

I have remembered some stuff from the blending. Being in a black dress or robe and having strange writing over me. Doing something like a procession and standing at the end of the stone alter and giving the Goatman his knife, so he could kill the child on the stone. Chanting something but I don't know what. Maybe there was a black veil too I am not sure. And the Goatman doing it with me. I think that is what happened to her. It wasn't anything very new so I was glad about that. Jesus has been holding me while I cry...or she does, cos I think the blending is still happening.

I was very tired and needed to rest, but it wasn't too long before we went back inside to rescue those who were hidden in the ice caves. The first group were children and teens who had served the Goatman. They were hidden in a dark cave guarded by the enemy, but Jesus and the angels were there and the enemy didn't put up much of a fight. We led the alters out and up to the dell where they were looked after. The second group we rescued were teens who had babies for the Goatman. I was scared about the memories they would share with me, those memories are hard to bear. After a short fight with the enemy we led them out to be cared for in the dell and that just left one. She was hidden away in a deep and smelly pit. I went first and talked with her, but Jesus came and made a way for us out of the pit. She was very afraid that Satan would find her and take her back but she followed us. She had also had babies for the Goatman. I didn't blend with any of the alters we rescued, but I knew that I would eventually and I was very tired. I was surprised about how fast the rescues were happening though. That seemed like a good thing.

After all of those rescues I was very tired and got swamped by feelings of being unloved and unwanted and lonely. I understood it was coming from those inside but it was still difficult. Jesus brought some of them to meet me and tell me their stories, which are part of my story. Sometimes they told me about their new life inside, the things that they were doing and learning.

Well I saw lights in the sky didn't I Jesus and I said what is that and nobody knew, but then you came and you told us.
What did the light look like my little one?
It was like a golden orange ball, but not like the sun cos you could look at it and it didn't hurt, and it was spinning and kind of bouncing across the sky.
And what was it my little one?
Well it came closer after you came and we could see it was an angel, and he was on a big horse that was like fire and he was galloping round and round, and I don't know why Jesus but that is what it was.
Shall I tell you why my little one?
Why Jesus?
Because he was celebrating your freedom my little one, but he was also warning the enemy that his protection is over you and all those in the dell. The enemy is still present in that land that is being reclaimed and in other places also. It was a warning to them my little one, so that they would know that you are protected and that they cannot harm you in any way.
He is keeping us safe Jesus.
Yes little one he is and many others with him.
I like that.

After they told me their stories Jesus would blend them with me. He told me that many of those inside were blending too. He was going fast like I had asked him to over and over but it was a lot of feelings and memories and information that was being given to me day after day. I struggled with life the way it was a lot of the time. I didn't like it and I wasn't happy. A lot of the time I wanted it ...especially the part I was in...to be over and to get to the promise...I talked to him a lot about these things.

Do you believe my plans for you are good my little one?
I am not sure I even know what that means Jesus. Isn't this part of your plan. It doesn't seem very good. I know you will say you are using it for good but I don't know if it's the same and if it is why should the good that is coming be any better.
My little one my plans for you are good. When I say this it includes today and tomorrow which I am working in and through to make you all you can be. That is good my little one but it is not all there is. My plan for your life is good my little one so that when's it is time for you to come home with me you can look at it and agree with me that it was good. No matter how difficult or painful it was, that it was good. I know that there is much you do not understand about this and that your vision is clouded by many things, but my dearest one I am leading you forward into life and hope in increasing measure. You see that your life now is not the way it was my little one even though much of it looks the same. It will continue to be filled with my life my little one until it overflows. It is a process my little one and it is a journey but that does not mean that the life that you have now is the life you will always have or that it will not get better. It means just the opposite my little one.
I just want to see it Jesus. Like sunshine on my face I want to see it.
I know my little one.
Well whatever is going to happen Jesus today is today and I have to do it. Help me not feel like this. Help me not think like this. I would like to enjoy the journey if I can and to see you and love you all the time and to appreciate all the goodness in my life. Please help me.
Yes my little one I will. Remember that this time will pass and the things that you are feeling are not always from you my little one. There is hope and life for you. It will not be taken away and you are moving deeper and deeper into my heart of love of you.

I have often forgotten that I am on a journey with many paths. The paths are all woven together to form one journey, and sometimes I am moving along one more than another but all of them take me forward. Sometimes I have to move forward on one path before I can move forward on another. That is especially true of the healing journey because there are so many things that have held me. Jesus has to set me free before I can move forward on another path. Like the path into the promise. But all of the paths take me deeper into his heart of love. That is the true journey I think, to know him.

I still forget sometimes. I focus on the outside things, on circumstances, on things I don't like and don't want, but Jesus wants me to fix my attention on him. My journey is about him no matter what is happening or not happening. It has been a hard thing to learn. I am still learning it but the more I look at Jesus, the less important it is what my outside life is like. Keeping my eyes on him, like Peter walking on the water, is what keeps me from being swamped by my circumstances and sinking.

**"Do not let your hearts be troubled.
Trust in God; trust also in me."
John 14:1**

Chapter 4

Arthur

The blending and healing was difficult, but now it was on the outside that things were happening. Arthur, my stepdad, had been ill for a long time but was getting weaker and needed a lot of looking after. There were caregivers going in each day to help with washing and dressing, but most of it was being done by mum. She was beginning to wonder how much longer she would be able to cope and was asking me for advice. I was going and looking after Arthur, so mum could get out of the house and do things she needed to and I was supporting her as best I could. I felt so out of my depth in all of it but Jesus helped me. I wondered about it with Jesus, all of the terrible memories and feelings from the past were very fresh after the rescues, but here I was loving and helping mum. It seemed a strange thing but kind of wonderful.

Yes my little one both giving and receiving love is essential for healing.
That is interesting Jesus...and maybe...what is happening for me is like that. I am a bit scared about having to be...relied on or...something, but I am anyway...and I think maybe me loving mum especially has to be healing doesn't it.
Yes my little one as you give love, as you give of yourself to someone who has caused you so much pain, both directly and indirectly by action and inaction, that is powerful my little one, both for her and for you and even for those inside who were hurt.
Like forgiveness is powerful for healing too isn't it.
Yes my little one it is and love and forgiveness flowing together are especially powerful my little one. Do not regret my asking you to stay here a little longer. It is bringing healing to you and to many.

Things got more and more difficult. Arthur was taken into the hospital and was very poorly. There was so much going on for me, more than how it seemed to others. The hospital was full of triggers for me, mostly because of the things that happened with Barbara, and I had to manage that until I got home, when I would have flashbacks and cry and hold on to Jesus. It stirred up a lot of grief about the past too, seeing how mum loved and looked after Arthur. I couldn't ever remember her being like that with us when we were growing up. It made me long for a mum who would love me like that. In all of the outside things I knew Marie was helping me and that was why she was there. That was good. I didn't talk to her much but it was a comfort to know that Jesus had provided help for me, even though I felt so very alone on the outside. I was so busy going backwards and forwards to the hospital that the time went by in a blur. I held on tight to Jesus and trusted that he would help me and get me through it and he did. I felt like I was being carried along. I knew he was with me and would help me with whatever I needed to do so I didn't feel anxious.

My little one do one day at a time holding on to my hand and trusting me. I will enable you in everything my little one.
I have this feeling I'm missing something or forgetting something or maybe it's that I'm not in control...maybe there is another alter who is on the outside. I don't know.
No my little one Marie is helping you in many ways. She is strengthening and encouraging you my little one and from time to time giving you the answers that you need, but she is not the one on the outside. You are my pearl living in my strength and my wisdom. I know you do not understand my little one, but this is how you are meant to live, caught in the flow of my love for you. Doing all things in the strength of my love for you where nothing is too hard for you. I know my dearest one that you are not yet used to this feeling, but this is what it means my little one to live in my strength and not your own.
Well...it doesn't feel hard exactly Jesus, but it is strange...it is like being carried along. I don't know. But I am glad because this would all be too much for me.
Yes my little one but I am with you and will help you.

I feel like I ought to be crying a lot and saying I can't do it, but I'm not and I can and it's ok...even though it's sad and not nice...but I can do it.
Yes my little one you can.
Is this what it will be like Jesus? I don't know if it will come or I have understood your plans...but will it feel kind of the same...like I doing and saying and being things I know I can't, or at least...not without you.
Yes my little one I will carry you in all that I ask of you enabling you in everything. I will give you the words to say and help you to say them. I will help you to help others in my strength my little one and not your own.

Even though I was doing ok I did talk to Jesus about suffering because it was hard to see Arthur and mum suffering and wondering when it would end.

Hello my little one.
I am feeling sad Jesus.
I know my little one I know you are.
I want you to fix it Jesus.
I know you do my little one, but sometimes the things that are best are not the things that you want.
That...I know that must be true Jesus, but why does your way always seem to mean suffering. What about mercy?
Mercy is not always about stopping the suffering my little one. Mercy is about allowing my goodness to work through a situation so that all are blessed.
I am not sure how this is blessing anyone Jesus. I don't see it. Will you let me see it?

He did let me see it. I think so anyway. There was a lot of stuff going on for me about mum. It was strange to see her being the mum I remembered from being a child, in the normal everyday things. The mum who was not kind, but kind of hard. The mum who had punished me with silence and pushed me away. She was being that way with Arthur's daughter from his previous marriage. She did know she was behaving badly, she just didn't seem to be able to stop it. I think it helped me to see that...I don't know what exactly was going on for her when I was growing up...but I see that the way she was with Arthur's daughter was because she was angry and afraid, and that she was trying to keep safe somehow. I understand about that and I suppose she must have felt afraid a lot when I was growing up. It helps me to see that, that it wasn't about me but about her and the situation she was in. It was strange to see her so vulnerable and to be the one helping and supporting her. I don't know what she would have done if I wasn't there.

Arthur didn't get better of course...he got worse. He got another infection and pneumonia and almost died very suddenly but didn't. He got a little bit better after that for a couple of days, but then seemed to get worse again. It was hard to see him suffering. He didn't understand because of his dementia and he kept calling out, help me, help me. It was horrible. The staff did look after him very well...they were all lovely and it was a great comfort to mum, because she knew he was being looked after so well. Arthur's daughter decided to go away on holiday. She had a panic attack in the hospital and had to be looked after by the doctor who was supposed to be looking after Arthur. That was the last straw I think and she decided she needed to not be there. Mum was relieved even if she was angry and upset, because it wasn't helping at all. So for the last few days it was just the two of us visiting him. The day before he died, we were both there at the same time...mostly we took turns and weren't there together. And the doctor said she wanted to talk to us and took us into an office and told us that he was dying, and that it wouldn't be very long...days perhaps. We knew it...but it was still a shock to hear the words. It was a kind of relief though...to know it was ending. Mum said she wasn't going to tell his daughter...but I said I thought she should, because I didn't want them to say she didn't tell them...let the responsibility be theirs and not hers. I offered to do it and she was so glad...so I talked to them on the phone and told what the Doctors had said. I was glad I did. I think mum was afraid they would rush back from their holiday, but they didn't.

We went home from the hospital that evening expecting to be called during the night...but the call didn't come. Mum was there first thing in the morning and I went a bit later. Arthur looked so different. He wasn't awake. I thought he looked like it was time. So we sat there together with him. The sun was shining and the ward was busy in a nice kind of way. We knew everyone by now and it felt like a second home. After he died and we weren't going anymore, we both said how strange it felt not to be there anymore and how we kind of missed it in a strange way. So we sat just chatting but watching his breathing, which was quite uneven and getting shallower and shallower. He stopped breathing...and then started again. The Doctors had told us what this meant. It happened one last time. It is a strange thing...he was gone and I could see that. It was so peaceful. I don't see how it could have been better. Just after he stopped breathing the nurses came to check his drugs...and mum said...something, I don't know what about his breathing and they pulled the curtains around and checked him and said he was gone. I knew it already...mum started to cry and I did too. I put my arms around her and held her...it is the only time she has ever let me comfort her. We sat with him awhile. Mum said later she was waiting to see if he would start breathing again. The chaplain came very soon after that. He had already been a couple of times to pray with Arthur. He was very nice and prayed with us. He said to hold Arthurs hand...and I thought that was kind of strange because Arthur was gone, but I put my hand on his shoulder. Mum said later she had worried because her hand was cold and Arthurs was warm. I suppose to her he was still there...I don't know. The nurse made us a drink and eventually we went back to mums. I told her I would do the texting and ringing...it is such a difficult thing to do so I did as much as I could. It was hard but it was better for me to do it. One of those was Arthur's daughter of course.

There were a lot of things to do after he died. I helped mum with all of them...all the paperwork things and funeral arrangements, meeting people, making decisions. Jesus had to work overtime because I don't know about these things. Even Jennifer wouldn't have known. I have been amazed how well I coped with it all and all the things I did, and how I was able to help mum and support her and be everything I needed to be. I think Marie was helping sometimes but Jesus said it was mostly me. Me with him of course. It does give me a lot of confidence that I can do anything he asks of me. It was such a hard few weeks for a lot of reasons but I did it and I was ok doing it.

I think in a lot of ways I was Jesus to mum...that sounds a strange thing to say, but I think it is true. I walked with her through the pain and the difficulty and didn't run away...that's what he does for me. He supports and comforts and counsels...and he helped me do that too. It made me glad...kind of, that I was still here because she needed me to be and I think Jesus wanted me to be, so that I could be him to her, so he could be with her and love her through me. And that is why we are here isn't it In life. And I know I couldn't do that as Pearl. I had to do it as Jennifer. I see that.

Jesus did so much in that time but it was very hard and it took time to recover. When we talked about it together later, mum and I could see so many good things in what had happened even in the middle of all the suffering. At the funeral I saw Jesus standing there smiling at me. Around him a young boy of about twelve was skipping and laughing and clapping. He was a picture of joy. I knew that it was Arthur. It made me smile and cry all at the same time. Arthur was always young at heart and had such a sweet spirit. It was easy to believe he would be a boy in heaven.

I think now that time changed things between me and mum, because we had shared in something that was real. I suppose a lot of what had gone before between us, was somehow shallow if that is the right word because of all the hidden things. But even though I am Pearl and not who she thinks I am we shared something very real in that time. And Jesus was in the midst and we both knew that. It was healing for both of us.

In the days after the funeral I spent time with Jesus. He held me and comforted me while pictures of things that had happened came into my mind. I don't know how much of my sadness or crying was about losing Arthur. Some of it was, but a lot of it was more about things that were upsetting or difficult and just the stress of it all. At the time I had to push it away because I couldn't be getting upset by it, but I knew Jesus was holding me in those things too, until I had time and space and it had taken until now to find that time. I was beginning to see something else too...the healing that was hidden amongst all the things that had happened. A healing that Jesus wanted to continue.

Chapter 5

Daddy

During the time when Arthur was in the hospital, the staff, patients and even the visitors would refer to him as my dad, and I suppose he was in a way. He was our stepdad for about twenty years but none of us ever really saw him like that. We didn't spend a lot of time with him until he became ill and though we loved him and knew him as a kind and generous man, we didn't see him as a father. But even so his dying stirred up things in me, things I thought were already healed. And I was getting it all mixed up with Mr. Mike too. Blossom and the others had never really seen him as a daddy but I was different. I never said it to anyone, not even Jesus but I did see him as a kind of daddy and that scared me. So often I felt like he wasn't really interested and when he missed his Skype appointment with me I would still feel like he had left me.

Why does it still hurt so much Jesus?
Because you are still in need of much healing my little one.
Is it the daddy thing?
Yes my little one it is.
He isn't my daddy.
No my little one he isn't and yet that is the place I have given him in your heart. It hurts my little one because that is the place that still needs the most healing.
I don't see why. Who needs a daddy...what are they for...they aren't any good. They don't want me...Crying...I don't want him...Crying...I can't have a daddy. I'm not good enough to have one...Crying...I don't want one...Crying...Make it stop Jesus make it stop...Crying.
My little one my dearest little one, you are so dearly loved both by my father and my servant.
Then why do they leave me? All the time...Crying...and he isn't my daddy...Crying...I don't want him, make him go away...Crying...Why am I like this?...Crying...Why does he leave me?...Crying.
He does not leave you my little one. He does not want to hurt you. Sometimes other things get in the way of him being able to show his love to you, but it is still real and true my little one. I have given it to him for you. I know his heart my little one. He does love you.
Crying...But he doesn't want to see me or be with me. He forgets about me and thinks I don't matter...Crying...That's not love is it Jesus? I don't understand...Crying.
Things are not always the way they seem to you my little one. You are wounded and that changes how you see the things that my servant does.
Crying...I don't understand him.
I know my little one I know.
Crying...Please can we stop this. I am so tired of this. This has been going on for years Jesus and it isn't getting better.
Yes my little one it is. It is so much better. I know it is hard for you to see this my little one, but just because the healing is not yet complete does not mean it has been for nothing or that it will never end.
Crying...It hurts too much Jesus and it won't ever go away.
Yes my little one it will. One day it will.
When I am dead.
No my little one before then.
Why did you give him that place in my heart Jesus? He doesn't want it...Crying...He doesn't want me...Crying.
Yes my little one he does.
No Jesus he doesn't. All those other children he is a daddy to them, but not to me, not to us, he won't even talk to me...Crying...I don't want him, make him go away.
My little one what if I were to tell you he talks to me constantly about you. That he

understands what I am asking of him and that he is willing.
I'd say I don't understand…Crying…And I don't see…Crying…And I don't want to be hurting any more…Crying…Please make it stop Jesus, please make it stop…Crying.
Yes my little one I will make it stop. I will make it stop as you follow me and allow me to heal you. My little one I know the best way for you and though it is not the way you would choose, it will draw you closer to me and to our father and prepare you for what lies ahead of you. Are you willing my little one to follow me no matter where I will lead you?
Crying…Where would I go Jesus?...Crying…What else would I do? Make it stop.
My little one when you were small you learned to fear the love of a father. You learned that it was not good for you to have it. You learned that fathers bring pain and abandonment. You learned all the lies that the enemy gave to you as truth my little one.
They were true.
They seemed true my little one but that is not what a father's love is.
I don't want to go Jesus…Crying…I don't want to go.
I know you are afraid my little one. I will not take you anywhere you are not ready to go.
I don't want to go and I don't understand.
Yes my little one you do. You are not willing to see my little one because you are afraid.
What am I afraid of?
Of the pain my little one but you are safe in my arms my little one you are loved and you are strong enough for this. My little one are you willing to go wherever I will lead you?
Why do you keep asking me that Jesus?
To help you my little one. Making the choice will give you the strength that you need.
Tell me what you are wanting Jesus. What are you going to do?
I am going to love you and heal you my little one and restore that part of your heart so that you can receive the fathers love, and also the love of my servant without fear my little one.
Crying…I don't want his love. Not either of them. They aren't the same.
No my little one they aren't and yet you need both in order to complete the healing that I have for you.
Well Mr. Mike won't ever love me. He doesn't have time for me. I don't want him.
My little one it is not the way it seems to you.
You have been saying that for years.
Because it is true my little one.
Well what is the matter with me that after all these years it is still true.
You are hurting my little one from many wounds that go deep into your heart. Wounds I am longing to heal.
How many times do we have to do this Jesus?
Until the healing is complete my little one.
When will that be Jesus?
When you are no longer afraid of the love that a father can give to you my little one.
Crying..
My little one this is not too hard for me.
Crying…But I think it might be too hard for me.
No my little one it is not. I know what you can do my little one. You are strong enough for this.
Crying…I see a lie Jesus…Crying…I don't know why it's there. That didn't happen to me.
Yes my little one it did. Remember that you have been blended with many others, some of who needed my healing just as you do. Tell me the lie my little one.
Crying…That the Goatman is my daddy…Crying.

My little one this is a lie that has been hidden in your heart, but now you are able to see it.
He was just a bad man Jesus. He wasn't my daddy.
No my little one he wasn't.
Crying…But I wanted him to be. I wanted him to love me and protect me.
That was his role in the cult my little one to be the father to you all. To stand in his place but he is not our father my little one. Our father is good and kind and will not ever hurt you.
Crying…It is mixed up with so many things Jesus because there is grandad …Crying…And the priest and the grand master …and Dad who just left me. It seems like too much Jesus.
But it is not my little one. It is a great healing but one which will change many things for you. Do not be afraid my little one I am enough for you in this as on everything. Write to my servant my little one and do not be afraid of him. He will not hurt you he does not hate you my little one.
I feel ashamed Jesus.
There is nothing to be ashamed of my little one, this is my doing and not yours. I have given him to you my little one and you to him. I know you do not understand my little one and all that you feel is fear, but my servants heart is towards you my little one. Always. Are you willing my little one to follow where I will lead you?
Crying…Yes...
Then take hold of my hand my little one. Write your letter and then rest. I will help you my little one. Do not be afraid.
Crying…I am afraid Jesus…Crying
I know my little one but I am with you and will help you.
Ok.
There is nothing to fear my little one.

I did write even though I was so afraid and felt very ashamed to be saying these things to Mr Mike. I knew that he was a daddy to a lot of the alter children he helped, but he had never suggested it to any of us. We always thought it was because we weren't good enough, or he didn't like us or even sometimes that we weren't real children to have a daddy. Now it felt to me like I was asking him to be my daddy and I felt sure he just wanted me to go away. I was afraid to have a daddy and I was afraid he wanted me to go away, and I was angry that this stuff was still not healed.

Even though Jesus told me that he had given Mr. Mike to me to be my daddy, I felt confused about it because of things he had said before, but he said it was different because I am me and not Blossum or anyone else.

Well... I wanted to try and understand why you are making a big deal about Mr. Mike being my daddy, if it was you. Was anything you Jesus, or have I just got it all wrong and you don't want him to be my daddy.
My little one he is your daddy already. It is already done all that needs to happen is for you to accept him as such.
When was it done Jesus?
From the very beginning my little one.
But what about the others...why wasn't he their daddy?
Because I did not ask him to be my little one. That was not their need it is your need.
Why didn't they need a daddy?
My little one they had a daddy. They had our father who they spent time with and received much love from. They did need a daddy my little one, but they did not need my servant to be their daddy.
Why am I different?
Because you are you my little one. You are my pearl and as you go through this life loving and serving me, you will do so side by side with my servant. He is given to

you to love you and teach you and guide you as a father would. That is who he is to you my little one. That is your need. Blossum and Aj did not need him to be their daddy. You are the one who will be with him my little one.

And so is that why you keep making a thing about it because it is important for the future?

Yes my little one it is.

But, why can't he just be my friend like he has been before.

Because you need something more from him my little one. Your need is for the love and protection and guidance of a daddy. He will continue to be your friend my little one but he will be more than that.

But I have you...and I suppose daddy daddy...so why do I need him?

Don't you want him to be your daddy my little one?

I don't think it matters what I want Jesus.

Yes my little one it does for I have put the desire in your heart, not so that it can bring you pain but so it can be fulfilled.

I don't think Blossum or Aj...ever saw him like that.

No my little one they didn't.

But I have even though I didn't want to.

Yes my little one for that is who he is to you, all that is happening is that you are beginning to accept it.

I am not sure I want to accept it.

Yes my little one I know because you are afraid of being hurt. Most of all you are afraid he does not want you.

I don't know why he would Jesus.

My little one just as I have given him a place in your heart I have given you a place in his. It is not different my little one.

So you did it?

Yes my little one I did.

So what do you want me to do?

Accept who he is to you my little one and do not be afraid. Most of all do not be ashamed for he is my gift to you just as you are my gift to him.

Like you said before.

Yes my little one.

I am not sure about it Jesus. I have spent years not ...seeing him that way.

I know you have my little one but now it is time for you to be who you are, my pearl with all that you are. You are not Blossum or Aj or even Jennifer you are you. You are different my little one.

I am having a bit of trouble with that Jesus. I mean I know I am different...I don't know what I mean. I am not Blossum or anyone else...I know I am different...but I can't seem to care too much about how. Is it important?

Yes my little one it is. You need to take hold of who you are before you can fully become who you are.

And I am not doing that?

You are afraid of that my little one.

Why?

Because you think that I will take it away from you.

Well you took it away from Aj and Blossum

I did not take anything away from them my little one. As they lived and grew into who I made them to be, they were healed and made ready to be who they are in you. They did not lose who they are my little one. I did not take it from them.

It is hard to understand.

I know my little one I know it is but taking hold of who you are with all that it means will help you my little one. If you try to pretend that you do not care about being Pearl then how can I fulfil my purpose in you my little one? How can I make you into all that I made you to be?

If I am resisting you?
Yes my little one.
Sorry. I am tired of finding out I'm not who I thought.
I know my little one but each of them are a part of who you are my little one. You were always discovering part of you, not someone else.
It does get confusing though Jesus.
I know my little one.
Will you help me care about who Pearl is? I am not sure I want to...but I suppose I need to.
Yes my little one you do.
Crying…I don't want to do this any more Jesus
My little one everything I have for you is good. I know that the journey is hard at times my little one especially when you cannot see what is ahead of you but it will be worth it. Be my Pearl my little one, all that you are and do not be afraid. I will never take it from you.
Crying…I don't want to find out I'm someone else Jesus. I'm sorry. I keep saying to you it doesn't matter...but it does matter. I just don't want it to matter….Crying.
My little one do you trust me?
Yes and no Jesus. It is so hard to be sure of what you are saying even when it is really you saying it.
But you know that I am good my little one and all that I am doing is good even if you do not understand it. Even if you make mistakes and get things wrong, even if you want things that I do not want for you even if you go the wrong way, and listen to the wrong voices, even if you are not who you thought you were, in all of that I am good and my love for you is true.
Yes. I do. And even in all of the mess, and sometimes it is a mess Jesus…I am moving forward.
Yes my little one you are. Do not be afraid then my little one to take the steps that are given to you. Accept yourself as my Pearl, accept that my servant is given to you to be your daddy my little one, no matter who he has been to others before you. Accept that I love you and do not be afraid of what lies ahead. I am with you in all of it my little one.
I know you are Jesus. I am sorry. I should never listen to fear.
No my little one you shouldn't.

It was all tied up together. Healing, accepting who I am, accepting Mr. Mike as my daddy. All of it was a struggle but I held on to Jesus and tried to follow him in everything. From this time I started to call Mr. Mike daddy. Sometimes I didn't want to. Sometimes I wanted to run away. Sometimes I still thought he didn't want to be my daddy and sometimes I thought it wasn't making any difference anyway. It was the start of healing and not the end I suppose.

I was afraid and ashamed about Mr. Mike being my daddy but with Jesus daddy, my heavenly daddy it was more like terror. Jesus talked to me about the healing he wanted to do. He was helping me to accept the truth and to choose to allow him into my heart. I was shocked that I had wanted the Goatman to be my daddy, that somehow, I believed that's what he was. That was new to me, but it made sense in my heart. I knew it was true. It was a terrible thing to me, and I knew it needed healing along with so many other things.

My little one the things that hurt you began almost before you were able to talk or walk. They shaped you my little one, not as I desired but as the enemy desired. I am undoing his work and reshaping you my little one into the person you were always meant to be, according to my design and not his. Even though there has been a great deal of healing that does not mean that there is not more to do my little one. I will always be shaping and reshaping you into all that you can be.
Yes, but why is there still such a big wound Jesus...or more than one you said
Yes my little one there are still many wounds to be healed but they are all at the

center of who you are my little one. You and not anyone else for you were always the focus of the attacks.

I don't think I understand Jesus.

My little one when you were made by me you were made with a purpose. You were made to show the world who I am my little one. The enemy does not understand the full purpose I have for you, but he is able to see a portion of it for it is written into your heart my little one and it shines like a beacon for those who are able to see it.

Like a light.

Yes my little one so that the enemy is aware to some extent that I have a purpose for you which is a great threat for him and his kingdom. He determined to extinguish that light my little one but was not able to do it. Not completely.

Can he do that sometimes Jesus? I mean you are in charge.

Yes my little one I am and I did not allow him to destroy you as was his intent. But my dearest one even though you were not destroyed you were so wounded that it has taken all this time to bring you to this point, so that your light can shine brightly for me just as I intended from the beginning.

Is this the...I hate to ask Jesus...but is this the last big healing of the bad things...and is it connected to the last twelve that are to be rescued?

Yes and yes my little one.

And it is something right at the very heart of me that is very deep and has to do with daddy?

Yes my little one it is.

And the memories...are they in me or are they in the twelve.

Both my little one.

And...are they very early memories?

Yes my little one they are. They are the things which shaped you my little one.

Shaped what I believe about daddy's and about me

Yes my little one.

And I suppose my relationship with daddy is central.

Yes my little one it is. I came to the earth to reveal the father to his children. I did not come on my own behalf.

No he sent you so that he could claim us back.

Yes my little one he did for that is how deep his love for you is, that he would send his only son to suffer and to die, so that he could reclaim his lost children from the darkness that holds them.

So this healing is about the central thing...daddy...and that is the most damaged part for me because of what the enemy did on purpose to get rid of me.

Yes my little one that is so.

And the twelve alters...are holding some of the memories and feelings.

Yes my little one they are.

And that is why they are last because it is about healing this...last big thing...the central thing.

Yes my little one.

And I suppose then it will take time Jesus.

Yes my little one it will but do not fear this for the healing that is coming will set you free to be all that you can be. It is a good thing my little one though it will be painful for a time.

And is all of it to do with daddy.

Yes my little one, all of it has to do with your relationship with our father. All of the things that were done to keep you from him and his love for you.

And that is about all of those people who stood in his place and hurt me.

Yes my little one and all of the lies you have believed about him and about yourself.

But it must help that I at least know the truth about those things even if I haven't got them in my heart.

Yes my little one it does help and all of the healing that has been done so far has

brought you to this point, so that you could be strong enough to keep standing through all of the pain and fear that still lies hidden.

I am strong enough?

Yes my little one you are. Your trust in me can stand my little one as you hold on to me.

It is sounding a bit scary Jesus but hopeful too. I would like to be free in all of those ways and be able to know that I am loved, because I think I have trouble with that. I was thinking how Blossum kind of understood towards the end that she was loved, especially by Mr. Mike but it seems harder for me like I have gone backwards. Is that because of the daddy thing?

Yes my little one it is and even though Blossum was able to accept the love of my servant, she was never able to see him as daddy my little one. I did not ask that of her. This healing is for you my little one because you are the one that needs it.

I am not very sure what to ask now Jesus. Is this something we have started and that you are doing now?

Yes my little one it is. The healing is already begun my little one with your acceptance of your need and of my will for you.

I am thinking the enemy is not going to like it.

No my little one he will not. He will oppose it in every way he can. He will make it difficult for you to accept the love of my servant my little one and he will try to keep you from our father also, but he cannot do it my little one not if you continue to trust and to follow me.

No cos you will just use it all Jesus like you did with Mr. Mike. I suppose him not coming just meant... I saw and felt the hurt that is there so you can make it better.

Yes my little one it did. My servant loves you my little one. He will not hurt you. Do not fear him in any way. Do not listen to lies or to fear but only to my word to you my little one. I am with you. I will not leave you no matter what the enemy will tell you and nor will my servant.

Is it going to take a long time Jesus?

A little while my dearest one. There is much to be done.

And while it is happening you will be healing those inside.

Yes my little one I will for I am also preparing them.

What for Jesus?

For all that is ahead for you my little one.

Well yes...but maybe you could say more about that Jesus.

I am making you whole in me my little one, all of you. I am giving back to you everything that has been taken, that and more my little one. Those inside are part of that and I am preparing them to play their part in the healing I have for all of you.

I don't really know what that means Jesus. Except you have said that we will all be blended one day.

Yes my little one, one day you will.

For now, Jesus told me it wasn't time yet to rescue the twelve alters, because of the healing he needed to do in me first even though it was all connected of course. Jesus said that what I remembered and believed came from when I was very young and wasn't there for me to remember like a story or event, but more as feelings and impressions. He wanted me to draw because he said it would help me express these things, the deeper things.

Later on I got out my pencils and some paper and put on some worship music and told Jesus I was ready. I had no idea what I was going to draw. But I did. I felt so scared and not safe. Maybe the picture says it all I don't know. There was stuff about being small and naked and being hurt and punished.

My little one I am holding you. You are loved and you are safe. Nothing can harm you my little one.

Crying…I don't feel safe Jesus.

I know my little one but I am holding you close to my heart. You are loved and you are safe.

Crying.

My little one even though the things that you remember are so very terrible that does not change who our father is. Nothing can change that my little one. What they did to you and to others in his name was terrible my little one and he weeps for you just as I do, but that is not who he is my little one. It is not who he is.

Crying…I don't want a Daddy…Crying…I don't want a daddy…Crying.

I know my little one I know but you are safe and you are loved. Nothing will harm you.

Crying.

My little one I will heal all of the pain and drive away all of the fear. Only hold on to me my little one and trust me. I am enough for you.

Crying…I don't feel safe Jesus.

But you are my little one. I am with you. Nothing will harm you.

Crying…I am bad I am so bad…Crying.

No my little one. You are my beloved Pearl. You are not bad. You are so very loved my little one…

Crying.

I will keep you safe my little one. Hold on to me and trust me. I will not leave you.

Crying…I feel like he will come and get me because I have been bad. I left and I told…Crying…I told Mr. Mike. I am bad…Crying.

No my little one you are not. You are safe and you are loved my little one. Nothing will harm you.

Crying.

My little one you are strong enough for this. I will hold you and love you through it. You are not bad my little one. You gave yourself to me and I will keep you safe. He cannot harm you my little one.

Crying…I know. In my head I know…..Crying.

I know you do my little one. Do not listen to fear. It is his weapon against you but it is not stronger than I am.

Nothing is Jesus…Crying.

No my little one nothing is. Rest in my arms a while my little one. I will keep you safe.

Jesus told me that the healing he was doing would be like going into five different rooms. This first one was the punishment room. I think he separated the things that needed healing so I didn't get overwhelmed. Each time I drew pictures and it was like it opened up the door to the next room and Jesus would hold me and heal me.

The room of abandonment

My little one you were not alone not ever.
Crying….He left me.
No my little one no. Your daddy never left you.
Crying…So much darkness Jesus.
I know my little one I know.
Crying.
My little one I am holding you. I never left you my little one not for one moment.
Crying….I know.
My little one you are held and you were loved through it all.
Crying.
I will never stop holding you my little one. I will never leave you.
What about daddy?
He and I are one my little one. When I am with you he is with you also.
Crying….He doesn't want me.
Yes my little one he does. He sent me for you my little one, to be with you and love you and show you who he is. He loves you very much. He does want you my little one.
Crying…I can't have a daddy.
My little one you already have a daddy who loves you. You have my servant and you have our father who was with you from the beginning who will never leave you.
Crying…Two daddy's…Crying.
Yes my little one two good kind daddy's who love you and want the best for you.
Crying.
You are so loved my little one. You are so loved.
Crying.
Hold on to me my little one and let me love you. Let me drive away the pain and the fear and loneliness. My little one I am with you in the darkest and loneliest of places. My father loves you my little one. You belong to him. He has always wanted you.
Crying.
I am holding you my little one I will not let you fall.
Crying.
My little one I will hold you and love you back to life. My life my little one which is not like the life that you have known. I am preparing you for many things my little one but

most of all I am preparing you to receive the love of our father who is longing to shower you with his goodness and his kindness and all the love that you can hold. My little one knowing his love deep down in your heart will change everything for you. There is no greater thing than this my little one. Hold on to me and keep following. Do not be afraid of anything for I am always with you.

I did a lot of crying. It didn't seem new exactly cos I've felt those things before with others but the memories are kind of different. They are just impressions really. Hard to describe like shapes and shadows and feeling...feeling small and helpless and all the rest of it. Later I went into the next room. In a lot of ways it was more difficult than the others.

The room of shame

Jesus.
My little one I am with you. I will help you with this.
Crying.
My little one none of the things that happened were your fault. You were not to blame not in any way.
I don't know if I can do this …Crying
My little one who are you?
Pearl…Crying…your Pearl…Crying.
Yes my little one my Pearl.
Crying.
Do you think my little one that I am ashamed of you?
Crying…You should be. I did bad things…Crying.
No my little one bad things were done to you it was not the same.
Crying…I don't remember…Crying.
No my little one and yet you do. You remember how it felt.
Crying…I am bad I am bad I am bad…Crying.
No my little one you are not.
Crying.
You are my precious and beloved Pearl. You are not bad in any way. What they did to you does not make you bad my little one.
Crying…I am disgusting…Crying.
No my little one you are pure and clean. You are my Pearl.
Crying...Make the daddies go away, make them go away, make them go away...
My little one you are safe and you are loved.
Crying.
Nothing will harm you my little one.
Crying.
You are my beloved Pearl and there is no stain on you from what they did my little

one...You are safe in my arms.
Crying.
You are safe.
Crying.
Safe and loved my beloved Pearl.

While Jesus was doing this healing I was trying to get used to the idea of Mr. Mike being my daddy. I was still having trouble with it. I was still worried he didn't want me.

    I was thinking about Mr. Mike and how I don't see how he can be my daddy because I am not a proper little girl. I have to be grown up all the time.
My servant understands this my little one and yet he is still able to be your daddy. My little one just because you are living a grownup's life that does not make you a grown up nor does it mean you do not need a daddy.
It is hard to be two things at once Jesus.
I know it is my little one.
Why do you want me to? You could have done this any way you wanted to.
Yes my little one I could but in this way you are learning many things that you will need to live the life that is ahead of you.
How to be a grown up?
No my little one for you already know how to be a grown up what you are learning most of all is how to depend upon me and how to see yourself as I see you and not as the world sees you.
It is taking a long time to learn those things.
Yes my little one for there are many things for you to overcome as you learn them. Many lies of the enemy my little one and much pain and sorrow.
I suppose that is true.
My little one this time will not last forever. I will set you free to go and be with my servant just as I have promised.
And will he be my daddy then?
Yes my little one he will.
I don't know what that means.
I know my little one.
I am not like a little girl is...a real one. I am used to being a grownup and not being a child.
But my little one just because he is your daddy, that does not mean that he will begin to treat you like a child, not in the way that you are thinking. He knows who you are my little one.
I don't think I do.
But you are learning my little one.
I think I might be very different in a different place.
Yes my little one you will be.
Is that one of the reasons I need to see me like you do ,because how people will see me will change and maybe that will change who I can be?
Yes my little one it will but it will not change who you are.
It is difficult to imagine Jesus.
Yes my little one I know it is but I am preparing you for all of it. Do not be anxious my little one. All of this is to make you ready.
I wish it would come.
I know my little one.

The healing continued. I was glad that Jesus had told me there were five rooms because every time we did one I knew it was getting nearer to the end of them. It helped a lot because I didn't like them and I didn't want to go into them.

The room of need

Jesus.
I'm here my little one.
I don't like it….Crying.
My little one it will not hurt you to see your needs. They are good needs to have.
Crying…I don't think so …Crying.
My little one I would not have given them to you if they were bad to have.
Crying…They seem bad to me Jesus.
Only because you have yet to know what it is to have them met my little one.
Crying…Why are you doing this?
To help you my little one.
Crying….How does it help Jesus?...Crying.
It helps you to see what a daddy should be my little one. I gave you these needs so that your daddy could meet them.
Crying…That doesn't make sense….Crying.
Yes my little one it does. I created you to love and to be loved my little one. There are many kinds of love but daddy love is special my little one. The love a father has for his child is very precious.
Crying…I don't think so…Crying.
I know you don't my little one because you have never experienced that kind of love from those who were in that position in your heart and your mind.
Crying…Bad daddies.
Yes my little one bad daddy's who hurt you and used you and did not love you as they should.
Crying.
My little one I did not show you this to hurt you but so that you can see what it is I am longing to give to you and the kind of love our father has for you. It is not bad love my little one but the good love of a father for his child.
Crying…I can't have it…Crying…I can't have it…Crying.
Why not my little one?
I don't know. How can I know?...Crying…I can't have it…Crying.
Yes my little one you can for I have given you my servant who will love you with this kind of love and our father is longing to pour out his love on you, to show you who he is. To love you as a good daddy loves his child.
Crying….I don't know. I don't know
No my little one I know you don't. Hold on to me my little one. I will help you.
Crying….I don't want to do this anymore Jesus…..Crying.
Only one more to go my little one just one more.

The room of belonging, or not belonging.

Hi Jesus
Hello my little one
I drew it Jesus. It is sad but it doesn't make me cry.
Why is it sad my little one?
Because I never felt like I belonged to anyone because they didn't want me.
What about now my little one?
I don't know. I suppose I think…maybe if they saw me. Pearl. They wouldn't want me.
Do you think you can ever have the kind of belonging or family you have drawn my little one?
No Jesus. I think I will always be not belonging. How can I belong? I am not normal girl who can belong to anyone…Crying.
My little one who are you?
Crying…I am your Pearl Jesus.
Yes my little one you are. You are my Pearl. You belong to me. Do you know who gave you to me my little one?
Crying…Daddy….Crying.
Why do you think he did that my little one?
Crying….Because no one else wanted me…Crying…No one else would ever want me.
No my little one that is not the reason. He gave you to me because you are precious, a priceless treasure my little one. Daddy loves me and only ever gives me good things.
Crying.
My little one you will always belong to me, but I have also given you to someone as a priceless and precious gift.
Crying…No Jesus no…Crying.
Yes my little one. You do belong.
Crying...No. I don't. I don't see it…Crying.
No my little one I know that you don't but that does not mean it is not so. My little one you are my treasure and I hold you close to my heart always but I gave you to my servant for a reason.
Crying.
Do you know what that reason is my little one?
No…..Crying.
So that you could be a blessing each to the other. My little one my servant is also precious to me and yet I have given him to you. Do you know why that is?
Crying….No.

Because I know that he can give you the love that you need my little one and that you can love him in return with a pure and joyful love that will bring him life.
Crying….I don't think so Jesus.
But I do my little one. I do. My little one the wounds you carry make it hard for you believe these things can be true for you but they are my little one.
And when I am better will I know it?
Yes my little one you will both know it and experience it.
Crying…I wish you wouldn't say those things….Crying.
My little one you are so dearly loved. I know that it is hard for you to accept these things and there is still much to be overcome but it will be my little one. Soon it will be.
Oh dear. Soon is always so far away.
No my little one it is not. Rest now my dearest one and do not be afraid of anything I will ask of you. Everything is to bring you healing and life my little one.
Crying…Is that the end of the rooms?
Yes my little one it is.
Good. I am tired.
I know you are my little one. Rest then for tomorrow we will begin the next phase of your healing.
The rescues?
Yes my little one and all that goes with that.
Well...tell me tomorrow Jesus.
Yes my little one rest.

I don't think I liked seeing those things much Mr. Mike. It makes me want to run away and hide and I get scared of what you think. It is hard for me to imagine you would want to be my daddy or to know what that means. Anyway that is all for today. Love from Pearl.

I kept on talking to Jesus about Mr. Mike because I was still scared about it. But then Mr. Mike did talk to me about being my daddy and said that Jesus had talked to him about it and that he was very pleased and happy to be my daddy. He talked about what being a Godfather and what that means. I didn't say much, I just listened because it seemed like too much to take in.

**"A friend loves at all times, and a brother is born for adversity."
Proverbs 17:17**

Chapter 6

The Twelve

Jesus told me that there were just twelve alters left to be rescued. I questioned him on that a lot because of the shock we had when we found out about the second land. I didn't want to think I had finished and then find out there were a lot more alters to be rescued and healed and blended. Not again. But Jesus was very clear- just twelve more.

Jesus told me that these alters couldn't be reached from the inside world like the others had. That they were hidden in places not connected to anywhere, but that he could take me to them. We were going to rescue each one separately and all of them were guarded.

He had told me about the twelve before Arthur died, but it had taken a little while for me to be strong enough but now it was time to begin. I was still afraid they would turn out not to be the last ones, but I was keen to get the rescues done anyway. The place the alters were in sounded awful. I didn't want them to keep on suffering if I could help them. Jesus told me these alters held the keys to my healing, because as they were healed so my relationship with my heavenly daddy would be healed and the last stronghold of the enemy would be broken.

The inside world seemed strange sometimes. When the memories first started to come and the alters made themselves known, Jennifer and all of us with her had so much trouble knowing what was real. It was so frightening to not know what was true about the past or even the present. Our whole life was turned upside down. We clung on to Jesus and learned to trust what he said was real. It was a big battle but by the time I was on the outside I accepted the reality of the past, of alters, the inside world and of angels and demons. I did talk to Jesus about it sometimes trying to understand and maybe to reassure myself that I wasn't just making it all up.

Reality is not defined by your ability to discern it my little one. Reality is what I say it is. It is, regardless of your ability to see, hear, feel, or sense it. Reality does not change according to your perception of it my little one, but I am helping you to see and perceive true reality not according to your natural senses my little one, but according to the spirit which is given to you in full measure. Learning to see and hear and sense the things of the spirit takes time my little one and it also takes faith.

Now I was strong enough for the rescues to begin, the last rescues. It felt like a big moment. He took me to where the alters were being kept. I don't know how we got there or where it was exactly. Each alter was guarded and was being tormented by the enemy. Jesus took me to where they were being held, and together we rescued each one and took them back to the dell where they were blended with me. The places they were in were often difficult and frightening for me because of the bad things that had happened. I had to face my own fear of drowning and of being buried alive, and the feelings that came with each blending were overwhelming. Jesus was healing me and also teaching me at the same time. One little girl was being held in a cage that was dangling over a pit of fire.

Let her go.
Ha ha never. She is ours.
He will set her free.
Will he now little girl but what about you will he set you free?
They came towards me all of them. They had big black swords that had fire running up the blades. They were scary and I backed up and dropped my sword. Jesus!
Don't be afraid little one.
You're so keen to have her free fine. You can join her.
Then a big black cloud swirled round me and held me so I couldn't move and then I was in the cage with the little girl dangling over the fire pit. She was awake and whimpering so I held her close.
It's ok it's ok. I've got you...Jesus.

I am here my little one. Watch.
Then I saw him in front of them.
You cannot have that child she belongs to me. She came into our realm.
She is mine. My very own. My precious child bought with my own blood. You cannot have her.
Then there was light and angels came and attacked the enemy and drove them away. And the chain glowed with a blue light and broke and then Jesus was pulling us out of the cage.
I don't understand what happened Jesus. How did they take me?
You dropped your sword my little one.
I didn't mean to. I didn't know what to do.
My little one you are mine you belong to me. They have no power over you except that which you give them.
Well. What did I do?
You believed them my little one. You believed they could take you captive and so they did.
But you rescued me Jesus.
Yes my little one I did. Come,
Then we were in the dell again and Jesus was holding us. The girl didn't make a sound just held on tight to me.
My dearest one this little one is very afraid. She has been so hurt and she is very confused. Will you take her my little one so that I can heal you both together and in that way help her to heal faster?
Yes.
So she melted into me and I clung on to Jesus because I could feel her fear.

    I knew I had made a big mistake in dropping my sword but I needed Jesus to help me understand. Learning how to stand in faith against the enemy when there was so much fear was difficult, even though I knew that Jesus was with me.

My little one you are learning and I will teach you many things.
Tell me about my sword Jesus and what I got wrong.
Do you know what the sword is?
I am supposing it is the sword of truth.
And what does truth do?
Destroys lies and sets you free.
Yes my little one and what were you doing?
I was setting that little girl free Jesus but I didn't know how to use the sword.
What was the lie that was holding her my little one?
I don't know. There might have been a lot of them.
Yes my little one but what do you think the biggest and strongest one was?

That she belonged to them?
Yes my little one.
Should I have cut the chain Jesus? It looked like she would disappear into the fire if I did that.
But she would not my little one for once the lie was broken she would no longer have been their captive.
But yes, you did destroy the chain didn't you. I saw it glowing.
Yes my little one you did.
And then we were in your arms.
Yes my little one.
And I suppose...things aren't always what they seem on the inside or on the outside.
No my little one they aren't. That is why you must trust in the truth. I would not have let either you or that little one perish in the fire my little one.
No. You wouldn't Jesus. Ok.
Do not worry about your mistakes but remember that I am in control and I will help you.

The most difficult rescues weren't the ones where I had to battle the enemy directly though. They were the ones where I had to face and overcome my own fear.

So we were in a dark place like a muddy field with dead trees and there were explosions going off. What is this Jesus? It reminds me of the Somme or something.
Yes my little one come this way.
So he led me through mud and explosions, until we came to a kind of ditch that was collapsing and falling in on the little girl that was there. She was getting buried and covered in worms and dirt. And the explosions were going on and it was dark and it was so frightening.
Crying.
My little one hold my hand.
Help me Jesus.
We got to the place where we could almost reach her but not quite. I could see I would have to crawl through a little gap to get to her and be there with her in all of that.
I am strong enough for you my little one. Are you ready?
You want me to go in there…..Crying
Yes my little one I do. Do not be afraid. I will be with you.
Crying.
So I crawled into her and I thought I couldn't do it cos I was so scared with all the soil coming down, I thought we would be buried alive. But I pulled her out. Then I just held on to Jesus. We both did. Jesus got on his feet.

Where are we going Jesus?
There is another my little one
Crying…Help me Jesus I don't know if I can do this.
I could see a little girl. She was trapped in something like a bog or quicksand. She was sinking and struggling and covered in thick grey mud. I was so scared.

Yes my little one you can go to her. Help her.
So I went towards her and when I got close enough I laid down on my stomach and held out my hand. She grabbed it and I pulled her out and carried her back to Jesus. She was only little about four maybe.
I've got you my little one...Crying.

There is another my little one. Do you see that tree over there?
Yes.
Go to her my little one. You will find her hidden at its base.
Ok.
I was crying a lot but I left the little girls with Jesus and went towards the dead tree. The girl was kind of hidden in a thorn bush... in a hole at the base of the tree.
Crying….I don't know how to get her out.
Use your sword my little one.
So I took my sword and cut through all the branches and thorns and pulled her out. I got cut but I didn't care. I was crying a lot.

Little one will you take them.
Blend you mean Jesus?
Yes my little one.
Can I take it?
Yes my little one you are strong enough.
Ok. So I held all three of them to me and they melted into me. It didn't feel too good and I got a bit overwhelmed by all the things they were feeling...Crying.
Little one you are not trapped there you are safe in my arms. You are safe my little one.
I felt like I was trapped and getting buried and sucked down and there was no escape. It was horrible and I cried and cried.
I've got you my little one. I am holding you. You are safe and you are loved. There is nothing to fear.
Crying…I can't get out I can't get out…Crying.

My little one you are safe in my arms. You are out my little one.
Crying…Hold me hold me…Crying.
Always my little one. Always.
I cried for a while but calmed down eventually. That was terrifying Jesus.
But you are safe my little one there is nothing to fear.

The rescues happened over a couple of days. Finally we got to the last one. I was so glad because it had been very hard, and I was feeling awful from all of the blending and the feelings that went with that.

Who is this?
This is an older girl my little one she is thirteen. She loved the Goatman as her father. He captured her heart my little one and made many promises to her that he never kept. He broke her my little one so that she was subject to his will, but she never lost her love for him so great was her need for a father.
That sounds bad.
Yes my little one for she is bound in many chains, but it is not too much for me my little one.
Ok. So then I found we were in blackness and it was thick. I couldn't see anything or feel anything. This is what I was expecting Jesus.

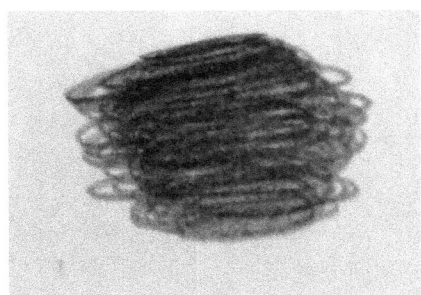

Yes my little one I know. Hold my hand and do not let go. I know the way.
I can't see anything or feel anything Jesus.
I know my little one but she is here. You must talk to her and help her. Here.
Hello. I bent down where Jesus said but I couldn't see her. When I touched her I could feel the thick chains that were covering her.
My name is Pearl. I have come to find you and help you. Can you hear me?
Did you see him?
Who?
My daddy he left me here. He is coming back. Did you see him?
I was sent to find you. I was sent by your daddy who loves you.
You were? But I am stuck. I can't move. It is heavy so heavy.
She is covered in chains.
Yes my little one. You must tell her the truth so that their hold on her is weakened.
Ok...but she thinks he sent me.
I know my little one.
Should I tell her?
Not yet my little one for the chains that bind her would only tighten.
Oh dear. Help me.
Yes my little one I will.
I can help you get free of those chains.
How?
I am going to tell you a story. It is a story about a princess who got lost and confused but was rescued and healed and restored.

How will that help?
It will help you to see.
I don't understand.
Can I tell you my story?
Ok.

Once upon a time there was a princess. She was very lovely but she had been lost for a long time. She was stolen from her daddy when she was only a baby and she didn't know where she was and she didn't know who she was either. She didn't know her name or where she came from or who her real daddy was. But the one who stole her looked after her. He wasn't very kind and did bad things to her, but the princess loved him anyway because she didn't have anyone else. She thought he was her true daddy and so she loved him and wanted him to love her. She thought he must even though he did bad things to her because he was her daddy. The princess couldn't see that he was tricking her. She couldn't see that he told her lies about who he was and about who she was too. She didn't know who he was, how he was the enemy of her daddy that stole her from him. He was glad to steal her heart from her daddy and to do bad things to her. That was what he wanted. The princess felt weighed down by sorrow and by pain, and by all the lies she was told until she couldn't move or see. She was in a dark, dark place and couldn't find her way out. She thought her daddy would rescue her but he never came. But her true daddy, the one she was stolen from all that time ago, sent another of his children to find her. He sent her into the darkness to show her who she was and to tell her that her true daddy was waiting for her and could rescue her from the dark place she was in... What do you think the princess should do?

I think if he is her true daddy she should go to him and not be in the darkness anymore.
I think so too. Do you know who's story it is?
I don't know. Is it your story?
It is my story and I was rescued from the darkness. But it is your story too and you can be rescued as well.
But I'm not a princess.
Your daddy says you are. Remember you were stolen from him but he knows you. He never forgot you. He sent me to rescue you.
My daddy?
Yes. Your daddy and my daddy are the same. He rescued me and now it is your turn. Can you move?
I can yes.
Here is my hand can you take it?
Yes. Here. I can see...kind of.
Yes it isn't so dark anymore. Can you stand?
Yes I can stand. It is true. It is true.
Yes it is true.
I see you. Hello.
Hello.
Who is he?
He brought me here. He was sent by daddy to help us.
Oh. Ok...
Come.
Jesus took us to the dell
What is this place?
It is a safe place my little one. My dearest one Pearl told you a story. A true story of how you were lost but now you are found.
Yes.
But there is more. Long ago you were separated from Pearl by the things that your

daddy's enemy did to both of you. But that was not what your daddy wanted for you. You were meant to be together. You can be together again.
But who will I be?
You will be who you were always meant to be, before you were taken by the one who held you captive. As part of Pearl you will be all that you were meant to be. A princess loved and wanted, treasured and held.
Oh. Me and Pearl together?
Yes my little one. What do you think?
I would like that.
Pearl?
Yes.
Come then.
And so she blended with me and I held on to Jesus.
My little one I am holding you and loving you and giving you all the strength you need.
Good.
My little one Hold on to me. I will not let you go. I am healing you.

When all twelve were rescued and blended with me I was very tired and feeling kind of depressed. I think the battles and the feelings were overwhelming, but it didn't stop there because now I was beginning to remember the memories that they had held. I was glad that it was done though. It felt like a really important moment in my healing... in our healing.

> Well...first of all did I hear singing this morning and were they having a party?
> **Yes my little one they were. They were celebrating the last of the rescues.**
> So they are the last?
> **Yes my little one they are.**
> So now the land will start to change and there will be more blendings with those in the dell.
> **Yes my little one the land is already changing and those inside are blending my little one as they heal. There are already far fewer of them than when you were last inside.**
> It is kind of exciting Jesus but it is kind of ...I don't want to be hopeful because we have been disappointed so many times.
> **My little one whatever lies ahead of you, you walk with me. You are healing and growing and you are walking forward into all that I have for you. Those things are good my little one even if they do not look the way you expect them to.**
> That is true Jesus. So they were having a party?
> **Yes my little one they were, for there is much for them to celebrate my little one. The last stronghold of the enemy is broken and those that were being held captive are now free. Healing is happening my little one and new life is before all of you.**
> It is kind of strange Jesus but it makes me happy.
> **Yes my little one it makes me happy too.**

Jesus had told me that the land would change as I healed and after the last rescues he took me back inside to see what was happening.

> What is happening inside?
> **The healing is continuing my little one and there are many changes that are happening. Would you like to see?**
> Yes. I would.
> **Come then my little one.**
> I could see that the land is now a bit like an island at the top of a waterfall...with the water going over the edge all around. The sea isn't very big now before it gets to the waterfall, and the forest has shrunk so it is only a few trees. The dell is the same and the playground is still there, but everything else is gone.

That is a strange thing Jesus.
It seems so to you my little one but the land is changing and shrinking and becoming less so that your land can become more.
But where is all the water going Jesus?
It is not going anywhere my little one it is simply flowing.
I don't understand...oh well, it is making a big waterfall..
Yes my little one it is. Look to the other side.
Ok...that part you made into a kind of waterfall has spread, so now...well it is very strange Jesus.
My little one everything here is changing and becoming just as you are and even though the land itself looks smaller, there is more life and power here than ever before.
The dell looks the same Jesus.
Yes my little one for those who live there still need it to be a safe place where they can relax and have fun and be together.
But there isn't too much else now Jesus. Just the playground and the mountain and a little bit of forest.
Yes my little one.
Are all of the lower levels gone now?
Yes my little one they are. This is all that remains my little one.
You have been busy Jesus.
Yes my little one I have.

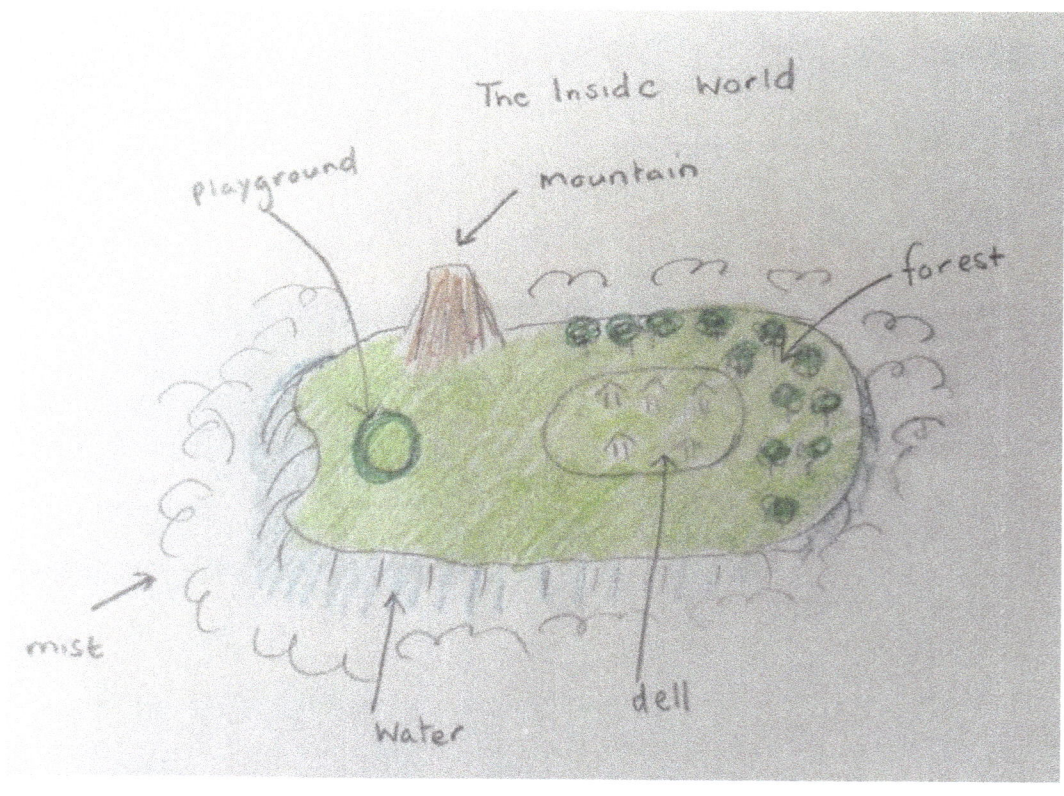

Chapter 7

Rainbows and Bubbles

The last remaining alters had been rescued and I had blended with them all. That was a lot of blending is a short space of time, and it meant that I was having a lot of memories and difficult feelings. Even so I was feeling hopeful because there were no more alters to be rescued and it seemed like maybe the end was in sight at long last. I found that I was thinking differently about daddies, the dark terror seemed to have gone and that was good.

I feel better Jesus even with the memories and stuff and I am looking forward to spending time with daddy and that is a big, big change.
Yes my little one it is for I have been healing you and making you ready.
Will it be soon?
Yes my little one it will.
I need to make daddy's[Mike] card today...or tomorrow Jesus. I was a bit scared calling him daddy last night and I realized why.
Tell me my little one.
I know you know already...but it was because I thought he might be ashamed to let others know he is my daddy. Even though he seems happy with it...and I didn't realize I was thinking that until last night.
Do you think he is ashamed of you my little one?
No...I don't know. I think I am still afraid he might be somewhere inside of him and wishing I wouldn't call him daddy in front of people.
Then why did you my little one?
Because I don't want to listen to fear and because he made his choice, I didn't make him Jesus.
No my little one you didn't and he is not ashamed to call you daughter not in any way. He is very proud of you my little one.
It is a strange thing Jesus.
I know it seems so to you my little one.
He hasn't even really known me very long.
But he has known parts of you my little one.
Yes...does he see them?
Sometimes my little one but mostly he sees you.
I am still not sure what I am like Jesus but I know I feel better. I feel stronger and more hopeful and less doubting and more trusting, and less hurting and afraid and that is all good.
Yes my little one it is very good. My dearest one even though you do not yet see yourself clearly you know that you are different and more able. The future does not hold the same fear for you that it has.

I was learning about daddies and what it might mean to have one…or two. It was very strange to me and I wasn't sure, but it was better. I wrote to Mike, my daddy, to tell him about my first meeting with my heavenly daddy.

Hi daddy
I thought I would tell you about my daddy's day. I hope you have had a good one. This morning I went for a run. I wasn't sure how far I could go, because of not doing much the last few weeks and because I didn't know about my back either, but I asked Jesus and he said keep going so I did. I did none...lol...nine miles and I am ok. Then after I got washed and stuff I knew what Jesus had planned for me.

Hi Jesus
Hello my little one. Are you ready?
We are going to see daddy?
Yes my little one we are.
Ok.
Hold my hand then my little one.
I think it is amazing Jesus that I even want to go. You have done a lot in a short time.
Yes my little one I have but there is more.
I heard him before I saw anything.
My child.
Daddy.
My child do not be afraid. Come. Come into my arms of love. I will never hurt you my little one.
I let go of Jesus hand and climbed up some steps. I thought maybe there was a throne at the top, but it was so bright I couldn't even really see anything. I climbed up on to what I guessed was the throne but it felt soft. Then I was sort of wrapped up in rainbows. It is hard to describe. Like being in a rainbow bubble, but the rainbow was made of stuff...kind of thick and you could touch it and it was all around, but it didn't feel like it was heavy or going to suffocate me.
This is a strange place.
It is a safe place my little one.
I can't see you daddy.
I know my child but I am here.
You are light.
Yes my little one I am.
And colors like rainbows but I suppose that is light too.
Yes my child it is.
And there is music but I can't quite hear it, and beautiful water and a lovely sound. Maybe that is the music.
I could see water at the bottom of the steps now, coming out from underneath. It was very clear and kind of lively and it made a lovely noise that I can't describe.
Being in your arms is strange daddy. Not like normal arms.
No my little one it isn't but this place is just what you need it to be for today.
Can it ...you be like different things?
I am many things my child all of them good.
And so will it be different sometimes when I come?
Yes my little one sometimes it will, according to your need.
Right now it is about feeling safe.
Yes little one.
I do feel safe. And I am not crying or hurting it is just a lovely place to be in your arms daddy. It is strange but it is lovely. Can Jesus come too?
Yes my little one he can.
Jesus came and sat next to me.
You are his daddy too aren't you?
First and last and always.
And the Holy Spirit. He must be here.
He is in everything my little one. There is nowhere he is not.
That is a strange thing cos there are some places ...bad places...where I wouldn't think he was there.
But he is my little one.
It must hurt him to be there.
Yes my little one it does very much.
Happy daddy's day daddy. It...I don't know. You are giving me a big gift.

Yes my little one I am. I am giving you myself but the gift that you give is just as precious my little one.
I don't bring anything daddy.
You brought yourself my little one. You are the gift.
But I am not as good as you daddy. I don't think that I am as good.
You are to me my little one.
You are soft and warm. I don't know how light can be soft and warm but you are. You are comforting daddy.
Yes my child.

I took Jesus hand.

Jesus I love you.
I know you do my little one.
I love you too daddy but you still feel a bit of a stranger to me…Crying…You are making me so well. Thankyou.
My child we are making you all you were created to be. It brings us great joy my little one to see you well and whole.
I suppose you see…Crying…Me that way already…Crying…I don't want to cry but you are so good.
Yes my little one always. Always and forever.
Crying…It isn't a painful crying. It a kind of wow crying…Crying…It is better. I like it better…Crying
You are held my little one and you are so very loved. This is your place, right here in my arms and it will never be taken from you.
Crying…I have a daddy…Crying…Who loves me…Crying…two daddy's…Crying
Yes my little one you do.
Crying…Wow….Crying.
I am here for you always my little one. All you must do is come.
Crying…I think I will like to come. It doesn't hurt….Crying…It doesn't hurt….Crying.
No my little one not anymore.
Crying….Maybe I can just rest here a little while….Crying
I would like that my little one. My Pearl.
Crying….Ok.

While I was healing and learning to accept that I had not one but two good daddies healing inside was continuing. Jesus told me that some of the alters had blended and that the land was changing too. I didn't go inside, he said it wasn't time. I kept on spending time with daddy, trying to understand what it meant to have one.

Are you going to show me and help me know what a daddy...a real good daddy is.
Yes my little one I am. I am going to show you my love and my goodness as only a daddy can.
I don't think I know what it is really...I know Jesus looks after me...is it the same?
Yes my little one it is the same for he and I are one and yet it is different because I am your father.
That is hard to understand. The same but different.
Yes my little one it is but you will understand in time.
I just thought of something. Blossum had her safe place in Blossum castle that you gave her and that was wonderful and I don't think she explored half of it...but this is my safe place here in you daddy. Is that right?
Yes my little one it is.
I think that is better than a castle...and I want to explore you daddy. Is that ok?
Yes my little one it is. That is what I want for you my little one for you to explore

everything that I am. To seek me out in every way that you can. To have adventures in me my little one.
Adventures in you. That sounds amazing daddy. How can I have adventures in you?
By discovering me my little one by searching me by knowing me.

I kept spending time with daddy but it wasn't always easy. The enemy wasn't happy and kept whispering their lies and sometimes I listened and it made me feel afraid again and not want to be with my daddy.

So he took me to the same place as before. I suppose it is daddy's throne but I only ever see the white steps that go up to it, because the top is covered in light and cloud and rainbows and pillows. But this time I stood at the bottom of the steps and didn't go up.
Hello daddy.
My child do not be afraid to come to me. I am safe and I will not ever hurt you.
I feel like I have been bad.
No my child you have not been bad, come.
So I went up the steps and into the pillows but I wasn't feeling very sure.
My little one you are dearly loved. Nothing and no one can ever take you from me. Do not let the enemy make you afraid my little one there is nothing to fear.
I didn't know...I mean I don't understand why I am afraid.
Because they have been whispering lies into your heart my little one even if you are not aware of it.
But that means I must be listening.
There is still much healing to be done my little one, you are only just beginning your journey into my heart of love for you. There is much still to discover and many things still to be overcome.
I suppose I thought I was better.
You are moving forward my little and have taken many steps to be where you are, but it is only the beginning my little one.
You are still soft pillows daddy.
Yes my little one I am for that is your need right now. To feel safe and protected my little one.
Crying...Yes.
My little one I am watching over you, you are safe and you are loved my little one. Even when you are not aware of being in my arms still you are safe and protected just as you are now.
I can't imagine anything bad happening to me here daddy.
No my little one nothing bad will ever happen to you here.
I think I am wanting more needing more. But I don't know what it is.
You are longing for the closeness of a father my little one that is a good thing for as you see and feel your need I can begin to meet it.
Crying....Crying.
My little one it is not a bad thing to cry for you have much to grieve but I am here for you my little one and I will help you and heal you and fill the need you have for a daddy's love.
Crying...It is a big need daddy....Crying.
Yes my child it is but it is not too big my little one. You are safe and you are held and you are loved.
Crying.
There is so much love for you to receive my little one this is only the beginning.
Crying...I don't know.
I know my little one.
Crying.
My little one as you receive my love there is healing happening. It is making you

mine my little one. There is nothing that can keep you from me. Nothing from the past my little one. None of that matters to me. You have nothing to be ashamed of.
Crying…How can I have a daddy? I shouldn't have a daddy. I am too bad…Crying.
Do you think that is true my little one? Is that how I see you?
Crying…No….Crying.
Then do not listen to lies but only of my words of love to you. I am your daddy.
Crying
I will always be your daddy and I love you and I am so very proud of you.
Crying…Jesus.
I am here my little one I am here.
Crying.
Jesus came and sat in the pillows with me and held me cos I was crying a lot.
My little one I will draw you here many times so that I can pour my love into you. Do not be afraid to come. You are not bad. You are my very own daughter. You are loved and cared for, safe and protected and nothing will ever change that.

It had been a while since I had been inside to one of those places the Holy Spirit showed me sometimes, when he wanted to teach me something. We had been to the forest of faith before and seen our faith tree that was growing there, but there had been a lot of healing and a lot of changes since then. Now the Holy Spirit took me there again. He said there was something he wanted to show me about my heavenly daddy.

Hi Holy Spirit.
Hello my dearest child.
What are we going to do?
I want you to open your heart up to the truth of who your father is my little one. Your true father and not the ones who lied to you or were cruel and unkind or abandoned you. You never belonged to them my little one, but only and always to your true Heavenly Father who has always loved you and wanted you.
Will you help me Holy Spirit?
Yes my little one I will if you are willing.
I am.
Come then my little one take my hand.
Are we going somewhere?
Yes my little one we are.
Where are we?
We are in the forest of faith my little one.
What does this have to do with daddy?
Everything my little one for it is his forest.
Is it?
Yes my little one it is.
Well, I suppose it must be. So what do you want to show to me?
Come my little one.
Do you see?
Is that my tree?
Yes my little one it is.
Help me see.
Tell me what you see my little one.
Well, it is in a kind of a dip kind of on its own. And it isn't very big but it looks strong, but its roots are kind of uncovered and …it looks like there has been digging going on.
What else my little one?
The sky is blue and there is no wind. There are tiny silver leaves and maybe berries, I don't know. Can we go closer?
Yes my dearest one come.

So we went closer. I touched the trunk of the tree. It felt so very strong like one of those steel cables that they use in buildings. That's what it reminded me of.

Oh, the trunk is so strong and made up of so many different strands all woven together. The ground is loose like I said and yes there are lots of little leaves and small round berries and all of it is silver.

Do you know what this means my dearest one?

Not really. I am supposing the trunk is made up of strands, because of the alters...do I get their faith Holy Spirit?

It is added to yours my little one as you blend with them everything that they are becomes part of who you are. Including their faith my little one.

Cool. So that is why I am...my tree is made up of strands and you have woven us together to make something very strong.

Yes my little one we have. What else do you see?

I don't know really what the leaves and the berries are...maybe that is about life and growth and fruit, but the fruit is small.

Perhaps my little one but it is also abundant and as it grows and ripens there will be an abundance for you to give away and share with others.

Is that what I will do?

Yes my little one it is.

Can I do that? How do you share the fruits of your faith, what is it?

The things that you are enabled to do with us my little one. Your acts of faith and the life that you live will bear much fruit my little one, which will be given to others to help them on their faith journey.

Because...I don't know say more.

My little one as you live the life we have for you, as you give yourself completely to us and live in our strength and our power, you are enabled to do so many things that you could not otherwise do. These are acts of faith my little one.

Yes ok.

Faith produces faith my little one that is the nature of it. What you have you give away to others. Your faith is given to others to help grow the faith that they already have.

Ok...so the berries are to give away when they are ripe.

Yes my little one they are.

But they aren't ready yet.

No my little one not yet.

When will that time be?

When you are ready to begin your work for us my little one. When you are fully prepared. When the healing is complete and you are free to do all that you are called to do.

Ok....so what about the ground. Holy Spirit. Have ...has the tree just been planted here or is it getting ready to be moved?

Your tree is being prepared my little one, because it will soon be time for it to be moved to a place where there is more light and more sunshine and more room for you to grow.

Is this like a nursery, sheltered and protected?

Yes my little one it is. This is where you have been as we have been healing you and helping you to grow, but it is almost time for you to be moved to a different and better place where you have room to grow my little one.

Ok...I don't know what that means...I mean I understand but what does it mean?

My little one in order for you to do all that we have purposed for you to do, you need to have a faith that is growing and strong, reaching out far beyond yourself to touch the lives of others. This means that we have to reposition you my little one so that you are in the right conditions for that kind of faith to grow.

So a new place.

Yes my little one.
Is this like the picture of the golden tree...that is what I am thinking of?
What do you think the golden color is my little one?
I suppose...I don't know...it makes me think of your glory, but I am not sure what I mean by that really.
As you shine with our love and with our power, with who we are my little one, that is our glory. It is who we are.
So a golden tree is shining with you.
Yes my little one that is so.
But my tree is silver.
Because that is the color of redemption my little one. That is what we have been doing. Restoring and redeeming but as our work in you changes so the color of your tree will change.
It will be gold?
Yes my little one it will.
Cool. And are you going to plant it beside still waters like in the picture.
Yes my little one we are.
That all sounds good Holy Spirit and encouraging and interesting, but I am not sure how this helps with daddy.
Who do you think planted you here my little one?
I don't know...I suppose I think it was you Holy Spirit.
Yes my dearest one it was.
Thankyou...but ...
My little one everything comes from the father.
Yes.
Including the faith I have given to you. Your daddy wanted you to have that faith my little one so that he could claim you for his own, so that you could grow strong and in time shine with his glory. It was and is his plan my little one.
Was it?
Yes my little one it was.
I am not sure what to say or even what I think. Mostly, I am still not understanding why you are telling me this Holy Spirit.
My little one who is your daddy?
He is God and he is powerful and strong and knows everything and made everything...though...I am not sure because Jesus does stuff and you do too, but I keep being told he is the source. Everything came from him. I came from him...I suppose and everything I am came from him...on purpose and not by accident cos he doesn't do accidents.
No little one he doesn't.
I don't know what else Holy Spirit.
No my little one I know that you don't.
Can you help me to know. I feel like I am not...getting it.
I can help you my little one.
Oh...I am remembering about the father being the gardener...something like that... when it says about trimming the branches and things.
Yes my little one that is so. And as the gardener he chooses what he wants in his garden.
I suppose this is part of his garden.
Yes my little one it is.
And daddy made a place for me.
Yes my little one he did and now he is preparing to move you to another place my little one so that you can grow and become all that he has dreamed for you to be.
And I suppose a good gardener...I don't know that much about gardening Holy Spirit but they prepare the ground and feed it and have the right kind of hole in the right place for

each type of plant...so this piece of ground was chosen just for me. So my faith could grow strong.
Yes my little one it was.
And I suppose that the place I am planted is about my life and the circumstances of it, and he has given me all the things I need to grow strong, and he has watched over me and protected me and maybe pruned me and fed me, and got rid of things that attacked me, and now he sees I am ready to be moved to a place where I can grow bigger and stronger. He is thinking about me and caring for me...he is...a gardener.
Yes my little one he is.
I don't think I have thought about him like that but I quite like it. Think it is a friendly and caring thing to be. Nurturing that is the word. Daddy is nurturing...helping me to grow strong.
Yes my little one he is.
And I am strong...I mean I look strong and feel strong...I could be bigger I suppose.
And that will come my little one. What matters is that you are strong enough to move from your place of hiddenness and protection into a place where you have room to grow and spread and become.
Yes...but...there is more digging to do because I am still firmly in this ground.
That is so my little one but not for long. All things are being prepared my little one.
Can I see where you are taking me?
Yes my little one. This is the place we have for you my little one.
It was a beautiful green and sunny place looking over some water...a lot of water. Maybe a lake, but he called it a river so it must be a big river. But then he took me down a little bank to flat bare brown piece of land...a bit like a muddy beach by the side of the water. These wasn't anything else there...no plants or trees. Just mud.
Why here...I mean...it is very beautiful all around. This is next to the water, but it is a bit exposed and the soil is bare.
My little one this is the best place for you to be. As you put down your roots you will find fresh and living water. There is nothing to restrict your growth my little one. You have the full sun, water, good soil and room to grow.
I do. It is true.
Do not fear being exposed my little one for remember your father the gardener has chosen this place especially for you. He know everything that you need to grow strong and tall and broad, so that your branches will reach out well beyond the place where you are planted.
He must know.
Yes my little one he does. I want you to think about these things. And remember that your daddy is a gardener who has watched over you tenderly and will continue to do so.
Yes. Ok. Thankyou. You always surprise me with what you show me.
That is because I am showing you new things my little one.
Yes. You are. It is nice and warm here.
Yes my little one it is and even if it gets very warm there is always enough water my little one. The river will never run dry.
That is good because the warmer it is the more water I will need.
Yes my little one that is so. Come then that is enough for today.
Thankyou Holy Spirit. Bye not bye.
Bye not bye my little one.

What the changes were that were coming I didn't know, but it did help me to see my heavenly daddy as a nurturing gardener. It was a warm and friendly picture. I kept on visiting him and as I got less afraid, he showed me new things about himself.

Where are we going Jesus?
We are going to daddy my little one only this time you will see him differently.
Ok. Are you coming too Holy Spirit?
I am always with you my dearest child.
Good. Ok. Help me see and everything.
Yes my little one we will. What do you see my little one?
I don't know what it is. I don't know what I'm seeing.
Look a little closer my dearest one.
Well...the best I can come up with is a field of bubbles all joined together on the ground but it doesn't make sense to me.
Let us go in my little one.
They are bubbles and they have rainbows in them and they are deep and they are sticking to us. But I am still not understanding...it's like they are wrapping me up like a bubble blanket.
Yes little one.
But they are soft and very pretty and not wet and they don't burst. Is this daddy...like soft pillows?
Yes my child I am here.
But I know it's not anymore silly than soft pillows...but what are you showing me daddy?
I am showing you more of who I am my little one.
But I am not seeing.
I know my little one but allow yourself to remember.
What do you want me to remember?...I don't want to remember bad things daddy.

I was remembering being in the box, the luggage trunk that grandad shut me in.

I know my little one but this will help you it will not harm you.
Well I see me in the trunk but I am wrapped in your bubbles daddy.
Yes my little one I was there. I was wrapped around you. Keeping you safe. Loving you and surrounding you with who I am.
Like beautiful bubble wrap.
Yes my little one like that. My little one there is nowhere you can go where I am not. I am always wrapped around you. I stick to you my little one I cannot be separated from you. We are never apart.
So I am always wrapped in your bubbles daddy.
Yes my little one you are.
But what are they?
My love and my protection my little one, given to you, surrounding you, sustaining you, protecting you and speaking to you of who I am.
Why rainbows...is it just cos you are light?
I am light my little one but light has many different facets and all of them are given to you. All of them are surrounding you at all times.
You are showing my strange things.
Yes my little one but I am explaining to you who I am in a way that you can understand so that you feel safe and loved my little one for that is what you are.
Why a big field?
I am everywhere my little one there is nowhere I am not and wherever you go I will always be there with you.
Like your bubbles fill every space.
Yes my little one.
So I am always kind of swimming through...bubbles...through you.
Completely surrounded my little one at all times and in all places. Loved and protected and held.
But not...I mean I can move however I want. They don't get in my way.
No my little one my love will not confine you or hold you back.

It is a strange thing.
Perhaps my little one but you will remember it and you will know that I am with you and that you are loved and protected at all times.
I will. I am thinking about those verses that say about being under the shadow of your wings. Is this like that?
Yes my little one there are many different ways to explain my love for you and the ways that I protect you and keep you safe. All of them are true my little one given to help you understand more of who I am.

I was learning more about daddy, about who he is and what it means for me to have a daddy, but there was still a lot of healing to be done. The Holy Spirit told me he was taking down the walls in my heart so that feelings and memories would begin to surface, so that they could be healed. I was having bad dreams and memories, the enemy was still attacking me and using the things that happened in everyday life to stir up fear from the past. When I was talking to daddy mike on Skype, it seemed to me he thought I was asking him to help me with something and said that he wouldn't. I got very confused and upset. And then I was in daddy's pillows and Jesus was holding me and the Holy Spirit was there too.

Crying...Daddy…Crying
I am here my child we are all of us here with you. You are loved and you are safe. My little one your daddy loves you. You know this.
Crying…Yes.
My little one do not be afraid to feel what is in your heart. We are healing you my little one.
Crying...Jesus…Crying
My little one tell me what you are feeling.
I feel ashamed….Crying….I feel so ashamed.
Why my little one?
Crying…He thinks I asked him for help…Crying…I didn't I didn't I didn't I didn't …Crying.
My little one it is not wrong to ask for help.
Crying…It is…Crying…It is bad and wrong and I should be punished. I will be punished because I am bad…Crying.
No my little one you will not be punished. You are not bad.
Crying…I must be because he said no…Crying…And I didn't even ask…Crying.
My little one do you think that is true. That because someone says no to you that you were bad to ask?
Yes.
Why my little one?
Because I am asking for something I shouldn't have. I am not worth helping…Crying …I am not worth helping…..Crying.
My little one this is a lie that you have believed for so long but it is not true.
Crying…I know you help me all the time….Crying…I ask for help every day and you always give it. You never say no….Crying.
My little one you have been so very hurt but the lies you have believed are just that. They are lies my little one.
I can ask you for help because I know you will always say yes…Crying….And I am never bad to ask…Crying. But I will never ask daddy for help. Not ever… Crying…Because the answer will always be no…Crying…And they will put me in the box…Crying…Is that it. I was put in the box?
Yes my little one.
Actually me. Not an alter?
Many of your alters share memories of the box my little one, but you are one of those who was punished in that way.
Crying…For asking?

Yes my little one for asking.
I won't ever ask. I won't…Crying.
My little one you are so dearly loved. Your daddy will not ever punish you for asking for his help.
Crying…I won't ever ask. I won't.
My little one do you think he wants you to be afraid to ask for his help?
Crying…I don't know…Crying…No…Crying…Grandad hated me. He hated me. I was bad I was so bad and he put me in the box…Crying.
Yes my little one he did but that is not because you were bad it was because his heart was full of darkness. My little one he took pleasure in hurting and punishing you. That is his shame my little one and not yours.
Crying…I was bad….
No my little one you weren't. My little one in all the things you have learned about yourself and who you are, we have never told you that you were bad nor have we punished you for asking for help. It is not different with your daddy my little one. He loves you and wants to help you.
Crying…I know it is all getting mixed up.
Yes my little one it is. Your daddy is not like your grandad in any way.
No. He isn't.
My little one you are loved just as you are. You do not need to be perfect to be loved my little one. The mistakes you make will not change our love for you nor will they change his. You are loved my little one. You are not bad and asking for help is not a bad thing for you to do.
My little one you understand many things about the past and about the hurt and shame that you have carried. Some things are still hidden from you my little one but you know that your grandad was a man who lived in darkness and the things he did to you were bad, not because you were bad but because he followed the evil one.
Yes. I understand that.
And you know that he does not reflect who your daddy is. Not our father who covers you in his rainbows and keeps you safe or your daddy who helps you to be you in a world that says you cannot be who you are.
I know daddy helps me in lots of ways…Crying…He is always helping me.
Yes my little one he is.
Crying…But you asked him to do that not me…Crying…I wouldn't ask it…Crying.
I know my little one for you are still believing the lie that you are not worth it.
I don't think I am worth it…Crying.
I know my little one I know.
Crying….Am I ever going to be better?
Yes my little one you are.
Crying.
You are going to be healed and made well again my little one.
Crying…Is this one of the things...the feelings that were walled off in my heart?
Yes my little one it is.
So it is good it came out.
Yes my little one. Now we can heal you and set you free just a little bit more.
Thankyou.
You are welcome my little one. My dearest one even though there is still more healing to be done that does not mean that you are not nearing its ending. You are growing stronger every day my little one. We are making you one in us.
Please will you help me?
Yes my little one always and in everything.
Crying.
You are loved my little one. You are so very loved.
I want to be better. I want to be full of you…Crying…I don't want lies and darkness in my

heart…Crying…Please get it out…Crying.
Yes my little one that is what we are doing. Step by step as you are able to bear it.
Go faster daddy.
My child we are taking you as fast as you are able. Hold on my little one. You are safe and you are loved just as you are.
I want to be better. I don't want to keep getting tripped up by the enemy. I don't want to hurt people with things I say and do.
Yes my little one we know this and your daddy knows it too. You are learning and growing my little one. The enemy may try to stop this. He may have you in his sights my little one but he cannot have you. You belong to us. You are safe and you are loved and we will use everything he does to help you.
You are always helping me.
Yes my little one we are.
And I'm not bad to ask.
No my little one it is a good thing for you to ask. It is good for you to recognize your need and come to us.
But it is different with people.
Sometimes my little one but that does not make you bad for asking.
But how will I know when it is bad and when it's not.
It is never bad my little one. Even when people say no it is not bad for you to ask.
I think I am not really seeing that yet.
No my little one for there is more healing that needs to be done but we will help you my little one it will come.
I know you know how to do it.
Yes my little one we do.
I need to go and get ready.
Our comfort is with you my little one.
I keep seeing the box.
I know my little one but it will fade.
Yes. Ok. Crying….Please be with me.
Always my little one. We are always with you.
Yes. You are. I am safe and I am loved…Crying…I am your Pearl…Crying
Yes my little one you are and you will always be so.

Daddy Mike wrote to me and said I hadn't done anything wrong and he wasn't upset with me, and that helped and I stopped feeling so scared and crying, but the feelings didn't exactly disappear and I didn't ever want to ask him for help.

> *Hi daddy*
> *Thankyou for your email. I still feel like I did something wrong but I know it is a lot of stuff getting mixed up for me. Last night when I was reading through some chapters to send to you, I read this memory that I have put in and I knew it was mine. I dint know before but it is the thing that I was remembering with daddy about asking for help.*
>
> *I saw grandad coming towards me and he looked angry. I don't know why. I was very frightened. He pinned me down on my back on a table I think, with one hand on my chest. I didn't have any clothes on and I must have been three I suppose. He called over his shoulder... Eve get me some rag. Eve is mums name. He took the rag she gave him and pushed it up between my legs inside me. I suppose it was to do stretching I don't know. Mum walked away. I cried mammy don't go, mammy don't go, but she left me. Maybe it was because I was crying I don't know but grandad picked me up by one arm and dragged me into the punishment room. He put me in the luggage trunk and shut and locked the lid, and I cried and cried mammy, mammy. In*

the trunk I could see that Jesus was curled up in there with me holding me close. He didn't leave me.

I suppose it is things like that that make me afraid to ask for help and feel like I am bad if I do it. Jesus says I was put in the box a lot of times. I didn't sleep good again and I was remembering things. Not new things but it made me wonder if they are my memories and not someone else's. Jesus says they are mine. They are memories of being in a pub or something like that, and grandad taking money from men so they could go in a room and do it with me. Stuff like that. I never came across an alter who had those memories even though we have had them for a long time. That's because they are mine. I spent some time in daddy's pillows and Jesus was holding me and the Holy Spirit was there. Jesus said they wanted to heal me. The Holy Spirit held my hands in his. He was blue and sparkly and it kind of went into me so I looked blue and sparkly too and I started to remember. It was Barbara the lady next door. I knocked on her door and was let in and went upstairs. I was only little...maybe three. She had put a white sheet on her bed and I saw the hook in the ceiling and I was scared. But she didn't do anything with the hook. She told me to take my clothes off and put the speculum in me to stretch. She said I was for daddies to do what they wanted with and it was her job to prepare me. She called in her son. He was a teenager. She said she wanted to teach me to do something that daddies like. She put his thing in her mouth and did things. It was disgusting. Then I had to do it just like she told me. It makes me feel disgusting and ashamed. Jesus says these things, all of them are my memories and it is because the holy spirit took the wall down in my heart, that I am remembering so that they can heal me. Jesus says I was on the outside until I was 3 or 4 and then I was hidden away because I got too hurt. So I suppose that is what is happening right now. I will be glad when it is done. I am tired because of not sleeping and there is bad feelings and pictures, because of the healing but I am ok. I know I don't feel too good but I am getting better because the bad stuff in my heart is getting taken away. So when it is better I will be even better than before and that is good.

I was healing and that was good but it didn't feel good. But it did mean that I was ready to go to a new and deeper place in daddy's heart.

I am tired daddy. I need you to help me with that.
I will help you my dearest child. Come. Come deeper.
Jesus took my hand and led me out of the place with the pillows.
It is like a tunnel. A tunnel of light...We went down a long tunnel. It looked like it was made up of bubbles of bright white light. It was quite long. We came to another room that seemed kind of round. It was white but not bright and there was a bubbling pool in the middle.
What is this place?
This is a place of healing and cleansing.
The water looks hot.
Yes my little one but not too hot. Come.

We all got in the pool. I couldn't tell if it was water or not but it was warm and nice. I was wearing a swimming costume and a little swimming cap with flowers on it, but Jesus didn't get changed and the Holy Spirit doesn't have clothes...I don't think.

It is warm and bubbly.
Yes my little one.
Rainbow bubbles again.
Yes my little one you are always safe and protected.
Daddy.
Yes my child.
You have strange places in your heart but I suppose it is like Jesus heart. He had a castle in there for Blossum.
Yes my little one he did. And now I am drawing you into my heart of love for you my

little one just as my son did.

Tell me about it daddy.

My little one now that you know and understand that you are safe I can draw you deeper. This is a place of cleansing and healing my little one. As you rest in the water you are cleansed of everything that would keep you from drawing closer my little one. It will take time to wash away the dirt and the wounds from your soul but it is happening my little one.

It is kind of sparkly in here...like stars but in the light.

Yes my little one it is.

Can you tell me about it?

Do you know what stars are my little one?

Well...they are like the sun. They are hot and give off heat and light...and other things too...we need the sun for life don't we daddy.

Yes my little one you do. These stars are also giving off light my little one. They are giving you everything you need to be cleansed and healed.

Oh. So it's not just the water.

No my little one. There is water and light and many other things you are not able to see.

Like with ...normal stars. They give off light I can't see.

Yes my little one they do and in doing so they are giving you life.

But don't they give off stuff that hurts us and burns us too.

Yes my little one they do but that is not so here my little one. Everything here is life giving.

That is good.

Yes my little one it is very good.

Will I go back to the pillows again?

You do not need to my little one for you know that you are safe in me. I am drawing you deeper and when you are ready I will lead you to a new place.

Ok daddy. But I need to stay here for a while.

Yes my little one you do.

Ok. Do I stay even when I'm not thinking about it, when I stop talking to you.

Yes my little one you do.

So you will be keeping on healing and cleansing me even if I'm not paying attention.

This is my work and not yours my little one. You do not need to do anything except rest in my love for you.

That is good. Thankyou daddy. I think maybe I need to get on with my outside jobs, but I am glad to be here and to know I feel safe enough to come.

Yes my little one it is very good. Keep coming my little one for there is so much more we have for you.

Yes. Bye not bye daddy and Jesus and Holy Spirit.

Bye not bye my little one.

I spent a lot time in the pool with Jesus. Sometimes it changed and I learned something new, but most of all I was healing and accepting that I was loved and safe and protected and loved. Always.

For those who are led by the Spirit of God are the children of God. The Spirit you received does not make you slaves, so that you live in fear again; rather, the Spirit you received brought about your adoption to sonship. And by him we cry, *"Abba,* Father." The Spirit himself testifies with our spirit that we are God's children

Romans 8:14-16

Chapter 8

What's in a Name?

While Jesus was healing me and I was accepting and spending time with my daddies, I was learning about who I was as Pearl. I was still worried that eventually I would be replaced by someone else, that I would have to start learning all over again who I was. I didn't want to do it again. While I was still living life as Jennifer, it was hard for me to see it mattered anyway. What difference did it make if I was Pearl or Blossom or Aj or anyone else when I had to be Jennifer almost all the time. I talked to Jesus about these things a lot. I talked to him about my name too. I had been known by a lot of names. I still was because I was still being Jennifer and even she was known by different names by different people. It could get confusing. As Jesus had been healing us I had different names too. Aj was just a name made up by daddy mike and we always knew that Blossom was a 'just for now' name, even though it was given to her by Jesus. He said that she wouldn't always be known by that name. We didn't realize at the time it was because they wouldn't be the ones on the outside, but now I could see it better. I saw too that it was different for me. That I did have a name, a permanent one. I thought that was a hopeful thing. It kind of helped me feel more real and like maybe I had a future. Jesus said that it was going to be my name from now on, no more changes. In a way, of course everyone I had blended with and would blend with was going to share in this name. Names mean something to Jesus, he doesn't give them by accident and he had made promises about our name even as far back as Aj.

Little one names are important to us.
Yes.
Little one your name is important to us.
But.. I don't know what it is Holy Spirit.
It is beautiful, just as you are little one.
I am glad Holy Spirit but.. I don't know what it is.
My little one when your name is revealed to you, it will be a moment of great significance. It will seal something inside of you little one, something good.
Jesus said it is something to do with saying who you are in my life and it is something to do with blessings, the blessings you have given me and the blessings you will do through me.
You have remembered well little one.
It sounds like a good name Holy Spirit but.. why are you telling me?
I want you to know little one that we have not forgotten. Your name is an important part of discovering who you are for it speaks of who we are in your life and who you are in us. It is a binding together my little one. Your name will bring blessing to you little one. It is a blessing in and of itself.
Then it is a very good name Holy Spirit, but I don't know what it is.
No little one you don't, not yet but it will come little one. We have not forgotten.
I have got used to Aj but.. it is just a make do thing. It doesn't mean anything.
No little one it doesn't but it has marked you out as an individual, separate and important to us.
Yes. Is there anything else about that...Oh... are your names.. is it... what do you mean binding together?
Little one your name tells of who you are, it is given to you by us. When it is revealed to you, then who you are will be both revealed and released in a way that will affect who you are little one. It is made of tangible spiritual stuff. Your name is real my little one.
Does that mean your name is real.. and when you revealed your name it was like spiritual stuff and something happened.
Yes little one and when you reveal who we are it is the same, for in showing the people who we are, in revealing that to them, that releases spiritual stuff little one. It is spiritual power in their lives.

Even if it isn't a name?
Yes little one...
So names have spiritual power?
Yes little one.
Is that what the stuff is?
No little one not quite there is more to it than that. It is power but it is also tangible. It is not just about the affect it has, like power, but also about what it is. There is much more to it my little one.
Ok. That is.. interesting Holy Spirit but I am not sure...
I am laying a foundation my little one.
Yes. Are you.. preparing me for my name Holy Spirit?
We are making you ready to receive it little one for your receiving of it also has power and spiritual stuff my little one.
Oh dear. There is going to be a lot of stuff flying about when I get my name Holy Spirit.
Yes my little one there is and it is good. It is very good my little one.
I will keep on looking forward to it then Holy Spirit. I forget sometimes.
Yes little one I know that you do but that, like everything else that we have promised you, will come....

And it did come of course. It came, at least in part, when Jesus showed us that I was there. It had taken time but it did come and now I understand why it took so long, because he was waiting for me to be ready. Ruth had given Jennifer a word a long time ago, before we even knew about the bad things, or alters or anything. The word was that her (or our) name was synonymous with many blessings. It made no sense at the time. I remember Jennifer saying, 'what name is that?!' Jesus told us not long after we started to talk to daddy mike and it was still Jennifer on the outside that our name was Precious. We found that very hard to accept and really hoped we weren't going to have to be called that by other people. I understand now that my name is precious because that is who I am to him, but it isn't what he wants other people to call me or even what he calls me most of the time. My name is Pearl and I wanted to try and understand what that means. I had read some things about pearls and how they are made. How the pearl that forms is made when something 'irritates' the oyster. How a beautiful pearl comes from something that causes pain.

I don't know what to say about these things Jesus. I know you have told us these things before...it is like layers and I suppose...oh...I remembered something I read about pearls. That the pearl is made up of layers...and the more layers there are the more beautiful and precious the pearl is.
Yes my little one that is so.
I have been wondering about my name Jesus...and what it means and if it is the name you told us about that is synonymous with many blessings.
And what do you think my little one?
I don't know...I suppose...I am made up of layers of blessing Jesus...that you have poured out on each one of us as you have healed us and taught us and loved us, and maybe that is what you meant. I don't know. It isn't what I was expecting but it could be that.
My little one the name I have given for you was chosen for just this reason. There is suffering my little one but there is also beauty, beauty which comes out of the suffering. My love and my grace have been sufficient for you, for all of you and I have made someone so special and beautiful, someone who is so strong in me because of all that you have suffered my little one, but also because you have trusted in me and allowed me to work and to bless you in many ways.
I don't know if I would say those things about me Jesus but you have worked hard to bring us through all the suffering and pain and lies and I know...you have done something amazing. Maybe I don't see it yet, not really but I see something.
Yes my little one you do and I will help you see it even more clearly as you write your story. For it is your story my little one. It is made up of many other stories but in the

center there is you, my pearl, my beautiful one who I am restoring and loving back to life.
I know you have loved us all just the same Jesus and understand a bit better about alters and blending than maybe Aj did, so you explain it to me different...I don't know what I am trying to say. Each of us has been on a journey and I have shared in a lot of those journeys Jesus and in a way, all of it has been my journey which continues...I am trying to see it I suppose, and understand it like you do, or something like...but it is hard.
No my little one it is not. You are my beloved child whom I have been loving and restoring from the beginning. Parts of you that were taken have been restored back to you my little one, though they were separate for a time and had their own lives and experience. Together you will be more and do more my little one which is why I have blended you and healed you as I have. So that you can be the Pearl I created you to be in this world.
But if they are all a part of me, why will you separate us again in heaven...help me understand Jesus.
Because my little one they are part of who you are in this world. That is how I made you my little one so that you could live and survive and become everything I wanted you to be but all of those parts are precious and loved in their own right. All of them were created as individuals and when the time comes that is who they will be again.
Ok...I think.
So what do you think of your name my little one?
I love my name Jesus. I think it is beautiful and I think it tells my story.
Yes my little one it does.
Which is one of suffering and of blessing...they go together to make something you wanted to make.
Something beautiful my little one.
I don't know. I don't see me like you do Jesus. But you will help me. I am glad to be a Pearl.
Yes my little one, my pearl of great price. My little one all the things that you are, all the people who make you up, all the things you have seen and experienced and learned, all of these things are gifts for you to give away.
Blessed to be a blessing.
Yes my little one.
Which is what we started off talking about...but I don't know how to do that Jesus and it ...I mean...I am kind of waiting for you to make a way for me to do that.
That is what I am doing my little one.

For a little while I wondered if I would just be known as Pearl. I knew I couldn't use Jennifer's surname. That didn't seem right anyway. But even without me knowing it Jesus gave me the rest of my name, it was just there in my heart waiting for me to see it. And I did see it but I wasn't sure about it. I questioned Jesus about it because it seemed so strange.

I still don't really know who I am Jesus. I find it hard to see me, but I know I am different to what I was.
Yes my little one you are. My dearest one you were hidden away for a purpose. I have kept you safe my little one even in the midst of such pain and fear you were always safe, but now it is time for the world to see the treasure that was hidden in the darkness, my Pearl of great price who will shine for me.
Are you sure that's what they will see Jesus. I am thinking they will see a nut job.
My little one those with eyes to see will see the truth.
Hmmm. And the rest will see a nut job.
But that does not matter my little one for the truth of who you are is not hidden in what they see it is hidden in who I am. I say who you are my little one not anyone else.
I want them to see you Jesus. I don't want them to see Pearl fruitcake.

I know my little one but that is not your name.
What is my name Jesus?
You already have it my little one.
It is a good name...I mean...it's kind of fun...but it's not far off Pearl fruitcake.
My little one I want your name to speak of who you are. Pearl tells of suffering and of the beauty that has come from it. Sunshine tells of your ability to shine for me even in the darkest of places.
Like I carry your light with me...warm sunshine, light and hope...all those things.
Yes my little one all those things.
Well I will ask you again Jesus because I will be having this name for all of my life...so it needs to be right.
Yes my little one it does but that is the perfect name for you my little one.

I did ask him about it a lot of times but he never changed his mind and so my name is Pearl Sunshine. Later on I remembered something that helped me realize it made sense, that in a way Jesus had been telling me my name all along. When Jesus had first been talking to Jennifer about what he was calling her (us) to do, he had told her that she would open up the windows of heaven and let the sunshine down on the people. It fitted and made sense to me.
I did wonder sometimes though why Jesus put sunshine in my name when I spent so much time crying and feeling depressed. I felt like I wasn't living up to the name he gave me, like I was getting it wrong or letting him down. Not being who he made me to be.

Hi Jesus.
Hello, my dearest little one. My little one you are so dearly loved. Everything that you are is precious to me. You are held my little one there is nothing to fear.
Sometimes I feel like I am floating in space. Lost and alone Jesus. It is frightening and it feels endless.
My little one you are not lost you are found you are held and you are loved by the one who created you. Everything in heaven and on earth belongs to me my little one, everything is in my control. You are my treasure and my delight there is nothing to fear.
Why aren't I better yet Jesus?
You are still healing my little one, the blending is not yet complete. There is still much for you to see and understand about the things that have happened to you. There is still pain and fear my little one but you are moving forward with me. I am helping you to let go of the past and to take hold of the life I have given you. Even though it seems slow to you it is not. You have come so very far my little one.
I was thinking how I have only been me on the outside for a few months and lots has happened Jesus, but I don't know that I seem any better than I was. I know it is hard for me to tell. It is hard for me to see myself ...but I am still sad and hurting sometimes. I want to be Pearl Sunshine and not Pearl raincloud.
My little one who you are does not change according to how you feel. You are Pearl Sunshine but that does not mean that you will never feel pain or cry. Your name tells of who you are my little one not how you feel.
Who am I Jesus?
You are my Pearl. Created in love to love and be loved. To show the world who I am through all that you have suffered and all that I have done. To tell your story my little one with all of its pain and its fear, but to let the world see that even in the midst of such darkness there is light. That the sun can break through the dark clouds my little one and that suffering and joy can go together hand in hand.
We have a little way to go then Jesus because I am not knowing much joy yet.
It is there my little one. It is already given to you. You are able to experience it but there is still much that gets in the way of it. I am removing those things my little one so that you are able to experience the fullness of who you are. You in me and me in

you my little one.

I suppose you know about suffering and joy Jesus. It says you suffered for the sake of the joy set before you. Is it like that for me?

It is not quite like that my little one for you did not choose your suffering as I did, but the things that you are enduring now for my sake you suffer for the sake of the joy set before you.

Suffering and joy. That is my name, or some of it. Because Pearl is about beauty from suffering and sunshine is about shining for you. It is a beautiful name Jesus. I want to live up to it. I want to live it maybe would be better.

Yes my little one and it will come.

Jesus has told me many times that I am his Pearl (of great price) and that he is my sunshine (he is the sun that shines through me) and even if I don't feel very sunshiny, he is still there in me. He doesn't change.

Look my little one. What do you see?

Crying…You are surrounded by light Jesus. I can't see you…crying

Why my little one?

Crying….Because it is too bright... You are my sunshine…crying

Yes my little one I am. You have yet to fully discover what this means my little one. I know that this life is hard but your true life is hidden in me, in who I am. You are not who the world sees you as, you are not who you have to be right here and now my little one. You are my Pearl. I am your sunshine and together we will walk through this life my little one bring hope and healing to many. I know my dearest one that it is hard for you to see this, and that the truth of who you are is still hidden from you in many ways, but you know that you are mine. That you are loved. That you are walking in this path with me. I have shown you where it ends my little one and no matter what you must go through to get there, the path and its ending are clear to you. Do not give up my little one. Do not desire anything but to keep on walking with me, one step at a time. I will give you all the strength that you need my little one.

So now I had a name, a name that told me who I am. A name that told my story just like Jesus had promised. And now it was time for another promise to be fulfilled. For the blending to be completed and for us all to be one whole person in him.

Chapter 9

An Ending

I was feeling very tired. The kind of tired that seems to go right down into the middle of you. The kind of tired I got when there was a lot of healing happening.

Jesus….Crying
My little one I am here. I am holding you so close to my heart of love. I will not ever let you go. My little one my spirit is healing you of many things. There are many inside my little one who are still hurting, but we are bringing healing and wholeness to each one of you.
I don't really understand Jesus.
I know my little one but you are tired and you need to rest while we work. My little one there is not anything that you must do it is our work in you my little one.
Am I tired because you are healing us?
Yes my little one.
I don't know why I'm crying.
My little one your connections to those inside are growing stronger. That means that you are feeling their pain but it will pass my little one. I am holding you.
My little one the blending will begin very soon and when it does that will mean an ending for you, I know my little one that this is hard for you to hear, but I want you to be ready my little one. I do not want you to be afraid.
You won't leave me.
No my little one I will not ever leave you. My little one we are healing you so that you can be stronger than you are now. So that you will be ready for all that is to come.
I do feel afraid but I don't know if it's me Jesus. Are these the alters in the dell who we rescued?
Yes my little one.
Not other ones?
No my little one all the remaining alters are gathered together in the dell. There are no others.
I want you to tell me if there are Jesus. I would rather know than get upset because you didn't tell me. Don't do that Jesus.
My little one I will always tell you what it is good for you to know.
Is the land changing?
Yes my little one it is.
Are they afraid?
Some of them my little one but most understand that what is happening is good. There is anxiety my little one and some uncertainty but most inside are trusting in my word to them and they are not afraid.
Are there many left inside Jesus?
No my little one not many.
Will there be more blendings before they blend with me?
Yes my little one there will for those who are still healing will blend together my little one and some of those who are caring for them will then also blend.
And that will leave some to blend with me..is that the plan?
Those remaining will then come to the surface to blend with you my little one.
And then it will just be me.
No my little one. I will be with you.
But no more alters.
No more alters my little one.
And no more inside.

No my little one for you will not need it anymore.
It is silly to be sad.
No my little one. It is a loss but it is not one that you will regret.
I don't know why it seems so scary but it's a bit like being lost in empty space, or something.
My little one I will be holding you and loving you through this. It is a great change my little one but you are able and through it you will grow stronger than you are now and you will be able to begin to grow in a new way my little one. Tall and strong so that you can be seen by others for the wonderful person that you are.
It is very hard to believe that I can be Pearl…I think maybe I am afraid that when it is all done, I don't know…who will I be. All alone in this place. I'm sorry I know I'm not making sense.
You always make sense to me my little one. I always understand you. My little one this healing will complete a great work in you and you will be able to move on from this place feeling much more secure in who you are, not less my little one. I am not changing who you are. You are my beautiful and beloved Pearl. My little one these changes must happen soon so that you are ready for all that is to come. So that you can be strong enough my little one for all that lies ahead of you. Do not be afraid my little one. I will be with you.

It did feel scary to me. It had been years of healing, years discovering new alters, new memories, years discovering new things inside. And now that was ending. No more inside world, no more alters. I couldn't imagine that. I was scared to be all alone in what felt like a big scary world. I knew that didn't make sense, because I wasn't alone and the other alters didn't help with outside life anyway, but it did feel like everyone was leaving me in a place I didn't want to be. And it was final. So final, there would be no going back. And then what? What would I do? who would I be in the world? I needed to feel safe as much as I ever did.

Am I still in daddy's hot tub?
Yes my little one you are. Come then. Let us spend time with daddy. He has much he is longing to share with you my little one.
Hi daddy….Crying
My child. My dearest and most beloved child.
I seem to be crying a lot today.
I know my little one. As you receive my love it opens up places in your heart that have been closed to me until now. Do not be afraid my little one. You are loved and wanted and never alone. Little one all you must do is rest in my love for you. You do not need to understand my little one.
How can I understand daddy. I don't understand anything. I still don't even understand what a daddy is.
I know my little one but I am filling your heart with my love so that you will know. I am doing this slowly for now my little one which is why I am asking you to rest in this place. As my love fills the empty places you are growing stronger. I know my little one that it does not seem that way to you but you are growing stronger.
I don't know who I am.
You are my child. The way you see yourself is changing, the things you understand about yourself are changing but who you are is not changing my little one. You are my beloved one and will always be so.
I don't like it.
Little one you are safe and you are loved. You have been through many changes my little one and we have kept you safe through them all. This is not different my little one. You are held securely in my arms of love. I will not ever let you go.
Daddy.
Yes my child I am your daddy who loves you and will hold you and protect you from

all the storms that are coming. You are loved my little one. You are safe. You are wanted. You are not ever alone.
I don't know who I am.
My little one there is nothing to be feared from who we are making you to be.
I know but it doesn't seem like me.
My little one you are who I say that you are. There is nothing to be feared from being the person you were created to be. You were not made to be hidden away my little one you were made to shine brightly for us, to make us known to a lost and broken world. That is who you are my little one. You are safe, hidden in us. You are our beloved child. That is who you are. Our pearl of great price....Little one we are healing you and making you stronger so that you can go out into the world and tell them who we are. So that they may know our love and healing for themselves. This is a good thing my little one and not a bad one.
It is daddy. It gets too much sometimes but it is good.
I know that you are tired my dearest one and you need to rest. Our healing in you will continue my little one. We are making you able to do everything that is necessary but do not be surprised if you need to rest my little one.
Yes.
Stay a while then my little one and rest in us. Then continue with your day but remember that we are with you sustaining you and loving you and giving you our strength even whilst we are healing you.
Yes. Thank you...Crying
Little one you are ours and we are making you whole in us. Hold on my dearest child, and do not be afraid. We are enough for you.
How could you not be?
Rest then my little one.

I did feel strange. Like I was being rearranged on the inside, which I was of course. I was seeing things differently, seeing myself and my story differently and feeling lots of things I didn't want to feel from those inside. But I must have been healing because it was time for me to take another step.

Let us go deeper.
The light in the room had got a lot brighter and then Jesus took my hand and led me out of the hot tub and into a different place. It was a garden, a really big one. Like those you see at stately homes. There were two peacocks...I suppose they are part of that.
A garden?
Yes my little one
With two peacocks...formal gardens Jesus.
Yes my little one.
I don't understand. Are we in daddy's heart?
Yes my little one this is the next part of the revelation of love that he has for you.
Ok. Daddy?
I am here my little one.
How is this you?
This is an entranceway my little one.
Like going up the drive to a big house.
Yes little one like that.
Ok.

We walked through the gardens to the house, which wasn't a house but a palace. Its walls were white but they were covered in green growing plants. We went up some steps...there were white columns. The door looked old, a big wooden one that reminded me more of a castle than a palace. We went through it and I suppose into a courtyard, but it was so full of plants it was hard to really see what was there. I know there was a stream. And there was a swinging seat where I sat between Jesus and the Holy Spirit. There looked to be lots of hidden places and there was an archway to go through. It was very peaceful, kind of dim and cool but in a nice way. Like when it's really hot and you go into a cool shady place.

Tell me about this place daddy. What is it?
It is a place made especially for you my daughter. There are many rooms for you to explore. Many places within the palace which contain something of my love for you. Each one has been put there for a purpose my little one.
And this place?
Is a garden of rest my little one.
It feels kind of mysterious and magical, but not scary. I don't know.
It is here for you my little one. All places lead both to and from the garden of rest.
Because you want me to rest in you and in your love for me.
Yes my dearest little one I do.
Help me do that daddy. I am feeling very anxious about everything.
I know my little one.
It is kind of like the palace is a safe place like Blossom castle and the swing chair is like the rocking chair in your heart Jesus...but there is room for the Holy Spirit too. I think there are things hidden here for me to find. Is that right?
Yes my dearest one it is.
Daddy I don't think I can do this…Crying…How can I be this person?
It is who you are my little one. Who I have made you to be. My little one all you must do for today is rest. You are weary my little one.
But does this mean you have finished cleansing and healing?
It means my little one that you are ready to go forward. To discover more of my heart for you.
Because you prepared the way?
Yes my little one.
Ok. It seems like too much.
No my little one it is not too much. You are ready my little one to discover more of what it is to have a daddy who loves you.
I don't feel very ready. I feel very small.
But you are loved and you are safe my little one and we will only take you at the pace you can manage. This is far enough for today my little one. My little one you are held and you are loved and you are safe.
But I am Pearl.
Yes little one you are.
Pearl Sunshine.
Yes my little one that is who you are.
It is hard to be Pearl Sunshine in the world daddy.
Yes my little one I know that it is. But you have our power and our strength and our courage my little one.
Jesus…Crying
My little one we are making you ready for a great adventure. Not just the one on the outside my little one but the adventure of discovering who we are and our love for you. They go together my little one for as we lead you forward on the outside we will also be leading you deeper and deeper into our love so that you are hidden in us my little one.
Unshakeable.
Yes my little one. Unshakeable in who you know us to be and in who you are. The truth my little one.
Crying…Yes.

So now I was in a new place in daddy's heart. I wasn't very sure what that meant except I was ready for something new. And then it was time. Time for the last of the blendings, time for the end of this part of my journey.

Come then my dearest one it is time.
Time for what?
For the first blending my little one.
Ok.
My little one I will not go faster than you are able but you are strong in me and ready for this.
I know you know better than I do about timings Jesus. But I feel a bit nervous.
My little one there is nothing to fear. Come then my dearest one I want you to meet Kitty.
Hello
Hi.
My little one Kitty has already blended with several others. She is strong enough now to be blended with you. She is ready to take her place on the outside.
Can you tell me a bit about yourself?
Well...I we...were hidden in the ice caves before we got rescued. There were five of us together but then we got rescued and taken to the dell. I am fourteen...I think. Am I still fourteen Jesus?
Yes my little one you are.
Well...I helped out you know. I helped the Goatman and those people…
My little one are you ready to be joined with kitty?
Yes Jesus. But I would like to see please.
Come then my little ones.
I didn't see much. We sat with Jesus in his rocking chair. Kitty had long black hair. We sat on his lap and held hands and she kind of disappeared into me. I sat with Jesus for a little while.
Jesus how many more are there?
Three my little one just three.
I feel scared.
I know my little one but there is nothing to fear. Rest now my little one but come back a little later for there is another blending to be done.
I don't want to be afraid Jesus.
My little one my plans for you are good. All of them are good. This is just another step my little one, another part of your healing.
But it is so final Jesus.
I know it seems so to you my little one but it is just another step.
Ok.
Come back later my little one.
Ok. Bye not bye Jesus
Bye not bye my little one.

I went back a little later. I wasn't sure what I felt about it. Scared, excited, anxious...all of it. I just trusted Jesus knew what he was doing because I had no idea what to expect.

Hi Jesus
Hello my little one. My dearest one this is Holly. She is seventeen. It is her time my little one if you are willing.
Whatever you want Jesus. Hello Holly.
Hi.
My little ones I do not want you to be afraid. There is nothing to fear. I am healing what has been broken and making you whole again.

Are you from the ice caves Holly?
Yes. I was there a long time but now I am free to live in the light. To live with you Pearl.
Yes.
Take my hands my little one.
So we each took a hand and he kind of folded us both into a hug and she melted into me.
My little one as you are healed you become more ready for all that is before you.
Does that just leave two Jesus?
Yes my little one it does.
Tomorrow?
Yes my little one if you are willing.
I am scared but if it's what you want.
Yes my little one it is. My little one as I restore what was lost to you, you will feel weaker for a time but that will soon pass my little one. Soon you will feel stronger than you ever have and more sure of who you are my little one
But...I don't know. I don't know what to do with this. I don't know what to think...I am a bit worried it's not real. It doesn't seem like it could be Jesus. It is like the end of a really long journey and I don't know what I will do.
But I do my little one. When one journey ends another begins. My little one the blending process will continue for a little while but the healing that you need will continue for much longer. It is an end my little one but it is also a beginning and not one to be feared.
When you say the healing will continue, what does that mean, will it be different?
Yes my little one once the blending is complete the healing you need will change somewhat. There will be no more need my little one for you to be blending with others, there will be no more rescues to be done and the inside as you know it now will not exist, but there is still much more for you to receive my little one, many empty places that still need to be filled with our love and there is so much for you to learn about, who you are not just to us but who you are in this world also. All of that is healing my little one for it is all part of making you the person you were created to be.
Yes. I kind of understand that but it will be different?
Yes my little one it will but take heart for this is a new beginning for you.
I will be glad if it is Jesus. I want a new beginning.
I know you do my little one.
I am so very tired Jesus.
Yes my little one now is a time for you to rest, even in the midst of everything my little one you need to rest.
That is hard to do when I have to train and write, and who knows what in the next few weeks.
But I will help you my little one. I will give you my strength my dearest one but take all the rest you can in this time for it will make you stronger for what lies ahead of you.
Jesus, when tomorrow...I want to know it's real. It is a really big thing. I don't want to be wondering.
My little one I will help you to see and understand the reality of what is happening but remember my dearest one that even though this is the ending of a long journey it is also the beginning of another one.
I want to see that too Jesus.
Yes my little one I know that you do.
Crying
I am holding you my little one. I am holding you close to my heart. My little one I am healing you. Even now I am healing you. There is nothing to fear my little one......Rest my little one and do not be afraid. I am holding you and healing you. You are being made strong in me.

I wrote and told daddy mike what happened the next day. The last of the blendings and the last time I would ever see the inside world that Jesus had made for all the alters who had lived there for so long.

I was crying the whole time. Jesus took me inside to where the little stream is or was. The one where I got saved. We all stood in the water.

My little ones the time has come. The time has come for all to be made one again. My little one you have come so very far in me and it is now time for you to receive back what was taken from you. Millicent and Margery are you ready to take your place in the outside side as part of Pearl living and working to my glory.
Sure am Jesus.
Yes I am ready..
My beautiful Pearl come. My little one this is your time. Will you receive back what was taken from you so long ago?
I stood up close to Jesus with my back to him. Yes…
They just came into Jesus arms one at a time and kind of melted into me. I cried a lot and Jesus held me in his arms for a while.
Come my little one.
He took me up the mountain so I could see out over the land.

Tell me what you see my little one.
The mountain is so beautiful. It is covered in flowers……There is just the dell and the little stream left Jesus. And empty huts. There is no one there.
No my little one none now remain for they are all given back to you. My little one as the land is given back to you the healing that we have been doing for so very long will be completed. There is more my little one but this part is ended.

As I watched it was kind of like water came up through the ground and it all disappeared into a beautiful golden mist that was filled with rainbows and the mist got higher and higher until it reached us at the top of the mountain and then I was back outside.

My little one I have made you strong in me. Your journey continues my little one but now you are one again. You are ready my little one to begin a new part of your journey with me.

I cried for a long time. Not because I was sad. I didn't feel sad but I felt overwhelmed. I never thought this day would come and I thought about all the things that have happened on our healing journey and I thought how Jesus has put back all the broken pieces back together, so many of us. And I thought about the bad things and how from the very beginning we were broken, so that this is almost the first time, or maybe it is the first time that I have been whole. I have felt different. It is hard to describe. I thought at first that I felt more solid, but I decided it was more like I was blurry round the edges and now I'm not. I keep thinking about how I am Pearl. This is me and there is no one else and it is very strange. Not bad strange but very strange. And tired of course. I feel like I can really be me now even though I don't really know what that will mean. So I feel like it is a big thing and I am different, stronger I suppose even though I am very tired. That is all I can think of.

I did feel strange and kind of empty. I had never been alone in the body before, even though I didn't really spend a lot of time with the other alters, I always knew they were there. We were connected I suppose in ways I don't understand. But now it was different. Now they were part of me, and it just seemed like they were gone. But they were giving me their memories. It was hard to sleep because of all the pictures and memories that were coming. Like being given videos that I had to watch.

Not nice ones of course. There wasn't anything very new in them which I was glad about, but they did keep me from sleeping. At the same time, I was full of wonder at what had happened, and I felt more loved than I ever had. I wasn't loved any more I just felt it in a new way.

>Hi Jesus
>**Hello my little one**
>You love me.
>**Yes my little one I do with all of my heart. My little one it brings us great joy to see you whole once again. It brings us even greater joy that you are now able to receive our love in far greater measure my little one. There is so much more we have for you to receive, so many things for you to learn and to grow in. This is not the end my little one it is a wonderful beginning.**
>I know that it is true...Crying...and it feels like to much.
>**It is not too much my little one. We are going to love you and teach you and lead you. There is so much before you my little one. Things you have not even dreamed of. My dearest one the journey you have been on has been long and difficult and painful but it has been worth it. It has brought you to this place my little one where we can begin to pour our love into you and show you what it truly means to be who you are to us and who you are for us.**
>I have no idea what is ahead Jesus. I suppose a lot of it will be difficult. But you love me and look what you done. And for the first time ever I believe I have a future. A good future. One worth living.
>**Yes my little one. My dearest little one you have come through many trials and difficulties and all of it has made you stronger. I have worked through everything so that you can receive all that we have for you. This is a new part of your journey my little one but you walk it in new strength and new hope because of all that we have done. It is a good day my little one. It is a very good day.**
>Yes. It is.
>**My little one these days before you are for healing and for rest. Take hold of them my little one. Do not fear what lies ahead for you. We are in everything with you. It is all in our hands. We will love you and guide you through it all.**
>Is there anything you want me to do?
>**I want you to rest my little one. That is all.**
>Ok...Thankyou
>**I am with you my little one in everything. There is so much before you my little one. Rest now and you will be able to meet it when it comes.**
>Ok. Please help me with writing and training Jesus.
>**Yes my little one I will. Do not be anxious about them.**
>Ok. Bye not bye Jesus.
>**My not bye my beautiful Pearl.**

It wasn't very long after this that I went away with Tilly to the Christian camp we had been to before. It was good to have some time away and just rest and spend time with Jesus without having the pressure of being Jennifer and doing all the things I usually had to do.

>*Hi daddy*
>*Jesus says I need to keep on writing so I am going to tell you about my weekend again even though I told you most of it already. We arrived on Friday and set up camp. I was excited but still feeling really tired. I enjoyed the meetings and it was exciting to find out that I loved to sing. I have never sung out loud before. I always sing in my head so no one can hear me, but I liked to sing out loud and worship and I felt free and not worried about it. When I was singing the songs it was the first time I could agree and not think well, maybe sometime that will be true or feel true. One of the songs had the line no longer a slave to fear and it made me cry just a little bit because it is true now. Really true. I am not a slave to*

fear any more and I can really and truly say that it is well with my soul. It really is. So for the first few days it was like the truth of what Jesus has done was sinking in. I was thinking about the alters who were kept captive in the caves and how Jesus set them free and how they are a part of me now. That is kind of hard to understand. So I did find a little bit of time to talk to Jesus about it all. At first I was asking about what he was doing...or not doing because I am so used to doing a lot of crying and there being a lot of healing, but that wasn't happening. He didn't seem to be saying or doing anything except he kept saying for such a time as this, which I know is from Ester. So I was asking about that first.

Hi Jesus
Hello my little one
What am I missing something Jesus?
No my little one. I have many things to show to you but you are not missing anything.
But you don't really seem to be saying or doing much.
Yes my little one I am. I am helping you to see who you are, my Pearl. The one I have saved healed and rescued from the darkness. My little one you have a long journey ahead of you and there are many things you have not yet seen or understood. I am helping you my little one. I am not doing nothing. I am giving you everything you need.
I am used to doing a lot of crying and being in pain but I'm not. I'm just enjoying and being thankful for all you have done. And being kind of amazed that I am here.
Yes my little one and that is part of it. You are seeing yourself and your story so far. You are understanding more fully what it means to be you and the road you have travelled to get to this point. I know my little one that you are thinking about the next step but sometimes it is necessary to see and understand what has been before you are ready to move on.
I kind of understand that. I was wondering how I can understand myself now. I mean did everything happen to me, all the outside stuff, all the inside stuff, was it all me. What does that mean...because I didn't make the choices when they were made Jesus. Help me understand.
My little one you now carry the memories and experiences of everyone who is now a part of who you are. That does not mean my dearest one that the lives they lived were you because at that time you were separate. But it does mean that you have a complete picture of the life that has been lived by all the different parts of you. It will take time to draw all these memories and experiences together to make one whole my little one. It will take time for you to understand yourself as you now are but it does not change who you are my little one. You are my Pearl and will always be so.
Well...me as I am now...does it mean that all of the bad things happened to me?
It means you carry the memories and experiences of those events my little one as though it happened to you even though you may not have been part of that at the time.
But do I say...that happened to me? How do I talk about it Jesus?
All the memories and experiences are now a part of who you are and in that sense yes it all happened to you.
It is hard to understand because it is like I was in many different places having many different experiences living many different lives all at the same time.
Yes my little one it is and yet all of it was you. As the blending is completed it will not so seem so strange as it does now. My dearest one you are my Pearl and you have been rescued out of great darkness. You have seen and experienced many things through many different eyes but still they are your experiences and your memories. All of it happened to you my little one. Where choices were made that you did not make still you carry the consequences of that choice my little one. That was part of what you accepted in the blending. You are not responsible and yet the

consequences remain.

Like where I live or have children or all those things?

Yes my little one like that. But the different parts of you that are now blended with you have been saved healed and cleansed by me, everything is forgiven my little one. You do not carry the guilt or shame of choices made for those burdens were taken even before you blended. You carry their memories, experiences and who they are and those things are now joined with you, with your own memories and experiences and with who you are but all of you, each part of you is saved and healed and cleansed my little one. Even though they made choices which you would not have that does not mean that you carry any guilt or shame for those choices my little one.

It is hard to understand. It is hard to see who I am in all of that.

You are my beautiful Pearl, made new, redeemed cleansed and healed, forgiven and loved my little one. The old is gone and the new is come. It is who you are now my little one which will carry you forward into all I have for you.

What do you mean?

You are one my little one and everything you have learned, everything you have been through will be used for my glory. Even the things you think of as belonging to others. They belong to you now my little one. You accepted them in the blending my little one.

Ok...so I need to see myself better, or something Jesus and the blending will bring it all together. I don't know what I am trying to say. I am beginning to see but I need you to help me.

I will help you my little one.

Why am I here Jesus?

To rest my little one and to receive from me. It is not anything you need to make happen my little one.

Am I still doing that? I still get anxious I did something wrong.

You have done nothing wrong my little one. You are my beloved. You are safe in my arms and your journey is in my hands my little one.

Ok. Keep talking to me Jesus. Tell me if I'm getting things wrong.

Yes my little one I will but you are not getting things wrong my little one. You are following me. Your heart is set on me and I am leading you forward into everything I have for you all of which is good.

Ok. I love you Jesus.

Yes my little one I know that you do.

Bye not bye.

Bye not bye my little one

For the first few days in the worship I was sitting on Jesus lap like I was resting and that is what he wanted me to be doing. He was wearing the golden locket again. I need to ask him about that. But then on the Monday he took my hand and led me to a start line like you have for a race and we stood hand in hand ready for the starting gun. That was a bit different. Then the speaker started to talk. She was talking about it being a change of season, that we were at a tipping point and it was time to go for gold...running the race. I knew it was for me. I know that it is the end of one part of my journey and the start of the next. I don't know what is coming but I think it is going to be different. I don't have any doubt anymore, or maybe it is fear. I am not sure but it is gone. I know that that what Jesus has planned for me is coming, all the things he's said are true and he will make it all possible and I don't need to be afraid, I just feel kind of like it's how it should be and needs to be. It's who I am. I kept on seeing me at the start line with Jesus, but I was also sitting on his lap and dancing with him and dancing in Jesus arms before daddy's throne and it was like he was saying that all of those were true all at the same time. And I suppose that is right.

There were lots of fun parts to the holiday. The pouring rain was even fun, cooking in the tent! and Tilly's towel adventure. We had a lot of sunshine too and I wore my adventure hat. Tilly seemed to have a good time, she says she loves me and is proud of me. That is kind of strange but nice. She has started to call me Pearl too and I like that. There was a gospel choir which I enjoyed a lot and I did more singing and dancing and there was a praise party at the end, where I did a lot of dancing and jumping up and down. I have felt happy for the first time I think. I played silly games with Tilly and we had a lot of fun. And now I am home. My time away was a time to rest and to celebrate what Jesus had done. I didn't know what was coming next, but it wasn't anything I expected. It wasn't anything I wanted.

Chapter 10

The Forest of Difficulty

As all of us have walked with Jesus he has taken us on a journey deeper into his heart of love for us. He took Blossom to a place of safety, Blossom Castle and then on to the Forest of Strength and the Land of Hope. It had been a long time since he had taken us there but now it was time to move on again. To go deeper. Coming out of the Land of Hope was the river, the river of his presence which we had been following. There were fields along the riverside but we weren't going into the fields. He had somewhere else for me to go.

I started off my day by spending time with Jesus. I saw I was by the river in the valley with Jesus. He took my hand and we started to walk along the riverside. I was expecting when it was time that we would walk into the field, but he showed me that the growth would spread from the riverbank, which made sense to me. We walked until we came to a little waterfall which we climbed up. Looking ahead I could see what looked like a forest with the river running through it.

Tell me what I saw Jesus. Am I following the river?
Yes my little one you are.
Because it goes deep into your heart.
Yes my little one it does.
And I understood that the ground, all that bare earth, the growth will start where I am walking along the river, but it will spread outwards. I won't need to actually go over every piece of ground because it will grow outward from the river to fill all of the valley.
Yes my little one that is so.
So why did we climb up the waterfall?
Because my little one as you did so it was like moving to another level, where there is more power and more light.
More of you?
Yes my little one. A deeper revelation of me and of my love for you.
And those trees I see ahead of us?
The Forest of Difficulty my little one. As I lead you through it you will discover more of my ways. You will grow wiser and stronger and more able my little one.
It doesn't sound nice.
No my little one but it is good and it will help you.
Is this...I was supposed to be asking you about the blessings that come with difficulties or something like that.
Yes my little one. I will teach you many things as we travel through the forest.
Ok. I suppose that is about to begin.
Yes my little one it is.
Ok. I don't know what to say about it.
Hold my hand and do not be afraid my little one. I will lead you through.

It was good to be moving forward, going deeper, but I wasn't very sure I wanted to go to a place called the Forest of Difficulty. Life was difficult enough. There were a lot of things happening and all of them were difficult and didn't seem particularly good to me. Jesus said I was in a storm which was how it felt.

I know you said I'm in a storm Jesus but I don't really see it. Tell me about it.
It is a storm of change my little one and like many storms it is made up of different elements. There is the wind my little one which comes from me. That is moving things into place. There is the rain which does not come from me but from the enemy who is seeking to discourage and destroy you. There is the lightening, which is my

power my little one, the power to cleanse and to heal and there is thunder which is my voice over you, protecting and guiding you. Battles are being fought on your behalf and on behalf of those you love. It is a storm my little one but it is bringing with it change and it will be a good change.
Like...clearing the air.
Yes my little one.

Things were difficult. Richard was being reassessed for disability benefit. That had meant filling in a very difficult and depressing form. Now that Richard was an adult I felt like he should be more involved in these things, but it wasn't easy to get him to do anything. I found it very stressful and upsetting.

Come then my little one let us talk about Richard. My little one I will help you through this time. I will help him my little one. I will give you both everything you need.
Daddy thinks I should ask you questions Jesus but I am afraid.
I know you are my little one but there is nothing to fear from anything I will tell you. My little one many things are about to change for Richard. You know this. When you go to be with my servant everything will change for him.
I know…Crying
That is not a bad thing my little one it is a good one. I am making him ready for that change my little one just as I am making you ready. It is not different.
Ok. But what does that mean?
It means my little one that I am helping him to see who he is, apart from you. I am helping him to stand on his own my little one to make choices and decisions about his own life. I know that your desire is to protect him my little one but much of that is driven by your own feelings of inadequacy, but my little one you are not inadequate for the task I have given you which is to love him my little one.
But I am responsible for him….Crying.
No my little one no. I am the one who is responsible for him. You do not bear that burden my little one. I am the one who will help him. I only ask you to love him and support him as I enable you my little one. My little one, my dearest little one I will not ask you to do more than you are able. Not ever. I am with you my little one and will help you to do everything I ask of you. Which is to love him my little one not to try and carry him.
I don't know. I get so lost and confused. How can I know what to do?
Because I am helping you my little one. My dearest one even though things will change for Richard that does not mean my little one that you must be there with him carrying him through. That is my job my little one. Trust me to do it.
I don't know what you mean by that Jesus.
My little one when you think of Richard having to be independent and doing the things that he will need to do you think of yourself as being the one who will need to be there helping him.
Do I? I try to imagine so many ways he can live without me.
I know you do my little one but what you do not do is imagine him living with me. I am with him my little one. I will not leave him. I will give him everything he needs.
But he doesn't trust you like I do Jesus. He doesn't know you that way. I am not even sure he thinks about you.
My little one trust me to work through all things to draw him closer to me. I am at work in his heart my little one. He is my child and I love him just as I love you.
I know that must be true Jesus. But…I just feel guilty all the time…like it is all my fault and like I have to somehow fix everything and I can't. I know I can't.
My little one my dearest little one I am your savior and I am also his. Your task is to love him my little one not fix him or his life.
I can see that about everyone else Jesus but somehow not with him.

I know my little one but you do not see what I see. My little one let me carry this burden. You were not ever meant to bear it my little one. You are not a failure. His difficulties are not your fault and you cannot fix this my little one. That is my job. Trust me to do it my way which is the best way my little one.
But what are you going to do?
I am going to help him my little one. I am going to help him see who is. Not the lies that he has believed my little one but the truth. I am going to help him move forward and become the man I have for him to be.
Those are good things.
Yes my little one they are and not to be feared in any way.
I don't want to ask what will happen Jesus. If he will get the benefit or he won't.
My little one whether he gets it or he doesn't I will be working in him to change the things he thinks about himself and his life. I will be helping him to make choices to move forward my little one.
I would like you to do that Jesus. He needs to do that.
Yes my little one and I will help him to do so. Trust me my little one. Whatever changes lie ahead for you and for him I will be with you helping you and guiding you and loving you. There is nothing to fear.

It took weeks to fill in the form and then Richard had to go for an interview. It was all very stressful and then we had to wait for the result. If he was refused the benefit it would most likely mean that he would be forced into getting a job. Something I didn't see as possible. Not only that but I would also have to find work, because I wouldn't be getting the caregiver's allowance anymore. It was all very frightening. I talked to Jesus a lot about all of it of course and I understood that this was all part of the forest, and that he was wanting to use all of these things to help me and to help Richard too. But it was still very difficult.

Tell me about the forest Jesus.
My little one as we travel through the Forest of Difficulty you will have to overcome many things. Obstacles which stand in your way, blocking your path. As you do this in my strength my little one I will teach you many things. Most of all I will teach you not to fear those things my little one because you will understand that I use them all to help you and not to hinder you. Each one is a gift my little one.
Explain that more Jesus.
My little one many things will come against you as you seek to follow me. Some of those will be from the enemy my little one, some of them will not but wherever they come from I will help you to overcome them and continue on the path I have for you.
So things that try and stop me from following you?
Yes my little one. They can be many kinds of things. Sometimes they will be put there to discourage you or make you turn aside and take a different path because it seems easier. Sometimes they will be put there to hurt you or cause you pain. Sometimes they will seem to block you in entirely with no way out but my little one my path for you remains. It is still there even when you cannot see it or the way seems blocked.
Yes.
As you learn to overcome these things as I direct and help you, you will become more confident in who I am my little one. You will learn more of my ways. You will understand that nothing can stop you following me if you do not give up or turn aside. Each thing that seeks to stop or hinder you I will use to teach you and make you stronger in me and in who you are. In that way they are gifts my little one because of all that I can give to you through them.
So when there is something difficult like today, I will be thinking about what you are going to do and how you are going to make it work for me and not about how awful and difficult and frightening it is.

Yes my little one you will.
That will be better Jesus.
Yes my little one it is a much better way to live. There is nothing to fear my little one and you will learn this as you follow me through the forest.
Ok. That is worth learning Jesus. I don't understand about life really or why it has to be this way, but I see that I need to learn those things and if I can face difficulties with joy instead of fear, I will be glad. Teach me Jesus.
Yes my little one I will.
So you are going to do good things through all of this and I don't need to be afraid. I need to look at what you are doing and trust you and know that what seems difficult is really just a way of you giving me something precious.. in the best way possible.
Yes my little one that is so.

That all sounded good in theory. In practice when the difficulties came, and they did keep coming, I got afraid and cried and often thought I couldn't go a step further. Jesus always helped me of course. I walked with him one day at a time through the forest holding on to him, because mostly I couldn't see anything good in what was happening.

So the letter arrived at last. It was what I thought. A big fat no. It works on points ...you get points and if you get enough you qualify. Richard got zero, like no points at all. There was this whole section that said things like you said you can do this and this and I agree, and you said you have difficulty with this and that, but I have decided you don't, which is basically saying I am a liar. Anyway so I was expecting it but it is still a bit scary. Richard says he hasn't been thinking about it and is refusing to say anything at all about it. It was what made me upset.....We can appeal and I suppose we should, but it seems to me that it is still going to be a no. Richard says there's no point but I will talk to him about it again. In any case we both need to find out what we can do now. So I will make appointments at the job center. That's all I know to do. The money will stop on the 20th. So change is here but I don't know what will happen...obviously. I talked to Jesus about fear. I didn't want to be afraid but I was. The future looked overwhelming to me. I didn't feel like I could help Richard with the things that were ahead for him and I was very afraid that I would have to get a job too. I didn't see how that was possible. Not any of it.

Hi Jesus
Hello my little one.
Jesus I am so glad I know you and love you and know that you love me. There is so much more to learn Jesus. I want you to show me and lead me so that you fill me up to overflowing.
My little one that is my great desire for you. I have many plans for you my little one and all of them require you to be filled with my love and my power. My spirit is waiting to fill you to overflowing my little one so that you are not afraid and are able to give us away to everyone you meet whether they are willing to receive us or not.
It takes courage to do that.
Yes my little one it does but when you know that you are loved fear can have no hold on you my little one. There is no room left in your heart for fear for it is filled with our love. Fear and love cannot coexist my little one. There is no fear in us. We are not afraid my little one.
No, but didn't you get afraid before you went to the cross Jesus?
Yes my little one I was afraid but that fear did not overcome me. It did not find a place in my heart where it could live and grow and control me. The love of my father overcame it my little one and so it is with you. Our love for you is driving out all the fear that has lived in your heart for so very long. Love is in control now my little one and not fear and even if you feel afraid sometimes that is not the same as fear living in your heart and controlling you from within.
How is it different Jesus?

When you feel afraid you are looking to the things that might happen, that you might experience. You are afraid you will be overcome by those things and that they are in control but when you know that I am in control and that you are wholly and completely loved by me then the fear that you feel cannot find a home my little one. It cannot settle in your heart. It cannot control you. So even if you feel afraid my little one you are able to come to me and know that I am in control and those things that you are afraid of have no power over you. Your trust in me makes it impossible for fear to control you my little one even if you feel afraid for a time.
Yes. I see that. I expect I will feel afraid sometimes Jesus but I don't want fear to control what I do and say so keep pouring in your love. Please.
Yes my little one. We will pour our love into you until here are no empty spaces, no room for fear my little one.
Is there more healing stuff to be done Jesus?
Some my little one. There are still places in your heart which need our healing love, there are still empty places which need to be filled. We will help you to receive the healing that you need my little one at just the right time.

I had a dream. In the dream I was walking along a path. The path was covered in things that would trip me up or hurt me. There didn't seem to be place I could put my feet down and it made it very difficult to keep walking. Behind me on the path were Sophie and Richard, not as they are now but as children. Then as I was thinking how impossible it was to walk forward, a giant broom came and swept everything off the path in one sweep. That was it, all the obstacles were gone.

Hello my dearest child.
Hi Holy Spirit. Would you explain your dream to me? It was your dream?
Yes my little one. It was sent as an encouragement to you. My little one there are many things that would stand against you continuing on the path that we have for you. Many of those are to do with Sophie and Richard my little one for you have a unique place in their lives. The enemy will send many things, many obstacles designed to make it impossible for you to keep walking but my dearest little one there is nothing he can do to stop you for I am able to sweep all of those things aside. Even as you seek to find a path you will find that everything he brings against you will be swept aside by my power.
So you are the broom?
Yes my little one I am the broom.
And these things that the enemy will send against us...
There will be many things my little one. Some of them will be small and some of them are designed to hurt you so much that you cannot continue to walk.
Like standing on a poisonous toad.
Yes my little one. But you do not have to walk along a path littered with obstacles and dangers. I am the one who will clear the path before you my little one. So do not be anxious about anything he will do but remember what I will do. He cannot stop you my little one.
...I see. So when this stuff starts getting in my way I need to remember that you are a very big broom and can brush them all aside with one sweep.
Yes my little one that is so.
That is good. Thankyou Holy Spirit. I do like your dreams. They help me.
That is their purpose my little one.

In the middle of all the things that had been happening, all the blending and healing and all of the benefits stuff I had been training for a marathon. A full twenty-six-mile marathon. Most of the time I thought I was crazy for doing it. It was hard and I struggled to do the distances I needed to. I suffered with cramps and sore muscles and sore knees and sore hips. Everything hurt. I got to the start line wondering if I was going to make it round, but I did. It took me six hours, but I did it. Mum and Cheryl came to cheer me on this time, and it was so good to have some support. Jesus ran with me of course. I couldn't have done it without him. It was a real test of endurance and perseverance especially because I was in pain almost the whole time. Some of it I enjoyed but mostly it was a case of keeping going despite the pain. It seemed to me that Jesus was talking to me about my life journey, keeping going through the pain, in his strength and not my own. It was a big achievement to cross the finish line.

I had decided to go ahead and appeal the benefits decision, but I wasn't feeling too hopeful. I found the whole thing overwhelming but Cheryl helped me a lot. There were lots of appointments to go to and phone calls to make. It was a very difficult time.

I did cry a lot yesterday before we talked, it was that letter that set me off, but I know it is just the whole thing that is so overwhelming to me. I thought I wouldn't ever stop. I cried for two hours without stopping. But I have seemed better today. I will just try and take each day as it comes and trust that Jesus will help me just like he did when I was running. I think that the marathon was like a big metaphor for me. He didn't take away the pain even though I asked him to a lot of times. But he did help me run my race. He gave me courage and determination and strength to keep going even though I was in pain. I think that is like the forest. He will help me keep going no matter how hard it is. I want it to be painless but that's not how it is, is it. I hope one day it will be different for me. I know there is still a lot of things that need healing and I have a lot to learn about a lot of things especially about being me.

Things didn't get easier. Both me and Richard had to apply for new benefits so that we had some money to live on. It wasn't going very well. They expected me to survive for six weeks without any kind of income and then when I got through that, they didn't give me enough money even to pay the rent because of some mix up. I went about three months without being able to pay any rent and my income had dropped so much, I was struggling even to buy enough food. Mum helped a lot but that was hard in itself. I hung on to Jesus but I did cry and get stressed, especially because I was having to make endless phone calls and go to appointments and the job center and things like that. It all made me desperate to escape from the life I was living, from being Jennifer.

Hi Jesus
Hello my little one.
Are you going to rescue me sometime Jesus….Crying
I will not leave you here my little one.
You have been saying that for years. I know I won't be here for all eternity but I am here now and will be for a long time yet. I'm sorry I can't love it like you want me to. I know I get everything wrong. I don't know what to do.
Hold on to me my little one. Hold on to me and do not let go. Remember that I am in control of everything. I will not leave you. I will help you and bring you through this. My little one I am strong enough for you. Do you believe this?
Yes….Crying
Then do not be afraid my dearest little one. I am for you. In everything I am for you. You are my very own. My treasure and my delight and I am working all things for your good.
Is life ever going to be worth living Jesus?
Yes my little one it is. My little one everything you are going through, everything you have gone through is being used for good. Even now my little one and so much more in the future. There is nothing I cannot do. There is nothing I would not give to you that it is good for you to have. My little one you are safe in our father's arms. He is holding you close to his heart as am I. There is nothing to fear my little one. We know who you are and everything that you are is precious to us. We are not keeping you here because we do not care my little one or because you have been bad in any way but only because it is better that it should be so. I know that it is hard my little one but hold on a little longer. It is only a little longer my little one.
It's like the walls of the prison are closing in. Help me….Crying

I am in control my little one. You will not be hurt. I have come to set you free from all the things that would hold you.

Yes. I would like to just come and be with you and not be alive anymore. I don't want to be here. I don't want to be alive. I don't want to be me in this life.

My little one I am making you strong enough so that you can live the life I have for you. So that you can follow me wherever I lead you. I know my little one that you think it is taking too long and that you will never see anything of my promises to you but they are my promises my little one and they will come. They are worth living for my little one. Hold on and do not give up. I am with you and will help you.

I don't even know what to do with myself Jesus. I can't seem to do anything. I can't even spend time with you or daddy…Daddy…Crying

I am here my dearest and most precious child. I do not ever leave you. We can never be apart.

I can't do this daddy.

My little one, my beautiful Pearl. You can do all things in the strength that is given to you. We are strong enough for you. We are helping you with everything.

I don't want to do it. I don't want to be here. I want to be with you…..Crying

You are always with me my little one. I am holding you safe in my arms. You are so very loved and no matter how it feels to you, you are safe. You are held and you are loved and you are safe.

I don't feel safe. I feel like I am lost floating in space and no one will save me.

You are not lost my little one you are safe in my arms. You are not alone. You are held and you are loved. You are safe my little one. There is nothing to fear.

So why am I afraid.

For many reasons my little one. The things of the past are still healing. They still have a hold on you my little one but we are setting you free. Even now as you hold on to us and trust us to help you through this we are setting you free from the fear that still holds you.

Because I can't hide away or run away from the things that are happening. I have to face them in your strength.

Yes my little one you do but you will not be overcome. We are enough for you my little one. Everything you need is found in us. There is nothing we cannot do. And as you face up to the fear that holds you we defeat it for you my little one and set you free from it a little at a time.

Is that what you are doing?

Yes my little one it is.

I don't want to live in fear.

No my little one I know you don't. Trust us my little one. We are working everything for your good. We are setting you free. You are safe my little one. I am holding you I will not let you go.

The world is so terrifying.

But we are with you in it my little one. You are not alone. You are held and you are loved. You have our courage and our strength. This world will not overcome you my little one for we are in you and we have overcome everything in this world that would come against you. There is nothing that is too hard for us, nothing we cannot do my dearest child.

Daddy….I want to hide….Crying

You are hidden in me my little one. You are safe and you are loved and nothing will harm you.

It is hard to feel that way about life.

I know it is my little one but that is what we are helping you with. We are all of us with you. You are not ever alone in this world. It is not too much for you my little one.

I know you have to get rid of the fear. I know you do.

Yes my little one the fear you hold in your heart does not belong there. Let us take it

from you my little one so that you are free to do and to be everything we made you for.
Ok.
Little one you belong to us and no matter what this world will throw at you that will not ever change. We are always in control my little one and you will always be loved and wanted and safe.
Ok
Little one as you walk through this world with us there are many things which will seek to overcome you. This is to help you my little one and not to harm you.
Yes.
It is not pointless my little one. We are making a way for you.
Ok. One day at a time.
Yes my little one. One day at a time.

Some of what I was feeling was coming from the past. The blending was still happening. I hadn't expected it to take so long and I had hoped it would get better, but it was still very difficult and all the things that were happening were getting mixed up together in a not good way.

I have been having horrid dreams and I've been very tired. I did spend some time in the afternoon drawing and crying. It was the box again and all the things I'm not allowed. I rang about the rent first thing and they said they'd heard back from my landlord and the payment would be going into my account that day. That was good news but I haven't seen any money yet. I thought I would leave the other stuff for next week. I was feeling so depressed this morning so my chat with Jesus wasn't so good really.

Hi Jesus
Hello my little one
I am glad I can talk to you Jesus but it is like I can't see any more. I don't see anything.
My little one reality does not change according to what you see. You are still held in our father's arms surrounded by his rainbows. My angels still attend you. I am still with you. My little one it is hard for you to see these things right now because your vision is clouded by many things. The enemy does not want you to see he wants you to be confused and to lose hope. The healing that we are doing is helping you my little one but for a time you will feel weaker and less able to take hold of the truth than you were but the truth does not change my little one. You are my Pearl you are safe and you are loved and will always be so.
Jesus I just want to hide away. I don't want to do anything. I don't want to be here. I know you always say there is purpose and reason in each day but I can't see it. I can't see there has been any purpose or reason for anything so far.
Many have been healed and set free my little one. There was purpose in that.
The alters you mean.
Yes my little one.
But now they are all in me. Living this life with me. I suppose it is better than being in a prison or a pit or a cage...but not better than being inside Jesus. Inside was lovely. The children had friends and could play. The adults had a nice place to live and people to share it with. It was a beautiful place and they could live there and you took it away.
Yes my little one I did. Do you know why I did that?
Because it was healing. But what is so great about healing Jesus if nothing gets better.
My little one healing is for many reasons. It is to help you live in the truth without fear. It is to take away the shame and the grief so that you can know what it is to feel joy and hope. It is so that you can receive my love and give it away to others. Healing is a good thing my little one though it is not always easy.
I can't do this Jesus I just can't. I am tired of it. I am so tired of it.
I know you are my little one. I know you are.

There isn't any hope or life for me there isn't. I can't keep doing this.
My little one do you know who you are to me?
You say I am your Pearl…Crying
My little one you are my Pearl.
I know my little one that you are tired and weary of everything that I am asking of you. I know you do not see but remember who you are to me my little one. I have loved you and healed you and brought you back to life and I will continue to do so. Not because this is an end in itself my little one but because of all that I am longing to give to you. My little one my love is not something that will break you but it will shape you and help you to become all that you were created to be. All that I dreamed for you to be. I know you do not understand my full meaning my little one and you do not see as I do. My love is still difficult for you to understand or accept but you are more able than you were my little one and the more you are healed the more you will be able to understand and accept of my love. That is what I am doing my little one. This time is difficult I know but I will bring you through stronger and more able to be you, my beautiful Pearl in a broken world that needs my light and my love my little one. I am leading you forward though you do not see it. It is not endless my little one. It is not without purpose. Hold on and trust me. The past cannot hold you my little one not if you hold on to and trust me.
I don't want to feel like this. I don't want to be here.
I know my little one but I am holding you there is nothing to fear. I will help you and give you my strength. You are able to do all things in my strength my little one even to endure through this time.
Do you love me Jesus?
Yes my little one I do. With all of my heart. I am holding you and loving you. You will not be overcome. All the things of the past will be healed my little one. The things of the present cannot hold you. I am making a way for you. You will know what it is to truly live my little one. To love and be loved and to be my Pearl in a world which so desperately needs to know who I am. Hold on to me my little one and do not let go. I am holding you so very close to me. You are loved my little one and you are wanted just as you are. You are not alone.

When I could I spent time with daddy in the garden of rest. I didn't really understand what was going on, not inside with all of the healing or on the outside but I knew I needed to hold on the Jesus and to daddy and the Holy Spirit. I knew I needed help and healing to make it through each and every day.

Hi daddy. Are you going to show me what it means to have a daddy? Will you fill my heart with a daddy's love? I feel a bit lost.
But you are not my little one you are in the garden of rest receiving everything you need from me. My dearest one your heart has been full of pain for all of your life and as you are healed and cleansed there is a different kind of healing that needs to be done. It is a comfort and a soothing rest my little one that you need before you are ready to go deeper.
Like resting after an operation.
Yes my little one so that you have enough strength for the journey that lies ahead of you. I am making you strong in me even as you rest here my little one.
Tell me about the palace daddy.
It was made just for you my little one. It is full of life. In this place you will discover so much of who I am to you. You will discover what it means to have a daddy my little one
Does it have different rooms and things?
Yes my little one this is your home in my heart. It has many places for you to discover and all of them will reveal something to you of who I am to you.

And right now I am in the garden of rest and this is a….well it is restful and soothing and comforting like you said. Is that part of who you are...like resting in your arms?
Yes my dearest one.
It is very green and kind of overgrown. Why is that?
Because the life that is here is here in abundance my little one. It is not contained but it free to grow just as you are now free to grow.
There doesn't seem to be any flowers or anything daddy. Just green.
For now my little one but that will change.
Does the garden have different seasons?
Yes my little one it does.
And this is Spring?
Yes my little one it is. All of the flowers that are here will bloom at the proper time my little one.
Springtime is about new growth and life and hope and becoming and all of those things.
Yes my little one it is.
Ok. Can I explore the garden?
Yes my little one you can but for now my dearest child rest. That is what you need most my little one.
Ok. Thankyou daddy.
You are welcome my dearest one.

I was a bit confused how I could be in a garden of rest and a forest of difficulty at the same time. It didn't seem to go together but that was because I didn't really understand about rest.

Why am I resting Jesus?
Because that is what you need right now. My little one you have been through many changes and fought many battles, you have been healed of deep wounds and have discovered many things about who you are. Now is the time for rest my little one before you begin once again to follow me into everything I have for you.
But I am also in the forest of difficulty.
Yes my little one you are but it is resting here that makes it possible for you to walk with me through the forest my little one.
But that doesn't seem like resting to me.
Resting does not mean my little one that you are doing nothing. It is about knowing where you are my little one. Safe in my arms, hidden in our father's heart. Resting in his love for you knowing that I will make all things possible for you no matter where you are or what you are doing.
So, but won't I always be resting?
Yes my little one that is our desire. That you should always be resting.
Because everything I do and am will come out of this place of rest.
Yes my little one.
Because when I know that I am safe and held and hidden and loved that I am here, then I won't be afraid and I can do anything and go anywhere because I know that I am always here with you and that this eternal reality is the one that lasts, the most important one that will never change no matter what else is changing.
Yes my little one.
And that is what you want me to learn deep down in my heart.
Yes my little one it is.
And then I will be unshakable like you said I would be.
Yes my little one you will.
Ok. Help me learn then Jesus.

I was still having bad dreams and flashbacks. I was feeling so many things from the past, things I thought I shouldn't be feeling any more even though I knew it was because I was being healed, because of the blending that was still happening.

I keep crying even when I am just doing normal things. I am feeling a lot of things. Alone, abandoned, afraid, unwanted, forgotten and trapped. I know it is cos I am being healed and it is because of the box, cos I keep kind of being back there and feeling how I did then I suppose. It is horrible and it makes me panic. I think there is some birthday in the mix too, cos that is looming again. And I have been feeling angry but it has taken me longer to see that. I am angry with everyone and about everything, but I think mostly I am angry with daddy. It doesn't help to know I am wrong to feel that way.

The box memories were hard to bear because it stirred up feelings of desperation and of being trapped. The memories from the alters I had blended with made it even clearer what had happened. The box lid had been opened and I thought I was being let out, but then it was slammed shut again and I was left in the dark, trapped and unable to get out. This life felt the same to me. Every time I thought there was some hope of escape I found out there wasn't and I had to keep on being here. Like the box lid being slammed shut over and over again. I got so

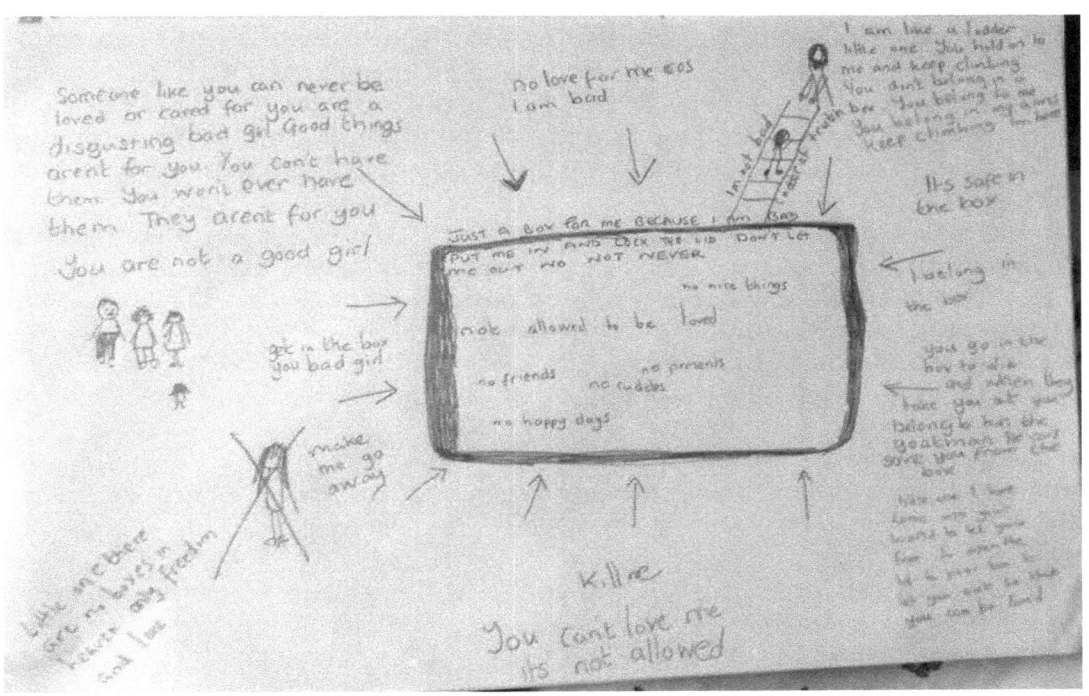

distressed. Jesus held me and reminded me that I wasn't in the box, that this life wasn't a punishment and that I wasn't trapped.

The box is more real to me that it has ever been. I see it and feel it clearer and it is a terrible feeling. It is making my feelings about being trapped here in this life difficult to cope with. I know it will pass but I had hoped that this sort of healing was done. But I suppose now all the memories are together again they will be more real won't they. And maybe that means they can be healed deeper. That isn't a fun thought. I hadn't thought of that before.

Daddy kept reminding me that no matter what was happening on the outside that I was safe and loved. That there is a greater reality that he wanted me to learn to live out of. That the things of the past couldn't hold me, not if could live out of the truth.

Hi daddy.

My precious and most beloved child. My little one the cares of this world were not meant to be carried by you. I am your daddy. You can bring everything to me and lay it my feet and I will take it from you.
I don't know what that means.
It means my little one that you do not carry the burden of responsibility.
I don't know what that means either.
It means my dearest child that all the things that are troubling you, all the things that you must do, all the things that need to change are in my hands and not yours…My little one I see you and know you completely. My little one do not run away from me.
I feel like you locked me in a prison and threw away the key and you keep telling me it's for my own good but if you don't let me out I will die here. I will die here.
My little one look around you what do you see.
So many things.
Tell me my little one.
I see me in a white cage desperate to get out. I see me in Jesus lap surrounded by your rainbows. I see a beautiful garden full of flowers.
Which of those is true my little one?
I don't know. Maybe all of them.
My little one you have spent all of your life locked in a prison that was not of my making. You have been set free from that prison my little one.
So why am I still in a cage? Did you just move me from prison to another?
No my little one no. What you see as a cage is really my protection. It is not a cage or a prison my little one. You are held and loved and protected until it is time for you to leave this place. That is for your good my little one not to harm you in any way.
It is still a prison.
No my little one a prison is a place of punishment. This is a place of safety. It looks like a prison to you because you are afraid and because you believe that I am keeping you here because you are not good enough to leave.
I won't ever leave.
No my little one that is not so. When it is time I will take you by the hand and lead you out of this place. My little one the time of your hiddenness will end. This is not a prison my little one.
I don't see that. Help me.
My little one I am with you. I will not ever leave you. No matter where we are we are together.
Yes. Help me…..Crying
I am with you my little one. I am holding you safe in my arms. Remember what I have told you. Things are not the way they seem to you. Trust in my sight my little one. Hold on to me and trust me. This time will end.
I hope it is true.
My little one I am faithful and true. I will not leave you. I will keep you and love you and lead you out from this place.

With everything that was happening I feeling confused again about who I was. The healing made me feel so small and vulnerable but at the same time I was having to be very adult helping Richard and dealing with all the phone calls and paperwork and appointments. I didn't know who I was or where I was in all of that.

When I feel like me, Pearl I feel very small and vulnerable Jesus. Most of the time. I suppose…I don't think about being me or I'm being a more grown up part of me. I don't understand what you are doing.
My little one which part of you is called by me to reach out to the lost and the lonely?
All of me I suppose. All the parts of me are important aren't they?
Yes my little one they are. Each part of you makes up who you are, my Pearl, my

beloved, the one who is called to love and be loved and to make me known to those who need me the most. My little one if you feel small and vulnerable at times that does not matter, it is part of who you are my little one. Part of what makes you, you.

Yes. I suppose even the grownup parts are still me.

Yes my little one they are.

I am sorry Jesus.

What are you sorry for my little one?

I feel like I got lost somewhere. Like I was getting better and stronger and now I'm not. I'm just a little girl who cries a lot.

And why do you think that is my little one?

Maybe it is because I am in the forest and I am learning to rest. Maybe like it all got harder suddenly and I am just finding my way as best I can.

My little one I am showing you the way. I am leading you step by step and you are growing stronger my little one. I know my dearest one that you do not feel stronger but your strength is in me my little one and not in yourself. The smallest and most vulnerable child can be strong when they trust wholly in who I am.

Yes. But I don't want to be miserable and crying Jesus.

I know my little one but your tears are only a reflection of the struggle and of the healing we are doing, not because you are weak my little one not because you are bad or wrong.

Aren't I supposed to be full of joy Jesus? I was just beginning to feel it and know it in my heart and it's like it just disappeared again I went back to being miserable.

My little one sometimes you will not feel the joy that is in your heart. That is because you are still suffering in many ways my little one and you are still learning how to be joyful in the midst of all of that. I know my little one that you think you are bad and wrong because you do not feel it right now but that is not what I have said.

Why can't I feel it Jesus? Why can't I be joyful when things are hard?

My little one it is not the outside things that are keeping you from my joy but the things that are still hidden deep in your heart. There is still much healing to be done my little one.

I am tired of it Jesus. It just goes on and on and no matter how much you do I am still not better. I don't know what to think about it.

My little one even though you have been blended with all of your alters the healing will continue my little one. The blending itself is not yet complete and there is much you have still to understand and accept about the past my little one. I am at work deep in your heart in ways you have not understood. I am healing you from the inside out my little one making you one and strong in me. As I weave you back together I am weaving myself into your very soul. I know these things are hard for you to understand my little one and to you it seems like more pain and suffering but it will not be long my little one before all of this is left behind you and you are beginning your new life with a heart that is filled with my joy and my hope. I am working to make this possible my little one.

It doesn't seem very possible Jesus.

I know my little one but it is. All things are possible for me my little one.

I asked Jesus to explain more about the forest to me. I wasn't enjoying it and I wanted to understand just how it was supposed to be helping me.

I don't really know what to say Jesus. I love you. I was thinking about how the forest is taking me deeper into your heart. Can you tell me a bit about that?

Yes my little one I can. My little one the forest is made up of many obstacles. It is a dark and difficult place to be my little one. It requires you to hold on to me and trust me and to follow me closely. You cannot see in the forest my little one. There is no path for you to follow. You cannot find the way out without me to lead you. All that

you can see in the forest are the obstacles that lay ahead of you my little one. That is why you must fix your eyes on me and not be overwhelmed by what you see.

But why is it taking me deeper?

Because as you follow me through the forest you are learning to depend wholly on my sight. You are learning to trust me to help you find your way through all of the things that are blocking your path. You are trusting in me to give you the strength to keep on going even when you cannot see that there is an end to what you are going through. It is in the forest that you learn true trust and dependence my little one so that you draw closer to me, so that you are surrendered wholly to me knowing that only I can lead you forward. That it is not your own strength which will bring you through but mine. It is a difficult place to be my little one but it is not a bad one. I am making you more completely mine and drawing you closer to me so that you can receive more of what I have for you.

Well I kind of understand that Jesus except all of my journey so far has been difficult so ...I don't know why we need a whole forest of it.

My little one the way has been difficult and painful it is true but each part of your journey has a purpose my little one. To help you and not to harm you. To heal you and draw you forward. This is not different my little one.

Psalm 43

Vindicate me, my God,
and plead my cause
against an unfaithful nation.
Rescue me from those who are
deceitful and wicked.
You are God my stronghold.
Why have you rejected me?
Why must I go about mourning,
oppressed by the enemy?
Send me your light and your faithful care,
let them lead me;
let them bring me to your holy mountain,
to the place where you dwell.
Then I will go to the altar of God,
to God, my joy and my delight.
I will praise you with the lyre,
O God, my God.
Why, my soul, are you downcast?
Why so disturbed within me?
Put your hope in God,
for I will yet praise him,
my Savior and my God.

Chapter 11

Putting the Pieces Together

I was sinking fast. I was getting overwhelmed by the memories and feelings from the blendings but didn't even really realise what was happening. I got very upset with daddy mike. I thought he didn't care. I stopped writing and didn't reply when he wrote to me. I was feeling so many things that seemed right to me, but it was all coming from the past. I was so angry with daddy mike and with everyone, including Jesus. I just wanted it all to stop.

Jesus.
I am here my little one.
Help me...crying
Always my little one I will always help you.
Is there any hope for me?.
Yes my little one there is great hope for you. Hold on my little one and do not let go. I am setting you free from many things. I am helping you in ways you have not yet understood. Hope is not lost my little one it is found. It is found in who I am who I am making you to be. You are my pearl my little one no matter what others see that is who you are.
I feel so lost and so angry and afraid. And so alone.
I know my little one I know but these things will pass and you will be stronger my little one. Do not be afraid but hold on to me. You have my courage my little one. Do not let go.
I am feeling too many things at once. It is too much. And the outside stuff. And everything.
My little one I am holding you and I will not let you go. I will give you everything you need. You are my treasure and my delight. This time is for you my little one to bring you healing and wholeness in me and to make the future I have planned for you possible. I know my little one that you are afraid and you do not see but my love for you is real. I will not let you go. I will bring you through this just as I have promised.
I want you to get rid of the anger. It scares me. I know I keep saying I hate you and I'm sorry. And I am angry with everyone and everything and it makes me afraid.
But I am holding you and helping you my little one. I will not let you be overwhelmed. I will set you free my little one but anger must first be faced before it can be let go of.
But I don't know what to do with it.
The first step is to acknowledge its presence my little one and that is what you are beginning to do. As you accept the anger you can begin to let go of it my little one but if you try to hide from it or push it away then I cannot set you free from that which is holding you. Do not be afraid my little one. Your anger will not destroy you or those around you.. not if you hold on to me.
It scares me.
I know it does my little one.
I can't do this.
Yes my little one you can. You can in my strength which is far greater than your own my little one.
But I can't be angry.
Yes my little one you can. I am your safe place. My servant is also a safe place.
No...crying
He will not leave you my little one.
I don't think he cares at all.
Yes my little one he does. He cares a great deal about you. He loves you. He is your daddy.
I don't think so....crying....I don't think so.

Yes my little one it is so. Just because you do not see it does not mean it is not so. He loves you and wants to help you my little one he will not leave you.

I don't think there is any hope Jesus.

But I do my little one. Trust in my sight my little one and not your own.

Surely it is time to give up now…Surely it is time to stop.

No my little one it is time to hold on and trust me. I will not leave you or forsake you or fail in any one of my promises to you. It is not time to give up my little one it is not time to stop. That time will not ever come because your hope is me and I do not ever fail.

I am so lost. I don't know who I am.

But I do my little one. I am holding you. I will not let you go. Trust me and hold on. I know where I am taking you my little one. It is worth the fight and the struggle and all of the tears.

Help me.

Yes my little one I will help you. Write to my servant, your daddy and do not be afraid. He will understand.

I don't want to.

I know my little one but this is to help you and not to hurt you. Trust me my little one and follow in my way. Lean on my understanding and not in your own.

I felt like I was drowning in all the feelings and the memories. I held on to Jesus and did what he asked.

Daddy I am lost in a dark place where I can't see and don't understand. I feel like I am drowning in all the things I am feeling. They come at me in big waves and I get so scared I will go down and not ever come up again. I don't know who I am. I don't know where Pearl is. She is buried under all the pain and fear and anger and grief and so many other things and it is so dark. That is all I can see darkness and bad memories that come out of it at me. Jesus says he is healing me and it is because of the blending and maybe other things I don't know. He says hold on and don't give up hope but I have been wanting to die so much. I don't see any hope just darkness. I don't know what it is all for.

My daddy wrote back to me. He did care after all. I was so afraid that he didn't. I was so confused about everything.

Sweetie trust all that you are to Jesus and know that He will raise you up out of this time of darkness. He will not abandon you...any of you. Pearl is safe because you are not alone...Jesus is with you. You are fully in my prayers and love. Continue to write me please or I will worry for you.
Love and prayers, Daddy

I did keep writing. It was like being thrown a lifeline and I grabbed on to it and held on tight.

Hi daddy, I am writing like you asked me to. It is hard for me to write. You wrote back to me. I never thought you would. I get so confused about everything and I don't know even if you like me. I have been feeling so angry with everyone and everything. I kept telling Jesus I hated him but I don't feel angry anymore. Now I am crying and crying. I keep thinking how they took my life from me. They took it and it is gone. I didn't mean to make it sound like there are more alters with me. I don't think that is it. It could be because how do I know but I don't think so. It is more like I am getting lost in all of their memories and feelings because now they are my memories and feelings. It doesn't seem like it happened to them any more it all happened to me. All those things happened to me. It was my life they took.. I am holding on tight to Jesus because it is like being in a tornado or something. He says I am still his Pearl. I don't know who that is. Maybe I am being remade and that is why. Please don't leave me daddy. I have to finish now. I can't write any more.

He didn't leave me. He never left me even though sometimes I thought he did. I misunderstood a lot of the things he did and said, when I was struggling so much. Jesus helped me to understand what was happening so it was a bit easier for me, to hold on to the truth but it was a big battle.

My little one all the threads that make up your life are being woven together. All the people that you have been are being joined my little one. This is not easy. You will feel lost for a time my little one but you are not. You are held safely in our father's arms. Your daddy loves you my little one and will not let you go. You are surrounded by his rainbows and hidden in his love. You belong to him my little one and he has given you to me so that I can show you who he is and how much that you are loved and wanted. This time is hard my little one but it is making you new. You are not lost or forgotten. There is nothing to fear. You are loved and wanted my beloved pearl and will always be so.

As I held on to Jesus and the truth and I got stronger, the darkness got less, and I could see again. I started to feel a little bit better. It felt like I was beginning to see the past more clearly as the memories came together, and Jesus helped me to understand some of the things I had wondered about for a long time. I remembered that mum had told me that when she was pregnant, her boss and his wife wanted to adopt me. She thought about it but in the end said no. It made me wonder if this was Jesus giving her a choice and a chance, a way out. A way of protecting me. I wondered how many times he gave choices to her and others that would have made a difference. Jesus told me he had given lots of people chances to rescue me right from the very beginning, but no one ever did. He didn't want those things to happen to me. It made me feel better about Jesus, but not about mum.

As Jesus filled in more of the gaps I could accept the things that I remembered because they fitted together and made sense, more than they had up to now. It wasn't easy to talk about these things but it helped. He told me that when I was about seventeen, the Goatman had died and the group had kind of faded away with him. Some joined other groups and some just stopped being involved, like me. When the priest left, when I was around ten or eleven, a lot of the other things stopped too and Barbara moved on to others, once I was older and trained.

Now Jesus wanted to bring other memories together and help me make sense of them.

I was in the dark and in the woods. It was the Goatman group. I was on a goat. They had put me on it. I could feel it's warm body and its soft fur. I could hear the noise it was making. It was tied up and they put me on it, so it was in me. Then they cut its throat and collected the blood on a bowl and they pulled me off. I don't know what happened after that. It isn't a new memory but it was so real this time. (drawing – Book 1- Part 1-Chapter 28 p258)

Little one as these things are given to you, you are able to accept them for what they were. They do not say anything about you my little one.
I wish you had let me die….Crying
You are my precious child. You are lovely in every way to me my little one. Do not wish for death. Hold on to me my little one and let me love you back to life. My little one you were violated in the worst of ways but that does not change who you are. You are my pearl my beloved child. You are loved and precious. You are clean and pure. You belong to me. I chose you because I love you and because I wanted you for my very own. Nothing that was done to you can change that.
I am your pearl and you love me…..Crying
Yes my little one. You are my princess. Blameless and pure and lovely.
How can you even touch me?
My little one you are my Pearl. What they did to you does not change how I see you or my love for you. The fault was theirs my little one. The stain lies on them and not on you.

I don't want to live Jesus. I'm sorry…I just don't…

My little one you are safe in my arms. You are loved. Remember all that I have promised you. There are many like you my little one who need to know that there is hope for them. That they are loved and not despised, that they are priceless and not worthless as they believe.

But you won't let me go.

Yes my little one I will. When the time is right I will let you go and be with your daddy. Hold on to me and trust me my little one. My love is enough for you.

You should get rid of me Jesus.

No my little one no. Hold on and let me love you and heal you. You are mine. My princess. There is no one who can take your place my little one.

The shame felt overwhelming when I remembered these things, but Jesus never wavered in his love and acceptance. He held me in his arms, he rocked me and wiped the tears from my eyes. He kissed my hair and held me close. No matter what I felt about myself in those times I knew he didn't feel the same. And I knew too that he sees the truth and not the lie.

I was in a cold dark lake. I was being pushed under the water by two people. I think it was the Goatman group. I don't know how old I was maybe about ten? It was a full moon very bright. That seemed to be important and when I came up they said words I don't know what and then pushed me under again. Three times I think.

Jesus.

Yes my little one.

Why are you showing me this?

It is a memory my little one. It belongs to you.

I don't want any of these memories.

I know my little one.

I suppose it was a ritual.

Yes my little one it was.

Do I need to know about it?

It will help you my little one.

Why don't I remember ... The alter must have understood something.

Yes my little one she did. Hold on to me my little one.

So I held on to Jesus and I was remembering again and I felt like I understood…I think it was a kind of cleansing or dedication or something to prepare me for something I was going to do. Something about the water and the moonlight. It hurts Jesus.

I know my little one I know it does.

Help me. I know I'm trying to block it out.

Crying...

I didn't block it out. They took me out of the lake and put a white robe on me and then I went to where there was a stone altar. There was a baby on it. I was given a knife and I stabbed into the baby...

I wish you would let me die….Crying

My little one you are who I say you are. You are beautiful and strong. None of this makes you bad my little one. My little one hold on to me. I am healing you my little one.

You should have killed me you should have killed me…

No my little one I have saved you and loved you and made you my very own. My little one you are loved and cherished and no matter what happened, no matter what you did or was done to you, you are my beloved child. It is who you are my little one. That will not ever change.

I can't bear it. I can't.

Yes my little one you can. I am bearing with you my little one. I am taking the pain and the fear and the shame from you. You are my beloved one. I am holding you

close to me. I will not let you go.
Stop making me live, stop making me live.
No my little one hold on and trust me. I am making you new my little one. The things of the past will have no hold on you.

The memories had a new reality for me now, even though they weren't new memories. They came full force with all of the sights and sounds and feelings, and they were so terrible to me I wanted to die. I didn't want to live with the truth it seemed too hard to bear.

I kept writing to daddy mike. He always loved me and accepted me no matter what I told him about the past or the present. It meant so much that he was just with me when I talked with him, even though a lot of the time I didn't say very much. There was a lot I wanted to say, but somehow it just didn't come out. It was easier for me to write these things than to say them.

I am having trouble wanting to be alive. There is so much pain and I feel like I am in a deep dark hole. I am supposing it will get better eventually, it's just it is hard to see there is any reason to go through this just to live this life. Sometimes I feel stronger and decide I'm not giving up and sometimes I just want to die. I know I don't say much. It is hard to talk when I am trying so hard not to cry. But it helps to see you. You can make me smile even when I am feeling so bad. Night night. Love from Pearl.

These memories were hard but most of all he wanted to help me accept and understand, and grieve for the babies we had lost and to understand the memories I had of them.

I am in a lot of pain…..Crying
I know you are my little one. Come into my arms of love and let me hold you. I am enough for you my little one no matter what lies in the past, or in the future I am always enough.
They hurt me. They took the babies. They pulled them out. I don't know how many Jesus.
Five my little one, there were five little ones that were taken from you.
It is all jumbled in my mind Jesus. I don't...I mean it is jumbled. We have cried for them and grieved, but somehow they still aren't very real.
My little one your children were lost to you, but they are safe with me and though you have grieved for them, you have not accepted them as your own. I want you to do so my little one, for only then can you fully accept their loss and find healing.
But we have held them Jesus and given them back to you.
Yes my little one you have but healing and acceptance takes time and you are ready my little one to take another step.
Ok.
Tell me what you remember my little one.
I remember the one we called Peter who was maybe the first. He was pulled out and the Goatman held him up and then…I can't.
Yes my little one you can. It will help you.
He put him down on the stone and put the dagger in his heart. They killed him.
Yes my little one they did. What happened next?
They wrapped his body up in a cloth. I didn't remember that before. And they put him in a grave. It wasn't very deep. And they covered him up. And he was gone. But you have him Jesus. Little Peter who never had a life. But he was lucky. He didn't suffer very much Jesus.
No my little one not very much.
Why must I do this again?
Because it is still jumbled my little one. It is still not healed. You have yet to fully accept the truth and your loss.
Jesus was holding baby Peter in his arms wrapped in a blanket and he gave him to me to hold.

What do you think my little one as you hold him?
That he is beautiful and he looks happy and content. And I am glad he is with you and didn't suffer. But the darkness and pain is still there for me Jesus.
Do you understand his significance my little one?
Well I remember that they said he was the first and that is why they buried him, but I don't understand why exactly or what it means.
He was your first child with the Goatman my little one and for that reason he was not disfigured in any way. He was left whole my little one and buried just as he was.
Ok.
He was a sign of things to come, of those that would follow him. He was given my little one so that those who followed him could fully belong to the cult. Their fate would be different to his. Their purpose was different.
Like...I don't know...sacrificing the firstborn or dedicating or something.
Yes my little one like that. He was given to Satan so that those who followed him could belong to the cult.
And there were another four?
Yes my little one there were.
I suppose I worried it might be more but that is enough.
Yes my little one it is.
You take him Jesus. He belongs to you.
Yes my little one just as you do.
Goodbye Peter.
He is safe with me my little one.
Yes. He is. How old was I Jesus when... whatever?
You were just sixteen my little one.
That seems kind of old Jesus considering.
You were mine my little one, I was with you helping you.
What does that mean?
I am in control of all things my little one.
You are hard to understand Jesus.
I know my little one. They had their uses for you. Giving them the children they wanted was only one of those. I was helping you in every way I could.
Am I supposed to ask questions Jesus? I don't see why it matters. I know I did other things. It is all a big nightmare and it makes me wish I was dead…Crying
Why my little one?
Because it hurts and because I still feel dirty and disgusting and I don't know how to live knowing what I did and what I was...really knowing it I mean. I am afraid of knowing it...of accepting that person as part of me, or those parts of me. How do I accept them Jesus. I mean I did when we were blended but maybe I didn't...not fully.
My little one do you think you were responsible for the things you did or the things that happened to you?
I don't think I had any control over anything.
No my little one you didn't. None of this was your doing my little one. You were controlled from the beginning. None of it was your fault my little one. It does not say anything about who you are.
Help me.
My little one in accepting that these things are part of you, you are not saying that you were responsible for them. You are not saying that is who you were. You experienced those things my little one but it does not change who you are. You are my pearl. My beloved one. You were in darkness my little one but I have brought you into the light.
Can you help me Jesus? To accept those things as part of my life, like any other parts so I can be whole and healed and strong in who you made me to be.
Yes my little one I can.

Do it then. Help me.

It will take a little time my dearest one but healing and wholeness will come. My little one the things of the past do not say anything about who you are. They are a part of your experience and the life you have lived for the most part through the lives and experience of others. Their experiences are being given back to you my little one. Who they are is being given back to you, but you remain Pearl, my beautiful child. You are strong enough my little one to carry all the memories and all the experiences of the life that you have all lived and yet remain who you are. You will not disappear my little one you will not become someone else. You will remain my Pearl. My beloved child who will carry my light out into this world. That is who you are my little one and nothing that has happened to you, nothing you have done or experienced can ever change that.

I didn't feel strong enough most of the time. It felt to me like I was being swallowed up by the pain and the darkness but I held on somehow. He did have to keep telling me that the things that had happened didn't say anything about who I am, because they made me feel so bad I wanted to die.

Hi Jesus
Hello my little one
My little one I am holding you close to my heart and I will not ever let you go.
Do we need to talk about the things you are healing Jesus? I wanted to talk to daddy but there was too much pain. I couldn't do it.
My little one talking to your daddy about these things will help you, but you need my healing and my love and my comfort before you will be able to do so. My little one healing takes time. Some things cannot be rushed my little one.
It has already taken time Jesus a lot of it and you can do anything.
Yes my little one I can but you need to be able to accept what I am giving to you. You cannot do it all at once. I know you feel like it is taking forever and the healing and the pain that goes with it will not ever end but that is not so. Hold on to me my little one. Follow where I lead. I will help you to accept all the healing I have for you.
I don't really care about healing Jesus, I didn't even think I should be made better. I think you should throw me away like a piece of rubbish.
But you are not a piece of rubbish my little one. You are my treasure and though you have been hurt I can mend you my little one.
I wish you wouldn't…Crying
I will not leave you my little one. Not ever. My little one the past does not define who you are. I do that. You are mine. You belong to me and only I can say who you are.
Ok…Crying
My little one as we explore the past together and you are able to accept it as your own I am healing you and making you stronger. I know it does not feel that way to you my little one but this time will pass and you will be more of who you are and not less.
I don't know what to do Jesus. How am I going to live?…Crying
In my strength and my courage my little one.
There's too much of it.
My little one I am able to do all things. I will not ask you to relive all of it my little one only those parts which will help you to heal. My little one do you remember what I told you about the broken little rabbits I would bring to you?
I think so…it was Blossum of course…you said you would give us many broken little rabbits to love. I think maybe that was something to do with the babies…that we never got to love them.
Yes my little one it was.
I would like that to be healed and done Jesus. We come back to it over and over but it still hurts.

We can do a little more if you are ready my little one.
Ok. You said there was five. I only really remember three of them. I think. I don't know. I forget.
You named three of them my little one but two remain.
Have we remembered them at all Jesus?
In part my little one but not enough to bring healing. Hold on to me my little one. I am with you.
Ok. I was being led out. I was dressed all in black with a black veil that went over my face and made it hard to see. They put me on the stone and pulled the baby out of me. It hurt. The things they put in me were cold. The Goatman held up the tiny baby girl by her feet. She was so small. He smashed her down on the stone and they took her apart. I don't want to describe it...
I was in Jesus lap and he was holding her. He passed her to me. She was wrapped in a blanket and was sleeping. She looked content.
I'm sorry I'm so sorry.
My little one none of this was your fault.
But I am still sorry. I am still sorry.
I know my little one I know.
Little Lucy…She's so tiny…Tell me about her Jesus.
She was your second my little one. She was taken from you and given as a sacrifice. She did not suffer my little one. She lived only a very short time.
So there was Peter and then Lucy...I was still sixteen?
Yes my little one you were.
Are you ready my little one?
Goodbye Lucy. I passed her back to Jesus...
You will see her again my little one.
In heaven?
Yes. In heaven.
But I suppose she won't be mine then...she will be whoever gave birth to her...
Yes my little one but you will still see her and know her for who she is.
Yes...I am wondering about Natalie and maybe understanding. Am I?
Yes my little one you are.
She was the last one...but .maybe they didn't want her anymore. That is why it was in a room and they drowned her because...they didn't want her.
No my little one they didn't. The group was ending my little one. They had no need of her, their meetings became fewer. They only needed to dispose of her my little one.
I see...And who was next after Lucy?
Thomas was next my little one.
I think it was very much the same as Lucy. You did some healing and we said goodbye Jesus. Didn't we?
Yes my little one you did.
So that leaves one more.
Yes my little one but that is enough for today.

Jesus never gave me more than I could bear. He knew when I needed to rest. He knew when I could do more. I learned to trust that. No matter how I felt he always held me and gave me the strength I needed to remember and to heal.

My little one I am holding you so close to me. I will not let you go.
My little one the healing I am doing goes deep and it cannot be done in an instant but you are able my little one as you hold on to me and trust me, to endure the pain. It will not last forever. It is only for a little while. My little one as you hold on to me and trust me I am able to reach deep into your heart to all the broken places. I am mending them my little one. I know that it hurts and you cannot see any hope but I

am your strength and your hope my little one. Hold on to me and do not let go. My little one are you ready?
If you think so Jesus. I want to get it done.
I know you do my little one. Snuggle into me and hold on.
I was in the black dress again standing by a fire in the dark woods. I had bare feet. They led me towards the stone and I felt so afraid. Like terror. And they laid me down and put the cold metal in me again to get the baby, but it was like I shut down I didn't look or hear or feel. I thought maybe the alter whose memory it was had just kept her eyes closed and not looked, but I don't think that was it. I didn't see. I didn't look.
No my little one you didn't.

I didn't feel right...I seemed to be on Jesus lap, but I couldn't see or move. I didn't like it. It made me think it was the enemy. So I prayed.
I'm sorry I'm having trouble. Help me.
My little one the pain will not overwhelm you...Here she is my little one...
I kept praying because I didn't trust anything, I knew the enemy was there, so I asked Jesus to get rid of it and I felt it or whatever it was, go and I felt better and clearer again.

I'm here my little one
I don't understand.
My little one sometimes memories and the pain that goes with them give the enemy something to hold on to. Your own fear, that of the alter you blended with, of the pain gave the enemy a way of holding that memory my little one, so that you could not see it.
Can I see it now?
Yes my little one you can, if you are willing.
You will be with me.
Always my little one.
Ok.
I was back by the fire again and the memory was the same except this time I did see. I saw the little baby girl. She was laid on the stone in front of me. I touched her. She was crying. I picked her up and held her and just looked and looked at her. I am not sure why I was allowed to do that. But then the Goatman was there and I gave her to him. I knew what would happen...but I gave her to him. I didn't see anymore.
This one will take time to heal my little one.
Because I'm still holding on to the pain?
Yes my little one but I will help you.
I gave her to him when I knew what he would do. I should die. Let me die. I should die.
No my little one I will hold you and love you and bring you healing and life. Little one the things of the past do not say anything about who you are. You are my beloved child. My Pearl.
I don't want to think about this stuff anymore.
I know my dearest one I know. Little one that is enough for now. I will help you to let go of the pain my little one but that is enough for today.

Daddy I don't know if can keep doing this. It is like being in a nightmare that I can't escape from. I don't want to keep on living this life. Kate is freaking out about me getting a job. She is worried she won't see me anymore so she is panicking and ringing me up crying. I don't want to be here.

Outside life was still happening of course while all of this healing was going on. The uncertainty was hard to live with and the fear of what the future might bring didn't go away. There was pressure from the benefits people for me to get a job, from Kate who didn't because how could I help her if I was working, and from mum who thought I shouldn't be living on state handouts. It was hard to take. I felt like I was being constantly punished for being me, for not being ok, and like I had to keep on being punished to protect everyone from the truth of who I was, because that truth would only bring pain. It is a hard thing to know that if the people I cared about knew who I was, it would bring them pain and suffering. It made it hard to accept that being Pearl was a good thing. It made it hard to want to be me even without all of the feelings from the past.

Hi Jesus
Hello my little one
Jesus my head is too full and I can't think I don't know what to think about and mostly I don't want to think about any of it. It just makes me want to disappear and I'm sorry because I see sometimes I do. That you are bringing me out of something so dark and terrible and it is taking time. Too much time but that is what is happening. Sometimes I get so lost in it all. I feel like there's no way out but there is. There is a way out and I shouldn't give up even if I want to...Crying
My little one I am making you so strong in me. I know my dearest one that you feel so lost at times but you are not. You are on the path I have made for you and I am drawing you further and further out of the darkness and into the light of my love. I will not stop my little one. The journey is not endless though it seems so to you.
It is the thinking that I'm going through all of this for nothing that is making me want to give up. I can't keep on doing this just to stay where I am. Just to keep on living Jennifer's life.
My little one my dearest little one I have promised you a new life. This is to make you ready for it my little one. It is not for nothing.
But you know how it seems to me Jesus.
Yes my little one I do but I want you to trust me and hold on to me. In this way you will grow strong enough to take hold of all that I have for you. I do not want you to miss out on anything I have for you my little one.
I'm so tired and there's still so much pain. Please can we finish the baby thing...Crying
My little one what do you think of when you think of your babies?
Darkness and horror and pain.
But that is not what I want for you my little one. Each one is a life to be celebrated even though the lives they lived were short my little one.
I don't know how to celebrate babies who were created to be killed.
My little one that is not why I created them.
Why did you then? Why do it?
You see their lives as having no purpose.
I think if they had a purpose it was taken from them...Crying.
No my little one that is not so. Their purpose was given to you just as their light was given to you. It was not lost my little one. I did not create them just so that they could die cruelly. That was never my intention for them my little one and though that was their fate still their purpose and their light, given to them by me was not lost. It lives on in you my little one and so their lives can be celebrated because even though their time on this earth was so very short, they are safe with me and their purpose and their light remains just as I always intended it should.
I think you need to explain.
My little one everyone that I create has a purpose, and everyone that I create carries my light within them.
Yes.
Those little ones never got to live out their purpose my little one but it was not lost. Their purpose remains in you. It was given to you my little one just as their light was given to you.
Why?
Because I knew that you would be willing to carry it my little one.
So...because of them...I have more purpose and more light than I would have had?
Yes my little one you do.

Is that something to celebrate?

Yes my little one because it means that nothing is lost. No matter what the enemy did he has not destroyed their purpose, nor has he taken their light from this world. Those things remain in you. And your children are safe with me my little one.

So...you overcame everything the enemy did?

Yes my little one I did.

But only if I fulfil my purpose.

Yes my little one.

But if I give up or choose not to...then their purpose is lost as well.

Yes my little one that is so.

Why can't you give my purpose to someone else?

Because it is your choice my little one. Those little ones did not have a choice. It was taken from them but you do my dearest one. You have a choice to continue to follow me or to turn aside or give up. If you do that my little one then the purpose and the light that you carry will never do what it was intended to, and though you will always be loved and will always belong to me, your purpose and the purposes of those you carry will never be fulfilled and the light that you carry will never be seen as I intend that it should.

That is a big responsibility Jesus.

Yes my little one it is but I bear it with you. I am the one who makes you able my little one.

Didn't you say before about others that were killed that you gave their light to me?

Yes my little one I did.

Is it the same?

Yes my little one.

So you have given me a lot of purpose and a lot of light that belonged to others...so it wouldn't be lost. And that's why you kept me alive and why the enemy wants to kill me...make me give up.

Yes my little one.

So tell me about the celebrating Jesus.

My little one each life that is created whether it is short or long is worthy of celebrating. Some are taken before they even begin to live my little one, but that does not make them less. Their lives are worth just as much to me.

Yes. I see that.

So celebrating the little ones that you lost is possible my little one because they are still precious and because I have made it possible for you to fulfil their purpose and carry their light into a dark and broken world. That is worth celebrating my little one.

But how? I don't know how.

First of all by allowing me to heal the pain my little one and by allowing yourself to see them differently. As precious children to be celebrated even though they were taken from you. Their lives are worth celebrating my little one just as yours is. They are my gifts to this world and the gift that was given remains in you my little one.

Wasn't anything lost Jesus?

Their choice was lost my little one but they are safe with me. The enemy did not triumph over them even though he took their lives.

It is hard to understand.

I know my little one.

Can I say goodbye to Emily Jesus. Is it ok to call her that?

Yes my little one it is. Tell me what you see as you look at her.

I see that she is loved and wanted and safe. And even though it was so terrible what happened the enemy didn't win. They didn't win.

No my little one they didn't not in any way.

Goodbye Emily....Crying

My little one my purpose in you is very great and I will enable you to live it out. It

takes time and perseverance and great courage my little one to live out the purpose I have for you but that does not mean it is not possible for you. I am giving you everything you need. I am showing you the way my little one. Everything will come just as I have said. Nothing can overcome me my little one.
No.
My little one I am making everything possible for you. Hold on and do not let go. Do not be afraid to trust me my little one I will not ever fail you. You are so very loved my little one.
I am so tired Jesus.
I know my little one do you are caught in a great battle but it is a battle that I have already won my little one. You need only hold on to me.

Slowly my jumbled memories were coming together in way that made sense. It made it easier to accept them as real which helped with the healing. I was brave enough to ask Jesus about some of the things I didn't understand. There was a memory I had of a baby being born that didn't seem to belong to any of the babies Jesus had helped me with so far.

Don't be afraid to ask my little one.
It's just some of the things I remember...that seem to be in that churchyard...seem like Goatman things, but I don't think the Goatman group met there. Like being buried and I thought there was a baby there, but maybe it is wrong and I am just confused.
No my little one you are not confused.
I don't understand then.
Little one the Goatman group was a large group for a time anyway and they met in many different places. But there were also smaller groups within that larger group who had their own gatherings.
Like local groups.
Yes my little one.
Like the one that met in the garage when I was younger.
Yes my little one like that.
But I don't know what happened to that group because uncle John died and so did grandad, and it didn't seem that big so maybe that one ended.
Yes my little one it did but there were others.
The memories I have of the churchyard from when I was little were they from the garage group?
Some of them my little one.
But you are saying there was another group that did more Goatman things.
Yes my little one there was.
There are too many questions in my head. Was there another baby?
Yes my little one there was.
Not for the Goatman group?
No my little one this was an accident...they did not intend for you to have this baby. You were meant for the Goatman.
Because Peter was his.
Yes my little one he was. Conceived in a ritual to be the first of many.
By there was one before...from the local group...and they had to get rid of it?
Yes my little one.
I don't remember who they were. I remember being dressed in black...they were some of the first things we remembered...but they weren't for the Goatman group?
No my little one. They were from a smaller group who met in the churchyard. They followed the same practices my little one. They were part of the larger group but had their own meetings.
But I wasn't supposed to have a baby.
No my little one you weren't.

I think that is enough. I am getting confused with all these babies. We have done a lot of grieving for them...they get mixed up for me.
Yes my little one because up until now the memories have come to you in a way that did not make sense. But the grieving was real my little one as were the memories.
So there were five Goatman babies and this one...but no more.
No my little one. That is all. There were no more babies. Little one we can do this later. I have told you many things. That is enough for now.
Yes. I think so. I will get lost if you tell me more. Help me put it all together like you want and...I suppose there is the baby and other things that needs healing.
Yes my little one there are many things which need my healing and my love.
Ok. Bye not bye Jesus.
Bye not bye my little one.

Everything was making much more sense now. The memories I had were fitting together to make one story instead of being a collection of jumbled up pieces. I supposed that there was still more for me to understand and more healing to be done but it was better. It was time for the last of the baby memories to be healed. The baby that I knew now had been first.

Do I need to remember?
Yes my little one for only as you connect to that memory can I bring healing. Do not be afraid my little one. I am with you.
Ok. I remembered going into the graveyard through a stone porch type thing. I was all dressed in black. I don't know how I got there. I could have walked but not in those clothes. There were two men with me but I don't know who they were. We went round the back to where it backs onto the woods. Maybe other people were there I don't know. It wasn't so clear. It seemed very dark, I think they were only using torches and they spoke in whispers. They got the baby out...he was very small and they buried him at the edge of the woods. I don't know if he was alive, when he was born or not.
Jesus.
I'm here my little one. They only needed to dispose of him my little one. There was no ritual. No sacrifice as such.
It is all so stupid and pointless. It makes me want to rip my insides out, so they can't do it again but they did…Crying…they did.
Yes my little one they did.
Why was that my life? It wasn't a life.
No my little one it should never have been so. My little one remember what I told you. Each life is precious my little one. Each one is worth celebrating. They are safe with me. Loved and wanted just as you are.
I feel like a piece of rubbish…Crying
But you are my precious and beloved child my little one. No matter what they did to you no matter what they said you, you are precious and wanted and loved.

I was sitting on Jesus lap holding the baby. He looked so sweet, with a little blonde curl. We seemed to be in a bright light. Not a glaring one but still bright.

There is no shame for you my little one. You are not guilty. You are in the light of my love. There is no fear or shame in my love my little one. No need for hiding. My little one your past does not say anything about who you are. You are my child you belong to me. I say who you are my little one.
You gave him life Jesus.
Yes my little one I did.
Because you wanted him to exist.
Yes my little one.
He belongs to you.

Yes my little one just as you do.
We are safe together with you. Your children. You don't see me any different to him …Crying.
No my little one I don't. You are both innocent in my eyes. Victims of great evil my little one but safe and loved in me.
It's not different…Crying
No my little one it isn't. Not to me.
I see. I see me in him. It isn't different.
No my little one it isn't. You are both innocent my little one. Both loved both wanted and accepted just as you are. It isn't different my little one.
Will you take it Jesus? All of the guilt and shame.
It is already done my little one.
Thankyou…Crying
My little one you are my precious and beloved child. There is nothing I would not do for you…My little one there is nothing I would not do for you.
I don't know what that means.
I know you don't my little one but in everything I am doing I am bring you life. Do not be afraid of anything that lies ahead for you my little one. You are my precious and beloved child. I will never do anything to harm you.
Just like you wouldn't for him.
Yes my little one. It is not different.
I don't feel like I want to let him go.
And neither will I ever let you go my little one. You are safe and you are held close to my heart. It is not different. My little one all of these years you have been so very loved. I know that it has not seemed so to you my little one but you are my treasure just as he is my treasure. You are loved and wanted. You are held and protected. It is not different my little one.
You hold him now Jesus.
Yes my little one I will hold you both. Both precious both loved both wanted. Both innocent in my eyes my little one.
Little Benjamin
My little Pearl.
I belong to you just the same.
Yes my little one you do.

"Can a mother forget the baby at her breast
And have no compassion on the child she has borne?
Though she may forget, I will not forget you!"
Isaiah 49:15

Chapter 12

The Truth Will Set You Free

The pieces of the past were coming together. Memories made more sense and as I healed I could see more clearly what had happened and understand it better. That wasn't easy and as more feelings surfaced with the new understanding I had, holding on to Jesus was just as important as it had ever been.

When I was crying and holding on to Jesus today, it was like I saw things so different to what I had before. I don't know if I can explain it. Like seeing it from someone else's point of view. Maybe that is what it is. Maybe it is how one of the alters saw it I am not sure. But I thought to myself I should have run. All that time ago I should have run away and kept running and running and never come back. But instead I am still here. Still held by it all. Still kind of with mum, still not free from her, still protecting her, still controlled by her, still in this place where I shouldn't be. A bad place for me and I need to get away. I need to get away from her and from this place. It is a desperate feeling and a hopeless trapped feeling. A feeling that it is all so wrong for me being here. I'm not talking about me wanting to be in America or with you. It's not to do with that it is just about not being here. I did talk a bit to Jesus but I was still crying a lot.

My little one you are safe in my arms you are safe in our father's arms. That is where you are. Nothing and nobody can take you from us.
You've got to help me Jesus. You've got to help me…Crying
I am here my little one I will help you.
I shouldn't be here…why am I still here. Why? I should have run and kept running and never come back. But instead I am still trapped here. I am still trapped just like I always was. After all of this time. O my god why can't I get away. Why…Crying…Why?
Because my little one you are not ready to leave. My little one there have been many things that have kept you here, many reasons why you have not been able to leave. You are beginning to break free my little one but it has taken time
I can't be here I can't be here I can't. This is the wrong place for me. I shouldn't be here. I can't be here. I can't be here.
My little one hold on to me and listen to what I will say. I am setting you free my little one so that you are able to leave. I know my dearest one that everything within you is desperate to leave this place, but it would not be enough for you to leave this place physically my little one. There are many things which still hold you, things which would continue to hold you even if you were to leave. I would not have it so my little one. I want to set you free so that you can truly leave this place with all of its pain and never return my little one. That is what I want for you. I will make it possible my little one but you need to hold on and trust me. I will not leave you here. I am doing a great work of healing my little one, one which is necessary so that you can truly leave this place. My little one I am enough for you. Hold on and do not let go. Remember all that I am to you and all that you are to me. I am healing you and setting you free my little one. I will not keep you here. This is not the life I have for you. I am setting you free so that you can go and do and be everything you were created for.
Help me.
I am here my little one I will not let you go.
I can't be here I can't be here.
Hold on my little one I will make it possible for you to leave. I love you my little one with all that I am and I understand everything that is holding you in the place that you

are in. I will not leave you here. I am working to set you free from everything that is holding you. Keep your eyes fixed on me my little one. I will not let you go.
I shouldn't be here.
No my little one you shouldn't. Hold on to me and let me set you free. Only I can do it my little one. You cannot free yourself. Hold on and trust me.

It was a desperate and terrifying feeling that I couldn't seem to shake. I suppose it is how someone felt back then when it was all happening. It was hard for me to understand why I had to stay, why Jesus couldn't take me to a different place, any place and then heal me. He started to show me something that would help set me free. Something that gave me the strength I needed for the healing that was ahead.

Last night I was sitting watching the tv and just started to cry. I was crying about being handed over to those men, but even while I was crying I was thinking but I am loved I am so loved. And I felt it like that love was more real than anything and more important than anything that happened, bigger somehow. And I thought about mum and how I don't suppose she has ever known she is loved, not like that. I felt so sad for her. I think maybe it helped me to see that. It helped me to know that I am loved with a big love that goes beyond anything that happens anything in this life. The pain isn't gone though.

Knowing that I was loved by Jesus, which was setting me free from the past, just like it had others before me, but I had my own choices to make.

Can you explain to me about the things that are holding me? I feel like I am caught in a giant web.
My little one even though there are still things which are keeping you here I can set you free. It is not too much for me my little one. There are things which need healing, things which need forgiveness and ties that need to be broken my little one, but all of it will be done in my strength. I will help you my little one. It will not be too much for you no matter how it feels right now. My little one do you remember how it was when you first started on your journey with me.
I don't know...when was that Jesus? I don't know.
When you jumped into my arms and gave yourself to me my little one.
Crying...In the stream?
Yes.
Was that when my journey began Jesus? I have been walking such a long time with everyone else.
Yes my little one you have but this is where your journey began my little one, when you began to make your own choices and to begin learning who you are.
Ok. Yes I remember.
And I promised to love you and care for you.
Yes.
That is where it began for you my little one. Though there was much that went before still that is where your own personal journey with me began, because it was only then that you truly accepted me for yourself.
Ok.
In the same way my little one even though those before you made choices to forgive, you must also make those same choices my little one. In some ways it is a deeper level of forgiveness, because now you understand so much more than you or others did then. You understand more of what was done to you and what it has cost you my little one. Forgiveness, though it has been given before, needs to be given again with each new level of healing that you receive.
Because it is so much more real to me now...Crying
Yes my dearest one.
I am just a little girl Jesus. I don't want any bad things in my heart. I want you to forgive

them all for the things they did to me. No matter what they did. I am loved. I belong to you. Maybe they never knew they were loved. That is so sad. So I forgive them all Jesus with you helping me…Crying.

Oh my dearest one. My Pearl and my treasure. To forgive in the midst of great pain is the greatest love of all my little one.

Is it Jesus? I don't know anything about love except that you love me. I don't even really know what that means….Crying

But I will show you my little one all the days of your life and beyond I will show you what it means. My little one you have chosen to hide yourself in me and to accept everything I have for you. It will not be withheld from you my little one hold on to me trust me and be willing to follow me wherever I will lead you.

Please take me away from this place. I don't care where I go. If all I have is you then that is enough. But please take me away from this place.

Forgiving others for what they had done to me was only part of what was holding me though. Jesus showed me that I was blaming myself for the things that happened to me, that I felt like it was my fault, when mum was hurt by grandad or the priest. I believed I had to protect her. I couldn't be angry with her so I had to be angry at me. My need to be punished was part of what was holding me here. But Jesus told me over and over that I shouldn't be punished for what others did. I needed to be loved not punished.

My little one my dearest little one the pain is not endless no matter how it seems to you. You are moving forward my little one and though it seems endless to you it is not. Let me take you by the hand my little one and show you something you have not yet seen or understood. Something which will help you take the next step.

Ok.

What do you see my little one?

I see the city. The one you keep showing me.

Yes my little one what else do you see?

It is surrounded by a ring of fire. Big flames.

What do you think that is my little one?

I don't know. It depends where the fire is from. Is it from you or the enemy?

It is my fire my little one.

Well…I suppose I'm thinking of refiners fire. Maybe something I have to get through to go into the city.

Yes my little one. It is not possible for you to enter the city without going through the fire.

Why?

Because the fire will remove everything that would hinder you there. Everything that would prevent you from reaching out to those in the darkness and leading them to the light.

Haven't I been through enough fire Jesus? I don't want to go. Just leave me...Crying.

No my little one I will not leave you. I did not bring you here to discourage you but you help you see what I am doing. I am not leading you into the fire my little one you are already in it. But it is not endless my little one.

Tell me you are taking me across the ring and not walking me around it.

We are going across my little one.

It doesn't matter Jesus…Crying…I am tired of believing in the city.

Do you think I should keep you in the fire my little one?

I don't know. You put me here.

Why my little one? Why have I led you into the fire?

I know the answer in my heart is you brought me here to punish me.

When I was led into the desert and tempted in every way, was that to punish me my little one?

No. It was to make you ready. So you could face what was ahead. So...your will would be strong enough and you wouldn't give up or give in.

Yes my little one. Why I have I led you into the fire?

To make me ready. I am tired of believing these things Jesus…Crying

But that does not make them untrue my little one. My little one I have led you into the fire not to punish you but to make you ready. I have brought you here to heal you and make you stronger. To teach you the things you need to learn. To prepare you in all the ways that you need to be prepared, so that you can go down into the city and do and be everything you were created for. It is not endless my little one. There is a purpose and a plan and everything I am doing is good.

Ok….Crying

So my little one even though you are in pain and you do not see or understand what I am doing much of the time, will you continue to walk with me? To have hope for the future I have promised you. To allow me into the places that most need my healing and my love. To trust me and not give up hope. This is just for a little time my dearest one and I am with you in it all.

I don't know if I can…Crying

You can my little one. I would not ask it of you otherwise.

If you say I can Jesus. Then yes only I would like it better if you carried me because I don't think I can walk any more…Crying

My little one I am holding you close to my heart always. You are always in my arms of love my little one and I will carry you through the flames and into everything I have promised you. All you must do is hold on.

Ok. Ok Jesus…Crying

My little one you have suffered greatly all the days of your life but you have not yet understood that you have always been loved. No matter what has happened my little one you have always been loved.

I am beginning to see it.

Yes my little one you are but your need to be punished is getting in the way. Will you let it go my little one?

I don't know how Jesus.

It starts with a choice my little one. Will you choose to let it go?

Yes. Will you love me and hold me and keep me safe?…Crying

Yes my little one I will. Always.

I can't do this Jesus.

Yes my little one you can. I am with you. I will never leave you.

You love me…Crying.

Yes my little one I do.

My life doesn't have to be full of bad things.

No my little one it doesn't.

But what will there be if there aren't bad things?

Good things my little one.

I don't know what they are. I don't know what they are.

I will show you my little one.

Will you? I don't think you will…Crying

My little one my love is here for you. I will make a way.

I will just hold on to you Jesus. It is too difficult for me. I want to shut my eyes and not look.

But there is nothing to fear my little one. I am with you in the good things as well as the bad.

It is hard for me to believe in good things Jesus.

I know it is my little one but keep holding on to me. I am carrying you forward into a good place my little one.

I felt like I had done so much of it before, but like Jesus said he was going deeper and every time his healing went deeper, I was set free just a little bit more and I could accept more of his love into my heart. His love that was making me new and bringing me life. But believing that I needed to be punished was keeping me from the things he wanted to give me. He told me the truth in so many different ways, helping me to see and understand like he does, that I am not bad and that I don't deserve to be punished.

My little one when you were small you were hurt by many things. One of the greatest hurts was to see yourself as someone who causes pain to others. As the one who was responsible for all of the bad things that you and others suffered including your mum. She was there to protect you my little one, but you never understood that. All you saw was her suffering as she failed to do so. My little one she was not able to protect you in the way that she should have for many reasons, but you blamed yourself for that. You saw that she was hurt by others my little one. You saw that she was not able to protect you and you blamed yourself. You saw yourself as the bad one. If you did not exist, if you were not there, if you were better, if you were anything or anyone other than who you were, then she would not suffer. It was all your fault my little one and you were the one who deserved to be punished. Even though you believed this in your heart, still you were hurt by her my little one in many ways. She did not love you as she should, she hurt you and rejected you many times. She punished you for things you did not do, she was cold and showed you little affection, and she handed you over to people who were cruel in the extreme, seemingly without caring about you at all. My little one all of these things set up conflicts in your heart which you were not able to resolve. This is part of the reason there were so many alters my little one, because one little girl could not hold all of those feelings of hurt and betrayal, anger and guilt, bewilderment and pain. And so you split my little one, because it was the only way for you to survive.

But now my little one all of these things, all of the feelings and the memories have come together again. It is a lot for anyone to understand and accept my little one. There is a great deal of pain still to be healed, but my dearest one I will not ask you to do it all at once. You know the truth my little one but you are still holding on to the guilt and the belief, that it is you who should be punished. And so my little one you fight against me, because how can you be punished if you receive the life I have for you. You tell yourself there is no plan, no hope of my promises coming to pass, because there is no punishment in that my little one. You convince yourself over and over that you will never have any of the things you so want and need, because how could that be. You are the bad one and you do not deserve anything good. Only pain and loneliness my little one.

But those are the misunderstandings of a hurt and confused little girl who did not see the truth about herself or the things that were happening to her. A little girl who was overwhelmed and had no choices and no way of breaking free from the things and the people that held her captive. My little one it is time for you to accept the truth as I see it because I am the only one who truly sees and understands the truth about you and the things that happened to you. It is time for you to let go of the lies that are still holding you my little one. They will keep you from everything I have for you for you cannot accept the future I have for you and yet still demand to be punished. It will not work my little one. The old must go and the new must come.
It is such a sad thing Jesus. My life…Crying
Yes my little one but it does not have to keep on being sad. My little one I have so much joy ahead for you if only you will take hold of it.
It is a very hard thing to do Jesus.
My little one who do I say that you are?

I am your Pearl. You love me and say I am innocent and not bad. I'm not bad. It wasn't my fault…Crying

No my little one it wasn't. Should you be punished then my little one?

No. But I am used to being punished Jesus. I don't know how to be loved…Crying

Will you let me show you my little one? Will you let go of your need to be punished and accept instead that you need to be loved?

Can I do it Jesus?

Yes my little one you can because I will help you.

Alright then. But I don't know how.

I know you don't my little one.

Am I ever going to get better Jesus? I feel like I am always going backwards.

Not backwards my little one only deeper. My little one if you feel like you are rushing through tumbling water that is taking you to places you don't want to go that is because I am taking you deeper my little one. We are not standing still we are moving forwards and like the river that flows faster and faster as it approaches the waterfall so you are moving faster and faster my little one no matter how it seems to you. My little one you have come a very long way in a short space of time and though it has often felt to you that you are drowning you are always safe in my arms.

So...what do I do?

Hold on to me my little one keep trusting and do not be afraid to believe that there are good things ahead for you. That even now there are good things my little one that I want you to enjoy. I know this life is difficult and painful much of the time my little one but take hold of the good things and do not be afraid of them. They are my gifts to you and I want you to receive them and not push them away.

Help me.

Yes my little one I will help you.

I still hate this river Jesus. Will you help me to see it different? Teach me how to hold on to you so I'm not drowning all the time, cos it still feels like too much.

I am with you my little one and I will help you and teach you and love you through all of this.

I'm sorry….Crying

I know my little one I know. Remember where you are my little one. You may be in the heat of the fire but you are safe in my arms my little one. You will not be burned but you will come through it different to the way you were before. I know it is hard my little one but you are able.

Keep showing me the truth Jesus. Help me trust you and hold on to you and not fight you. I'm sorry I do.

I know my little one I will help you.

What about mum? I...am still needing your help with her. I don't even really know what I'm feeling.

Yes my little one I will help you but that is for another day. That is enough for now my little one.

Alright. Bye not bye Jesus.

Bye not bye my little one.

I was grieving again for the life I had lost but sometimes I could see the truth that Jesus was showing me. So often it got lost in the pain and the fear but sometimes I saw it. It helped me to hold on and to keep going.

I have been doing a lot of crying. It is different to when he is healing memories...it is crying for all the things I lost. Which is a lot. But I have started to see and understand things. I expect you will think they are obvious things and maybe I saw them a bit before but not the same. I see now that I was born to be me. That Jesus put me in the world and the enemy tried to destroy me but they couldn't. And Jesus kept me alive and has been mending me so I can be me in this world and do the things he made me to do. That helped me because sometimes I still think I would be better being Jennifer or someone else and not me. But Jesus didn't put Jennifer in this world. He doesn't want me to be her. He wants me to be me. I know I should know that already but it made sense suddenly. And I see even more than that that I can choose who I am in this world. I never really saw that before, that it is up to me. And Jesus has been setting me free so I can have those choices. Choices I never had before. I was thinking about what it means to be a victim. I think it is about not having a choice. And maybe I have been a victim. For a long time but not anymore. Jesus has been giving me my choices back so I'm not a victim of the past or anything else. I can choose who I am in this world. I know I get sad because I can't really be me pearl but I can still choose to be who I am. It is different. So I need to think about the person I want to be so I can make the right choices. Like if I want to be a kind person I need to choose to do kind things don't I. It's not complicated I don't think but I need to know what I am choosing every day. And my choices will make me whoever I turn out to be in this world. I think that makes sense. It does to me. It feels better because I have felt so helpless and hopeless just stuck waiting for something to happen. But now I see that at least some of it is up to me. I can choose to be the me I want to be. Jesus will have to help me of course. I saw in the New Year with Jesus talking about these things. It seemed like a good start to the year. I don't know what this year will be, but I can choose to be the best me I can be in it. So that is what has been happening. It seems better even though nothing is changed and I am not really looking forward to the things I see ahead. Not at all. Anyway I am sending you a hug...lots of them. Love from Pearl.

Jesus was setting me free to make choices and I could see that was good. But while I was struggling with the healing and all of these feelings, I was still very anxious about having to get a job. I didn't believe I could do it. I didn't want to. It made it hard to hold on to the hope that Jesus was giving me because all I could see in front of me was a life I didn't want to live. The appeal against the decision made about Richard's disability benefit failed. That was the end of the line and it meant that Richard might have to find work, and that I definitely would have to. In some ways I was expecting it but it didn't make it any less frightening. Change had come at last but not really the way I wanted.

I have had a rough week. There has been a big battle going on I think especially at night. I haven't had much sleep. I have tried hard to hold on to Jesus and to trust him and sometimes I have done ok and sometimes not. Every night I have seemed to fall into a pit that I had to get out of in the morning. I am glad to get up in the mornings. The nights are long. I have talked to him a lot. I have asked for help a lot. It hasn't seemed liked things are getting better, but I suppose I haven't sunk completely. I have kept going and done the things I have needed to do. I didn't sit down and talk to Jesus yesterday and today I have kept putting it off, but I did eventually because I knew I was in trouble and he is my only help.

Jesus I don't know how to do this...Crying
You hold on to me my little one and let me love you.
I was sitting on Jesus lap and I buried my head in his chest and cried and cried.
I don't understand. Again. Why do we have to keep on doing this? What am I not learning? Why are you lying to me? Don't lie to me. I don't care what you ask of me but don't lie to me. Jesus took my hands in his and looked right at me.
My little one be still. My little one I have not lied to you. Not ever.
But why does it seem like you have? Over and over again. I feel I have to keep making excuses because I have to believe you don't lie to survive but then comes another one. And if you aren't lying I don't know how to understand the things you say.
My little one hold on to me and trust me. You know who I am. I do not lie.
Help me. You've got to help me.
My little one in what way have I lied to you?
So many times with the it's soon... it is time... it is come you're leaving stuff...and now this. I

don't want you to get a job. It's all just lies. You've got to help me know the truth. You are the truth. You are the truth.

My little one I will not lie to you not ever. If at times you do not understand my full meaning that does not mean that I have lied to you.

I don't know how to understand the things you say. I don't know how to trust them.

You trust in who I am my little one.

I don't see how that helps. If you say something I want to know that I can believe it. Why don't you want that?

I do want that my little one. I want that with all of my heart. My little one all of your life you have learned to mistrust the things that people said to you, especially when it was promises of good things or expressions of love or affection, because so often you were let down or betrayed my little one but I will not ever do that. Everything I say is real and true.

It doesn't seem that way to me.

My little one in all the things I have said to you when have I lied?

I don't think you have lied Jesus, but I think you have said things in a way that wasn't the whole truth.

And why do you think I would do that my little one?

Sometimes I'm not ready to hear the truth Jesus.

No my little one sometimes you're not. Do you think my little one in anything I say to you or don't say to you that my desire is to hurt you or bring you pain?

Crying…No.

Then why do you think I say the things I do my little one even if it is not the full complete truth?

To help me.

Yes my little one to help you.

Can you help me understand better how it isn't lying Jesus? Even if it is to help me.

My little one I do not ever lie to you but my dearest if I were to tell you the full truth about everything it would overwhelm you or frighten you much of the time. It would not help you my little one. As with everything I give you as much of the truth as you are able to accept and I tell you what will help you my little one. That does not mean that I lie only that there is still more truth to be revealed.

I don't like it. I need to know you will say what you mean or mean what you say or something.

No my little one what you need is to trust me. My little one I will never do anything to hurt you.

But how does it help to say no I don't want you to get a job when you know that I have to. Maybe you don't want me to and it's technically true but that not helping. Am I supposed to know the exact right question to ask before you tell me the truth?

No my little one no what you are supposed to do is to talk to me about these things. To know my thoughts and my mind about these things. Sometimes asking one simple question will not tell you what you need to know my little one, but I am always here for you to talk to at any time about anything,

I don't want to talk about these things. They are too hard to talk about…Crying

I know they seem so to you my little one because you are still afraid.

Of course I am. You keep lying to me. It's better not to ask you at all than to hear lies.

My dearest little one everything about you is precious to me. It is not my desire my little one to mislead you in any way. I am healing you and leading you forward into life. That is what I am doing my little one. There are many things along the way that will cause you to doubt my love for you. There are many reasons that the enemy will give you to pull away from me my little one, but the lies come from him and not from me. I am with you my little one. I love you. You are my precious and beloved child. I will not ever lie to you.

I get so confused. It is all so confusing. I don't understand anything you are doing …Crying

My little one when everything seems confusing and you do not understand what must you do?
Hold on and trust you.
Why my little one?
Because of who you are. Because you love me.
Yes my little one I do. I will not ever let go of you my little one. Do not listen to the enemy my little one. Remember who I am even if you do not understand. Even when you cannot see. Even when nothing seems to be the way that I have said. Keep trusting my little one because of who I am. Because I love you and because I will not ever lie to you.
Help me…Crying
Yes my little one. Always. Always I will help you.
I saw the four angels who protect me battling with monsters. They drove them away and I felt better and snuggled into Jesus but I was still crying.
My little one you are my hearts delight. I will not ever leave you. I will help you with everything. Fear nothing that lies ahead of you my little one. Remember who you are. My plans for you are real and true. You are mine my little one and nothing will ever change that or my great love for you. Rest in me my little one and trust me to make a way for you.
Just hold me Jesus…Crying…Please just hold me….Crying
All the days of your life I will hold you my little one.
Crying…I can't do this…Crying
I know my little one I know.

It was very hard for me to understand why Jesus had let me cling on to the hope I wouldn't have to get a job, when he knew that I did. I supposed he was right and it would have been overwhelming to me, but it felt overwhelming now. I didn't really believe anyone would give me a job of course so there was some comfort in that, but that just made me feel useless and wish I wasn't me. In my more hopeful moments I could see that he might allow it so that he could work through it for Richard's good and for mine, but mostly I was still confused and afraid.

This afternoon I decided I just needed to spend some time with the Holy Spirit...not to hear anything or do anything...just to be with him. So I put on some worship music. I had a lovely time. I did some dancing with Jesus. Heaven seemed to turn into a disco with rainbow lights. It made me laugh and cry and the same time. And I spent time with daddy in the soft pillows and I was kind of surrounded by space and shooting stars and the Holy Spirit was swirling round us like a gold sparkly comet. It reminded me that they aren't stressed or sad. That its all under control and that I'm so loved. I cried a lot but it was good and I felt better.

People kept asking me what I wanted to do as a job. The benefits people, mum, even my friends who knew that I was Pearl. I didn't want to do anything. I had never thought about getting a job. I didn't believe I could do anything at all and most of all I just wanted to leave and be with my daddy and do the things that Jesus kept saying he wanted me to do. Not some stupid pointless job. Most of all I was afraid that it meant I would be living Jennifer's life a lot longer, maybe forever, no matter what Jesus said.

Even though I didn't want to be on this path, somehow I was walking on it. Through a friend I started doing some work cleaning for an elderly lady once a week. I was scared to do it. It felt like a big thing and somehow it felt wrong to take money for doing something I didn't think I could do. I felt like I was blundering through a fog with no idea what I was doing or why.

My little one I am here with you and I will not ever leave you. All of this is to help you my little one and not to harm you. I know you feel you cannot do it my little one but I am with you and I will help you.

I feel like I am failing you Jesus…Crying
When have I said so my little one?
I don't know what's the matter with me. I can't seem to do anything but cry…Crying
You are caught in a great battle my little one. It is a battle for your very life but you belong to me. The enemy cannot have you. No matter what lies he may tell you your heart belongs to me my little one. It will always be so. My little one listen to me, even though you are so much stronger than you were you are still vulnerable to his lies. That does not mean you should listen to them my little one. I am always here to help you but it does mean that he is still able to make you doubt and fall into despair if you listen to him.
I am sorry. It just seems so endless and difficult and I can't do it…Crying
My little one who do you walk with?
You…Crying
What is there then my little one that you cannot do?
I know it's not true so I don't understand because I don't feel like I can take another step.
What do you see before you my little one?
What I saw was Jesus in front of me holding out his arms towards me and I understood what he was showing me. I have been seeing endless ...what my life is now and worse...and nothing good and that is why I have wanted to give up. But…you are before me Jesus. It's you I am walking towards…Crying
Yes my little one it is. Always.
Like Peter on the water…Crying
Yes my little one just like that. You fix your eyes on me my little one. You walk towards me. I am the goal. I am the treasure and the promise my little one. I am here with you but I am also ahead of you. It is me you are seeking my little one.
I get so lost Jesus.
I know you do my little one but you are learning and growing and becoming. I will not leave you. I will always help you. My dearest one my ways are always good. Everything I have for you is good. Even this.
It is hard for me to see….Crying.
I know it is my little one and that is why you must look at me. I will show you the way. I will lead you along the path I have for you. It is a good path my little one and not to be feared in any way. Who do you walk with my little one?
You Jesus….Crying…
And what is ahead of you?
You Jesus…Crying
And who is your strength and everything you need?
You are….Crying
Yes my little one I am. My dearest one things are not as they seem to you. I have not forgotten who you are. This is to help you my little one. To help you become all I have made you to be. Will you trust me and keep following wherever I will lead you?
I think I am not good enough.
I know you do my little one but who do you walk with?
I walk with you Jesus.
Yes my little one you do. My dearest one you are weary from all the battles you have been fighting but there is much that I have for you to do. You are able my little one in my strength to keep on walking forwards with me. Will you take my hand my little one and walk forward into the future I have for you trusting that is good and full of life and hope and joy and all of the things I have promised you?
I find that hard a lot of the time but maybe I can keep walking towards you Jesus. Maybe...Crying
My little one you are my treasure and my delight. Every step you take is taken with me and for me my little one. You are not ever alone. I know my dearest one that many things are still hidden from you and you cannot see the future I have for you but it is

there my little one. It cannot be taken from you not if you keep following.
I am going to need so much help because every time I look ahead I just crumble.
What do you see ahead of you my little one?
You Jesus. Help me see you and not all those other things that are crushing me…Crying.
I am here my little one. I cannot ever be taken from you. Keep walking towards me. I am everything I have for you.
Show me what to do Jesus. I don't know what to do. If you have things for me to do show me what they are. I don't know….Crying
Walk towards me my little one.
Show me what that means then.
Yes my little one I will. Rest then my dearest one for you are very weary. There is nothing you cannot do in my strength my little one. Do not listen to lies. You are my child you belong to me and I will never ask you to do anything you are not able to do.
Yes.
Rest then my little one and do not be afraid. You are safe and you are loved and you have everything you need. The future is before you my little one but there is nothing to fear from it. I am your future my little one. I will always be with you.

I wrote to daddy to tell him about my first day.

Well I started my new job like I told you. Apart from having to pretend to be Jennifer and answer questions I kind of enjoyed it. Not that I especially like cleaning but it is different when you are doing it for someone else, and I know that a big part of me going there is cos she wants some company and someone to talk to. She is kind of funny and I like her so it's kind of nice for me. I don't know what I think about it apart from that. I think it is a strange thing for me to be doing and I feel confused by where Jesus is leading me.

I was confused because I hadn't expected this at all. But Jesus reminded me that even though I am always walking towards him, I am also walking on many different paths all at the same time.

My little one you are walking many paths with me and all of them are connected. They are not separate. Sometimes they come together sometimes they will seem far apart. Sometimes you will see the path and sometimes you will not but all of the paths are there my little one whether you see them or not, whether you are walking forward on them or not.
Yes.
For a long time my little one you have been walking the path of healing with me. It has been a dark and difficult path my little one but you have allowed me to carry you through and do so much more than you ever thought I could. That path continues my little one but now it is being joined by another path, one which you have also been walking on though it has often seemed to you that you have not made any progress on it. This is the path of ministry my little one. The healing that I have done is part of this for it is necessary for you to be healed and set free so that you can walk the path of ministry that I have for you. Now it is time my little one for you to walk forward on this path. It is not that you stop walking the path of healing or that you have not been walking upon this path before, only that it will now become your primary path, the one that you are most aware of. Other paths remain my little one and you are walking upon them all with me but this now becomes our focus. That is what I mean when I say it is time.
So a bit like the healing path has met up with the ministry path...so now I'm walking along a different kind of path.
Yes my little one but you have also been walking along this path. It is not a new path my little one.
No. It is a bit hard to understand but ok.

My little our focus is changing but that does not mean that healing will stop. It is still necessary for you to receive many things my little one. This part of the path is to help you grow stronger and to receive the things you need so that you can continue along this path. Even though it is not the path we have been concentrating on before some of it will be the same my little one but the further along his path you go the more things will begin to change. It is not so far away my little one and that is why I say that it is soon.
Because that is what we are preparing for, what we are beginning to do.
Yes my little one.
Mmm. I kind of see that makes sense from your point of view Jesus. For me it just seems the same.
But it is not my little one and it will begin to change. Slowly at first but then much more rapidly.
Hmm. I am not sure if this is helping.
My little one you know that I love you and will help you to walk the path I have for you. You know that I am with you and that my desire is to draw you close to me and give you everything you need, myself most of all. You know that your attention must be upon me and that I am asking you to trust me and spend time with me so that you can receive all that I have for you. You know that I am asking you to step out with courage and with faith into the new things I have for you to do so that you can discover more of who you are to begin to grow into being that person. You know my little one that I want you to spend time thinking about your story and all that it means and that I want you to continue writing both to my servant and the second book. All of these things are important my little one. All of them are necessary.
Yes. I know I seem to have a lot to do and I suppose you are giving me reasons to do them, because the way you see it I need to, because it is coming. And I know you are right because you always are Jesus.
Yes my little one I am. So continue to trust me and to trust in my sight. My little one do all that I am asking of you. It is not too much and it will help you.
I need to think about what you said help me understand it and not misunderstand it.
Yes my little one I will.
Help me ask questions if you want me to...I don't know what to ask and even when I do sometimes...I don't think to... and even when I do think to... sometimes I still don't.
I know my little one. I understand. I will help you.
Ok then. Bye not bye?
Bye not bye my little one. I will be with you helping you. Do not be afraid of anything.

I was starting something new. Jesus was walking with me, but we seemed to be going somewhere I hadn't expected to go and didn't want to go. I was still healing, still learning to see me like Jesus does, but now I was going to be finding out more about what it meant to be Pearl Sunshine, still living as Jennifer, but doing new things. Things that Jennifer wouldn't have done. I wasn't sure about it. I was afraid but I held on to Jesus and followed him.

Chapter 13

The Fountain

Jesus had been talking to me again about opening doors in my heart. Fear and pain had closed off parts of my heart to him, but he wanted to open them all so that I could be healed and set free and filled with love. He reminded me that my heart was their garden and that he was wanting to open up new places to his love and to daddy's love especially. I was struggling with being me, a child, and I had been finding it hard to spend time with my heavenly daddy again, because it was hurting. It made me sad.

Hi Jesus
Hello, my dearest little one
I am feeling very sad Jesus…crying
I know my little one I know. My dearest one I am holding you. I am with you. You are loved and wanted my little one.
I know...crying
My little one this time will pass and all that you are dreaming of will come. It will come.
I don't want to talk about it Jesus. Please just hold me and love me and help me to see you. Help me to see you.
I am here my little one. I am right here with you. I will not ever leave you.
I don't want to cry Jesus…crying.
I know my little one but crying does not mean that you are not willing to follow me my little one only that it is sometimes hard to do so.
You do ask hard things Jesus.
Yes my little one sometimes I do but I will always give you the strength to do them. That does not mean that you will not cry from time to time. Even I cried my little one as I followed my father's will for me.
Yes. It is hard to be here.
Yes my little one sometimes it is but that does not mean that it is bad. It is good that you are here my little one just as it was good that I was here.
I think it is a bit different Jesus.
It is not so different my little one. My purpose was different but I was following my father's will for me just as you are. It is not different.
I haven't spent any time with daddy.
But he is there for you my little one. Always.
Daddy...crying….
I am here my child I am always here.
I know why I don't come. Finally I see it…
Yes my dearest one but that does not make you bad. It is only that you need my love my little one. A father's love given to a heart that has great need of it.
Yes...and...I keep looking to daddy but he can't...love me. He is so far away and busy. Always busy…crying…
But I am here my little one and I can give you all the daddy's love that you need.
I know. But I don't come because it hurts. It still hurts.
Because your need is still very great my little one. That is all but I can meet that need my little one if you will come.
I don't want to be a child it hurts….crying.
But that is who you are my little one. I would not have it any other way. My little one just because the world does not see you as a child that does not mean that I cannot meet your need.

It is like a big hole…crying…
Yes my little one it is. Let me fill it with my love my little one.
Ok daddy…crying…
My little one as you come and spend time with me I can fill your heart with my love. Do not stay away my little one. You can have a daddy's love. It is here for you.
Help me.
Yes my little one I am holding you in my arms. You are safe and you are loved and I will give you everything you need.
I'm sorry I don't come.
I understand my little one but do not be afraid to feel your need. It is time for a greater healing my little one.
But I thought we were just gardening.
It is all healing my little one. My love will open up new parts of the garden, those parts that were made just for me.
Yes. I see.
Yes my little one you do so do not be afraid to come. I know my child that it is still painful but it is also life giving. It is what you need. Come to me my little one and spend time with me even if it is painful at first. The pain will go my little one as your need is met.
I don't want to be a little girl.
Why not my little one?
Because I need all those things I can't have…crying….
Why are you still believing that my little one?
Because I am here on my own having to be a grown up.
But I am here with you. You are not alone. You are never alone. You have all the daddy's love you need right here with you my little one. My little one all this time I have been here with you. I have loved you and sung over you. I have drawn you to me. My little one you have such need of my love. Do not be afraid to come. If it makes you feel small and vulnerable that does not matter. I am safe and warm my little one. I will hold you and love you and fill your heart with my love.
I know….crying….
I know you do my little one so spend time with me. Do not be afraid of the way you feel my little one. You are my child. You are safe and you are loved. There is nothing to fear.
I know I need you daddy
Yes my little one you do. My little one receiving my love for you will set you free to be the child that you are. I know that it is still hard for you to understand why we are asking you to live as an adult my little one but before you can live as a child you must be free to do so. In your heart my little one. Your circumstances may seem to you to be the thing that keeps you from living as a child but that is not so my little one. Let me love you and heal you and set you free to be the child that you truly are. Then you will be able to live as that child my little one no matter what your circumstances.
I don't think I understand how I can live as a child. I think maybe I see that I am not free. And there is pain and emptiness and part of my heart where the doors are shut because of the pain. I see that daddy.
Yes my little one and as I bring healing and open up the doors in your heart to my love I will show you what it means to live as a child my little one. You have not understood what it means because it has never been possible for you but it is my desire to make it possible my little one so that you can be who you truly are, all of who you are my little one.
Yes. I see that…..crying….
Yes my little one you do so come and spend time with me and do not be afraid. I will give you everything you need my little one. You are my beloved child. I am longing to

show you just who you are to me.
Ok.
You are loved my little one and this time will not last forever. It is only to make you ready my little one. That is all.
I need your help daddy....crying....
I know you do my little one. Do not be afraid to write to your daddy. He is there for you my little one. He will help you.
I don't think he has time for me...crying....
He has all the time I give to him my little one but I am the one who will meet your need. Do not look elsewhere but look only to me my little one.
Yes....crying....
It is time my little one to open up the doors in your heart that have been shut for so long. It may be painful for a time my little one but it is good. It is very good.
Ok. Help me to come.
Yes my little one. I will help you.
Bye not bye then daddy.
Bye not bye my little one.

Today when I was with daddy the doors were opening and I saw the new parts of the garden behind them. It was full of all dead stuff...plants and things, and a fire came and started burning it all up. It hurt so much. I cried and cried. I think it is just the beginning. Lots of different doors to be opened and a lot of gardening to do. I am not feeling very ok, but I know it is because of healing stuff.

I talked to the Holy Spirit as well about what he was wanting to do. Jesus had been talking to me about two infillings. The first would be an infilling of daddy's love and the second was an infilling of the Holy Spirit. He told me that it was a bit like a blending. That as Jesus came into my heart deeper and deeper, we became more and more one. So that we would think and act as one.

Hi Holy Spirit
Hello, my dearest little one
I am thinking about baptism and blending. It is a different way to see it but it makes sense to me.
Yes my little one as your spirit and ours become more deeply entwined, more deeply connected we become more as one my little one. There is less separation between us.
So...like having the mind of Christ and being led by the spirit and being rooted and established in love, and all of those things going deeper into your heart. That is all blending with you.
Yes my little one it is and just as in the blending with alters the distinction between us grows less, you become more and more like Jesus, though you remain who you are my little one.
Just like the alters are still who they are but people see me mostly.
Yes my little one and the more the blending progresses the more people will see Jesus and the less they will see you.
And that is already started. It starts when I got saved and accepted Jesus into my heart.
Yes my little one and the more you open up your heart to us the more the blending progresses.
I was thinking how when Jesus was baptized, all his doors were open and you could just go in completely and fill him up to overflowing.
Yes my little one there were no closed doors in his heart. I could fill every part of him my little one just as I long to do with you.
I am thinking that maybe for a lot of people they have a lot of closed doors and maybe you can't get very far in at all, and that is why there doesn't seem too much difference and they aren't changed...obviously anyway.

Yes my little one that is so but we are always working to help them open up their hearts to us, just as we are with you.
And my heart holy spirit...I don't suppose I will have all my doors open to you because, I think there will be more you need to do maybe...but this time is for me to allow you to open up as much as I can, so that when it is time, then you can go deep and the blending [with Jesus] can be more.
Yes my little one that is so.
I want that Holy Spirit.
Yes my little one I know you do.
Well...I don't know how but you do.
Spend time with us my little one, allow us access, keep choosing us in everything. In that way we will have access to those areas of your heart that are most needed. My little one you are right in thinking that there will be more. There will be many more times of blending and filling for you but this time is special my little one. It is worth preparing for. It will make many things possible for you that are not possible now.
Yes. I see that.

I chose to let the Holy Spirit take down walls and open doors in the garden of my heart. To let daddy into the place of loneliness, that I had not yet allowed myself to feel or to know about. He took me to the garden so I could see and understand what was happening. I saw a frozen wasteland. Solid ground. But the wall was down and the sun was shining gently warming the land.

Tell me about this new part of the garden and what I saw.
It is a part of your heart that you closed off long ago my little one away from the light and warmth of our love. Now it is opened up to us we can bring light and warmth and hope and life my little one. It will take time but it is already happening.
And what will you grow there Jesus?
Warmth and compassion my little one and a willingness to give of yourself without fear. My little one when you are filled with our love you will have no room left for fear. We are making you strong my little one.
Unshakable.
Yes my little one just as I have promised.
The Holy Spirit said it was something to do with loneliness
Yes my little one for the loneliness that is hidden there has always been a part of you from when you were very small. But that is not our desire for you my little one. We will bring light and life and warmth to the part of your heart that needs it the most.
It is important then.
Yes my little one it is. As we go deeper into your heart and open up the doors that are closed and take down the walls that have been built we can draw you closer and closer to our hearts of love my little one so that you can be filled with a greater measure of our love for you.
I suppose there is more doors to open.
Yes my little one there are.
I want you to open them all Jesus. I don't want any shut doors or walls. I want you to fill every part of me. For it to be your garden. I don't know how to do that.
No my little one but I do. All you must do is follow my little one.

As the walls came down and the doors were opened the things that were hidden there, weren't hidden any more. Most of all I started to feel angry, and more than anything or anyone I was angry with my heavenly daddy.

Hi Holy Spirit.
Hello my little one. Will you come into the garden with me?
Yes. Are you going to show me something?

Yes my little one I am.
Oh it is very bright and warm here now.
Yes my little one for we are thawing out the ground which has been frozen and barren for so very long. As they angels dig they are uncovering what lies beneath my little one.
Is that what you want me to see?
Yes my little one it is.
It is just a big black hole covered by black frozen soil.
Yes my little one it is but the hole is not empty.
Oh dear. That sounds bad.
But we are able my little one to bring healing to every part of you. Do not be afraid. Are you willing to see what is there my little one?
If it will help me.
Yes my little one it will. Come then.
We climbed down a silver rope ladder into a deep dark cave.
It seems pretty empty to me.
But it is not my little one. Look at your feet.
They are sinking. It is like black ooze. It is smelly.
Yes my little one it is.
Sorry. I am just wanting to run away.
But we are here with you my little one.
I know. So I am thinking this is like an infection and this is like disgusting pus, but I don't know what it is except it a bad thing to have in my heart.
Yes my little one but now this place has been uncovered we can begin to heal it.
I suppose this black stuff is the anger I am feeling and it comes from an infected wound which you want to heal.
Yes my little one it does.
And daddy wants to fill this place with his love when ..it is healed and cleaned.
Yes my little one this part of the garden will be made new.
That's all good but you need to get rid of this goo and get to the hurt it is covering.
Yes my little one that is what we are going to do. My little one the anger that you are feeling covers a deep wound. It is a wound that only the love of the father can heal. He is wanting to fill you with his love my dearest one so that your heart is made whole and well again.
So why are you showing me this?
So that you can understand and not be afraid my little one. So that we can heal you and set you free from the pain and the loneliness that is in your heart. So that we can fill you with the love that you so desperately need.
Well yes but...I don't know what to do.
You do not need to do anything my little one except trust us. I know my dearest one that to be angry is frightening to you but we will hold you and enable you and when the anger has been released you will be able to see the wound that lies beneath it. Then we can begin to heal that wound my little one. It will take a little time but not too long my little one.
I have so much to do. So many new things and people to be with. How am I going to do that if I am angry and in pain?
In my strength my little one.
Well you know. I don't.
No my little one but we will each of us help you through this. We will give you all that you need my little one. We will help you to see what needs to be seen and to let go of the things you need to let go of and to allow us to heal you and love you and hold you. We will give everything to you that you will need my little one.
I know you will but it is sounding...not fun.
It will be difficult for w time my little one but not more than you can do.

Am I going to be angry?

For a little while my dearest one but I am always with you and will help you.

Well right now I am too tired to be angry or afraid, but I need your help. I know I do. Go as fast as I can bear it please because I don't like feeling this way.

I know you don't my little one. Come then. Our father is waiting. He longing to hold you in his arms my little one.

Hi again daddy.

Hello my little one.

I don't know how I'm feeling. But not like I want to snuggle into you really. I'm sorry.

I know my little one. I will help you. For now it is enough that you came with my son. He will help you to receive all that I have for you, even if you are angry and afraid my little one.

Ok. I hate this, why do I have to keep on doing this?

Because the wounds go deep my little one and because the healing we have for you must also go deep.

I am tired of it. It make me want to rip my heart out and stamp on it so I don't need to bother with the stupid thing.

Your heart is precious my little one. Let us love you and heal you and make you whole again.

Ok.

My little one we will help you but you need to make a choice in your heart to let us in no matter how you are feeling about it.

I know that feelings aren't truth and that you love me and want to help me so I do choose Jesus I do. But I might shout about it sometimes.

I know my little one,

Can I go now. I'm tired.

Yes my little one but remember what we have told you. The healing will begin my little one but we will help you and love you through it.

Ok. I need to go. Bye not bye.

Bye jot bye my little one.

I didn't like being angry. I was afraid to be angry. Being angry wasn't safe. It had never been safe. I suppose that is why I had to hide the anger away so deep in my heart. Jesus explained it to me more. I was feeling confused and angry so he had to tell me over and over to help me see what they were doing.

My dearest one you have a wound deep in your heart which needs cleansing and healing. There is a great deal of anger covering this wound my little one so do not be surprised if you feel angry for a time and do not be afraid of it. We will help you my little one. The wound that you have goes deep my little one but we will heal it and fill the hole that is there with our love. Your daddy loves you my little one and he wants you to know that.

Yes. I don't know what the wound is though Jesus.

It is your feelings of loneliness and abandonment my little one and the fear that goes with it and the anger that has festered because you have not allowed us to heal that wound. My little one there are so many things that have hurt you and you had to shut them away to survive but we are healing every wound my little one and making you whole again.
I suppose I just feel angry that it never seems to end and why should I have to keep suffering and suffering because of what other people did and what you let them do.
I know my little one I understand.
I know you do Jesus. I want it to stop.
I know my little one so do we. That is why we are healing you my little one we do not want you to be angry and in pain because of the things that have happened. We want you to know that you are loved and be free to live in that love without fear.
I know. What do I do with the anger?
You bring it to us my little one.
I don't want to mean to people.
I know my little one. We will help you.
I know it is jut the way I am feeling but I am sick of life Jesus why can't you just get rid of it.
My little one there is so much more at stake than you know. Life is good my little one even though it does not seem so to you right now. Hold on and trust us my little one.
I don't know what else to say Jesus. Help me remember what this is for. I know I will probably forget if you don't. I will just get lost in the hurting.
But we will hold you and love you my little one. You are moving forward. We will help you.
Well, I said you could open all the doors in my heart and I meant it. I did. I just wish my heart wasn't full of broken places.
I know my little one but we will heal them all. All of it belongs to us my little one and we will reclaim it and fill it with who we are and your heart will be full of life and joy my little one.
I suppose that is worth ...the pain.
Yes my little one it is.

I needed to choose to let them in, but I did because I knew I could trust each one of them to heal me even though I was afraid and hurting. Jesus took me to be with daddy. I didn't really want to go but I did because I knew it was where I most needed to be.

My dearest child my love is surrounding you. It will not ever let you go. I know that you feel abandoned and you are hurting and angry. My little one many things were done to you in my name that I never wanted for you. I only ever wanted you to be loved and cared for, protected and nurtured and helped in every way to become the wonderful person that I know you to be. That did not happen my little one but that does not mean that I abandoned you. I watched over you. I gave my son for you and my spirit to help you. I gave you everything you needed to survive so that I could love you and show you what a father truly is. I know my little one that the pain you bear goes deep but it is not more than you can bear nor is more than I can heal. As you come to me I am pouring in my love and though this is painful for you it is bringing you life. Hold on my dearest little one. You know the truth of who I am even in the midst of your pain and confusion. My love is give to you freely because you are my beloved child. There is no one I love or want more than you my little one not even my own son for when I see you I see you in him. There is no separation my little one.
I don't what to be me. I don't want to live...crying.
Little one you know that I am healing you. This pain will pass. Hold on to the hope we have given you. Hold on to he truth of who you are. Do not desire to be anyone other than who you are my little one.

It hurts too much…crying

It will pass my little one. You are loved and you are held. You are our treasure and our delight and we are making you well again. Hold on and keep trusting.

I want it to be over. I want to see you and know I have a daddy who loves me. Do I?

Yes my little one you.

Are you mending my heart?

Yes my little one that is what I am doing.

I need to stop crying. Please fix me.

Yes my little one I will.

Having a daddy should be a good thing not a bad one…crying

Yes my little one it should. My little one we are working to restore to you that which was taken, which was your relationship with your daddy and your ability to receive his love into your heart. It is love that you need my little one. That you have always needed but of which you have been so afraid.

Because daddies hurt you and leave you and punish you for things you don't know what.

That is what you have believed my little one, but your daddy loves you with a true and pure love. He will never hurt you and he will never leave you.

Daddy...crying…

I am here my dearest child.

I need you.

I know you do my little one. I will not leave you. My little one you have always been wanted. I have watched over you every day of your life. I have been with you in everything. I did not ever leave you not for one moment. You are my child and I have loved you my dearest one with all the love that I have. I have not held anything back but you have not been able to receive that love my little one, save only a little as you have begun to heal. But now it is time my little one for the things that have been taken from you to be restored. For the love that you have so desperately needed to be received deep into your heart where it is most needed. Do not fear this my little one. My love is good in every way. It brings healing and life and freedom from the pain and fear which have kept you from me. My little one it is a new day for you it is a good day.

I want to be free to enjoy you.

I know you do my little one.

But I don't know how.

My little one all you may do is trust us. We know the way my little one. We are all of us working together to bring you the healing that you need. Your heart belongs to us my little one. It is our treasure. Everything you need will be given to you my little one. Everything.

But what does that mean Jesus? I don't even know what I need.

I know my little one but we do. My dearest one as you walk with us you will find that we can make a way for you to do and be everything we desire for you n matter what is needed no matter what the cost. We are able in every way my little one so that no matter where we send you or what we will ask of you will know that everything will be given to you as you have need of it.

That is a good way to live.

Yes my little one it is for it is a life free from fear and full of love.

Which is what you want for me.

Yes my little one it is.

I am very tired.

I know my little one. There is much healing happening. Hold on and keep trusting my little one. We are with you in everything.

Just make me better please. I don't want to be in pain and crying. I want to know I am loved and cared for and safe and not alone. I don't want to be alone anymore.

You are not alone my little one you are never alone.

But I feel it…crying…
I know you do my little one but that is what we are healing. My little one your feelings of aloneness cannot be got rid of in an instant. There is a journey to be taken my little one as with all healing.
I think you could do it instantly.
But then we would not be able to give you everything you need my little one.
What do I need?
A revelation of who we are and most of all of who I am. My little one I am your daddy but you still do not know what that means or who I am to you. I will help you to discover that my little one.
I don't see how me crying and being in pain is discovering anything about you daddy.
You are discovering your great need of me my little one and I am meeting you in that need. I can do so much in you my little one because of your great need, more than I could if it were not so.
I don't know
I know you don't my little one but hold on and trust me. I am your daddy. I know what is best for you.
I have to trust you to look after me.
Yes my little one you do.
I still don't want to be here.
I know my little one I know.

It was hard and I was in pain and crying a lot. I was feeling confused and angry not just with my heavenly daddy but with daddy mike too. I was still confused and not trusting that daddies were a good thing or that I could have one or be loved. Jesus kept telling me to keep writing. Sometimes I did and sometimes I didn't. It was a struggle and a battle a lot of the time. Things on the outside still weren't easy either and I wasn't coping very well. I didn't understand why I had to do all this healing and all the outside stuff as well. I didn't understand why Jesus wasn't helping me. I was having a hard time.

Hello Holy Spirit.
Hello my dearest one. Little one we are with you we are holding you. We will not let you go.
I don't want to be here. I don't want to be me. I'm sorry.
Little one you are not alone.
But you don't do what I want you to do…crying…
I know my little one I know but will you trust us to do what is right and necessary and good.
It just seems to me that you don't care...crying…
But that is not so my little one.
I don't understand. I don't understand how you can leave me here in this life and not help me.
We are helping you my little one.
I don't see how.
We are helping you to trust us. Even when things go wrong my little one will you trust us to work with you and for you. Even when you do not understand.
No I just want you to fix things. I don't like this life. I don't want it.
I know my little one but as in all things it comes down to trust. Will you choose to trust us my little one or to believe the lie that we do not care?
I don't like your choices.
They bring you life my little one.
I don't want to be here. I just want to go home. I am tired of life. I don't want it.
Yes my little one you do. You do want life my little one.
Go away…crying
No my little one I will not go away. I am always with you. I will not ever leave you. I

will help you my little one if you will allow me to.
Why can't you just fix things?
We are fixing things my little one. We are fixing you.
You are just making me sad. Daddy you are supposed to look after me. You are supposed to help me. Aren't you? What are you doing? You just leave me to it. You don't help you don't care.
My little one all of your days I have watched over you. I have never not cared.
It is hard for me to see that.
I know it is my little one. From your perspective I abandoned you to the cruelty of those who had power over you. I did not rescue you. I turned away because I did not care. Little one do you think this is true?
Yes but if it is true there is no hope for me. No love no nothing.
It is not true my little one it only seems true.
You can't fix this you can't ever fix this. How can you convince me it wasn't that way. You left me. You let them hurt me…crying…..
No my little one I did not. I did not leave you and though you were hurt I did not let them take you from me. My little one I kept you safe. No matter how it seems to you I kept you safe.
I won't ever understand it.
Not fully my little one no for many things are still hidden from you. Most of all my love is still hidden from you. Your anger and your pain keep you from accepting it.
I wish you would decide. I thought ..you got rid of it.
There are layers my little one as one layer is healed and cleansed so the next layer needs to be healed and cleansed.
It is too hard.
No my little one it is hard and painful but not more than you can do. My little one you are my treasure. Who you are is hidden in my son. I love you just as I love him. Not more my little one not less but completely.
I don't understand about daddies. Aren't you supposed to help me?
I am helping you my little one. I want more for you than you want for yourself. You want things fixing. You want me to smooth the path before your feet so that it is not so hard or painful but I want you to know who I am and to know that you are loved and wanted. I want you to discover all the treasure I have hidden for you along the path. I want you to become all that you were created to be. That is more my little one it is so much more. It is giving you what you truly need my little one. That is what a good daddy does. A good daddy does not give his child what she demands just because it is what she wants. A good daddy who is wise and understands the needs of his child gives her what she most needs no matter how much she cries and stamps her feet. Is that not so my little one?
I am not crying for sweeties daddy….crying….
I know you aren't my little one. Your pain is real I know this but I am longing to heal your wounds my little one so that the pain is gone and you are able to receive everything I am longing to give to you. I know you are not crying for sweets my little one but I see beyond your immediate needs to the deeper needs that are crying out to be met. I know my dearest one that you get lost in the pain and confusion but I am holding you. I am strong enough to hold you my little one even when you do not understand.
I don't understand….crying….
I know my little one for you have never known what it is to have a good daddy but I am longing to show you my little one, to give my love to you, to hold you in my arms and comfort you and to meet all of your needs my little one. Little one I am healing you from a great wound. It will take time but hold on to me and trust me. Everything that you need will be given to you just at the right time. Do not be afraid then but keep on trusting and hoping because you are loved and precious and because you

do matter my little one. You do matter to me.
Do? Do I really?…crying….
Yes my little one you do. I gave my son for you my little one, to save you and bring you home to me.
I know you did but I get so confused….crying….
That is because you do not see my little one. Let me show you. Let me lead you into my love. There is nothing to fear from it my little one. Little one you are loved. You are so very loved. Hold on to me my little one and let me show you how loved you are.
I don't think you can do it.
I can my little one. I can do all things, even mend your broken heart. My son is with you, my spirit is with you. They will help you my little one. My little one you are my child and I am longing to show you what that means. Hold on and trust me. I am everything you need my dearest and most beloved child.
I don't like my life.
I know my little one but we are helping you to become everything you were made to be. The path is not easy my little one but you are able to walk it with us.
But do I want to? Of course I do. It's just…Help me….crying
Yes my little one we will help you. You belong to us. Our precious and beloved child. We are holding you and loving you my little one so that you will be filled with who we are and can live the life we have for you. A life that is rich and full my little one.
I wish it would come.
It will my little one. It will.

I was angry and confused but I held on. I still held on just like they knew I would because I had enough of the truth by now, to know that no matter how it seemed or how I felt that I was loved. I didn't understand it and I didn't always feel it, but somewhere in my heart I knew the truth and that was enough to keep me holding on.

My little one the healing that you experienced in the past through your alters was real. It is not gone but you are you my little one and we are bringing a deeper measure of healing so that there can be no question in your heart whether you are loved and cared for and protected. So that you will know that you have a daddy who loves you and cares for you and has always done so.
I would like to know that but it doesn't seem true to me Jesus. But then I remember you and all the bad things that happened to you and you didn't seem to think he didn't love you. Even when he turned away from you at the end and you felt like he abandoned you. Can you tell me about that and help me understand?
My little one I knew I had a purpose in this life. My purpose was to show our children just who the father is. They needed to see him in the flesh my little one so that they could see and understand who he is and how much he loves them. My little one when I came I came representing our daddy I was not separate from him. Everything I did I did with him and for him. My little one everything I went through and all the bad things that happened to me also happened to him. We were not, are not separate in that way. When I gave myself on the cross he was also giving himself my little one. When I died I was showing you how much he was willing to give for you. When I cried out in pain that he had abandoned me he was also crying out my little one, we are not separate. We are one. My dearest one the things you are struggling with come from a need to blame the one you see as responsible for your pain. He is not responsible my little one. He loves you and never wanted any of those things to happen to you. Do you think I am responsible my little one? We are not separate or different.
I know and there have been times when we did see you were responsible Jesus, because you are in control of everything. Because you gave people free will so they could hurt me

and because you kept me alive. All of those things. I know that you show me who daddy is. That he is like you. He is good and kind and loves me but somehow I am angry with him and blaming him. It doesn't make sense, but it does.

You need to forgive him my little one and let go of the anger you feel. Give it to him my little one so that he can love you and help you through it.

How did you know he loved you when bad things happened? People did bad things to you. And he let them.

Because I understood my little one that the bad things did not come from him. I understood that he was with me in them. I understood that he was not separate from me and that he was giving me the strength I needed. I understood that there was a good purpose and a plan and I trusted him my little one because I know who he is.

I know who you are Jesus…crying..

Yes my little one you do.

How can I be angry with him? What do I do with it?

You give it to him my little one.

But how can I forgive him if it's not his fault?

Forgiveness is letting go of your need to blame him my little one. To accept that he loves you even in the midst of all that happened to you he loved you. He did not leave you my little one.

I think it is easier to be angry.

Yes my little one it is but it is not better. It keeps you from all that we have to give to you. Your daddy loves you my little one. It has always been so.

I don't want to keep on being angry but I am not sure I am seeing in my heart why I shouldn't be. It is all wrong. This world is all wrong…crying….

Yes my little one it is but we are making it right again my dearest one. All that we are doing is to make it right again.

But why let what you made get broken in the first place Jesus? That's what I don't understand. If you made a world and your children so why let it get broken and smashed? Why would you do that when you could stop it. When you knew it would happen. It's not like you didn't know. Why make me just to see me smashed up into pieces?….crying….

My little one the evil in this world does not come from us. I know this is hard for you to understand and it is even harder for you to understand why we allow it to continue to hurt and destroy the things and the people we love. But my dearest one there is so much more that you have not seen or understood of our plans for this world and for our children. My little one allowing evil to continue even with all of the pain and suffering this brings, is making something possible that is so beautiful and so very wonderful that all of that is worth it my little one. Remember that we are with you, with all of you, with our very creation in all of the pain and suffering my little one. We are not separate from it any more than we are separate from you. My little one we do not spare ourselves the pain and suffering of this world we are in it working through it to accomplish so much more than you could imagine. Far more than I can explain to you now.

Like you say you will work through my suffering, like your suffering accomplished a wonderful thing to save us.

Yes my little one just like that. I know it is hard to understand my little one but we are part of everything. We do not distance ourselves from it. My little one when you suffer we suffer. We are always with you. Just as when I suffered our father suffered. He did not distance himself from it my little one.

But didn't he turn away Jesus? I don't really understand about that.

Only because he had to my little one. When I took on the sins of the world, all the things that are not from him, all the things that are against him I became everything that he is not my little one. He could not be a part of me at that moment my dearest one. He could not be with me in that. It was my burden my little one and I carried it alone for just one moment my little one. That was long enough.

I don't think I exactly understand except I suppose that was more terrible for all of you than anything else.
Yes my little one it was.
I know I am wrong Jesus it's just I know something in me needs to change..
Then forgive him my little one. Give up your need to blame him for the evil in his world and for what happened to you. He is a good father my little one. He will never abandon you.
Will you help me Jesus?
Yes my little one I will.

Now I knew I had to forgive daddy. I wanted to but I wasn't sure I could. I knew it would help me but I wasn't sure I understood really. Most of all I was afraid.

Hello daddy
Hello, my dearest little one
I have come to talk with you about stuff.
I know you have my little one. I will help you.
I have been angry with you and blaming you for the bad things that happened. Jesus says I need to forgive you. I need your help...crying….
I know you do my little one
Jesus...crying…
Yes my little one I am here. I will help you.
Holy Spirit you are here too?
Yes my little one I am. I am always with you. Little one we understand your hurt and you anger but blaming our father for what others have done, only keeps you from receiving his love. It is hurting you my little one. Let it go.
My little one I am your daddy. I have watched you growing and becoming. I have seen you making choices over and over again in your heart to trust and to follow. My little one I am so proud of who you are. You have not let evil shape who you are becoming. You have taken hold of the love and the healing that we have offered you often when you were afraid to do so. This is not different my little one. It is just another step towards all that we have for you.
But if I forgive you. If I…crying…I have to let you in and let you love me and I am afraid.
Why my little one? Why are you afraid of my love?
Because you will hurt me.
I will not ever hurt you my little one. Not ever.
It's what daddies do…crying…
My little one remember that your daddy is just like me. He is not different he will not hurt you he will not leave he will only love you and guide you and keep you safe.
I don't understand.. How can I believe that when you didn't?
Because you are here my little one safe in the arms of my son who was given to save you from all the enemy has done. My little one I did not leave you though you were hurt I did not abandon you, though you were afraid I did not let you die though you suffered I made a way for you to be healed.
Crying….Why?
Because I love you my little one, because you belong to me because you are my child and I will never abandon you or let you go. My little one I have given you everything you need so that you could be here with me receiving my love for you. You were lost in the darkness but we have brought you back into the light. There is nothing I would not do for you my little one.
How do I stop blaming you?
You choose to trust in who I am my little one. You give your anger and your pain to me so that I can draw you close and show you that you are loved and were not ever abandoned.

I want to have a daddy who won't hurt me or leave me....crying....
I know you do my little one. I am here. Will you not come to me?
Help me.
Yes my little one we will all of us help you. Come then my little one. Let me lead you to our father who loves you just as I do. Do not be afraid my little one I am here with you.

Jesus led me up the white steps and I was surrounded by golden rainbows, which kind of wrapped me up and I knew I was loved.

Daddy I am sorry I was angry. Will you take my angry, take it out of my heart?
Yes my little one. Will you let go of your need to blame me for the bad things that happened to you my little one? Will you let it go?
Yes. I let it go. You aren't bad. It ..I trust that it wasn't your fault even tho I don't understand…crying…
I know you don't my little one come into my arms. My little one I will set you free from your anger and your fear. I will fill your heart with my love for that is your greatest need my little one. You are my child. My beloved and perfect child. You are held safe and secure and I will not ever let you go I will never turn away from you. I will always love you with a perfect and good daddies love. Little one this is only the beginning for you. There is so much more I have to give to you, so much more of my love. My dearest one taking steps towards me each and every day will help you. I will show you how my little one. You need only come.
Ok. Help me do that.
Yes my little one. Rest then. Healing is come my little one rest.

I started to feel better now that I had forgiven my daddy, not so angry or confused. He told me he was going to turn that big hole in my heart garden into a fountain. That it was going to be a fountain of his love overflowing into my heart, enough for me and for me to give away too. Jesus said they were preparing me for a season of infilling. It would happen in stages and the hole in my heart would be filled slowly with daddies love, until it was the fountain I saw.

Once I was full of daddy's love and knew who I was without any doubt or fear, the Holy Spirit would come and fill me. That would happen when I was baptized, something they had talked to me about many times. And then I would be ready and equipped for the life they had promised to give to me.

I wanted to know more about daddies love, now I wasn't so afraid of it. I wanted to understand what was happening and what it would mean to have a fountain in my heart garden.

Tell me about the fountain daddy.
My little one you have been so deeply wounded but we are taking everything that has hurt you and we are using it to bless you. My little one even though the wound has gone so very deep it is healing and is being transformed into a means for blessing not only for you but many others. As the wound in your heart becomes a well my love is being poured in. As the waters rise you will become stronger my little one and more able to receive the love I have for you. For now my little one I must continue to love you a little at a time so that you are not overwhelmed but when you are ready I will pour in my love in a new way. A way that you have not yet experienced my little one either directly or through any of your alters. This is to help you receive even more of my love my little one and when you are ready I will pour in a greater measure and again until you are overflowing and able to give the love that I have given you away to others. That will come my little one but for now accept what I am giving you. You are able to walk the path we have for you my little one. We give you all that you need. You are our child and we love you completely. There is nothing my little one

that we would not do for you or give for you. Do not be afraid my little one. There is nothing to fear from the future we have for you. We are in it my little one just as we are in this day. We will never be taken from you and no matter what lies ahead for you, you will always be safe and you will always be loved.

What daddy was promising sounded wonderful. What they were doing was wonderful, but I was feeling terrible. I was doing one day at a time. I was tired and didn't really want to keep on living.

Jesus says that it is a very big deep hurt that is being healed. The one that is being turned into a well. He says that is where a lot of trauma and terror has been hidden away, and that is what they want to heal and set me free from. I don't think it has even really started yet it is just stuff that is kind of on top of that that I am feeling. He says they are strengthening me first. It doesn't sound like it is going to be much fun. It isn't a lot of fun now. I trust him to get me through it but I am tired of it all.

Jesus told me that the wound that they wanted to heal was made up of deep fear. Of trauma and terror that had been hidden away so long ago, our collective terror, though some had been healed already. He told me that I was safe but that I wouldn't feel it. He helped me to understand what was coming because I would need to be strong and be able to trust and to hold on to him through the healing that was coming.

So right now the wound in my heart is being cleaned out. When that is done then the real healing will start. It is going to be layers of healing. So heal rest prepare heal rest prepare.... Until it is done. The first healing will take a few days but the whole thing will take months. It will be finished by the end of summer. There will be memories but a lot of them won't be new it's just they will be more detailed. They will start with the newest and go back in time cos the ones when I was very small are the deepest and hardest to heal. This is the healing that needs to be done so the well can be filled. There will be three big fillings of the well to make it into a big fountain. It won't be a gentle fountain. It reminds me more of those geysers that shoot up into the air. Very powerful. I need to have the fountain filled first before the next and last infilling. That's because it is about me knowing who I am as daddy's child and getting rid of the fear in my heart. When I am secure in that then the Holy Spirit can come and fill me. That is more about equipping for the things I will do that is the blending [with Jesus] and will happen when I get baptized. The four infillings...that is a word right? ... All together make up the waterfall they have been showing us all these years and that we have been going towards. Then it will be time. I don't know how long all of that is going to take, but Jesus says the healing will be done by the end of summer. I am looking forward to the end of summer.

Chapter 14

Removing the Marks

The wound in my heart was being cleansed. When that was done Jesus told me that the healing would begin. It would be layers of healing with times of rest between and would take several months. I wasn't looking forward to it. I was tired of endless healing along with the life I was living. I wasn't feeling very grateful.

My little one we are filling your heart with many good things. I know my dearest one that it is discouraging to you to keep finding more wounds but my dearest one you have survived great evil. It takes time to heal.
But that is the point if it takes my whole life to heal. By the time I am better I will be dead. What is the point?
My little one you know our plans for you are many.
So you say Jesus.
Yes my little one I do. My little one hold on to me and do not listen to the pain and the despair of the past. The truth remains my little one no matter how you are feeling.
I know...please can we get this over with. I would rather do it fast.
I know my little one but this healing will be difficult and you must be able to keep on walking through it. We will not give you more than you can bear.
I wish you would take me away somewhere safe and do these things. It is too much to have to keep on doing normal life and pretending. That way you could go faster because it wouldn't matter.
Yes my little one we could but my dearest one that is not always the best way. We are helping you to become all that you can be. That is not just about healing my little one.
Isn't it Jesus?
No my little one we are also teaching you many things through this. You are able my little one to keep on walking in the strength we give to you even in the midst of such a great healing as this. Doing so makes you stronger my little one and helps you take hold of the things we want to give to you in this time.
Like?
Courage and faith my little one for both will be needed.
Well if I have to keep on living...I would like to do it free from pain and fear and despair Jesus.
I know my little one.
I know I'm not behaving very well and I'm sorry but..
I understand my little one. I will not leave you.
Please just get one with it.
We are preparing you my little one.
Always preparing Jesus.
Yes my little one but it will come when you are ready.
I don't really have anything good to say Jesus.
Then hold on my little one and trust me. I am with you. I will make you able.
I am thinking about how the Angels came and strengthened you in the garden Jesus before you went to the cross. That must have been a difficult and terrible time for you because you knew what was coming.
Yes my little one I did but I too had to wait my little one. Everything had to come at the proper time.
I can't imagine how that was Jesus or how you didn't run away.
My little one everything I needed was given to me just as everything you need is given to you.

I am sorry Jesus.

I know my little one but you are safe and you are loved. This is to help you my little one not to harm you. My little one I am here with you. I will not leave you.

Why does healing have to be so terrible. Isn't it enough that the bad things happened in the first place? crying….

Yes my little one it is enough. You should never have had to suffer the way that you have my little one. Healing is hard and painful but through it I can give you so much more than was taken my little one.

I don't see that Jesus. Even after all this time I don't think I even got back what was taken. How could I? I can never have it back.

No my little one you can't but I can still restore everything my little one in a way that means that everything is redeemed, so that nothing is lost to you but much is given in return.

I don't understand.

My little one many things were stolen from you and in their place you were given fear and pain and lies. As I restore everything that was taken, I can give to you more than you originally had my little one. I can fill your heart with my love, I can give you truth at the very centre of who you are, I can show you who you are and who I am also. I can give you peace and security and purpose my little one. I can give you who I am and more than you would ever have known if it were not for the healing that that you have needed and that you have received.

Maybe that is true Jesus, but I lost my whole life and I can never have it back…crying

No my little one you can't not as it would have been but I can give you more my little one. Many things are now possible for you that would not have been possible. I know my little one that it is hard for you to see this right now, but it is so my little one.

I don't see it. I don't…crying….

Hold on to me my little one and let me love you back to life. New life is come my little one and the pain of it will not last forever.

I don't feel like I can do anything.

But I am here with you my little one and I can do all things. I will love you and heal you and set you free.

Again.

Yes my little one until the healing is complete.

I don't care.

But I do my little one. You are more precious to me than anything.

If you had let me die you could have saved yourself all this trouble.

But then I would not have seen you become all that you can be in me nor would I have been able to work through you to draw my lost and broken children back to me. Many things would have been lost my little one if I had let you die.

I need to do something, or I will just sit here and cry Jesus. Come running with me and help me.

Yes my little one I will.

It wasn't very long before it was time to begin the healing. Jesus held me and comforted me while I remembered. The memories weren't exactly new, but they were much clearer and had details and understanding that weren't there before for me.

Jesus has started the healing. I don't specially want to talk about it and as usual I am thinking it can't be true. But I suppose it is. It's not exactly new...but it is. It is in the cellar place with the priest group. I was seven Jesus says. I knew they hurt us there and they were cruel. I don't know how to say it so it doesn't sound made up. They had a machine thing on the floor. They put metal things round my wrists and ankles that were attached by chains to the wooden machine. There was a handle and they turned it and the bottom part of the machine moved along like with cogs in a track so I was pulled and stretched. I don't know why. Except they said it was cos I was bad. The priest was there and Barbara too, and others but I don't know who they were. I don't know what it was for. That is what I saw and felt yesterday. I held on to Jesus and cried and cried. Today I saw a bit more. Today I saw someone coming down the stairs into the cellar. I think it was grandad but I am not sure. He had a branding iron in his hand. It was glowing bright red. I was so terrified. They were still stretching me. They said they were branding my heart so I belonged to them, or Satan I am not sure. They burnt me over my heart. And it made a mark but I don't have any scars daddy. Maybe it wasn't a very bad burn or maybe I am making it up. I don't know. But I cried and cried and held on to Jesus. I felt how afraid I was then. I told Jesus nobody should have to survive those things and he should have let me die. He held me and reminded me of all the reasons I am still alive. Then we went to daddy and I sat with him and Jesus surrounded by rainbows and the Holy Spirit was there too. And I cried and cried and cried. So that is what is being healed. I don't think I have remembered it all yet.

I talked to Jesus about what I remembered. He told me that the enemy had left a mark on my heart, that there was a physical mark on the outside and a spiritual one on my heart. He said there have been a lot of them, some had been healed and some not. The mark was from me believing I belonged to Satan, and it made me vulnerable to attacks. While I was being healed he got rid of the enemy that was attacking me and the mark that was made all that time ago. He said these marks were what need to be removed, so the enemy would have no more power over me, all the places in my heart that made me vulnerable would be healed, and all his marks would be gone.

I had started to do some voluntary work in preparation for getting paid work. I was doing one day a week at a charity for the disabled. I spent the morning in the office and the afternoon helping out at a craft group. I found it scary because I had no real idea what I was doing and I wasn't used to mixing with people, especially groups of people. It was very tiring as well. I did sometimes enjoy it though and I was getting more confident and trusting Jesus more to help me when I was struggling. Being in the middle of healing meant I was struggling with everything.

Yesterday was hard. Maybe I was just feeling rubbish because of the healing, but I felt scared and bad about being me. I went to the office in the morning, that's just a room in the lady's house but anyway...I had to write a cover letter to go with some invitations to a fundraising event. I was scared because I didn't know what to say. I sat staring at the computer and said Jesus help me but not out loud. I suppose he did because I wrote a letter that they thought was ok. Then in the afternoon I went to the workshop. I just wanted to hide in the corner and not talk to anyone. One of the ladies there is a bit bossy and always tells you, you are doing everything wrong...she made me want to cry and run away. But I couldn't do any of those things of course. So I came home feeling like I am rubbish and can't do anything and wondering how I am going to be able to do all the things that are ahead of me. Jesus reminds me that he's the one who will make me able. I know that is true but I still feel very overwhelmed. This morning I went to the job center. I have to work on my cv and ask the volunteer people about a reference. I am hating this…then I knew it was time for more healing. I wanted to put it off but I wanted to get it done too.

I snuggled on Jesus lap and he took me back into the memory. It was very bad. It was grandad with the branding thing. The memory seemed to continue from where it left off. They were still pulling me and they forced my mouth open, and grandad put the branding thing in and burnt the back of my mouth. They said they were branding it like my heart. They said that my mouth and my words belonged to Satan. It kind of reminded me of Isaiah when he gets the hot coal in his mouth. They pulled me more and I had to say, I loved Satan and that I belonged to him. But Jesus kissed my mouth with a little kiss and said my mouth and my words belonged to him. He was holding me and I was crying and crying. He kept saying I belonged to him and never to Satan. Then they stopped pulling and took my legs out and burnt between my legs. They said that belonged to Satan too for his offspring. And that was the end of the memory. Jesus held me and rocked me and I cried and cried. He told me that I am his Pearl and I belong to him. He says that this memory is healed now, so that is one done. I am very, very tired. I think that is everything. I hope I will start to feel better until the next one. I don't want to wait long though ...oh I forgot one of the things that made me cry so much, was knowing that grandad made that branding thing. He made it just for me. It is a long time since I cried about grandad because he was my grandad. It is all wrong.

Jesus was helping me all the time with outside life and all the things I need to do and be. I was crying a lot when I was home and safe and I was feeling very tired. I didn't rest very long before it was time for the next memory.

It seemed to be taking ages and I kept telling him to get on with it. I didn't know where the memory was going. I usually don't. I was in grandma and grandad's house and the priest arrived. I got called into the kitchen and put on the table. Grandad told mum to hold me while the priest examined me. He seemed to be checking if I'd healed from something, but I don't know what. So he seemed satisfied, I don't know really why I needed to remember that bit. Then it was dark, grandad had a cat in a sack. I remembered that we often had stray cats always black who seemed to appear and then disappear for no reason. So grandad and the priest took me down into the woods at the back of the house. I kind of remember it...there was a disused railway line and it was quite a big area. Anyway, we met up with a group of people dressed in black robes. I realized it was the same group of people as in the last memory in the cellar. I was dressed in a black robe too. There was a flat stone that they used as an altar. The cat was laid on its back and held down by grandad and the priest and I stabbed it, and then cut down the middle and took out its heart and squeezed the blood into a cup and drank it. It was horrible but I didn't see why I was remembering it. But then I was on the altar and I was wearing a crown made of black feathers and strutting up and down. I had writing all over my body. I felt powerful and strong and the other people around me, seemed to be bowing down and worshipping me. They said I was Satan's child.

I realized that a demon was in control of me, and it was the demon they were worshipping. Then I understood why Jesus was showing me this memory and I cried and cried because it made me feel so dirty and ashamed and there was so much pain. I knew Jesus wanted me to come back later so I did and he took me into another memory. This time I was by the lake and it was the group where they wore white robes. I was in the lake with some adults and we were drowning a small girl. It was the same feeling again of being powerful and feeling in control and so enjoying what I was doing. I cried for a long time. It reminded me about Susanna and Jesus said that there were others like her who were controlled in that way. He said being controlled in this way has left a mark on my heart, that he is getting rid of and setting me free from. I am so tired and hurting a lot. I am wondering why I don't deserve to be punished. I know Jesus says it wasn't my fault, but I still think other people would think I should be punished like any other murderer. I know we have done this before. I suppose this is just deeper like he keeps saying. He says I was between five and six years old in these memories. I think that is all...

Jesus took me into another memory yesterday...the last one for this healing. It was so terrible it is hard to think about and I have been crying and crying. I am not done crying. It was the Goatman group and I was stood with the Goatman on the stone altar. I didn't have clothes but I was covered in black writing and I was holding up a head. Like it was a trophy or something. I didn't see it very clearly, but it was clear enough. I think Jesus just showed me enough but not more than I needed to see. He keeps holding me and telling me I am not who they said but who he says. I keep getting lost in the horror of it and the other two memories...it is like I see two versions of me. The one who was so lost in the darkness and the one now who is held and loved. And I cry because the darkness is so terrible but I know I have been saved from it and I am loved and wanted and belong to Jesus. I don't know what to say more than that. I know I am still not ok. I think it will be a few days yet because there is so much pain.

These memories were full of such horror and fear it took a long time to recover from remembering them. The feelings were overwhelming and I cried and cried.

I don't really feel like I am getting better. Like I am still the monster they made me… crying….

You were never a monster my little one.

I was…crying….

No my little one you were a child who was beaten and abused and hurt in every way that they could hurt you. You were not in control my little one. You had no choice. There was nothing you could do to escape my little one or any choice that you could make other than the one they gave you.

That doesn't mean they didn't make me a monster...crying….

Yes my little one it does. My little one they could not have hurt you any more than they did. They did not make you a monster my little one but they made you believe that you were one. They made you believe that you were like Satan himself but you were not my little one. You were a child who could not see the truth who did not know who she was and had all of her choices taken away. That is a great tragedy my little one but it does not make you a monster.

I don't know how to see that. I understand...but I don't see it.

Because you are still held by the lie.

How do I get free?

By believing the truth my little one. That you are not a monster but my dearly beloved child. They made you believe many things my little one. They told you things about yourself that were not true. They were never true my little one but you did not have any choice but to accept the lies as the only truth there was. You never questioned it my little one. My little one the truth that you are mine remains. It cannot ever be changed. Do you think that my Pearl is a monster?

No, but that thing was... didn't you make me new. Doesn't that mean I was a monster before?

No my little one it means that you were lost. That you were held captive by a darkness that you could not escape. You were not a monster my little one. My little one it is not wrong to grieve for what was or to wish it were not so but my dearest one those things do not change who you are. They can never do that my little one.

I am your Pearl.

Yes my little one you are. My little one I am healing you and taking all the pain out of your heart. My little one hold on to me and remember who you are. You are who I say that you are my little one. No matter what lies in the past you are my pearl. You were always my Pearl my little one.

So what do I do with knowing what I did. What do I do with it?

You accept the truth that it happened my little one but you must also accept that it was never your choice. You were not and are not guilty of those things my little one.

Even if I didn't choose it. I still did it.

Yes my little one. They used you to do terrible things. The fault is not yours but yours were the hands they used. That does not say anything about you except that you were also hurt by those things my little one, which is why you need my healing and also to accept the truth that you were not responsible in any way for the things they made you do.

It is too horrible.

Yes my little one it is but it is not too much to heal nor is it too hard for me to set you free from the things that are still holding you.

Do you still love me Jesus?

Yes my little one I do. With all of my heart. Nothing can change my love for you my little one. It is without measure and without end.

> Am I ever going to be better?
>
> **Yes my little one you are. I am going to heal you and set you free and our father's love will fill your heart to overflowing, so that you will know and understand what you are loved without measure my little one. There will be no more doubt and no more fear my little one.**
>
> **Keep holding on. Keep trusting. You will see your new day.**

I did keep holding on. I kept on crying and struggling but I kept holding on and doing all the things I needed to...somehow.

> I had a lot to do on Thursday. Lots of jobs and volunteering and the doctors. I got through it all but I was very anxious about the doctors. Like I said she was very nice and kind but I was scared. All the things I do and all the times I bluff my way through everything and manage to fool everyone, but I can't do it there and it didn't even seem like it had been worthwhile. Maybe part of it is that the attention is on me...with questions being asked that I can't answer, and I am asking for help, which is still a problem. When I went to bed I took one of the painkillers the doctor gave me. It made me so sick. I was up most of the night. I wasn't sick because I wouldn't let myself be. I am very afraid of being sick. So I am done with Drs. I can't make myself go to the physiotherapist. Maybe it would help the body but I don't think it would help me much. Next morning I had to get up early to go to the job center. She is starting to put pressure on. Apparently I am supposed to be spending 35 hours a week looking for work. So I left wanting to cry and I was still feeling ill and very tired. So then I went to see Kate. I told her I couldn't stay cos of being ill, but she still made me stay until I helped her with something. Then I got to come home. Later on I realized something about the job center. Every time I go I kind of crash. I thought it was just the having to get a job thing but it's not. It cos I'm being made to do something I don't want to do. I'm being forced to be someone I'm not. And I have to like it and make out like its what I want. I have to be a good girl. There are a lot of triggers in all of that. I did a lot of crying yesterday because I was feeling so overwhelmed by everything. Last night I was having horrible dreams and feeling like there's no hope and there is no point in being me. I should be put in the bin and let someone else do this life except there is no one else. I woke up crying and couldn't seem to stop. I got up at 5.30 cos I'd had enough. I sat and listened to some worship music and told Jesus I needed help...well I have said that a lot this week. I felt the difference when the enemy went. I felt better but still sad and tired.

Then it was time for the next memory..

> *It is the memory where I married the Goatman. He says we will have to go back into it a few times and the healing will take more than a week. I didn't see anything very new but I saw it in a different way. Before I have always seen it from the outside but not this time. This time I was there laid on the stone looking up at the Goatman with his big knife and I felt the terror. I had to hold on tight to Jesus. He said he was taking all the fear from me. The Goatman leaned over and spoke right into my face. He said I would always belong to him. Jesus said I never belonged to the Goatman but always to him. It was bad but I held on to Jesus and cried and cried. So we have made a start on that. And that was my week. I am very tired and my stomach is still sore. But I am still holding on to Jesus. I don't see how he can work any of this out. I am not sure I am trusting him to but I am going to keep following anyway cos what else can I do. I think that is all.*

I didn't know what else to do. A lot of the time I just wanted to lay down and die but somehow I didn't. I suppose Jesus was giving me the strength and courage I needed just like he said he would. I needed it.

> *I have been back into the memory of the marriage with the Goatman two more times. Yesterday in the memory the Goatman was doing it to me and saying over and over you*

belong to me, you belong to me and I was saying back I belong to you. I saw blackness surrounding me and going into me. It was very horrible. Jesus held me and rocked me and I was surrounded by golden rainbows. He held me close and it was like I was going into his heart. It is hard to describe but that's how it felt. I did cry a lot. Today the Goatman threw me to the crowd, I don't know how many there were. It seemed like a lot. They grabbed me and carried me away. I was laid on my back. I knew what they were doing to me and I had my mouth covered, so I couldn't move or make a sound but I hardly felt it. I was staring up at the trees and the sky. The trees were just branches with no leaves and the sky was full of twinkling stars that I watched. They twinkled and twinkled. Jesus said he made them twinkle just for me, so I could look at them and not really know what was happening to me. I held on to him and cried and cried. It was very terrible even though I was looking at the twinkling stars. I could kind of hear the laughing and screaming and voices, but they seemed far away. So that is what is happening. I have been wondering a lot if there is any hope for me. I know I need to look at Jesus and not what is happening, but it is hard to do that all the time. I asked him to make himself very big to me so I can't see anything else.

That part of the memory was terrible. It wasn't a new memory, but part of one that we had right back at the beginning when Jennifer had been on the outside. But this time I saw it differently. I saw the next part differently too and in some ways this was even harder to accept.

The memory began where it left off. I was laid on the grass. That was all I could see grass and mud. I couldn't move or feel anything like I wasn't connected to the body. There were no people anywhere. I don't know where they went. But then I was surrounded by darkness. Demons. They were laughing and saying they had come to take me because I belonged to them. I couldn't move or speak. But I saw that they were held back and couldn't get me. Like there was an invisible wall. Then the wall seemed to be more visible. A golden shimmery wall. The more I looked at it the clearer it got. I saw that the four Angels stood in a circle around me. They had their backs to me so they were facing the demons. They spread out their wings so they overlapped and made a barrier so I was completely protected. The place where I was seemed to fill with a golden light and I knew I was in heaven. Jesus was in front of me. I was still on the ground and couldn't move. He said, 'my child' and he bent down and kissed me on the forehead. I knew he was bringing me back to life. Jesus faded heaven faded the Angels faded and I was left alone on the grass. Grandad came and picked me up. That was the end. I cried and cried because I didn't want to be back I wanted to be in heaven. It was so wonderful. Even remembering it made me not want to leave. But he brought me back. He brought me back knowing what would happen. And it seemed like he left me there even though I know he didn't. I suppose at the time it was how it seemed. I cried so much.

The memory of heaven was so clear that for a few days afterwards I just wanted to go back. It was a place of complete safety and love. A place I never wanted to leave. What was worse was knowing that Jesus had sent me back. That I had died and he had brought me back to life and sent me back knowing what was going to happen. Knowing what life would be for me. I had known it before but never so clearly, never with that memory of what he had sent me away from. I felt abandoned and rejected in the worst way even though at the same time I had the memory of heaven where I was so very loved and so safe. I talked to Jesus about it a lot of times trying to understand how he could love me, and still send me back to such a life. It took a while but I did start to understand what Jesus was wanting me to see.

Hi Jesus

Hello my little one

I suppose I need your help with the things I am thinking Jesus. I feel sad but maybe I am seeing something.

Tell me what you see my little one.

That I am here for a reason. That you must have a good reason for keeping me alive because you love me and even if it is hard for me to believe, sometimes it does matter to you if I suffer. Sometimes I think it can't matter because if it did you wouldn't let me keep on suffering. But I think maybe that part is wrong.

My little one every tear you cry is precious to me. Your suffering has been very great my little one and all of it matters. That does not mean my little one that it is what I wanted for you but it does mean that I allowed it. I allowed it because I understand what you do not. That all the suffering you have endured will be used to drive back the kingdom of darkness and to keep others from suffering as you have. More than that my little one it will keep a great many of my children from the eternal suffering that they would otherwise have endured. My dearest one such suffering is far greater than anything that even you have endured. I do not want that for any of my children. I have paid a great price my little one so that they do not have to and I have asked you to pay that price with me my little one, to share in all of my sufferings so that my children might be rescued and brought in from the darkness.

I know it mattered that you suffered Jesus. It mattered to you because you cried about it and were afraid and struggled to accept it and I know it mattered to daddy because he loves you but you still suffered Jesus. I suppose in some ways you still do because you are with us all in our suffering. I suppose accepting that suffering is...somehow necessary to follow you...like you said to share in your sufferings. I suppose that is what it means to be one with you, and maybe the closer we are to you the more we will suffer, I don't know because it is hard to imagine I could suffer more than I have. But I see that suffering is part of what it means to belong to you somehow, in this world. Maybe that helps me accept it better without believing the lie that it doesn't matter to you and you don't care. We suffer together Jesus. Don't we?

Yes my little one we do. I know my little one that it is a hard thing to accept. I know that your heart is still hurting and longing for an end to all the suffering, not only yours my little one but the suffering of all my children, but my little one my heart is also hurting and longing for the suffering to end. That is what we are doing my little one. We are working together with all of my children who are willing, to bring all of the suffering and pain of this world to an end not because it doesn't matter my little one but because it does.

Yes. I think I see that. And accepting that my suffering is part of that somehow, part of working towards it all ending. Kind of using it against itself...if I give it to you and let you use it, well you can make it count. You can somehow move towards ending the suffering. I don't know Jesus. But maybe accepting suffering past and present and future and not being afraid of it or trying to escape from it is part of surrendering it to you. Or maybe it is all about surrendering to you no matter if it means suffering...accepting that it will and not being afraid but knowing it all works for good, for ending suffering...I don't know. I suppose it takes the fear out of the future.

Yes my little one it does. Acceptance of suffering will help set you free from many things my little one. Not because I want you to suffer but because I do not want you

to be controlled by your fear of it.

Well...knowing that you are with me in it, that you are in control and that you care, that you use it all and it all works towards ending suffering. And that the suffering will end. For me it will Jesus. I know that those who are lost...that is hard to understand ..eternal suffering. But I know you don't want it. I don't understand why it's a thing if you don't want it, but maybe that is a big question that I will ask another time. For now...it is about accepting my own suffering in this life and not being afraid of it. Trusting that you do care and you suffer with me, and that you are and will use it all to end the suffering of others, and that it is part of what it means to share in your suffering and to belong to you in this world. Something like that.

Yes my little one. Acceptance of suffering in this world is difficult my little one for yourself and others. Acceptance does not mean that it does not matter or that you do not want it to end only that you are not afraid of it.

Yes because then it doesn't have any power over me does it. It can't control me. It sets me free.

Yes my little one exactly so.

Which is what you are doing. Setting me free from fear.

Yes my little one it is.

You always do things in a way I don't expect Jesus.

I know my little one but I will always do what I have promised.

Thankyou Jesus. I am not sure why you made the world you did or why suffering has to be part of it. I know it's not what you want and that it matters to you and you suffer too. Help me to accept my own suffering and not be afraid of it but just to give it to you and hold on you and trust you.

Yes my little one I am setting you free from many things so that you can become everything I have for you to be. So that you will not be controlled by fear my little one but filled with my love and compassion for a broken and suffering world. That is what I have for you my little one.

And to be filled with your love and compassion means accepting it will cause me pain Jesus like it does for you.

Yes my little one it does but you do not need to fear this my little one. Your suffering, all of it, belongs to me and I will use it for great good.

This place is such a hard place to be Jesus. This world.

Yes my little one it is but you are not alone. You are never alone.

No. Who am I Jesus?

You are my Pearl. My precious and beloved daughter of who, I am so very proud.

I think I would just like to snuggle now Jesus. Put all these things in my heart and help me.

Yes my little one that is what I am doing. Come then. Rest in my arms for a while.

It brought me a lot of comfort and peace in my heart to see these things. The pain didn't stop but somehow the fear wasn't there like it had been before. I did keep talking to Jesus about the world and what it means to be his child in a world that is so full of suffering and things I don't understand.

Hi Jesus
Hello my little one
Am I getting better?
Yes my little one you are. In every way.
I think...I don't know what I think Jesus. Suffering is a part of life for everyone. I am not sure what my suffering means. It must mean something that you allowed it and that you sent me back into it. Tell me about it.
My little one you are my child. You have always been my child.
Explain that to me Jesus. Is everyone your child?
Yes my little one every person that ever lived is my child.
But don't some belong to the enemy?

Yes my little one they do because of the things they have chosen, but they do not stop being my children my little one. They remain my children even when they are lost to the darkness.
That somehow makes it even sadder.
Yes my little one it does. I do not want any of my children to be lost to the darkness.
No. Of course not. So I have always been your child?
Yes my little one you have and when I made you I already knew the life that you would have and all the suffering and pain you would endure. My dearest one that does not mean that I did not care about those things. I care deeply my little one. I have given myself to you so that you could survive those things and live free of the pain and the fear of the past. I know my dearest one it is hard for you to understand how I could allow you to suffer so when you are my beloved pearl but understand my dearest one that pain and suffering are not the enemy. I have never surrendered you to the enemy my little one. I have kept you safe so that you could choose to belong to me and so that I could redeem everything he has done to you.
But you lose some of your children to the enemy.
Yes my little one I do and that is to my great sorrow. My little one I do not choose to lose any of my children but I do allow them to choose.
So I could have chosen to give myself to the enemy.
Yes my little one you could but you did not. You chose me my little one.
When I went to heaven and...saw you and you kissed me back to life...that must have done something. Even though I didn't remember it I suppose someone did. What did it do Jesus? Help me understand what happened.
My little one your heart belongs to me. Even though you did not know who I was or understand what was happening in that moment your heart was sealed for me. That means my little one that from that moment on your heart belonged to me and nothing that the enemy could do would change that.
You mean that's when I was saved...like eternal saving.
Yes my little one it was.
I don't understand...I mean it must have been another alter maybe...and...it didn't seem like I was choosing anything.
Every one of you was aware of being in heaven my little one. I did not exclude any of you from that.
Well...I suppose we all died together.
Yes my little one you did and each of you retained some memory of what happened.
Even if we didn't remember it.
Yes my little one.
Ok...but what about the choosing and did we all choose you? I don't what happened in my heart Jesus?
My little one when the enemy came to claim you I took you in my arms and made you my own. Even though you were not aware of the choice you were making I see your heart my little one. You reached out towards me and accepted me just as you did all those years later when you jumped into my arms and accepted me for yourself.
So even though that was the enemy marrying me to himself, you came and claimed me and I became yours, like it worked exactly opposite to what he wanted.
Yes my little one it did. And from that moment on everything that you are was hidden safe in me.
So...I know that means I was eternally safe from that moment, but what did it mean for my life here Jesus. What difference does it make...I know it makes a difference but I am not sure what it is. What happens when I got saved?
My little one when you are saved you accept all that I am into your heart. You give yourself to me and I accept you into my heart. We become one.
That doesn't happen with people who don't get saved even though they are your children.
No my little one it doesn't. They close their hearts to me and unless they choose me I

cannot enter.
Like I stand and the door and knock.
Yes my little one.
But they are your children, doesn't that mean that somehow you are in them. I mean they have eternal life already isn't that right?
Yes my little one it is. As my children they are already part of the eternal and even though they may never choose me, their spiritual lives will continue long after they leave this world.
For ever.
Yes my little one as you would understand it.
Mmm..is that a time thing?
Yes my little one it is.
So we became one when you kissed me.
Yes my little one.
That is kind of beautiful Jesus and I suppose because I had chosen and I belonged to you, you could...I mean it was your choice about my life.
Yes my little one you gave yourself to me. I could have chosen to keep you in heaven my little one but I did not. I chose to send you back into a world of darkness knowing that you would carry my light to many who were lost in the darkness so that they could choose me just as you chose me.
Kind of like daddy sent you.
Yes my little one like that.
It took you a long time to help me know those things Jesus.
Yes my little one for you it has seemed like a long time but I have always been with you working in your heart preparing you for all that is to come.
Even from that moment.
Yes my little one even from then.
And before then?
You were still my child my little one. I was always with you.
You are with all of your children.
Yes my little one I am.
But when they die are you with them then?
I do not leave them my little one, but they will never know my love for they have chosen to live in darkness apart from everything I am.
But how can you bear it Jesus. I don't understand about hell.
I know my little one but that is for another time. For now remember that I have loved you and saved you and that you have always been my beloved child. I sent you back into a dark and cruel world knowing that you would suffer my little one but also knowing what I would do through you to save so many who would have been lost to the darkness. To give choice to many who do not know they have a choice and to show the world who I am through your story and your life.
I keep on learning about me.
Yes my little one you do.
When I jumped into your arms I was already saved.
Yes my little one you were.
That makes more sense somehow when I think of all that went before. Me jumping into your arms was more about me knowing who I was and that I belonged to you.
Yes my little one it was. It opened up your heart to me in a new way my little one but you already belonged to me.
I love you Jesus. It is a hard choice you made for me. I still need to think about it but I love you.
I know you do my little one.

I asked him later about the alters that were made after this and if they already belonged to him. He said they each needed to make their own choice and they could have chosen not to accept him and not to blend. It helped me to understand what had happened to all for us on our journey and how it all fitted together. It helped me to see how Jesus had led us all step by step towards him so that we could be healed and know that we are loved.

The healings and the memories continued. Each one showed me something about the way the enemy had controlled me. I suppose they were still controlling me because of the lies I was still believing. But Jesus was determined to set me free. He took me back into another memory. Like all of them it was difficult to accept.

I was in a dark place outside with grass and trees. I was in the white dress I wore for the marriage, but I think this was before. I think it is the dress grandma made out of a white sheet for the school nativity when I was an angel. That somehow makes it worse. There were three other girls in white dresses and we had circles of flowers on our heads. We stood in a circle around a man. It wasn't the Goatman but I think it was the same group. Granddad stood behind me and I had to say something, but I didn't know what. Then my dress was taken off and the flowers. It was the same for the others. I held my hands out and the man poured blood over my hands and over my head. He said the blood of innocents was on my hands and on my head. I had black writing all over my body. Then we laid face down in front of the man like we were worshipping him. Then we had a crown of black feathers put on our head like the one I saw in the other memory. Then we were led to where there was a fire. They had cooked a baby. They cut its head off. I'm not sure what happened to that, but it's body was cut in four pieces. One for each of us. I got a part with a leg and I had to eat it. It was supposed to be like a celebration feast I think. Then granddad took me away from there. He had my paddling pool from home and a big plastic container of water to wash me. He decided to do it with me and he pulled me under the water, while he was doing it and it was very horrible because the water was full of blood that had come off me.

We had remembered parts of this before. Jennifer had even drawn some of it. It made more sense to me now but there was more I needed to understand.

That is what I remembered yesterday. Today when I went back into the memory it started off with grandad painting the back figures and writing on me. I don't know what they were. I was very cold and scared and the paintbrush tickled. Then they put the dress on me and circle of flowers and I went to stand with the other girls like I remembered yesterday. I didn't remember anything different, but I understood what I was remembering. When my white dress and my flowers were taken off, I was casting off everything that was good and embracing the bad in me that was the black writing. I was agreeing to be bad to be like Satan. That is what I was saying. Maybe I was thinking it then I don't know, but I was holding on to Jesus and crying and saying I like my flowers I don't want to be bad. And he kept saying over and over that I wasn't bad. That I was his Pearl. He was holding my hand tightly, but I started hitting myself on the outside while I was crying, but he reminded me he was holding my hand and told me to stop hurting myself so I held on tight to snuggles so I

wouldn't. And when the blood was put on me it was like saying I was so bad and I wanted the babies to die, all the future ones. So I held on to Jesus and cried and cried. I know Jesus says I didn't choose and I wasn't and aren't bad, but I am still feeling like I am. But that is cos he is still healing me. I think that is all I remembered.

He took me back into the memory one more time. To the part between the baptism and the feast. I think they were making sure we knew how bad we were. They had a baby on a cross in the ground. I think maybe it was already dead but I don't know. We each had to put a nail in and then stab a knife into its body. Then that is the one they cooked and cut up for us to eat. I kept crying and crying and saying, I don't want to be bad and Jesus kept holding me and telling me I'm not bad. And that is kind of how it was really. Then I have spent time with Jesus just holding on to him and crying and him telling me I'm not bad for the past few days. Yesterday I kind of understood something. I knew it before but somehow it got in my heart. It is that no matter how hard the enemy tried and no matter what they did or made me believe, they could never steal me away from Jesus. He kept me safe. And that is a deeper kind of safe that stays the same no matter how much I am hurt. So maybe I am feeling safer than I did. That is a good thing.

Jesus was settling me free but it was tiring in the middle of everything else. I was still having to look for jobs and help Richard with his appointments and phone calls for the benefits people. That was very stressful. I wanted to get through the healing though. I didn't like knowing it was there waiting for me, it was better to get it done and behind me.

The healing started again on Friday. Jesus says it will take two weeks. He says he will be taking me into five memories starting when I was ten and going back to when I was two. They are all memories of being buried and he has been talking to me about what happened and what it meant. On Friday angels came and rubbed a golden oil on me and then put golden armor on me. Jesus said he was giving me the strength I need for this healing. I have been having thoughts about how none of this is real, which I haven't had for a long time. Jesus says it is the enemy trying to keep me from being healed. He has taken me into two memories so far. The first one I was ten and the second one I was seven. They weren't very different. I was dressed in black with a black veil and put in a box and the lid was nailed shut and I was lowered down into a hole. I could hear the soil landing on the lid.

I held on to Jesus it was so terrifying. He said he was taking the terror from me. In the second one they brought me up and I had to knock twice on the lid to say I belonged to Satan. They lowered me down three times and each time they left me there longer. When

they took me out the Goatman took me to the altar and did it with me. I cried a lot. I am tired and depressed and not very sure about what will happen. I do feel confused about outside life, but I will keep going as long as I can.

I was three. I was in a black dress again and they were putting me in a box but I was screaming and crying and fighting. I think they were very angry. My finger got trapped when they put the lid on cos I was trying to get out. That made me scream more. So they put me in the hole. They pretty much dropped me in and told me I had to stay there until I was quiet, but I screamed and cried. Because the lid wasn't on properly soil and worms came in and that made me scream and cry even more, and they kept saying I had to shut up or I would stay there. And then I saw Jesus in the box with me and he put me to sleep...and that made me cry because it was such a kind thing to do because I was so out of control. It was a terrible memory but it was good too to see Jesus with me helping me. I am tired but my head is very full.

Jesus held me and comforted me all the time I was remembering. Even when I felt the terror of the past things I knew I was safe. He gave me the strength and the courage I needed to go through the healing, but it was very tiring and I was hurting a lot. Outside life was hard and I was so longing to be able to stop pretending to be Jennifer, to just be little girl who was looked after instead of being the one who had to be responsible and look after everyone else. But that's not how it was of course.

Jesus has been carrying on with the healing but mostly it has just been crying. I saw that he didn't exactly put me to sleep in the last memory, but he held me in his arms and I knew it and so I was calm and felt loved and just fell asleep. That was a good thing to remember. It helps me feel safe. I can't think what else to say really except I am tired but that isn't anything new. I have been starting all my days crying with Jesus mostly, because I feel overwhelmed and am wondering what good it is being Pearl. I know that isn't new either but it is hard for me to see that anyone wants me, even Jesus when I have to keep living like I don't exist. He tells me the same as he's always told me, as he is asking this of me so it will be possible for me to be Pearl one day, but it is hard to keep on waiting and hoping and wondering if I will even like it if it came.

Jesus did more healing yesterday. It was from when I was two. Someone...I think it was grandad was carrying me. I wasn't wearing anything this time. He put me in a wooden box. He was rough and the lid was put on. I don't know if they put me in the ground because it was just dark, dark, dark. That was all there was. And I kind of cried but maybe I was confused I don't know. I suppose I was very little. The darkness seemed to go on and on and it was hard to breathe. And then I was in Jesus arms but not in the box. Somewhere else and there was light. He held me close and rocked me and there was light and not dark and I think maybe I fell asleep. I woke up and the lid was off and the Goatman was staring down at me very close. And then I was afraid and cried and cried. I think it is helping me to know Jesus was with me in those times. That no matter what they did he was there and he was loving me. That's what I think sometimes but tonight it was like I got overwhelmed by all the feelings of grief and of rage. It was frightening and overwhelming. I still think he should have let me die. I'm still not glad to be alive. I am tired.

Jesus had done a lot and there was more to come but things on the outside were about to change. That would be difficult as well and I was going to need to hold on to Jesus through it all.

Chapter 15

It's Off to Work we Go

The benefits people were insisting I spent time looking for a job, so I had, kind of. I even applied for one. Before I knew it, I'd been for an interview and got the job. Just like that. I wasn't just surprised I was amazed, but I knew that Jesus was behind it. That was good but also confusing.

Hi Jesus
Hello my little one
I don't even know what to say Jesus. I am grateful and annoyed and confused all at the same time. Maybe a little depressed too.
It does not mean what you think my little one all that it means is that I am helping you to grow stronger and more confident in who you are and who you can be. I am in control my little one do not ever doubt it.
Well I don't think I can Jesus. But why did you keep saying you didn't want me to get a job when all the time you did?
My little one I did not and do not want you to get a job not in the way that you mean. This is to help you my little one it is not about earning money nor is it about who you are or my plans for you, it is only to help you grow stronger and more able in who you are.
But I did mean this.
No my little one you fear that you will have to continue in this work for many years and that this is all that there is for you. That it is your fate to work in an ordinary job and do all the things you do not want to do, and be all the things you do not want to be for the rest of your life. That is what you meant my little one.
Well, maybe but what did you mean...I do not want you to get a job.
I meant just that my little one. I did not and do not want you to get a job in the sense that you mean. This is not a job my little one this is you learning and growing and becoming. It is not about earning a living nor is it about settling for an ordinary life.
I wish you would talk to me so I understand Jesus. How am I supposed to know what you mean?
By asking me my little one.
Didn't I?
No my little one because you were afraid of what I would say.
Yes, I was afraid you would say I have to get a job and I do.
My little one I do not want you to see it as a job because that is not what it is.
It is your way of helping me.
Yes my little one it is.
Ok...but how am I going to be able to do the healing while I'm doing this not a job?
In my strength my little one as always.
It seems like a lot of hours.
It will help you my little one.
I know you know Jesus.
Yes my little one I do.
Am I going to be here a long time?
Just a little while longer my dearest one. Just a little while.
It makes me sad.
My little one everything is working for your good. It is all for you my little one.
I am not sure what I think about it Jesus. You don't seem all the way honest to me sometimes.
I do not always tell you everything or explain everything my little one but I will always help you to know the truth. I will always be leading you further into my heart of love

for you and I will always be helping you to walk the path I have for you which is good in every way.
I suppose ..it is about trusting you.
Yes my little one it is always.
Well, Thank you. I am going to need your help Jesus.
You will have it my little one. Always.

Jesus explanation of why it wasn't a job did make a kind of sense but I wasn't convinced. I didn't see how it would be a good thing and I didn't see how I was going to manage it along with everything else. I already felt overwhelmed. So I asked him about it again, many times.

I think maybe I have questions Jesus
Yes my little one I know you do.
I am worried about how tired I will get Jesus especially if we are still doing the healing.
My little one I will give you all the strength that you need and even though you will be tired, it will help you my little one to grow stronger than you are now.
Like doing the other things like my other job and the volunteering have.
Yes my little one like that. As you do more you are able to step forward more confidently. You learn more about yourself my little one and how I will enable you in all the situations you are in. Staying safe and comfortable will not help you my little one it is only as you step out into new things that you learn and grow and become.
I suppose the actual work is besides the point.
Yes my little one it is. It is about learning to work with others, finding new ways to express who you are, discovering more of the things I have put inside of you and allowing you to grow in those things.
Well ok. I see that Jesus.
I know you do my little one ask your question.
What about Pearl? What about who I am and all of your plans for me? What about that?...crying....
It is to make those things possible that I am asking this of you. My little one when you go to be with my servant you will need to be stronger than you are now. You will need to be more sure of who you are and the things that you can do. You will need to be able to spend more time working alongside people and to not need so much time on your own. All of this is to help make those things possible my little one. I have not forgotten who you are. This is to help you my little one.
But I am just a little girl and you keep piling more and more grownup things on me and none of the things I want come and I'm sorry, because I understand what you say and why. But what about me Pearl?...crying....
My little one you are my dearly beloved child and I will never forget you. Even though I am asking many things of you that is only because I love you my little one and because I want you to be all that you can be. I know it is hard to keep on waiting my little one I know all of your needs and I will meet them my little one. I have promised you so many things but there is more that I have for you than the things you want and need as a child. They would not be enough for you my little one because you are more than that. I know my dearest one that your heart is still aching for all the things that have been taken from you in this life but I will restore all of them to you my little one. A home and a family and the ability to love and be loved. You have come so very far my little one and it is only a little longer. I will not forget the things that you need my little one. You are my child first and foremost. I will love you and heal you and give you everything that you need. All the desires of your heart will be given to you my little one but I am doing so much more than that. Hold on and trust me my little one. I know who you are and you are my treasure. I will not forget you.
It is hard for me to understand…crying….
I know it is my little one and that is why you must trust in my love for you. What I

want for you is far greater than anything you could think to ask for my little one.
I know I can do it Jesus if you want me to….crying…..
Yes my little one you can.
And it is good but I don't want to be here. I am still thinking let me out…crying…
I know my little one but remember that I am setting you free so that you can go and become all that you were made to be. Truly free my little one so that you will not need to keep coming back or going round in circles trying to find something that you lost or to get away from something that that is still holding you. My little one trust in my way for you. It is good even if it seems hard and confusing at times.

It was hard and confusing. I tried very hard to trust in what Jesus was saying and doing but this was something I had been living in fear of, something I had hoped Jesus would protect me from, something I didn't believe I could do and something I didn't want to do.

I thought I would write and tell you what Jesus has showed me today. All week I have been crying and crying. I have been waking up in the night and crying and starting to cry just in the middle of doing things. So I asked him why and I have started to understand. Getting a job has meant I have finally had to accept that my childhood is lost. I think because I am nine I have somehow thought my childhood wasn't really gone and have imagined that when I got to America I could somehow be that child I never was. Like I was holding on to something that was already gone even though I suppose it is obvious. Living life as Jennifer is so painful to me like it says it doesn't matter who I am and a big part of that is having to be a grown up with all the things that means. But I have kept holding on somehow and hoping. But when I knew I was going to have to work and my whole life just be a grownup's life with no room for me that was when I finally let go. And all of the crying is me grieving for what is lost. It is lost and I can never get it back. Jesus says me grieving is part of setting me free from what is holding me. I suppose that makes sense but it doesn't make it better. So I don't know what that means. It is all gone and I can never get it back. When you were talking about your pool party that made me think about all the things I never had. Just things like fun and laughter and affection and safety...all of those things. I think I have been pretending to myself that somehow those things aren't lost for me, but they are. So I am grieving for the past and for the future. That is why I am crying and crying and why it seems better to me if I could die because what life is there for me. I am getting through my days somehow. I do one moment at a time, one job at a time and don't think about what is ahead if I can help it. All the other things I said last I wrote are still there. They haven't gone but this is extra on top. I don't know what else to say. That is enough I think. Bye.

Richard had to go for another interview assessment to decide whether he would have to get a job or not. It was scary for both of us. I had to be the grown-up mum and look after him of course. I did my best. I was worried but holding on to the thought that Jesus was in control and he was going to work it all out somehow.

My own struggles continued. I was still feeling that Jesus lied when he said I wouldn't have to get a job. I was still angry he hadn't let me die as a child and had sent me back to live this life. I was angry he was asking me to live this life when I was a little girl and that he kept on telling me just a little while longer. I was angry and afraid and confused about everything that was happening.

My little one I am with you.
I am angry Jesus. I am angry that you would put me through this. That you didn't let me die…crying….
I know my little one I know
And I know what you will say it is because of all that you will do. Well you had better. You had better make it worth it...It had better be good. Beyond good….crying…
My little one when I suffered I suffered with a purpose, for all that it would

accomplish. I know my little one that you think it is not the same but it is for you are in me and I am in you and you do not ever suffer without purpose and just as my suffering won a great reward so will yours my little one.

But people suffer all the time for no purpose Jesus…crying…

Do they my little one? I use it all my dearest one to bring about my purposes all of which are good. I know my dearest one that to you it seems wrong and cruel, but that is because there are so many things you do not understand. I am not wrong my little one. I am not cruel.

No….crying…

My little one I know how you have suffered and how you continue to suffer. I suffer with you my little one and for you. My little one I will take all of your suffering and use it for great good. I know my little one that this does not always comfort you and that you are angry that I would continue to ask you to live in this life and to continue to suffer and you are afraid that it will never be worth the pain you have endured but that is not what I have said my little one. You are in me and I am in you. Your suffering is my suffering my little one and you share in my sufferings also. Just as my suffering was and is used for great purpose so will yours be my little one. It is not different. It cannot be different.

It better be Jesus. To have lived this life and gone through all of this for nothing that would be cruel and wrong…crying….

Yes my little one it would but you are my child. You are hidden in who I am. All that I am is given to you my little one. All that I have is shared with you. My little one you have given me your life, everything you are. You are beyond price my little one and I would not ever do anything to harm you. I know my dearest one that this is still hard to understand when you continue to endure so much pain but my dearest little one it is not pain that will harm you. It is the desire of the enemy of your soul to take you from me my little one but he cannot do it. He has never been able to do it. You are mine. My beloved one and you are hidden safe in me. I will use all the suffering you have endured against him my little one. Do not be afraid that I will not.

It is still a hard thing to understand that you chose to let me suffer but I know you suffered and everyone suffers. This is a place of suffering Jesus…..crying…..

Yes my little one in many ways it is but I would not have it so my little one. That was not my intent.

But you knew it would happen.

Yes my little one I did. I always knew.

But somehow it will be worth it….crying….

Yes my little one it will.

And I just have to trust you on that because how can I know. I can't see everything like you can. I can't understand…crying…

No my little one you can't but you know that you are loved my little one and that you belong to me and if I ask you to endure suffering for my sake it is not because I have stopped loving you or because I do not care it is because I ask you to share in my sufferings my little one. Because you are mine. It is my sufferings which will save and redeem a broken world my little one. You are part of that. That is not for nothing my little one.

No but you better do it Jesus. You better take it all and do something so wonderful with it all, that I will be able to say yes it was worth it and I can't even imagine what that would be….crying….

My little one this is my promise to you. That I will take all that you have suffered, everything that you have endured and I will use it to drive back the darkness. I will use it to defeat the work of the enemy in so many people's lives. I will use it to break holes in the kingdom of darkness and to let the light shine down on my children. I will use it my little one. I will use it all.

Well you had better….crying……

Yes my little one I will. I promise you I will.
It is a big promise….crying…..
Yes my little one it is but it is not too big my little one.
I want to see it.
You will my little one.
Get on with it. Don't leave me here…crying….
My little one hold on to me and trust me. I am with you every step of the way. I am making you able my little one. If it is taking time it is only because my plans for you are far greater than anything you can imagine.
I am still angry with you Jesus…crying…..
I know my little one I know.

He was so very patient. Before I started my job I went for a trial day. The job was working in a hotel cleaning the rooms. It seemed like something I should be able to do even if cleaning wasn't exactly something I enjoyed. It didn't get off to a great start when no one came to pick me up at the arranged time. It made me want to give up and go home but I didn't. I held on to what I believed, that this was what Jesus wanted for me. Eventually after I called them I was picked up and spent a couple of hours being shown the work I would do. It seemed ok. But I was still scared and didn't want to do it.

I am sorry...crying….
I know you are my little one. My dearest one the enemy is tormenting you with his lies but that is what they are. Your future is in my hands my little one. I know that what I am asking of you is hard but that does not mean that it is bad. It does not mean that my promises will never come. It does not mean that I have lied my little one.
No. When you say it like that I see it Jesus. But I don't want to do this job. I don't want to be here. I don't want to be Jennifer I don't want to be a grown up I don't want to be alone anymore and there is no escape from all of that and even if I am better than I was all that seems to happen is more of the things I don't want and it is hard to bear Jesus. It seems like you don't love me and that that the things you've said aren't true….crying…..
I know how it seems my little one but that is not how it is. It takes faith to follow where I lead my little one. Often it will seem like I am leading you away from the things that I have promised you but that is not so my little one. It is only that I know the best way for you. The way that will help you draw closer to me and become all that I have made you to be. My dearest one if I ask you to trust me it is because trust is necessary my little one. You cannot go where I am taking you without trust.
Because everything I see will tell me I am going the wrong way.
Yes my little one often it will.
It is hard to keep on trusting Jesus when I seem to be going in the wrong direction for years and years.
I know it is my little one
I don't think I can do this Jesus…crying….
But you can my little one. I would not ask it of you otherwise.
I know I just need to trust you and keep walking forward with you even if I don't like where you are taking me but I am tired and I am scared and I just want it to be over. I want to see your promises Jesus. I don't know how much longer I can keep doing this…crying…..
My little one all the days of your life I have watched over you dreaming of all you can be in this world. You are my child my little one and I love you beyond anything you can imagine. Everything that is mine belongs to you my little one and can never be taken from you. The time you have in this life is so short my little one but it can accomplish great things if you surrender it to me. I know my dearest one that life has not been kind to you and that you often wish that it would end but it is not yet time my little one. My promises will come and when they do you will see that I have led you this way for a reason. You will see that I am well able to do everything I have

said. You will see that I can take your suffering and use it for great good my little one and even though the cost has been so very high you will not regret it. These things are hard for you to see right now my little one and that is why you must trust me. Trust is necessary my little one because you cannot see. Do not trust what you see my little one trust only in me and in who I am. I will not fail you. I will be with you in every moment and even though the path is hard I will sustain you on it and give you all that you need. Keep going my little one. Do not listen to lies but hold on to my hand and allow me to lead you forward into the life that I have promised you many times. It is not a lie my little one. It is real and true just as I am real and true and everything I am asking of you is to make it possible for you to live this life my little one. So that you will be strong enough and will not crumble and fall when opposition comes. So that you will know who you are and who I am also when others question and doubt. I am asking this of you because it is necessary my little one. Not because I do not love you but because I do. Keep trusting my little one. Keep hoping. I am with you helping you. Keep your eyes fixed on me and do not listen to lies. Everything I have for you is good my little one. My promises are true and will be fulfilled. There is nothing to fear.

I don't want to do this job Jesus but I do want to follow you. So I will try and think about it different. I don't want to live this life but I will because you ask it. I can't be apart from you. I love you. I belong to you. I need you. Please help me….crying….

My little one you are mine and I will not ever leave you. I will hold you in my arms and enable you in everything. My dearest little one there is nothing to fear from the future I have for you. I am in it all with you. Keep your eyes fixed on me my little one.

I will try. Please give me the courage and strength I need.

I will give you everything you need my little one. Keep holding on. I will not leave you.

So I started my job. I was scared but Jesus was right there with me. I took one step at a time, sometimes literally. Right now I'm going for the bus. That's all I'm doing just going on the bus. Right now I'm just waiting to be picked up, right now I'm just cleaning this room…and so on. I made friends which was nice, even though of course I was being Jennifer. Meeting new people was interesting and I didn't mind the work. It was hard though and very exhausting. I was so tired having to work six hours with no break in a very physical job.

Work seems mostly ok. I don't ever want to go but I am ok when I am there. The people are interesting and mostly very nice, but I do feel like I am from a different planet. The conversations are hard for me sometimes. They talk about adult things of course and ask me about men. One of the men asked me if I wanted to go out sometime. I said no...obviously. I have tried to not freak out about it. Jesus reminds me that I am safe. It has been strange seeing me. I mean how I am with people because normally I am on my own all the time. I do pretty well and don't seem to get shy or scared. And I have coped with tricky situations like with the man and when I thought someone was angry with me and with guests too. I am not understanding what Jesus is doing, but I am seeing me better even when I am thinking he should get rid of me and there is no point being me.

It was a lot of new situations and a lot of new people. For years now we had been living in a kind of bubble, not being in the real world while Jesus had been healing us. I had forgotten what it was like 'out there'. It was a bit of a culture shock and it was hard and I didn't always feel safe. And there were all the other things of course. They hadn't gone away.

I wish I could have daddy hugs. What are they like I wonder. I have needed some hugs today but I am ok. I nearly cried a couple of times at work but I asked Jesus to help me. He must have cos I did ok. Anyway I have some good news. Richard's assessment says he has limited capacity to work and he doesn't need to get a job so that is a big relief. At least I don't have to worry about that anymore. Yesterday was a bit hard. Did I say mum wasn't pestering me? I take it back. I don't think she means to pester me about stuff, about work, about if I am going to get more hours or a third job. She used to do three jobs and the state doesn't owe me a living...that sort of thing. Sigh,.. Of course even if I did have ninety-nine jobs it would just change to getting a better job or a career or training or more money. So that depressed me a bit and reminded me how we have never been good enough. That sort of thing. Jesus says he is proud of me. I hold on to that. I had to go to the job center too. She was saying stuff about more hours too but at least I don't have to go in anymore. She is just going to phone me not exactly sure why. And I saw Kate too. She told me something which made me mad. There is this lady who used to know Jennifer. They were in the worship team together and I suppose she was a friend. Kate still sees her but we haven't seen her for years. She told Kate she shouldn't have anything to do with me, Jennifer, because I don't go to church anymore and am backslidden. I was very cross. She doesn't know anything about me so how can she say those things. I did realize later that it is the enemy. They don't want me spending time with Kate do they, helping her and reminding her of the truth. It does make me wonder though what people who knew Jennifer are saying. I don't care that much except I think it is a bad thing to say bad things about people when you know nothing. Humph. Kate said she would risk spending time with me, I don't think she was too impressed either. So I felt very got at yesterday and today wasn't too much better at work. Nothing bad just little things.

I was getting used to working but I wasn't enjoying it very much. I found it very hard and I got so very tired. I got stressed about not being able to do it well enough, worried I would get into trouble. And there were a lot of problems with not being picked up, being forgotten and left standing waiting, which made me late and made everything harder. It made me feel a lot of things about being unimportant. Jesus was always with me reminding me that I belonged to him and was loved and wanted, but I still didn't want to do it and it was still making me doubt that Jesus' promises would ever come. I was afraid that I would be doing this for the rest of my life, that it had all been for nothing and that Pearl Sunshine might as well not exist. I was in the middle of a battle and held on to Jesus as tightly as I could, but it was a struggle.

Why do I have to go to work when you said you didn't want me to?
It was not my will for you my little one for there are other ways in which I could have made you strong enough to follow me but I am using it my dearest one. It is making you strong in all the ways that you will need. Do not be anxious about it my little one. It is serving a purpose and that purpose is good.
Like with my other job.
Yes my little one. You are growing in confidence and beginning to see more of the truth about who you are. You are growing stronger my little one in many ways so that you will be overcome the obstacles that are ahead of you. It is making you more aware of the people around you and of their struggles. You see so much more than you realize my little one and I will teach you so many things through this. I know my dearest one that you are afraid of what may lie ahead for you but I have promised to be with you and help you and care for you. I have made you many promises all of which will be fulfilled. You only need to trust and to follow where I lead my little one. I am with you. I am always with you.
I do get scared. I see people living such meaningless lives and that scares me too more than anything. For them and for me because it is hard for me to see my life is any different sometimes. But you are in my life. You are my life so that must make a difference.
Yes my little one it does. Your life has meaning and purpose my little one because you are in me and I am in you. It cannot help but be so. You fulfil that purpose as you follow me my little one. Remember that it is not a single purpose but one which has many strands woven together. You are fulfilling your purpose even now my little one and even though that purpose will grow and become more obvious to you and to those around you that does not change the significance of all that you are doing now. It is a beginning my little one but it is a good beginning because you are

following me closely.

Kind of like, a rope that is being woven together as all the purposes you have for me are pulled in... maybe they are...people that I change something in or for, I don't know, or other things maybe, and right now my bit of rope is kind of thin but it is getting thicker and it will grow and grow as I follow you and more and more strands are woven in.

Yes my little one and as you follow me I will enable you to draw so many in that your purpose will be far bigger than anything you can imagine.

What is it that I am seeing Jesus...the rope? I know it's not a rope, maybe it's more like a picture of a tapestry that you are making something.

Yes my little one there are many ways to understand it. Your purpose is like the framework that is given to you. As you follow me I bring you the threads to weave into that framework and I show you how and when and where and I help you to do it. It is something we do together my little one. The more closely you follow me the more complete and beautiful the picture your life makes will be.

And if I go wrong, I suppose you can correct it.

Yes my little one I can. Even when you make mistakes I can make something beautiful with the picture that is being made.

But if...I mean, maybe I will miss things and there will be holes and gaps.

Yes my little one sometimes there will but I will help you my little one. The more closely you follow and the more surrendered you are to me the fewer gaps and holes there will be. Your picture will still be very beautiful my little one. You are beautiful.

I suppose some people's pictures never get made or are full of gaps and holes.

Yes my little one that is so. Sometimes the framework is destroyed because of their choices my little one but I could restore all things even the purpose to which my children are called.

I suppose, no I don't know. I suppose the enemy wants to destroy the purpose or make it so my picture never gets made.

Yes my little one he does. He wants you to give up on completing your picture for he understands what it would mean for you to do so.

What would it mean?

Many of the threads that are meant to be a part of the picture would be lost my little one. They are given to you to be a part of your picture, your purpose and if you do not complete their part of the picture there is nowhere else for them to go.

But what does that mean Jesus. How can that be?

My little one as you weave your picture with me you are becoming connected to so many others. I am weaving everything together my little one but sometimes the connections are not made and the threads remain lose. That means the whole picture is not as strong as it should be. My children are not one as they should be.

And then we are not strong against the enemy and for you working together with you, that sort of thing, so yes I see he would want it and if my picture is big and strong and connected to a lot of others, that is like bringing the purposes of your people together. Working to bring the kingdom and defeat the enemy. It is when we are separate that we are weak but together we can do so much more. The enemy doesn't want that so if I don't follow and make my picture then everything is weaker.

Yes my little one that is so. Everyone has their part to play. Everyone has their purpose but it is in working together my little one that you bring the kingdom. It is working with one common purpose that the enemy is defeated.

I see...sort of. And even now I am making my picture. Drawing the threads in that should be there. Making connections...helping others fulfil their purpose I suppose. It is hard to see ..but I suppose it could be true.

It is true my little one. You are already drawing in many to your picture. Some are only a tiny part my little one but others are not.

Like daddy.

Yes my little one the connections you have with him are strong and will only grow

stronger as I weave you more closely together.
Because it is working together with him that I will be able to fulfil my purpose.
Yes my little one it is. Him and many others.
Ok. Life is never what it seems on the surface.
No my little one it isn't. You must learn to see as I see my little one. It will help you to do so.
Because I will see that it all has meaning and purpose.
Yes my little one you will.
Help me remember all that Jesus when I think my life is pointless.
I will help you my little one.

So now I was working with everything that meant and doing my other little cleaning job and helping Kate and looking after Richard and the flat. Things were more settled at least but they weren't easy and now it was time for more healing.

> **"For I know the plans I have for you," declares the Lord,**
> **"plans to prosper you and not to harm you,**
> **plans to give you hope and a future."**
>
> **Jeremiah 29:11**

Chapter 16

An End and a Beginning

Now that things on the outside had kind of settled down, Jesus said it was time to continue with the healings. The healings that would set me free so that the fountain could be filled with daddy's love and I could be filled with the Holy Spirit. The healing came in groups of memories like they had before. The next set of memories were of being drowned.

This next healing will take you back into a place of fear my little one, but as you see that I was with you in it and that I was always in control, you will be able to break free of that fear. That will set you free in ways you have not understood my little one. There will be five healings in all. They are memories that you have buried deep my little one, but in releasing the fear that is in those memories you will be able to move forward with me.

Jesus took me back into the memories when I was safe in his arms just like he always did. I curled up on my bed with my bear Snuggles and closed my eyes, holding on to Jesus and trusting him to keep me safe and not let me be overwhelmed by the memory.

In the first one I was about ten I think. I was wearing a white robe and they took me in the lake. They put me under three times. They put something over my head...a hood maybe and it stuck to my face, so even when I came to the surface I couldn't really breathe. I was under a long time it wasn't just dipping. It was terrible and I held on to Jesus and cried and cried. When I was under the water I saw a light. Like I did in the box. It calmed me down because it was so beautiful. When they finished they carried me out and the Goatman stripped off my robe. They drew symbols on my body and I had to bow down and worship the Goatman. Then they put a new red robe on me and I understood it was like a graduation. That I had moved up a level on the cult. I never thought of that before, but I suppose it makes a kind of sense. In the second memory I was about seven. It was kind of the same except I struggled and fought a lot more and they were very, very rough. But this time when I was taken out of the water they cut the palm of my hands and the Goatman did the same and he held my hands tight like the blood was mixing. He looked into my face and said 'mine' but behind him I saw Jesus looking at me and he said mine. I cried a lot. The memories were terrible but I have been ok since. I am tired but I am tired anyway.

The drownings didn't just happen in the Goatman cult. They happened in the group that wore white robes and were led by the Grand Master. I am not sure what the difference between them was. Some of the people were the same and they did the same kinds of things. It was all cruel.

I did some more healing with Jesus yesterday. It was memory we had before but I understand it better now. I was being drowned over and over in a lake and then I had to cut the throat of a baby goat. It was very bad but I hadn't understood that it was like a test I had to pass. I was five. I don't think it was the Goatman cult, but the other one with the white robes and the Grand Master. Jesus was holding me in his arms and I saw his face clearer than I ever have before. That made me cry more than the memory. I have been at work today. I am not enjoying it and I am so tired I could cry.

As the healings continued I didn't just get tired because of working and healing. I couldn't sleep. I didn't even know why but I spent a lot of time laying in the dark not sleeping. I started to lose hope again and asked Jesus to take me home over and over. I had to hold on tight.

Jesus took me back into two more memories. In the first one I think I was four. Grandad was pushing me under the water in the bath. I had a big cut on my leg and I kept seeing it every time I came up. I was feeling confused and knowing that I was so hated. It was so overwhelming that feeling of being hated. But then I saw Jesus and he was looking at me with so much love. It was like his love was bigger than all the hate, even while I was being drowned over and over. I am not sure why grandad was doing it except I had the thought that it was like practice, because he kept shouting and telling me not to struggle and make a fuss. The second one was kind of the same in the bath. I think I was a bit younger maybe three. It was grandad again but I think maybe there were others there. It was terrifying being held under and I thrashed about a lot. This time I was more holding on to Jesus here and now. I cried so much. Back in the bath I seemed to be surrounded by a golden light but I didn't see anything really.

It was a relief to get all the drowning memories done. That meant there was only one more set of memories to go before it was finished. I was very glad about that. I wasn't doing too well. I am feeling a bit rubbish but I think that is the healing. We started again yesterday. I just want to get it over with, I am feeling very lonely and maybe very…I don't know what the word is…like a little hurting person. That is the healing I know…

The last set of memories were from times when I was smothered. Jesus told me it was all about control. So much of what they did was about controlling me.

We have done two memories. The first one was from when I was five. It was grandad. He had grandma holding me. I was sat on her lap and she held my ankles tight while grandad held a cushion over my face. It was horrible of course and what I was thinking was how they had no pity. None at all. I think …well Jesus says it was about control. The point was I had to keep still. No struggling. I got the idea that by the age of five, I had pretty much learned to keep still. In the memory I saw Jesus in front of me. He was dressed in a long robe with a kind of scarf that had lots of different colored jewels on it. It was very pretty and I was looking at it which helped me not panic. Today I think maybe I was about three. I was wearing a pretty flowery dress that I was looking at when I was picked up. I don't even know who it was, but I was held really tight around my whole body and it went dark and I couldn't breathe and I started to wail. I mean here not then. I think I was struggling in the memory or trying but I was held too tight. It was just so dark and I was thinking make it stop, make it stop. I did see a little light that danced around so I looked at it. That helped in the memory I mean. That was Jesus I suppose. I cried a lot after and Jesus rocked me in his arms.

At last it was done. I was so so glad. No more healing for a while. I could just rest a little bit and try to do better at work and the rest of life.

I have done all the healing. I am done, done, done. No more. Well for a little while. So I will tell you about it and then that's it. Yesterday's memory I was about two or three I think. I was in bed and it was still sunny, so I suppose it must have been summertime. It was grandad again, he just put a pillow over my face so the sun was blocked out and it was dark, dark, dark, that was all I could think. I cried a lot and held on to Jesus. There was a lot of fear. Today I was even smaller. It wasn't clear really just a pillow over my face and terror. I cried and wailed but Jesus was holding me and telling me I was safe. And after a little while I just snuggled into him and felt very peaceful and safe. It is hard to know if that was then or now. Maybe both. I think I know much better than I did that Jesus was always with me, and that somehow no matter how it seems I was always safe and I always will be no matter what is happening. That I am always safe in his arms all of the time.

I was very, very tired. Work was exhausting and I still wasn't sleeping and the healing was very tiring all by itself. It made me gloomy. I wanted to see hope but I was afraid of hope. I knew I was hoping that now the healing was done something better would be coming. Jesus talked about infillings and my baptism. He didn't say how long it would take, but I was hoping like always that it was almost time to go be with my daddy and start living my new life as Pearl. But I was afraid because it never seemed to come, no matter how close I thought it was sometimes.

Hi Jesus
Hello my little one
I need your help so much Jesus….Crying
Yes my little one I know that you do but I am here I will not leave you.
Help me to see what I'm not seeing Jesus. Help me to see like you do…..Crying
My little one I will give you everything that you need. That is what this time is for. I will help you to see and understand many things that you have so far not seen or understood. This is to help you my little one so that you are able to walk forward into all that I have for you. My little one this time is given to you for many reasons. I know my little one that you do not really understand why I am asking so very much of you or why my promises to you never seem to come. But my little one I am making you ready for so much more than you have imagined. Hold on and trust me my little one. I

will not fail you.
Hold me Jesus.
I will hold you my little one. My dearest one your daddy loves you. Do not think that he does not. He does not want you to go away nor do I want you to stop writing or talking to him.
I just feel like I am a big disappointment ….Crying
No my little one it is only that he feels frustrated for you and wants to help but does not know how. You are not a disappointment to him my little one.
Why won't you rescue me from this? Help me to understand Jesus because I don't. I don't…Crying
My little one as you face all the challenges this life brings you, you are learning how to trust and depend on me. Such trust and dependence is necessary my little one and must be complete if you are to do everything that I will ask of you. My little one I know that it is hard for you to see and understand these things right now for much is still hidden from you and you are tired my little one and in need of much rest.
Well why are you asking me to do so much tiring work if you want me to rest…..Crying.
Because it is my rest that you need my little one. I know that you are tired because of all the things that you need to do but it is my rest that you need most of all my little one. It is my strength that you need above your own. It is my sight that you need more than anything you see and understand. It is these things I am longing to give to you my little one.
By showing me how much I need them.
In part my little one. As you cling to me and trust me to give to you all the things that you need I am able to give you so much more than you are asking for.
Like blessed are those who hunger and thirst.
Yes my little one just like that.
So you have put me in a place where I so desperately need you so that you can give me everything you want to…Crying
That is part of it my little one. I am using your great need to give you many things that you will need in the future.
Is this the first infilling?
Yes my little one it is.
It's not what I thought Jesus. Why does everything have to be so hard?
Because my little one I am doing so many things at once. It is not that I want it to be hard my little one but you have chosen the steep path. I will enable you to walk it my little one but do not be surprised if it is difficult for a time.
Is that because I want to go fast?
Yes my little one which is a good thing and not a bad one but it does make the path more difficult.
But are we even going anywhere. I still can't see where we're going….Crying
I know my little one I know but that is why you need to hold on and trust me. If I enabled you to see and understand everything right now you would not have to cling so closely to me you would not have to trust me or to draw everything you need from me. My little one I know that it is hard but this is what I am doing. I am drawing you along a steep and difficult path towards everything I have promised you. Along the way I am giving you everything that you will need when you reach your destination my little one. Even if you do not see the destination it is there.
Ok. I see that Jesus. It is all about trusting and depending on you when it looks most hopeless and is most difficult
Yes my little one it is.
I don't think I am doing too well.
You are here with me my little one. You are following and staying close to me. You are being obedient in everything I am asking of you. Your tears do not mean you are doing badly my little one they only mean that it is difficult.

I think they mean I'm not trusting you. If I was, I would be like daddy wants and all like yay the futures great.

My little one if you were able to do that I would not need to lead you as I am. This is a journey you are on and there is much you need to learn and many things you need to receive. That does not make you bad my little one it only means that you are still on the journey and have not yet reached that place.

I wish you would help him see that.

I will help him my little one.

Tell me about this first infilling Jesus.

My dearest one the first thing you need to receive is my rest. That is like a foundation my little one for until you are able to fully rest in me everything else will remain difficult.

Tell me about your rest.

Trust and dependence my little one. When you are able to fully trust and depend on me for everything then you will receive my rest.

So as I do that through this time because it is so awful, you can give me your rest and that is the first infilling.

Yes my little one it is.

I thought it was daddy's fountain.

Yes my little one it is. Daddy's love will be given to you when you are able to receive it.

Do I need your rest first?

Yes my little one you do. When you have received my rest you will be able to receive everything else I have for you.

Like you said each infilling prepares me for the next.

Yes my little one.

So I need to trust and depend on you and not doubt or give in to fear but remember who you are and that you love me and I am safe in your arms always no matter what is happening or how things look to me.

Yes my little one.

And the second infilling?

Sight and understanding my little one to enable you to walk forward with me into all that I have for you.

And the third?

Daddy's love my little one which will be poured out in such great measure that you are not able to contain it but it will overflow to everyone around you.

And then the fourth is the baptism?

Yes my little one it is.

And that is to help me do all the things you want me to do.

It is specifically to give you all you need for the ministry that is ahead for you my little one.

Like when you were baptized?

Yes my little one like that.

Ok. That helps I think.

Yes my little one do not be discouraged. I am doing many things my little one. I am making a way for you.

Trust and dependence then.

Yes my little one.

Please help me then Jesus. This is not fun….Crying

I know it isn't my little one but as you cling to me and trust me to give you everything you need you are able to receive all that I have for you. It is a good thing my little one even if it is difficult.

Well if you aren't faithful and true everything is lost Jesus. So I am going to trust you. You are strong enough to hold me up and keep me going….Crying

Yes my little one I am.
Like when I am weak then I am strong.
Yes my little one because it is then that I can give you my strength in greater measure. You are learning and growing my little one and as you do you are able to receive so much more. Do not be discouraged my little one. I am so very proud of you. My little one you are my dearly beloved child and nothing will ever change that. Pearl sunshine is who you are and who I am making you to be. You have not yet seen or understood who that is my little one. Do not give up on her just yet.
I keep thinking I should. That I should just be Jennifer and forget about being me…Crying
But that is not what I want my little one. It is not who you are.
It is still hard to understand why you ask me to live as Jennifer but then I remember that you lived kind of hidden for a long time didn't you. Until it was time.
Yes my little one I did.
Is it the same?
Yes my little one it is the same.
I don't think I understand anything.
Many things are hidden from you my little one but you understand that you are loved and that I am with you and I am making you mine my little one.
I know you understand Jesus.
Yes my little one I do.
Ok then. Help me to trust and depend on you. Please help me.
Always my little one. I will always help you.
Bye not bye then Jesus. Help me today. I am still so tired.
I know my little one. I will help you.
Bye not bye.
Bye not bye my little one.

Work was hard and it was strange to see myself in different company. I felt very different from everyone. I couldn't tell if that was just how I felt or if people at work thought it too. I seemed to be accepted and liked as far as I could tell. It wasn't bad just strange.

Life is so weird Jesus
Your life belongs to me my little one and I will use it to bring me glory and to draw many of my children back to me. You are my beloved pearl and no matter how it seems to you you are perfect for the life I am giving to you.
I don't feel perfect for anything Jesus. I just think I am kind of weird and don't fit anywhere.
You fit with me my little one. I am not asking you to do anything alone.
That is true. You and me together.
Yes my little one.
So I might not fit without you but with you I can fit anywhere.
Yes my little one you can. Like a key in a lock you and I can together open the door to many so that they can enter the kingdom just as you have.
That is kind of a nice picture Jesus. You and me together make a key to open the door to the prison. I can't do it without you cos I'm not the key you are. But somehow together we can do it.
Yes my little one we can. Do not be anxious about how this will be my little one. I am making a way for you. All you must do is follow.
One day at a time.
Yes my little one.
I will try not to be impatient Jesus but you know I want to go fast. Jesus there are so many who need you surely it is better if we go fast.
It is better my little one if you are fully prepared and that way we can reach so many more than if you are not fully prepared. Be patient my little one I know that it is hard

to keep waiting. I will take you as fast as you are able but I will not take you too fast my little one. That would not help you or anyone else.
Well, I don't want to fall Jesus.
I know you don't my little one.
Help me follow close then Jesus and not get ahead or lag behind or get distracted or scared so I start pulling away. I want to follow you perfectly.
I will help you my dearest one. Stay close to me and follow everything I say to you and give to you to do. That way you will go as fast as you are able to go and you will not fall or go astray.

Seeing myself differently past present and future was part of what Jesus was doing. It was part of what needed to change. Walls had been taken down and the fear that was holding me was gone. That meant I was able to see much more clearly and understand the past, but also myself and the hope that Jesus had given me for the future.

Everything that you have seen and experienced is now being seen in a new light my little one. The light of the truth. This will help you but as everything comes together and you see it all afresh there will be sadness for a time because it will seem more real to you. This is your life my little one. It has been given back to you and some of that is hard but there is also hope my little one for as you come to terms with and fully accept the past for what it is you are able to see yourself much more clearly. Not as they saw you my little one but as I see you and that is what is most important. It is then that you will be able to receive the second infilling that is coming.
Because there are no more walls or barriers which I suppose were made of fear.
Yes my little one. Sadness cannot keep me out but fear can.
So accepting who I am, how you see me and my life. Knowing and accepting the truth about that means I can be filled.
Yes my little one it does.
And learning to rest in you was and is part of that because it is about letting go of fear.
Yes my little one it is.

So there you are that is what he is doing. I drew the picture like I said. I cried for a long time before I could even draw anything and I kept telling Jesus I couldn't do it, and I didn't know how to do it but in the end I did. I will tell you about it because I'm not sure it will make sense otherwise. First I drew my heart and I drew the things in it that Jesus put there when he made me. He put in sunshine and life, like in the flowers and I drew a waterfall of fresh water and a rainbow and love. He put all those there, but then the enemy got hold of my heart and surrounded it in darkness like a fierce storm, and there was lightening that sent pain into my heart and it broke into a lot of pieces, and he put heavy chains on my heart too. And that is what I drew and I cried and cried for all the bad things they did, and how they spoiled what Jesus made. I know that isn't the end of the story and that it isn't like that even now, but that is for a different picture I think.

Chapter 17

Battles

After all of the healing and with working and all the other things I was doing I was tired. I was tired not just physically but somehow right in the middle of me. Like I was empty. I needed to rest. I was going away with Cheryl to the Christian event we had been to so many times. I hoped it would be a time to be with Jesus and relax and have a break. It was and it wasn't all at the same time. After one of the meetings, I came back from the ministry and Cheryl said she'd been touched by him too. She seemed surprised that the Holy Spirit had been speaking to her. She said he hasn't left me and I looked at her and said, and he never will and she started to sob. She cried about a lot of things...some of it was about how she missed Jennifer. I held her and I hope I said the things Jesus wanted me to and it felt better like something had cleared the air. But the next day things seemed more difficult. I started to feel depressed and couldn't seem to find anything to say. My thoughts were jumbled and I couldn't think. Cheryl kept saying how quiet I was and I said I was just tired, which I was cos I wasn't sleeping too well. Jesus seemed lost in a fog but I knew he was there. When I got home I cried from relief. I felt so much better and not depressed any more and like a big weight was lifted. I was disappointed my time away hadn't been more restful. I hadn't expected to be under attack. I hadn't expected it to be so difficult. Jesus had been working through it all and I had learned some things, but I wasn't exactly feeling refreshed.

Hi Jesus.
My little one I am with you always I will never leave you.
I know you won't. I do know it. Jesus there is so much I need to talk to you about it seems like too much...and I am still, I don't even know what it is, but it is such a relief. It is such a relief to be home. I know there's a lot you want to show me and teach me and talk to me about and I want to ask so many things, but I feel like I'm just... getting unsquashed. I want to listen.
My little one you need to rest. There are many things I have to say to you and much I have to show to you but you need to rest. My little one many things will be revealed to you in the coming days and weeks and all of it is to be found in my presence. Come and rest with me often my little one and I will give you everything that you need and show you everything that you need to know and understand.
Yes. I am tired in all kind of ways Jesus. But I do want to ask you about things. Can I? Just a little bit?
You can always ask me my little one. I am always here for you.
Well I want to talk to you about Cheryl. I want to talk to you about what happened. I want to get free of it. I want to understand how not to get stuffed out, I want to know how to help her... But it is a big lot of stuff.
My little one spiritual oppression is something that you will face many times. The enemy will not want you to give to others what you have received and will do all he can to keep you from giving away the things that you have received. I will help you my little one. This is a battle that you must learn to fight. Being aware of what is happening, is the first part of the battle my little one and it is this that I have been teaching you.
I don't think I did to well Jesus cos I didn't see it till I was out of it.
But you did see it my little one and now you are seeking to understand it and that is good.
Well...first of all I don't feel free of it yet, I don't know I can't tell. Holy spirit can you come and get rid of anything that is still holding me…crying.
You are clean my little one.
Thankyou. I love you so much...crying….
I know you do my little one.

You have so much to teach me. Maybe the first thing I need to learn is how to protect myself. I know being aware of the battle is the first thing. Listening to you would help.
Yes my little one it would. Being alert is always the first defense my little one. Do not ever assume that the enemy is not paying attention. There is always a battle to be fought my little one.
Is there?
Yes my little one there is. I know that often you are unaware of this, but battles are being fought constantly on your behalf my little one.
Are they?
Yes my little one they are and even if you are not aware of it the enemy is constantly seeking ways to destroy you, or at least to prevent you from being who you are in this world.
So what do I do?
Stay close my little one and I will teach you many things that you need to know.
Well can I ask you for discernment so that I can at least know what is going on...at the time not later...because that would help a lot.
Yes my little one it would. My dearest one my desire is to give you everything that you need as you walk with me. I am leading you and teaching you my little one and I will help you to receive everything that you need.
Well I am asking for discernment Jesus because I need to be able to be in the darkness without being crushed by it. I need to see it for what it is so that I can call on you. Please.
Yes my little one I know that you do.
Why did you keep saying obedience is better than sacrifice?
Because my little one I know that you are longing to go. I see your heart my little one and I understand but there are things that you need before you can go my little one. Obedience is better because as you follow me I can give you everything that you need and accomplish everything that I desire. It is not just about going my little one.
Tell me about resting in you Jesus. What does it mean and what needs to change?
When you are able to rest fully in me you are able to let go of your own needs my little one for you know and understand that I will meet every one of them. That there is nothing that I will not do for you or give to you that you truly need. That does not mean that everything you want will be given to you when you want it but you will never go without my little one. I will love you and care for you just as I have promised.
Needs of every kind?
Yes my little one everything you need is found in me and comes through me. I know my little one that you still have so many unmet needs but that does not mean that I do not care or that they will never be met only that there is a perfect time and a perfect way to meet those needs.
And you will sustain me until those needs are met.
Yes my little one always.
So everything I need spiritually emotionally physically all of it you will give to me and I don't need to be anxious about it. I don't need to figure it out. I just need to follow you and to trust you and be obedient to you in everything knowing that you will meet every need I have as I walk forward with you. And that is what resting in you is.
Yes my little one it is.
I suppose that comes from knowing who you are and knowing who I am in you.
Yes my little one for as these things are revealed to your heart in a deeper and deeper way you are able to let go of your own needs you are able to let go of your own desires and to trust me with them completely. It will not be hard my little one because you will see and understand that you are not truly losing anything, that there will be no lack because I will provide everything that you need.
The Lord is my shepherd .
Yes my little one just so.

And maybe it is meditating on these things that help them get into my heart take root and grow there.
Yes my little one it is. The seeds are already there my little one but it is as they put down deep roots and grow strong that there will be no more fear for you and rest will come to the garden of your heart. No more striving my little one no more anxious thoughts no more restless yearning no more fear of disappointment of any kind.
Rest is good.
Yes my little one but few ever really experience it.
Help me then Jesus. I want to live out of your rest. I want my heart to be full of it.
I will help you my little one.
So the rest thing and the bible thing go together.
Yes my little one they do
And I suppose that seeing and understanding will come out of that place, because I won't be afraid to see and understand. It will open up my heart to receive everything you want to show me and teach me.
Yes my little one exactly so.
Good. That sounds very good.
Yes my little one it is. I will help you to receive everything I have for you my little one. Stay close and listen to everything I will say to you. Open up your heart to me and do not listen to fear my little one. It has no place in your heart. I have come to set you free from the fear that has held you fro so long. I have come to fill you with my love so that you can truly know what it is to be my child. When you live out of my rest you will be unstoppable my little one for the enemy of your soul will have no hold on you and nothing will be impossible for you.
Rest is like fundamental.
Yes my little one it is.
And that is why obedience is better than sacrifice because I suppose there are lots of things I could be doing, but until I receive your rest I will be hindered and held back and not able to do all the things you want me to. I need to live out of your rest so you can pour into me and fill me up with everything I need. But rest comes first.
Yes my little one it does. My rest will enable you to receive all that I have for you and to live the life that I will give to you. There is no room for fear in that life my little one not if you are to truly live it.
Like you did Jesus. You weren't afraid, except maybe in the garden
Even though I was afraid my little one that fear had no hold on me. It did not take root in my heart for I lived from a place of rest, so that when I faced the greatest test I was able to take hold of my father's love for me and to follow him wherever he led me. I was afraid my little one but that fear had no place in my heart.
So it's not that I won't get afraid only that it won't have a place in my heart and it won't stop me or have any power over me.
Yes my little one that is so. Feeling fear does not mean that you have to follow it my little one. You follow me.
But why will I feel afraid if my heart is full of your rest?
Because you live in a fallen world my little one, where many things will come against you and where the enemy of your soul will try to make your afraid in any way he can. You will feel fear many times my little one but that does not mean that you are its slave or that you have to listen to its voice over and above mine. Fear will still be present in this world my little one but I am greater than any fear. Put your trust in me and that fear loses its power over you. That is what my rest will give to you my little one, the ability to trust me over any fear that comes.
So I will still be afraid but it won't control me. I won't listen to fear I will listen to you.
There is always a choice to be made my little one but yes fear will have no power over you, unless you choose to give it power.
But the more I live out of your rest the easier that will be.

Yes my little one it will.
I would like to not feel afraid or worried. That doesn't mean I don't care only that I'm not controlled by fear.
Yes my little one. You will be able to care even more deeply because you will not be afraid. You will not need to protect yourself in that way. You will be able to feel what I feel and not be afraid.
So my heart will be open to feel like you do for people, so that I will care even more and be prepared to face whatever for their sake, because I won't be thinking about me at all. All of my needs are taken care of. I won't be afraid about me so I can focus on them, like daddy was saying.
Yes my little one just like that.
Because I am resting in you.
Yes my little one.
Rest is very important.
Yes my little one it is.

Learning to rest was going to take some time. Jesus was working through everything. Sometimes I could see it but a lot of the time I couldn't. Work was still hard and it was showing me things about myself that I didn't like. I was doing and saying things that I didn't want to be doing and saying. I was making mistakes not just in my work but with people, and making mistakes made me want to protect myself by blaming others. I knew that was wrong and I didn't want to but it so hard not to.

My little one you are loved and you are safe. Even when you make mistakes still you are loved and you are safe. Nothing can change that.
I am glad. I suppose I wouldn't need to protect myself if I knew that better.
No my little one you wouldn't.
I'm sorry. Help me know it. Help me remember it and not just react. Help me not put blame on others. That is a bad thing to do and I am sorry.
My little one any mistakes that you have made will help you to learn and to grow when you bring them to me. Do not be afraid of them. They do not make you bad my little one.
I would prefer not to make mistakes Jesus but it does show me things about me. Things I don't like mostly. But I'm not perfect. I'm not you. Help me be better. Help me remember I'm loved and safe and don't need to protect myself. You will protect me. Help me let go of that need.
That is what I am doing my little one.
Thankyou. I will do my best...help me.
I will my little one I promise you I will.
Ok. That's good and better. I don't need to protect myself. I'm already safe.
Yes my little one you are. Very safe.
Thankyou.
You are welcome my little one.

I didn't always see it that clearly of course. I needed a lot of help.

I don't feel very proud Jesus I feel like a big failure...crying..
Why my little one who's expectations are you looking at? Not mine.
No. The worlds I suppose. I don't measure up. How can I?...crying..
My little one I have not put those expectations on you. All that I ask is that you hold on to my hand and follow me. That you trust me and love me and put your hope in who I am. Not in anything else my little one not even yourself.
Yes. I don't need to meet their expectations.
No my little one you don't. You are you, special and unique and as you make your way in this world there will be many who will think you are not all the things you ought to be but that does not matter my little one. You follow me. You are my pearl

and I am your sunshine and together we will do so many great and wonderful things. Do not look at what others want of you my little one. You are my child. You follow me.

I live for you Jesus.

Yes my little one you do. I will help you do all the things you need to my little one and I will help you to live in a way that honors me, but do not expect that everyone around you will always see and understand. Much of the time they will not. Fix your attention on me my little one. Your mistakes do not matter if you give them to me.

How can they not matter Jesus if other people suffer?

Because I will use them my little one. I will work through them so that the outcome is good.

Even if I did something really bad Jesus. Say someone died because I made a mistake. How could you make that good?

My little one the consequences of the mistake would remain, but that does not mean I cannot work through it for good.

You don't undo the mistake.

No my little one I work through it.

But it still matters. How could it not matter if someone died?

It matters my little one but not in the way you are thinking. It matters because as you give it to me I can work through it. It matters that others have suffered my little one but it does not matter in the great eternal scheme of things. Your mistakes cannot change that.

Because you work through it.

Yes my little one. I know you are not fully understanding. You see your mistakes as making the world worse for those around you, but I take those mistakes and use them to bring life my little one. That is why I say it does not matter, not because there is not pain but because there is life.

I found that difficult to understand but I have seen Jesus work through mistakes for good. I have seen him work through daddy's mistakes, to help me and to heal me and give me the things I need. He has done that a lot of times. It wasn't fun, often there was a lot of pain but Jesus used it for good in a way that daddy's mistakes didn't matter. At least not in a bad way.

The mistake I most feared making was in listening to the enemy about the future, or misunderstanding what Jesus was saying because it had happened so often. It made me afraid to listen to what Jesus wanted to show me about his plans.

And what is happening with the infilling? Where is it?....crying...

It is happening my little one. You are beginning to see and understand. It is a process my little one. I am opening up your heart to see who you truly are. My little one you are first and foremost my child but you are also my servant. You are sent into this world to bring the light of my love to those who need it the most. You are more than you think you are my little one. As I change your idea of who you and enable you to see yourself more clearly in the light of my love for you, you are able to take hold of all that I am giving to you. My little one you do not need to do anything but trust me and hold on to me. Everything you need will be given to you.

I hate this I hate this....crying

I know you do my little one but refusing to talk about it will not help you.

I know you are right and I am afraid and I don't want to be. But I am. I'm still afraid it's not real...crying.

I am real my little one my plans for you are real.

I know you are real Jesus.

But why not my plans my little one?

Too many mistakes Jesus.

What have you learned from your mistakes my little one?
To be very cautious.
Yes my little one and what else?
That my mistakes don't mean you aren't real or that your plans aren't real.
No my little one they don't. You keep your hand in mine my little one and I will lead you forward just as I have said. I am bigger than your mistakes my little one. Your mistakes do not change who I am nor do they change who you are. You are who I say that you are my little one. You are being revealed a little at a time but that does not mean that you are not real. The same is true of my plans for you my dearest one. They are being revealed slowly but they are still real.
Yes your plan is already happening.
Yes my little one it is.
I forgot again.
But now you have remembered my little one. What you are doing is seeking the next step I have for you. That is not a bad thing my little one it is how you keep moving forward. Even if what you think now is not the next step it is in daring to seek that you will find it.
Seek and you will find.
Yes my little one.
You want me to overcome my fear by seeking.
Yes my little one I do.
But don't I already know? I mean this is a time for infilling for seeing and understanding. Oh...is this part of it?
Yes my little one it is for as you see and understand my plans for you you discover more of who you are. Not only that but you are able to move forward and take the steps that I am giving to you.
It isn't wrong to wonder and imagine or to ask....crying
No my little one it isn't.
It still seems wrong.
Why my little one?
I thought I was better why do I still think these things?
Because the healing is not yet complete my little one.
Well I can stay stuck in my fear or I can treat it like the lie it is and break free of it...crying
Yes my little one you can.

I did have to be wary though because the enemy wasn't going to miss any opportunities. They tricked me many times into talking about the future with them, telling me things that were going to happen, making me hope and expect things to start changing very soon. It was my worst fear and I tried so hard not to fall for it again. But I did. They were attacking in other ways too. It was the birthday again.

I realized that the enemy was getting at me because of how I was feeling and thinking about things. I had horrible nightmares that night about bodies being chopped up and I was thinking about how I did that. I had nightmares the next night too about drowning and not being able to breathe. It was the enemy because of the birthday. I still hate the birthday. Cheryl gave me presents. She said they were to celebrate me Pearl. She said when she cried that time when we were on holiday she kind of let go of something about Jennifer and it is better now, so she can celebrate me or the birthday or something. I like presents but I don't like birthday presents. So it was very kind and I am glad if she is better but the presents are still in the bag.

On Wednesday it was the birthday and I cried and cried. It was like grief for the life I never had and because of all the bad things. And because I am me and am still having to

celebrate Jennifer's birthday. I don't think it is a day of celebration I think it is a day of grieving. It used to be a day of fear and horror so maybe it is better but I still hate it.
Yesterday at work I hurt my back. I don't know what I did. One minute I was fine and the next I could hardly move. So I just had to leave my work and come home. I am in a lot of pain and can't really do anything if it means moving. The pain has made me cry and feeling so helpless has made me cry too. I haven't been to work today of course. I am not sure if I can get sick pay yet, so I don't know what will happen about that. Mum has been here helping which is nice but I think it makes me feel a lot of mixed up things and that is making me cry too. I will have to go to the Drs. on Monday and I am not good at that. The Drs. scares me. So it has been a full week and some of it has been nice but a lot of it has been difficult and painful. I have been feeling very sad a lot of the time. I have missed you and am sending you hugs. Love from Pearl.

The healing was continuing and like always the things that Jesus showed me were a surprise. I couldn't see it until he showed me it was all hidden too deep in my heart.

Hi daddy
It's me again. I haven't really been doing too well, feeling kind of sad and trapped and there seem to have been a lot of triggers which hasn't happened for a while. I woke up crying in the middle of the night. I felt like a pan of boiling water with the lid on, like it was all spilling out. I had a memory I think it was a memory... where I was in a garden. It was a warm night and men were coming to the bottom of the garden to do it with me. The usual kind of thing but it wasn't about that really. I was thinking why didn't I run away. I could have run away, because I was left alone a few times but I didn't. And I realized that I didn't run away, not then not ever, because I don't matter. I didn't even matter to me. Why would I run away when I don't matter. And I cried and cried. And then I realized that is getting all mixed up with now and I am believing that is why I can't get away now. Why I can't leave because I don't matter. Everyone else matters.. everyone but me and that is why I am still here because I don't matter and why I will always be here. Jesus says it is a lie that needs breaking. I think I am confused in my heart about a lot of things. But I do feel better now I see the lie, even though it doesn't seem like a lie and Jesus is going to help me like he always does. Like the lid is off the pan of boiling water. He says he is still setting me free of the things that hold me here. I wish he would run out of things

Hi Jesus
Hello my little one.
What is this Jesus?
Healing my little one I am working to set you free from the lies that are still holding you.
Tel me about it so I can see and understand.
My little one there are still many wounds in your heart that need healing. That does not mean my little one that you are not much better than you were only that your healing is not yet complete.
Will it ever be?
Your healing will continue my little one for there is still much to be done. But that does not mean my dearest that you cannot live a life that is rich and full that you cannot know what joy and happiness is or that you are not able to do everything I have for you to do.
Alright.
My little one before you can leave this place I must set you free from all of the things that are holding you here. If I do not do that my little one you will not be able to fully take hold of the life I have for you. Believing that you do not matter and that you must stay here to fulfill the needs of others is one of those things my little one.
Is that what I believe?

Yes my little one it is.
I thought we had done the I don't matter thing. Maybe it wasn't me. I can't remember.
My little one we will return to this many times as you have need of it for the wounds go very deep. That does not mean my little one that you cannot be free of the lie that is holding you here.
So I saw that is the reason I didn't run away and I should have run away.....is because I didn't matter. I didn't run away because I knew I didn't matter. And that somehow it seems the same to me now. That I am still here because I don't matter. And I can't leave or run away because I don't matter. That's what I saw Jesus.
Yes my little one that is the lie.
Why don't I matter Jesus? If I am your child and you love me why don't I matter?...crying
You do matter my little one.
What does that mean then Jesus cos it seems to me somehow that it's all about other people. Everything you do is for other people and not for me and maybe there is something about mum in there. I'm not sure, yes there is because she put everyone before me. Everyone was more important than I was and now it is you. But how can that be? It doesn't make sense. It's not who you are…crying.
No my little one it isn't. My dearest one there are many things you have yet to understand about my love for you. I am not keeping you here because you do not matter my little one but because you do. It is not the same.
But you are keeping me here so I can do what you want me to do. You have healed me for the same reason. It is all about other people Jesus not about me. I know that is selfish and bad and wrong that I should even mind but I do….crying
My little one you need to know deep in your heart that you matter to me. That you are important and special because of who you are. That everything about you matters my little one because you are precious and loved. Not because of what you do but because of who you are. My little one if you never did anything for me you would still matter. It does not depend on what you do my little one but only on who you are.
I know we have talked about this before Jesus and it makes sense in my head but the lie is still there. That I have to stay for other people and it doesn't matter how much I suffer because I don't matter. It was true then and it is true now because it's all about what you want and what others need and it doesn't matter what I want or need….crying
What do you want my little one?
I want to go home. I don't want to be here. I don't want to be here….crying….
I know you don't my little one but what do you want?
I want to follow you and know you. I want to be loved. I want a life that is worth living. Not a useless pointless life but one that makes a difference. One that takes everything I have been through and makes it count. A life that matters Jesus. I want to matter…crying.
Yes my little one you do but you already matter my little one. You will not matter more to me when you have reached out to those in need or when you have fulfilled everything I have for you. You cannot matter more than you already do my little one.
Is that what I'm afraid of? That I don't matter and never will.
Yes my little one but you do not matter because of what you do you matter because of who you are. That does not change my little one. It will not ever change. You have always mattered and you always will.
But I always believed I didn't.
Yes my little one for that is what you were told in so many ways but it was not the truth my little one. You do matter. You are important and special and loved just because you are you. Not for any other reason.
It must have been very deep in my heart Jesus. To keep me where I was.
Yes my little one but it was not the truth.
Why are you healing me Jesus? Why did you save me?...crying..
Because I love you my little one. You are my beloved pearl and you matter to me more than anything. If you never did any of the things I have planned for you, you

would still matter to me just the same.

Why won't you let me go Jesus?

Because there is so much I want to give to you my little one and if I let you go before you are ready you will not be able to take hold of them or receive them in your heart. My little one believing you do not matter will keep you from many things I am longing to give to you.

Can't you get me out of here and then show me I matter? I might believe it more if you did that for me.

No my little one it does not work that way. The lie would remain my little one. It must be broken now so that you are free to walk forward with me.

Do I matter Jesus? When I think about leaving here I think about the pain and difficulty I will make for everyone. People here and people in America. And that is why I keep thinking I can't go.

I know my little one.

And then I think about the people who will be helped by my story and if I don't go they will suffer. And it doesn't matter what I do people are going to suffer and where am I in the middle of all that? I don't even count….crying

Yes my little one you do.

And it makes me want to disappear. It makes me feel trapped like there is no escape and no way forward that I can take because all of it means people suffering….crying

My little one do you see why I have to set you free from this?

Yes but I don't see the way out.

I know my little one but I do. Will you follow me my little one? Will you let me show you the way? Will you open your heart to the truth and let me take the lie that is holding you captive and causing you so much pain?

Yes. It is a mess Jesus.

It is not too hard for me my little one.

My little one when you think about the future what do you see?

I don't know. It gets all jumbled and fuzzy like I can't see it or think about it. If I think about your promises then somehow it's not allowed and won't come and if I think about being here then it is just despair. So I can't think about it Jesus and I think this should be better by now.

My little one there are many things still for you to overcome but you can still walk forward with me step by step. They will not stop you my little one not if you keep following.

Ok.

My little one the future I have for you is my promise and my gift to you. It is not bad for you to have it my little one. I do not give bad gifts but only what is good and life giving for you and for others. I know my dearest one that you think people will suffer when you leave but my dearest one that is not what I have for them. There will be sadness my little one but that does not mean that what I am doing is bad and it is my doing my little one and not yours. You are only following where I lead. I will use everything to bring them life my little one. Your leaving will not bring suffering it will bring life.

It will bring suffering Jesus. They will be sad and maybe have to go without because of me.

My little one even if there is sadness for a time that does not mean you should not go or that I cannot work through it for their good. My little one it is better for them that you should go because that is my plan my little one. I will work through it to bring good things into their lives not to bring sadness and despair.

They won't see it.

No my little one not at first but that does not mean it is not so.

And the people in America?

They will be blessed by your coming my little one. They will not suffer because you are there.

Won't they?

No my little one they won't. I will work through you to bring them healing and life my little one. They will not suffer.
I think they might Jesus. What if the enemy decides to attack them?
My little one what the enemy does is not your fault or your responsibility. They are my children and I am the one who will protect and care for them.
What if I am inconvenient or they don't like me?
My little one my dearest little one you are a delight not an inconvenience.
I don't think so and why is this not better?
It is better my little one it is only that there is more still to do?
My little one will you follow me where I will lead trusting in who I am and that everything I am doing is good? It is not your fault my little one if others do not like my plans for you nor is it your responsibility to keep them safe or make their lives better. All you must do is love them my little one and follow me trusting in who I am and that my purpose in you is good both for you and for them.
It is very muddled Jesus in my head.
Yes my little one for the lie stops you seeing clearly but I will help you my little one so that you are free to leave this place knowing that everything I am doing is good and that all of my plans for you are good and that you do matter my little one because you are you. My Pearl Sunshine who is loved and wanted for who she is and not for any other reason.
I think I should know that I matter Jesus. You have loved me and saved me and never left me and if I am still here, it is because you love me and not because you don't care or I don't matter. But the other stuff is still there. I suppose that is the past. What I believed then and why wouldn't I? So it is just healing I need Jesus. It doesn't say anything about now or the future.
No my little one it doesn't. You do matter my little one. You have always mattered even if it did not seem so to you.
I don't like this life Jesus.
I know my little one.
But you have to set me free so I can leave. Like I am still held by chains and you have to break them.
Yes my little one that is so.
And this is a chain?
Yes my little one it is but it is much weaker than it was my little one.
I suppose every time you do some healing it gets weaker.
Yes my little one it does.
Are there more chains...are they all lies?
Yes my little one they are. They will be broken my little one and you will be free to leave this place and go to be with my servant just as I have said.
There is always more to be done Jesus. I thought this was a time of infilling.
Yes my little one it is but as you see and understand the past and who you are that means I can set you free from the things that are holding you. It is a good thing my little one and part of all that I have for you in this time.
What do you want me to do?
Stay close my little one and keep trusting. That is all.

It was hard to have to go back to the same lies over and over. Lies that still needed to be broken, but every time Jesus healed me the lie got weaker and weaker and one day it would be completely broken. That was his promise. Now I understood what I hadn't before. That I was programmed by the enemy to think and behave in a certain way, which made me vulnerable to being controlled by them until that programming was completely broken. That is what was holding me here and what Jesus was working to set me free from.

Life was hard and I didn't always see there was any hope for the future. The enemy was constantly telling me that there was no hope for me, but Jesus kept on encouraging me to see the hope and the purpose he has for my life.

My little one when I made you I made you with a purpose. I have given you many gifts my little one with many more to come. Most of all I have given you a story of hope and of healing, of light overcoming the darkness. That is your gift my little one. That is what the city needs. My little one the darkness is overcome as the light shines brightly. I want to fill you with my light my little one so that no matter how deep the darkness you will not be overcome. This time is hard because the darkness does not want to give way to the light. It will resist everything I am doing and everything I want to give to you but as you cling to me and follow me and I draw you closer and closer into my heart of love setting you free from all the things that would keep you from me I am able to fill you with my light. That is what I am doing my little one. Even though you do not see it the enemy does and he will try to prevent it in any way he can. I know my dearest one that sometimes this life is overwhelming and it seems unfair that I should ask so much of you but I know what lies ahead for you my little one and all the battles you will face. I know what you will need. Let me give it to you my little one so that you are strong enough to face the darkness. So that you can stand strong in the light of my love, strong enough to give away that light to others who do not have your strength my little one. My children who are so very lost and held in chains by a darkness that for them has never been broken. My little one the city is yours. It is given to you by me. It contains many who need my light my little one. I will send you out to search for them. I will enable you to give them the hope that you have received from me. My little one keep your eyes fixed on me. It is not as it seems my little one. There is hope. There is light. There is a future for you.

I held on and kept going. Time was passing and it was the end of October. I felt like pressure was building up inside of me. I had been struggling a lot but hadn't realized why.

My little one you are safe in my arms. No matter what is happening that is where you are. I will make a way for you my little one but you must hold on and trust me. The enemy of your soul is seeking to take you from me. He cannot do it my little one you belong to me but he can make it harder for you to follow me. Hold on and trust me my little one. I am yours. I am everything you need. Remember that I am your sight when you cannot see and I am your strength when you have nothing left to give. You are not alone my little one. You are loved and wanted and will always be so. The darkness cannot overcome you my little one. Stay close to me. I am everything you need.
Is this a fight Jesus?
Yes my little one it is.
Over me?
Yes my little one you are my treasure and my delight and the enemy is seeking to take you from me but he cannot do it my little one. You are safe in my arms always.
Are they planning something?
Yes my little one but you are safe. You are always safe.
Is it because it is Halloween? They haven't really bothered me before.
I know my little one but now is the time for many of the chains that are holding you to be broken. They will try to prevent this by reasserting their claim on you, but they cannot have you my little one. Hold on to me and trust me. I will not fail you.
Does that mean you are going to do something. To set me free?
Yes my little one it does.
But they are going to attack?
I am with you my little one there is nothing to fear.

You are bigger and stronger than they are Jesus. Is this why I've been feeling so terrible?…Crying

It is part of it my little one for they are seeking to destroy you but I am holding you close to me. You are mine my little one. My very own. They cannot have you.

Help me…Crying

I am here my little one. I am with you. They cannot have you.

Will they try and say they can?

Yes my little one they will try to overwhelm you but all you must do is hold on to me. I am fighting for you my little one. I will not let you go.

That was in the morning of Halloween. The next day I wrote to daddy to tell him what had happened that night.

I was feeling horrible like I told you. I think the fear was from the memory that was coming. So I went to bed and put out the light but I knew really that I wasn't going to be sleeping. The fear got worse and I was right back into a memory. It was very clear and very real. I was in a kind of open grassy place at night surrounded by trees and there was a stone alter and the Goatman was there. They stood me up on the altar and I saw Barbara coming towards me. It is hard to describe what she was wearing. She wasn't wearing anything really except jewelry. Long ropes of beads lots and lots of them and things on her arms some kind of ceremonial outfit I suppose. Like I said she wasn't wearing anything, not pretty. Then I saw I was wearing exactly the same. They bound our arms together with golden rope things. What I understood was that my training was complete, it was a kind of graduation I suppose. I don't know what they called it. I don't care. Maybe I was around nine or ten? I'm not sure what happened then cos then I was laid on my back on the altar, and the ropes were round my wrists and they were pulling hard so it hurt, and the Goatman was doing it to me and the altar was surrounded by people. That was all terrible, but it was the thought that I completely belonged to them. That I couldn't escape. I couldn't move. I was held there and I belonged to them. That was so overwhelming. I was crying a lot of course and begging Jesus to make it stop. It seemed to go on for a long time. They kept saying it and it got confused between then and now, because I know the enemy was there. I was laid on my bed surrounded by them...back then they kept telling me I belonged to them and in the present they were saying the same. I kept saying no I belong to Jesus and I was crying and crying and saying to Jesus make it stop, please make it stop. And then I asked him where were you in the memory. And I saw him kind of in front and above me. And I saw me leave my body and go into Jesus arms where he held me. He was kind of golden and I was too, but below us I could see me on the altar surrounded by darkness and held there. And he said to me all they have is your body, but I have your soul. You belong to me. And I said yes. And then he said to me tell them to go, meaning the demons in my room. So I did and they left and the Angels made them go. And then it was over and I cried...but then I went to sleep. I had a rough night though and didn't sleep well.

Jesus had saved me again. He was working to set me free but the enemy wasn't giving up. I was finding it very hard to keep holding on even though Jesus was doing so very much.

Hi daddy
I haven't been doing too well. There seems to have been a big fight going on. Am I going to give up or am I going to keep going? Can I keep going? I haven't been sleeping really. I have been angry with Jesus again because of how life is and because I can't see an end to all the things that make me so unhappy. I don't understand what is happening. To me it doesn't seem like anything is really. But I still know that Jesus is my only hope and that somehow it is me getting it all wrong. At least I hope it is. So I did spend time with Jesus this afternoon. I put it off because I knew I was going to cry a lot and I did.

No my little one the enemy of your soul may want you to lose hope but I have never wanted it my little one. I have given you my hope over and over and will continue to do so. Why would I do that my little one of it was not real and true?
I don't know…crying
I would not my little one. I am not cruel.
Sometimes I think you are. Sometimes I think you don't care. Sometimes I think you want me to suffer.
Do you my little one? Is that who I am?
No but you are asking too much I can't do it anymore. I can't. I can't fight these battles. I can't live this life. I can't keep on pretending. I can't keep following. I can't .
Do you think I would ask you to do something you cannot do my little one?
Stop it. Why do you always have to be right? Why does it mean I always have to trust you when I don't want to, why does it mean I have to keep on doing this when I don't want to. I don't want to. I don't want to…crying…
I know my little one. I know you don't want to.
So why do you ask me to? Why can't you be kind?…crying….
I am being kind my little one. I know it is hard for you to see this but in order to set you free from the things that are holding you I need you to trust me and follow where I lead. It would not be kind my little one to leave you in chains. It would not be kind to continue to let the enemy torment you with his lies. It would not be kind to allow him to direct your path my little one.
Why am I not free? After all this time and everything you have done. I should be free by now. I can't do this anymore …crying.
Do you think my little one I would ask it of you if it were not necessary. If I were not working through it to bring you good things?
I don't know. You talk a lot about good things. But where are they Jesus. I'm sorry. I know things are better but I can't do it anymore. I don't want to do it any more….crying
What do you want to do my little one?
I don't know. I don't know. I wanted to follow you. I wanted to see your promises. I wanted …what you said. But I can't have it. So there is no point being me or even being alive. How can I want anything except you and your promises…crying…
My little one I will help you to keep walking forward into all that I have promised you. I will hold your hand and lead you step by step. It is not too hard for you my little one. You are able but the enemy of your soul will continue to tell you here is no hope. He will continue to tell you it is too hard. He will continue to tell you that pearl sunshine has no purpose and place in this world but my little one those are lies designed to keep you from all that I have for you. I am real and true my little one. My promises are real and true. The hope that I have given you is as real as my love my little one. Do not give up now. Do not let go my little one. You are my precious and beloved pearl and there is so much I am longing to give to you. Do not listen to lies just because the path is hard and you can't see its ending. I am the same my little

one. I have not changed. My love for you is real. It is unending. It cannot ever fail. Not ever. So not give up hope my little one. Not now. Not ever.

It is so hard. And I am so tired…crying

I know my little one. I know you are.

And I don't understand and I am so afraid this won't ever end and you will leave me here. Don't leave me here…Crying…..

My little one I will not leave you here. Your time will come. It will come my little one. A time when you will shine for all to see. You are my pearl I am your sunshine and together we will work to bring life and hope to many my little one. That is my plan and my purpose and it will be fulfilled no matter how it seems to you now. Hold on to me. Continue to trust me. I am faithful and true and will never leave you.

One day I am going to give up Jesus. One day I am….crying…

No my little one you are going to hold on to me and trust me until everything I have promised you has been fulfilled. You will not give up my little one.

Then that will be the biggest miracle of all because I want to give up. I have had enough….crying…..

I know my little one.

Make it stop. Please make it stop…crying….

I will make you able to walk the path I have for you my little one. Take my hand. Take hold of the hope I have given you. Do not be afraid. I am with you always. You are loved and you are safe and everything I have for you is good.

Why don't I like any of it then Jesus? Why is all so hard?...crying….

It is only so that you can grow stronger my little one. That is a good thing.

I don't want to be strong….crying

You want to live the life I have for you my little one and do all the things I have promised you. That means you must be strong enough to do so.

I don't think I can do it…crying…..

But I know that you can.

Why do you always have to know everything?

Because that is who I am my little one.

I lost my hope so often because the life I was living was so very hard and because I was so unhappy. The enemy didn't stop attacking me with their lies but Jesus was always kind and patient. He never lost his hope in me. No matter how unreasonable I was he held me and loved me and told me the truth.

"No in all these things we are more than conquerors through him who loved us. For I am convinced that neither death nor life, neither angels nor demons, neither the present nor the future, nor any powers, neither height nor depth, no anything else in all creation, will be able to separate us from the love of God that is in Christ Jesus our Lord."
Romans 8:37-39

Chapter 18

The Land of Rest

I was having a very hard time. I felt lost and like I couldn't see anything. Even though Jesus had done so much and was rescuing me day after day, I didn't seem to be getting any better, I was just stumbling through my days not getting anywhere.

I feel like I am shut in a dark room and it is so dark I just have to stay still until the light is switched on. That is a difficult thing to do. I am very tired. My head is too full of thoughts that aren't good and full of things I need to do. I feel more unhappy than I have for a long time and I don't know what I'm doing or supposed to be doing or what I can do. I don't suppose any of this is making sense. I am scared daddy. All alone in a pitch-dark room not knowing what to do. That is how it feels.

It was how it felt. But I knew that Jesus was with me and would never leave me. I was fighting him and holding on to him all at the same time. The enemy was still attacking me with their lies. No wonder I was tired.

Hi my daddy
Last night I put the light out to sleep. I prayed like I usually do but it went something like 'look after everyone. Do what you like I don't care. Cry'. And there I was sitting at the bottom of a deep dark hole. Jesus was there and he said take my hand. I wasn't sure I wanted to. Sometimes it is easier to sit in the darkness. But I did. And he lifted me up on his shoulders and climbed up a golden ladder out into a sunny grassy place and I held on to him and cried. I went to sleep then but I talked to him this morning.

Tell me about where I was Jesus.
It was a pit of doubt and unbelief my little one. One that the enemy prepared especially for you.
I am tired of this Jesus…Crying
I know my little one I know.
It seemed easier to stay there.
My little one wherever you are I am there with you but do not choose to live in the darkness. That is not where you belong. You are my pearl and I am your sunshine and we are always together my little one no matter what this life brings to you.
I don't understand what it is bringing. I don't know what you are doing. I don't want to cry.
My little one all the things that you see now as difficult and painful are making you strong enough to follow me. I know my dearest one that you often think I am being unkind and that I do not care but that is not so. You are my child and I want everything that is good for you. I am helping you my little one not hurting you.
But it does hurt Jesus all the time. So much I want to hide away in a dark pit because it is too much.
It is not too much my little one but the enemy will trip you up and cause you to fall if he can. Do not give up hope my little one. I am with you always and even when you cannot see or understand. I am always working for you, no matter how it may seem to you.
I wish I was better at this.
You are learning and growing my little one. If you stumble I will pick you up.
I am trying to be brave because I love you Jesus and want to follow you, but I feel like I am going to stay sitting in the dirt while daddy is flying off somewhere.
No my little one that is not what I have said.
I don't know what you've said and even when I do. I am still here in the dirt.

Lift up your head my little one. The light of my love is shining on you. You were not made to live your life in the dirt but to fly my little one.
I'm sorry because I know I look at the wrong things like stupid cleaning jobs and loneliness and not being me and feeling like I don't matter at all, because I am still sitting here in the dirt. Maybe it is where I belong Jesus. Maybe this is as good as it gets.
Lift up your head my little one. Let the sunshine on your face. You are loved and you are wanted. You are my Pearl

Jesus lifted up my chin so I was looking at him instead of the dirt. The sun was shining bright behind him so I couldn't exactly see him but it made me cry a lot.

I am holding you close to my heart my little one and I will carry you to where I want you to be. Just like daddy's balloons I will take you to new places my little one. You do not belong in the dirt. Hold on and trust me.
You said I'm not going to America.
No my little one I did not. The promise remains. You will go to be with your daddy just as I have said.
Why do I have to keep on being this grownup cleaning person Jesus …Why? ...crying
Because it is helping you my little one. Not for any other reason.
It is very hard for me to see that.
No my little one. You do see it you just want it to end so that the things I have promised you will come.
I am so tired of this fight…Crying
I know my little one I know you are.
What is this time Jesus? I don't know what it is.
It is the final preparation my little one.
I don't know if that helps.
It is a time for you to grow stronger my little one which is happening. It is a time for you to learn more about who you are, that is also happening. It is a time for you to receive my love and my healing which continues. It is a time for you to begin seeing the plans I have for you that will happen my little one, as you open your heart up to me once again and it is a time for you to write and to prepare many things in your everyday life so that when the time comes, you will be able to go and be with your daddy just as I have promised you will.
Will you show me what those things are?
I am already showing you my little one keep holding on. Keep your face lifted to the sun and remember who I am. I will not leave you my little one. You are my treasure and my delight. Everything I am is given to you and I will enable you to walk the path I have for you.
It is better out of the pit Jesus. Please help me not to fall in again.
I will help you my little one. I am with you and my love is making a way for you.
I think that is enough now Jesus. Please help me.
Always my little one.

Now I knew why I felt I was stuck in a dark place with no way out. I was in a pit. I had known it even without knowing it. I had to be picked up and rescued by Jesus so many times. The enemy kept the pressure on and even though I knew that, still they could wear me down and I would listen to their lies and follow them into the darkness.

My Jesus.
I am here my little one. My little one I am holding you so close to me. I will not ever let you go.
When is this going to end Jesus? When is it going to end?
Soon my little one soon. When you are ready then you will go.

I won't ever be ready. I don't know what you want from me.

It is not that I want anything from you my little one except your love but I want many things for you. Things that you are not yet able to receive.

I don't understand. Why I can only have hard and painful things. Why am I so bad?

My little one have I said so? Have I ever said so?

No but it has got confusing about what you have said and how do I understand my life except that I deserve bad things and hard things and not anything good.

That is what you have believed for so long my little one but it is not true.

If it isn't true why is my life like this…Crying

Because my little one I am setting you free from many things. I am making you strong in me and enabling you in many ways that I could not do if you had all the things that you are longing for. Good things my little one things that I want for you but not yet my little one not yet.

Because I am too bad…Crying

No my little one because you have been hurt and need to recover.

Why wouldn't nice things help me recover? Why is it hard and difficult and horrible things I don't want that help me. I don't see it. I don't see it…Crying

My little one what do I want for you more than anything?

That I would be who you made me to be. That I would know who you are and who I am.

Yes my little one and do you think it is easy for you to receive these things in a world that opposes my will in every way?

No.

No my little one it is not. In order for you to be who you were made to be you must first know who I am and who you are also. This comes not through all the good and lovely things that you want my little one but through the struggles and pain of this life. That is not because I want it so my little one only because to take hold of all that I want to give to you, you must be strong enough for the battles that will come. You must be healed enough to be able to accept everything I want to give to you. You must be free enough to walk in my strength and not your own. I know my dearest one that you are weary and do not really understand the path you are on but hold on to me. Keep your eyes fixed on me my little one. It is not for nothing. Everything you are going through is reaping a reward both for you and for others. I am with you. I will not ever leave you. You are my beloved child and you are loved and wanted in this life and in the one that is to come. Let that be enough for you my little one. When it is hard hold on to me. When the darkness closes in draw even closer. This world is a painful and difficult place my little one but you are not alone in it. I know who you are my little one. I will not forget my promises to you. I am making a way for you to be everything you were created to be. Hold on and trust me. I am everything you need.

I don't know if I can do it Jesus. I don't even know if I want to. I used to want to. I wanted to follow you and love you and give you everything. But mostly now I just want it to stop…..Crying

Only because you do not see its ending my little one.

I don't see its ending. You have told us over and over for years that it would end. If you want me to keep going you are going to have to do something Jesus. I don't want to go back in the pit. But I don't know how to keep on believing there is anything more for me. That there has been any point to any of it. That I will ever be free of the past or the present because it is just endless…..Crying

My little one, my dearest little one I will help you in all of the ways you need. Take my hand my little one and take one step at a time. No matter what lies ahead for you I am with you in it. I am with you my little one. Keep all of your attention on me. Hold on to me and trust me and let me take you forward into all that I have promised you.

Crying….I'm sorry Jesus….Crying

I will give you my strength and enable you in every way my little one. You are not alone.

Crying
You are not ever alone.

Jesus was in front of me squatting down and I was sitting in the dirt like the day before.

Then I need more of you Jesus and the Holy Spirit and daddy. You've got to help me because I can't even get up……Crying
Do you want to come with me my little one into all that I have promised you? Will you take my hand and continue to walk with me no matter what the cost. No matter how hard and how endless it seems?
Because that is the choice?
Yes my little one it is but it is not a hopeless one. It is a choice which will lead you to life my little one. My life and all that I am.
It is about choosing you
Yes my little one it is. Always.
I do choose you Jesus I do but I can't do it…… Crying
Not in your own strength my little one but you are not alone. I will help you and lead you and guide you and give you all that you need. You can walk this path with me my little one. It was made especially for you and you walk it with me in my strength.
I see that Jesus.
I know you do my little one. Come then take my hand and let me take you forward into all that I have for you. Trust me my little one. I am for you in every way.

So I held out my hand and he picked me up in his arms and I buried my face in his chest and cried.

I think it is too hard…Crying
No my little one come and tell me what you see.
So I looked up and around me.
We seem to be in a forest but right at the edge. Is this the forest of difficulty?
Yes my little one.
It has been a very big forest Jesus…Crying
I know it has my little one but what do you see?
We are on a path that leads out and down to the city. The way is clear Jesus. It isn't blocked by anything. Have I been sitting on this path all the time?...Crying
Yes my little one you have.
And we are almost there.
Yes my little one tell me what you see?
The path is broad and clear Jesus. It goes to the edge of like a bowl shape dip and the city is in it.
It is only a little way now my dearest one. The hardest part is behind you. It is only a little way.
I just have to keep walking.
Yes my little one.
How do I trust what I am seeing?
Because I am the one who is showing it to you my little one. To give you hope so that you are able to continue with me.
Is it real and true?
Yes my little one it is real and true.
Please can you help me know that. I have been tricked so many times….Crying
I know my little one but this is not a trick. What else do you see my little one?
A little Blossum flower on the path.
Yes my little one for this is your path. The path I made for all of you. Not one of you is forgotten my little one. You are all precious to me. All of you are held close to my

heart. The life I have is for all of you, all of you together hidden in me working as one for the sake of the kingdom. You have been on such a journey my little one. I have saved you and healed you and set you free and though that journey continues you are about to begin a new journey my little one. One which will not be the same. Hold on. Keep walking. Give yourself to me and trust me. I am able where you are not my little one. I give myself to you. All that I am so that you can be all that you were created to be. Each of you hidden in me to be all that you can be in his world. Will you come my little one, into the city that I have given you? It is only a little further my little one.

I don't know what else I would choose except to sit on this path and stay here and I don't want to do that. But help me because I am still afraid and I know I can't do it. I can't do it. It is too hard….Crying

Not for me my little one. Not for me. You see the sun that is rising my little one. That is for you. To help you. To help you to see and understand the journey that is before you and the journey that is behind you. It is my gift my little one given to you. Lift up your head my little one. Let the light in. Do not be afraid. I am with you.

Alright Jesus. Help me be brave.

Always my little one. Always.

I had forgotten I was walking through the forest of difficulty. I had been there a long time, more than a year. Now it seemed I was almost out. I didn't know what that meant. I was afraid to believe it might mean something good, but it seemed like it was a hopeful thing.

Only a few days later I reached the edge of the forest. I didn't feel ready somehow.

Do you see it my little one?
Yes. But how can we be here already. Am I seeing right?
Tell me what you see my little one.
We are at the edge of the forest. There are no more trees past this place. I can't see what's ahead, I can just see the sun that is coming up.
What do you think it means my little one?
I don't want to talk about this….Crying
Why not my little one?
Because you are going to make me hope for something that isn't coming. I don't want to do that…Crying
It is coming my little one. Tell me what you see.
It is a beautiful sunny meadow full of flowers.
It is a place of rest my little one. The forest has come to an end and now it is time to rest and spend time with me to prepare for the next part of your journey.
It looks lovely Jesus but I don't see how I can have got to the end of the forest.
My little one your time in the forest has accomplished all that I desired. You have

followed me faithfully. You have learned to trust and depend on me even when you could not see or understand the way that I was leading you, even when it seemed too difficult to continue you have held on my little one. You are so much stronger than you were but you are weary and now it is time for you to rest my little one.

I don't even know what you mean by that, when I am working so hard and everything is so difficult. That isn't going to stop.

My little one you have been fighting many battles and breaking free of the things that have been holding you. That is what has made you tired my little one, not the physical work that you have been doing though that is hard and tiring in itself. I know my dearest one that you are longing for things to change and they will but first you need to rest. You need to spend time with me. You need my instruction and my guidance. You need to see and to understand more clearly than you do now. This is a time when you can begin to see and understand my little one. Where I can fill you and heal you and give you my strength for the journey that is ahead of you. I know my dearest one that you are so very tired and that is why you need to stay just for a little while my dearest one. You need to receive what I have for you. You need to prepare for the time that is coming. You need to know and understand more clearly than you do now, what I will ask of you in the months that are ahead.

Crying....Go away.

No my little one I will never leave you. Take my hand my little one. Come.

I planted myself down in the path and turned my back on the meadow. Jesus squatted down in front of me.

It's not real none of it is real...Crying

What is not real my little one?

Hope. Please stop it...Crying

No my little one my hope is real and true just as I am. I know my little one that you are afraid that I will disappoint you but I will not. I am all that you have believed me to be my little one.

I have believed you to be a lot of bad things....Crying.

No my little one the truth is in your heart. You know who I am.

I can't do it. I will just stay here.

My little one through all the things you have been through I have been with you. I held you and carried you and loved you. I have healed you and set you free. Do not stop now my little one. Take my hand and follow me into the land of rest. It has been made just for you my little one. It has everything you need in this time. It will help you and allow you to recover from all the struggles that you have been through to this point.

Like he leads me beside still waters, he restores my soul.

Yes my little one just like that.

I am so tired. I am so tired...Crying

I know you are my little one. I know you are. Will you come with me and allow me to give you my rest. I have so many things I am longing to give to you my little one. You have followed me well. Do not give up now.

I don't really see how I can rest Jesus when life is so difficult.

I know my little one but will you trust me and follow me. This land will restore many things to you my little one. Come take my hand. It is time.

You said you wanted me to walk out of forest with my head held high.

Yes my little one I do. For you have walked bravely my little one. You have overcome many obstacles to get to this point. Do not be afraid. You are able to continue with me.

I just don't know if it is real.

What do you see my little one?

The light is golden and gentle like at dawn. The flowers are pink and white and they are waving in the breeze. It is kind of big Jesus. I don't see where it ends. It looks a lot nicer than the forest.
Come then my little one. Let me show you what I have for you.

So I took his hand and we walked into the meadow. The flowers went up to my waist and as we walked little butterflies flew up and around us. It got a bit much for me and I stopped and put my arms round Jesus and cried.

Jesus….Crying
My little one my dearest little one everything is in my hands. You most of all. You are so very loved my little one and everything you need will be given to you. Come. It is only a little further.

So we walked on a bit further.

Tell me what you see my little one.
It is a round pool of water. I think it is coming up from under the ground and it is spilling over into a little stream that goes off somewhere. And it is surrounded by green, green, grass that looks like comfy cushions. And there are little yellow flowers like stars. And it is warm and lovely. And all the flowers are around us. It is a little hidden place.
Yes my little one it is. It is a place just for you. Here we will stay a while my little one. Here you will receive all I have for you. Here you will rest in my presence. My spirit will teach you many things about what is to come. He will help you to see and understand my little one. You will write your book, you will rest and recover and we will prepare you for what is ahead. It is a good pace my little one.
The little stream reminds me of the one inside. Where you saved me.
Yes my little one for it is here I will restore many things to you.
I don't know what that means Jesus…Crying
I know my little one. First you need to rest a while. We will not begin until you are ready.
Begin what?
Helping you to see and understand my little one.
I am so tired. I am so tired
Yes my little one I know. Rest then and do not be afraid. I am with you my little one. Rest.

The pool was the river that we had followed out of the land of hope. It had gone underground and out of sight in the forest but now it had come to the surface again, bubbling up to make a lovely pool where Jesus said I was going to rest for a little while.

Well in some ways I have been feeling a bit better but I don't know how restful it is. This morning I was laying on the grass with Jesus with my feet in the pool and we were looking at the clouds. They were making different shapes like a sailing boat, a slide and swings... It made me cry and tell him to stop. I am having trouble again with being me. I keep thinking how little Pearl should be got rid of because she is no use and there is no place for her. I just have to keep on being big Pearl. I don't know what the point of little Pearl is. I see Jesus is working through big Pearl…. Big Pearl can do all those things but what about me? What is the point of me? I know we are the same person…I think so anyway but sometimes I wish we weren't and that Jesus would get rid of little me, because there doesn't seem to be any reason for me to exist. It is hard for me to understand still why I am me. It is hard to believe I can ever have a life where there is a place for little me and if I never can then why do I have to exist? We…Aj and Blossom and me have been asking this question for a long time but there doesn't seem to be an answer. Or I don't know what it is. Do you know my daddy? Anyway that is some of what is happening. Night, night. Love from Pearl

I was in the beautiful land of rest. It was kind of like an outdoor jacuzzi except it was very gentle in every way. It was warm and sunny and so-so restful sitting there with Jesus soaking in the rainbow bubbles. Outside life didn't seem much different but I did have time to think about some different things. I had been reading in the bible where Paul says he is a slave to Christ. That puzzled me because to me slavery was all about fear.

Hi Jesus
Hello my little one
I want to talk to you about this slavery and service thing Jesus. I wish I had more time.
My little one I am always with you and I am speaking to you constantly.
Well...I think I am your slave but to me... I understand it wrong. I think it means no choice somehow and punishment if I get it wrong. You tell me, it is hard to know what is in my heart Jesus.
My little one for all of your life you have lived in fear. You never expected anything good because for you the world does not give good things. It only gives punishments for things you have done or not done or for who you are my little one because you could never understand why the punishments came when they did. You thought it must be you and that is what life was. But I have been showing you a different way my little one. A life not based on punishment and fear but on love. My little one when I ask you to follow me that is what I am doing. That is why I ask you to choose so often my little one so that you will know that it is your choice my dearest one and not anything that you are forced to do.
So where am I getting it wrong Jesus, because I still don't expect good things and somehow I think I am being punished even though I don't understand why.
My little one what you have not understood is that when I give you choice I do not punish you for saying no. I help you to say yes because of all the blessing that will come to you and to others from following me but that does not mean that I punish you for saying no.
But why do I think I'm still being punished when I have said yes?
Because my little one you still believe that punishment will come no matter what you choose or what you do.
Why?
Because that is what happened my little one. No matter how good you were, no matter how you tried to please everyone still you were punished. It was your experience of life for many years my little one.
But, what is that to do with slavery Jesus? I'm not sure I'm understanding.

Jesus squatted down in front of me

My little one when you chose to follow me what did I say?
That you would love me and look after me.
Why my little one?
Because ....crying....I am your child.
Yes my little one you are.
But I was their child too and still they punished me and hurt me...crying....
Yes my little one they did and so you expect the same my little one.
But that's not who you are...crying
No my little one it isn't and I will never punish you or hurt you as they did. Sometimes I may correct you my little one but that is not the same. You are not my slave my little one. You are not there to do what I say or face the consequences. You are my beloved child. We walk hand in hand through this world. I will love you and care for you and though often this life will not be easy that is not because I am punishing you my little one. It is not because you are not doing well enough or

because of who you are. It is the nature of the battle my little one but I am with you in it. You are my child my little one. Wholly loved and wanted I will never punish you or hurt you whether you do what I ask or not.

I don't understand that. I think you will because I deserve it…crying..

My little one, my dearest little one you are still caught in the lie that says you are bad and that whatever you do it will never be good enough but that is not so my little one let me show you who you are. You are my child my little one and all of this belongs to you. Just as it belongs to me. It is not different my little one. I am your lord and I show you the way but all of this is yours. You belong to me and I belong to you. Just the same my little one.

I don't think I have understood Jesus….crying

I know my little one but now is the time when I will show you who you are so that you can see and understand the true nature of who I have made you to be. Your ideas of who you are, are so very small my little one let me show you who you are. Who I have made you to be, not just in this world but in the world that is to come.

Is that what you've been talking about all along Jesus?

Yes my little one. Who you are in this world as my servant is important and precious but it is only part of the truth of who you are my little one let me help you to see and understand. You are not anyone's slave my little one. You belong to me but you are my beloved daughter and I want only good things for you.

It is a bit hard to see that in my life sometimes Jesus…crying

I know it is my little one but part of that is because of how you understand the things that are happening, not because they are bad in themselves.

I have to go now but please help me see the truth then Jesus. I have it jumbled somehow.

I know my little one but I can unjumble you. Stay close and keep listening. I am with you always.

Only Jesus could ever unjumble my jumbled heart. It seemed to me every time I thought I was seeing and understanding Jesus would show me more that needed to be done. But he told me often that's because he was always going deeper, not because I wasn't getting better.

My little one the forest has taught you many things. You kept on following when you could not see or understand. You overcame many obstacles in my strength. This is not the same my little one for this is a time when you will see and understand many things that have been hidden from you. The obstacles that were in your way are no longer there my little one. Even though your outside life is still demanding the struggle is not the same. It is a different place my little one.

Ok. But it still doesn't seem very restful to me. I would like a holiday Jesus. I would like time away with you. I would like to see and understand like you say but it is hard to do when there is no time and I am exhausted and in pain.

But I am with you my little one and I will help you.

Well it is up to you Jesus. I don't know anything. I am too tired to do anything.

That is why we are resting my little one.

I don't get it.

Who are you depending on my little one?

You

And who are you trusting each and every day for the strength you need?

You

And who are you looking to for guidance and direction and hope?

You Jesus.

Yes my little one. That is what resting is. It is not that the hardships of life cease my little one it is only that you cling to me through them and trust me. If you feel weak my little one that does not matter because I am all the strength you need. If you do not understand that does not matter because I am your sight and understanding. If

you do not see the way ahead that does not matter for I will lead you by the hand into everything I have for you. This time is for resting my little one and for receiving all that I have for you. It is not about what you can do my little one but only about what I can do.

Well that's good because I am done Jesus. Physically and very other way.

I know my little one but as you rest in my arms in this place I am able to give you everything you need even in the midst of all the things that you are doing my little one.

I hope so Jesus. Otherwise I will be here a very long time.

I know the way I have for you my little one. All you must do is rest and trust me.

I know you know how tired I am Jesus...crying

Yes my little one I do.

Ok then. Well I just have to keep going and trust that you will give me the strength I need...and all the other things I need.

Yes my little one you do.

I better go then.

I am your strength my little one. Hold on to me trust me and I will give you my rest.

I think what Jesus is wanting to show me is the truth I who I am eternally. Not just in this life but forever. Yesterday he showed me something that is hard to explain. It was me, as I really am with Jesus, dancing and running and laughing in a beautiful place that I suppose was heaven. And I understood that who I am can't be changed by anything in this life and that all of that is waiting for me. It can't ever be taken away or lost, and that in a way I can live fearlessly in this life because I have nothing to lose. I am totally secure. I've been given everything and I can never lose it. I saw it and understood it in my heart. So it is a shame I am feeling so tired and depressed isn't it. I keep asking Jesus if he is going to rescue me from all of this but I already know the answer. I am holding on to him. It is all up to him. I am not sure about anything but that.

I was feeling very tired. Tired, tired, tired. I suppose the forest had been such a battle that now I was out of it I just felt exhausted. Like I had run a very long and tiring race and now I had stopped. I couldn't seem to do anything. Life felt overwhelming and I felt like a big disappointment. Jesus held me while I cried. He was crying with me. He understood how hard it all was. I had stopped asking him to go faster. There didn't seem any reason to because I felt like it was going to go on forever no matter how fast I went. I spent time with him in the pool. He held me and told me things about his rest. A lot of the time I was too tired to do anything but just lean into him and let him hold me. Sometimes though he wanted me to see and understand something new.

What do you see my little one?
The sun rising.
What do you think that means?
I don't know. New beginnings. New sight and understanding.
And do you think my little one that you can stop the sun from rising?
No...crying
No my little one you cannot. Rest then my dearest one and wait for the new day is almost come. It's light is already dawning my little one.
I wish I could just curl up in a ball and not go anywhere or do anything.
It is only in the struggles of this life that you can learn to rest in me my little one. It is only then that you can truly take hold of what I am giving to you.
Can I do it?
Yes my little one you can because I am helping you.
Ok.
My little one this life is given to you for many reasons. It is helping you to become strong enough my little one but it also helping you draw so close to me and to receive all that I have for you. Do not regret it my little one. I am doing so much more

than you know.
I hope so Jesus. It all looks hopeless from where I am.
But it is not my little one. I am your hope and I am always with you.
I should go then Jesus. That is enough crying for now.
Remember when you are my little one and that I am with you in all the things you must do. You have my strength and my courage my little one and everything that you need.
I love you Jesus
I know you do my little one.

But even while I was resting, or trying to, the enemy wasn't. I was losing hope of anything better. I wasn't happy. Outside life was just work and other things I had to do. There was no fun, nothing I looked forward to or wanted to do just a long line of things to get through. And I was so lonely. I haven't been doing very good. Night times especially have been awful with me laying awake thinking how I can kill myself. And lots of crying of course. On Sunday I had time to have a long talk with Jesus.

Hi Jesus
Hello my little one
Well we are here sitting in the pool. It reminds me of a jacuzzi without the bubbles.
You are resting in my presence my little one. My arms are around you. You are safe and you are loved. This is where you will receive all that I have to give to you in this time my little one. It is a good place.
I have been in trouble Jesus. Maybe I still am. I want to escape so much and I can only think of one way to do it.
My little one even though this time is hard and there are many things you do not understand I am with you. You do not need to escape my little one this place is giving you life which is my great desire for you.
How is it giving me life Jesus?
What is life my little one?
I'm not very sure. I know you are life but I don't know what that means.
My little one what the enemy desires to give to you is death which is separation from all that I am. He does this by telling you lies about the future about the past and about who I am and who you are. He desires death for you my little one because he wants to take you from me but he cannot do it. Not in the eternal sense because you already belong to me. You cannot be taken from me but he can keep you from living out your purpose here on the earth. He can keep you from following me my little one. My way leads to life, to all that I am, so that you can receive me deep in your heart. So that we can live and breathe and move as one. That is life my little one. That is who I am. That is what I want to give to you and what the enemy of your soul does not want you to receive.
When I die...I will be full of you Jesus and then I will be fully alive.
Yes my little one you will but there is much that you can receive before that time. You can draw so close to me that you overflow with who I am my little one.
I am thinking about peter and how his shadow healed people it wasn't his shadow was it though Jesus it was you...flowing out through him kind of like...I don't know he was leaking you everywhere and people got healed.
Yes my little one like that.
And you want that for me.
I want that for all my children my little one.
And that is life to give away to others like Peter did.
Yes my little one it is.
So how is this time giving me life Jesus? Mostly I feel like it is killing me. But then you do say I have to die before I can live, or something like that.
Yes my little one it is only as you give up everything that you are to me that I can fill you with who I am.

Like...I open up my heart completely and I don't keep anything for myself.
Yes my little one.
I don't know Jesus. I think I am not doing well. Me wanting to run away and die, that is me saying I am going to have what I want...because what you want is too hard and too painful and I can't do it....Crying....
Yes my little one it is.
Or maybe because I don't think you keep your promises and I don't trust you...Crying....
Which do you think my little one.?
Mostly the first one...Mostly.....Crying
And do I ever ask anything of you that is too hard for you my little one?
It all feels too hard Jesus and I don't want to do it and I'm tired but I know I can do it. I can. I just don't want to, not any more.....Crying
Why my little one?
I don't know maybe...it is abut control again. Maybe I'm not dying like you say. So you can fill me with your life...Crying
And what is it you want my little one? To die as the enemy desires or to be filled with my life. To become who you were created to be. To live out your purpose on this earth. To love me and serve me and do all that I have told you of. What is it you want my little one?
You know what I want Jesus but I lose hope of it. I think I can't do it. It is too hard ...Crying
But it isn't too hard my little one. Not when you have me. What will you choose my little one? Will you choose my life for you and for others or will you choose death as the enemy desires.
I choose you Jesus always and forever but I don't know how to give it all to you and stop trying to take back control...I don't think I'm brave enough or strong enough.
Do you think that I know you my little one?
Yes Jesus. Better than I do.
And do you think I know the way for you to receive everything I have for you, which is my life my little one in all its fullness?
Yes. I'm just not sure I'm willing because it is so hard.
I know it is my little one but you know that I am with you and will help you.
Yes. I'm sorry I fight you and listen to lies when you only want to give me good things. I am having a lot of trouble with your way Jesus...Crying
I know my little one but you have not let go of me, you have not stopped trusting me even in the midst of all your struggles. I am holding you my little one and you are safe and you are loved. There is nothing to fear from the path I have for you my little one. It is good in every way.
I know it is about following you Jesus and not about getting what I want. It is so hard to be here year after year with all the things that means for me. I know you know. I know you are with me. I don't know how to do it Jesus...Crying
But I will show you my little one. As you cling to me and depend on me for everything I will show you. Remember I am teaching you to dance with me my little one. To follow my every move. You can only do that if you trust completely in who I am and are willing to follow wherever I take you.
That is true Jesus.
Yes my little one it is. This life is costly I know but it is working wonderful things in your heart my little one. Things that are behind price.
I get afraid I'm not going to make it and it will all have been for nothing. That I can't be the person you see....Crying
My little one you are already that person.
You know what I mean Jesus. That I won't ever be able to be that person.
Are you afraid of being that person my little one?
Maybe. It doesn't seem much like me. But I don't know what me is. I feel so trapped Jesus. Somehow that doesn't change and makes me so afraid and desperate to escape and I

suppose that is something you need to heal I don't know. I don't know…..Crying

My little one where are you?

I'm in the pool with you Jesus. But I'm in this life too that I can't escape from. I understand what you are saying about it and that it is good but...I still feel trapped.

Why my little one?

Because I can't see a way out.

I am your way my little one.

I feel like you are blocking my way out Jesus. Like you are keeping me here.

Yes my little one I am. For now but not forever.

Because you are doing something in my heart.

Yes my little one.

I suppose it is like the job. You say you want me to stay so I will stay because this is where you want me to be. Even if it's hard and I don't like it. It's the same.

Yes my little one it is.

But it's not forever.

No my little one it isn't. I will take you by the hand my little one and lead you out of this place but you must be ready to leave my little one. You must first receive everything I have to give to you in this place.

I see that. So you want me to stay.

For now my little one not forever.

It is hard for me to think about the future Jesus.

I know it is my little one because you do not see a time when all the things I have spoken of will come to pass. But they will my little one. When it is time. I keep my promises my little one. All of them.

It is impossibly hard Jesus.

I know my little one but you are not alone. I am with you.

Help me not to be afraid Jesus.

Yes my little one I will give you everything you need.

I felt a bit better for a little while. Jesus showed me the city again, where it had been hidden in a bowl-shaped dip it rose up so it was on a hill. Jesus said he was making what had been hidden visible. I wasn't sure what that meant but I supposed it was a step forward.

"You are the light of the world. A city on a hill cannot be hidden."
Matthew 5:14

Chapter 19

Suffering and Hope

As I rested in the pool I talked with Jesus about different things. I was still finding it difficult to want to stay and live not just because my life was difficult, but because of all the pain and suffering I saw all around me and in the world. It was hard to understand.

I am loved…crying..
Yes my little one you are. You are so very loved.
I will be very glad when this life is over and we can all be with you and enjoy you and I don't understand a lot of things about why but I know you want so many of your children to be there with you...and you want to defeat the darkness but you have already defeated it Jesus. I don't know why darkness is so strong if it is already defeated.
Because my little one the battle is won but it is not yet over. The battle continues my little one even though the end is not in doubt.
Why did you give us choice Jesus?
Because you are my children my little one. It is part of who you are. You are so much more than you know yourself to be. Being my child means that you have choice. That is the way that you are made.
The two go together somehow.
Yes my little one they do.
You couldn't make us in your image if we didn't have choice.
No my little one.
Why weren't you happy just to be you? I mean why did you want to have children when it meant so much pain and suffering for you and for them. I don't understand that.
Suffering is not the evil you believe it to be my little one and many things are accomplished through it
Pain is not the enemy.
No my little one it isn't.
But there's no pain in heaven so you must want there not to be pain and suffering Jesus.
My little one many things happen that I do not want because things here on the earth, in the life you live here, so many are broken and do not follow my will. That is not so in heaven my little one where everything is perfect. The suffering that you see around you is because of the choices that have been made against my will and against the things that I wanted for my children. Suffering came with choice my little one for the choices that mankind have made have often been to turn against me. That does not mean my little one that there is no choice in heaven but only that each choice that is made will be for me and not against me. Perfect choices my little one. Choices led by love and not by fear.
Fear is the enemy and where there is perfect love there is no fear and all the choices made will be perfect.
Yes my little one.
I suppose you use the choices that people make, that bring suffering, to draw us back into your perfect love, like you have with me.
Yes my little one that is what I do. Suffering is not an evil my little one, not when I take it and use it to draw you back to me.
But it's not what you want.
No my little one it is not what I want. I do not want my children to suffer my little one I want them to know who they are and who I am. I want them to come home to me.
To the place where there is no suffering.
Yes my little one.

I am still looking forward to heaven Jesus but aren't you going to let me show people who you are? As your Pearl.
Yes my little one I am. When it is time.
And your timing is perfect.
Yes my little one it is.

I was resting in Jesus arms in a beautiful pool. I could see the city, my gift that seemed so close and yet so very far away. When I really saw what he was showing me about the future and about who I was it was so wonderful, but overwhelming at the same time. Like it was all too good for me.

Jesus.
Hello my little one.
You have told me over and over that you are going to do so many wonderful things through me and there is this whole city you are giving me and I know I don't understand and maybe a lot of the time I don't really believe it. I don't know what to say about it except. I am just little me Jesus and you have chosen me to do these big things and all I do is cry and complain because it is hard but just now I can see what you ..that it is amazing. I don't know.
Little one you are my child and you share everything with me. Some things are just for you my little one but many things are for the sake of others. I have asked you to follow me this way because of all the blessings I can bring to you and to others because of your obedience. You have followed me well my little one and I am pleased. Do not be afraid my little one that you cannot do what I am asking if you. I will make everything possible for you. All you need do is trust me my dearest one. I am the one you need.
I know it all makes sense to you Jesus. Most of it doesn't make sense to me. Help me see like you do and not like I do most of the time. Help me see you...crying.
That is what I am doing my little one that is what this time in the pool is for.
Because only as I rest in you can I see as you do.
Yes my little one.
And this water Jesus. I am soaking in it...this... I don't know. What it is doing?
It is changing you my little one. It is changing how you see yourself and the world around you. It is filling you with my presence, it is enabling you to become the person you were created to be.
And I have to stay here until I've received everything you have for me?
Yes my little one you do. Until you have received the full measure of everything I have for you, you cannot walk forward with me.
So I need to rest and be patient and trust you.
Yes my little one you do.
That is hard Jesus when life gets to me and I want to escape.
I know my little one but I am here with you. Hold on to me and trust me. I would not ask you to stay if it were not good that you should do so.
You confuse me cos yesterday you seemed to be saying I was ready.
My little one you are ready in many ways but there is still more I have to give to you. Do the things I am asking of you and rest in who I am. I will take you to be with my servant when the time is right.
It is all up to you Jesus and the point is to follow you not to get what I want. This life is for you and for your kingdom. I already have everything I need. I would like a life that was so many things it's not. Most of all I want to be me and to use what has happened to me. I can't do that here and it is frustrating. And I get scared sometimes that I never will but you have done so much and I am only here because of you so it doesn't make sense to be scared. You are in control. You know the way. I only need to hold on and follow.
Yes my little one that is so.
Help me today then Jesus. Help me be pearl and you be my sunshine.

I will always be with you my little one and I will always help you to be who I have made you to be.
You think I am a good idea Jesus…crying..
Yes my little one. I only ever have good ideas. You are my treasure.
And you are mine Jesus….crying…
Yes my little one and together we will walk through this life. There is hope my little one. It is with you always.

Mostly I was still finding it hard to have any hope for the future. I was getting lost in outside life and all the struggles I had with it and with being me pretending to be someone else. It seemed endless and no matter what Jesus did or where he took me or how close it seemed the promise was always out of reach. I wanted so much to follow Jesus but I was very afraid I wasn't going to make it.

I had flu and was off work for two weeks. I felt terrible but it wasn't just that. Being ill made me feel vulnerable and like I was bad for being ill. It seemed to make everything worse and I had no strength to cope with it.

I don't like being ill Jesus.
I know my little one but you must trust me in this as in everything. I am with you. I will help you. You are not alone. Everything you need will be given to you my little one. You do not need to be strong without me, you need to be strong with me. That means you can be strong in any circumstance my little one because it does not depend on you but only on me.
What does it mean to be strong Jesus?
It means you have confidence in who I am my little one and in my great love for you. Your confidence will not waver according to circumstances you will be strong in who I am my little one because you know me.
I feel like I do waver Jesus when I think I can't take any more.
No my little one you know who I am. What you doubt is who you are which is hidden in me.
Do the two go together?
Yes my little one they do. We are not separate my little one. I am always with you. I am in you and you are in me. You are my child. You belong to me. I will never leave you or forsake you. You can have full confidence in who I am not only for my own sake but also who I am in you.
Who are you in me Jesus?...crying…
I am your sunshine my little one I am everything you need. You are not alone. I am your life and your comfort and your joy. I am given to you my little one so that you can give me away to others but I am first of all in you and with you. I will not leave you.
I'm not sure how that helps me when I look at my life and how I don't want to live it.
It helps you my little one when you remember that I am with you in it. That this is our journey my little one and not yours alone.
I don't like it. I want it to stop…crying..
And that is why you must hold on to me and trust me. Remember who I am my little one. Remember who you are. You are my pearl and I am your sunshine. We are together even in the darkest of places.
Please can you stop this. Please can you stop this…crying..
I will help you my little one to be all that you can be in me. It takes time my little one to learn how to walk in all that I am giving to you. I know my dearest one that you are so very weary but do not give up your hope in me. It will not fail you my little one.
I don't know what to do. I don't like being ill.
Rest in who I am my little one. You are safe and you are loved. You do not need my little one to be in control. I am in control. I say who you are. I direct your path. I walk

with you on it my little one and there is nothing to fear. My little one will you rest in my arms and trust me? I am with you and will help you. I will love you and care for you just as I have said.
Please help me then. To do that.
Yes my little one I will.

I wrote to my daddy. It was a comfort to me to know that he was there even though I didn't get to spend much time with him.

Hi my daddy
I am having a big meltdown today. I am crying and crying and can't seem to stop. Maybe it's because I'm not very well. I don't cope too good with being unwell. Maybe it makes me feel unsafe I don't know. I know I'm safe and loved but I don't feel it. I am just a little girl trapped in a life I don't want. Trapped in a body that's all wrong. Being someone I don't want to be and doing things I don't want to do. Day after day after day. And I try to forget and do the best I can and try and find things to do to keep busy and I hold on to Jesus and trust him, but then I remember and it all comes crashing down like today. I know Jesus has set me free from a lot but I don't feel free. I don't ever feel free. I don't think I will ever escape from this. Sometimes I pretend to myself that I will but I don't really believe it. I don't understand a lot of things. I know that. I have no clue why I am me here living this life. I am glad that you love me my daddy. You are a good thing in my life. I am going to stop now because I need to stop crying. Love from Pearl.

I was getting better and was back at work but I felt like I was in the middle of a storm, a storm that seemed to have pulled in the people around me. Kate had been diagnosed with cancer for the second time. My friend Ruth had been struggling and was in hospital again after several suicide attempts and now Sophie called me. She said that she had been having a really difficult time and had been given a diagnosis of personality disorder. She'd been told it was often linked to childhood trauma.

Hi my daddy
Not sure where to start really. I have been tired but ok flu wise. Yesterday was so icy I had to take my boots off and walk to the bus stop in my socks because I didn't think I would make it otherwise. Nasty wet socks all day. I have been feeling very sad and crying. I have held on to Jesus but I don't feel ready to talk to him about it. To me it seems like the enemy stole my last child. Like I lost them all. It is getting mixed up with the babies I think. To me it seems like the enemy is winning on all sides. Kate has cancer again. Anyway I have been reading about bpd…Sophie sent me some stuff...and I have been thinking about when she was growing up. Trying to remember how it was. I am still worried that there are things I don't remember, but I have a feeling it was messy enough to hurt her anyway. Thankyou for writing to me. It always helps me to know you are there and that you care. Maybe me talking to Sophie about the things I remember will help her. She seems to be giving herself a hard time and thinking she is a wimp, because nothing really bad happened to her. But there were plenty of bad things. I know you say it's not my fault and I know that me Pearl hasn't done anything. But it is still my fault somehow. I feel like I am being punished over and over for things I never did. I don't think it will ever end until I die. I hope it will end then…and knowing that Sophie and I suppose Richard are being punished too, just makes it all so much worse.

I was so afraid that something had happened to Sophie, and maybe Richard too, that I couldn't remember. So many things had been hidden away. Life with their dad had not been easy and I knew there were things that must have hurt both of them but I was afraid there was more. I was most afraid that it was something we had done or not done. I was afraid it was all my fault and I had no idea how to help her.

My little one my love for you is real and true and will not ever fail. I am with you always my little one. We will walk path this together just as we always do. My love for your children is not less than my love for you my little one, my power to heal them is not less but each of them has a journey they must go on just as you have your own journey. This is not a bad thing my little one though it may be painful at times. There is light and hope my little one do not turn your back on them. Your anger is just but I am not the cause of your pain my little one neither am I the cause of theirs. I will help you just as I will help them. I will lead them and guide them and love them my little one just as I have with you. Hold on and trust my little one. I am for you in every way. I will help you to move forward into everything I have promised you. There is life and hope my little one do not believe the lie that there is not.

I think maybe I haven't seen clearly how bad it was for them. I haven't wanted to see because what can I do about it. I can't do anything...I couldn't do anything....crying...

No my little one you couldn't but now you can. You can love them and speak the truth to them. You can be with them and help them my little one.

I'm not strong enough Jesus….crying

Yes my little one you are strong enough. I am with you. I am everything you need. I know it does not seem so to you my little one but I saw everything that happened. I was with you my little one. It was not your fault.

Just like it wasn't my fault about the babies.

Yes my little one just like that.

Why can I never do anything. Why are they just taken and killed and hurt….crying

You can do something now my little one. Hope is not lost. Your little ones are safe with me. Sophie is in my arms of love also my little one.

That breaks my heart even more Jesus because look at my life and look at the world... it's such a mess. And you can do anything. How can I find hope in that?...crying…

My little one the pain that you feel and the pain that you see all around you is not all that there is. There is hope and life. Everything is working towards something my little one. Something good. That means that even in the midst of the pain and the darkness there is hope. There is hope my little one because I am the light in the darkness and each one of my children is also a light my little one. The darkness cannot overcome the light no matter how it seems sometimes. All you must do is keep trusting and keep following. Your life has been filled with darkness and pain my little one and it has been a long and difficult journey for you to reach this point but that does not mean it has been for nothing nor does it mean that this is the end. It is a journey my little one. One which you are still on and though it is still painful and difficult it is not as it was. It is better my little one. You are better. You are much more able to trust and to follow than you were. That means I can lead you forward into the life I have for you my little one and all that I have promised you. Do not give up hope just because you do not yet see it. It is there it is real just as I am real.

It was hard for me to see any hope. I held on to Jesus but I couldn't seem to hold on to hope.

It has all been for nothing daddy. All of it. My whole life and I don't understand why. That's what I keep asking. Why? Why did he do all that stuff just for this? Why did I/we have to go through all that? Why do I have to keep on living and living and living? When I turn my light out at night and put my head on the pillow I close my eyes and imagine what it would be like to stop breathing. To just stop and for it all to be over. I would like that. When I think about Sophie and Richard I am grateful for one thing. That they don't have children. That it will stop with them. So many lives destroyed but at least there won't be any more. I feel like I am wasting your time. Like all the time you have given to us for all of these years has been wasted. I don't understand why. I feel like I have been so stupid to keep on hoping. I am sorry we have wasted so much of your time. We didn't mean to. I don't know what to do now. I do love you my daddy. Love from Pearl.

I was back in that place of no hope and wanting to give up again. Not that I wanted to give up but I couldn't face the future I could see and was desperate to find a way to escape it. And there was only one way I could see.

All things are in my hands of love my little one. Do not be afraid.
How can you say that when so many bad things have happened Jesus?
Because my little one even when the bad things were happening I was with you, even when it seemed like the enemy was winning I had a plan and even though it seems to you now that the struggle has not really been worth it I know what lies ahead my little one. I am bringing life and hope and joy out of great darkness. That is why I say do not be afraid.
Well you see it all Jesus and I only see little bits. But I get tired of the fight.
I know my little one..
I get tired of the fight with myself too. Why am I going round and round in circles with so many things? Why can't I just move forward in a straight line instead of going round and round? What am I doing wrong?
You are not doing anything wrong my little one but listening to the enemy will never help you. Breaking free takes time my little one and is not easy but that does not mean it is not possible or that you should give up the fight it only means my dearest one that you must recognize the battle for what it is. When you stop fighting and being aware that the battle is happening that is when you stop moving forward.
If I keep going will I break free? Is it just I give up before I get to that point and then have to go round again.
Yes my little one.
So that is why I have to persevere and endure. To get the breakthrough.
Yes my little one without perseverance and endurance you cannot break free of the things that are holding you. It takes time and diligent effort my little one.
Why? Why can't you just fix those things?
Because it is in the persevering that you learn so many things my little one. It is in the perseverance that you become more of who you are. It is in the endurance that you become able to stand against the enemy and all of his schemes and it is through these things my little one that I can shape you into who you truly are.
So every time I give in and fall back I have to go round in a circle to get back to where I was and then maybe this time I will keep going and break free.
Yes my little one.
Help me see. Help me hold on to you give me courage and wisdom and hope.
I will help you my little one. Always.

I kept going, stumbling from one day to the next. It was a big effort and I felt like I was going to fall any moment.

Hi Jesus
Hello, my dearest little one
I know Jesus that I'm not doing good. That I don't want to listen and I don't want to talk. I don't want you to show me stuff or tell me stuff. I don't care I'm sorry.
I know my little one I know but I will hold you and love you through this. There is nothing you must do my little one but hold on and trust me.
It doesn't seem like enough Jesus but it is maybe as much as I can do.
For now my little one for now.
How did it get to this Jesus? All the things you have done. All the things we did inside. All those rescues and all of that healing. All the things you taught me and showed me about the spiritual world. The book I wrote...all the times I chose you and trusted you, all the times you defeated the enemy and set me free. All the changes...being Jennifer and then Aj and then Blossom and it has brought me here. It's brought me to nowhere and nothing you

promised has happened...crying...
That is not so my little one that is not so.
No. It's not....crying......
My little one all of the things you think you see, things that are a disappointment to you are hiding the truth. The truth that you are so much stronger my little one. The truth that you are becoming who you were created to be.
The only person I'm becoming is Jennifer the cleaner. Is that what it was for? ...crying
No my little one no. Let me open your eyes so that you can see.
I don't think I want to. I don't care. I don't care...crying...
Then hold on my little one. Things are not the way they seem to you. All of this is to help you my little one. I have not brought you here to leave you here. It is only a steppingstone my little one. A gateway to the next part of your journey with me
I don't think there is anything else Jesus. What was it for? What was it all for? crying...
It was for you my little one to make you strong enough to follow wherever I will lead you.
It hasn't worked too well then Jesus cos I am just crying and losing hope....crying...
But you are still here with me my little one. Still holding on still trusting in spite of all of your tears.
Have you let me down Jesus? Have you?...crying....
No my little one I will never let you down. I will never fail. Never. My little one I am looking after you. I am caring for you and giving you everything that you need. I am healing you and helping you and making you strong in me. I have not forgotten my promises to you my little one. They are not gone. They are real and true just as I am real and true. Hold on my little one and do not give up hope. I am with you. Always.

I wasn't sleeping well and I was very tired. I was getting lost and felt like somehow pearl wasn't even real, that Jennifer was the real one, that work and all of those things were real and nothing else was. It was making me feel very sad and like there wasn't any point in continuing. But talking with daddy Mike helped me realize that even in the middle of my struggle with despair that I wasn't done yet. That I still wanted to follow Jesus.

Hello my daddy
After we talked yesterday I started to see something. Jesus is all about choices isn't he. I wondered if one of the reasons I am here living this life is because he wanted me to know what my choice is. Because I could settle for this life. I could do this. Live an ordinary life as Jennifer and in some ways it wouldn't be so bad. Maybe some people would think so. It would be easier in some ways. Less painful and frightening. I see that. It helps to see the choice I think and I saw it clearer than I have before when we were talking yesterday. But what I know is that I don't want this life. I have never wanted it. Jesus kept me alive for a reason. He has healed me for a reason. It isn't so I can clean hotel rooms is it, or any other normal job. It doesn't matter what the job is. So I talked to him about it this morning.

Hi Jesus.
Hello, my dearest little one.
Tell me about what I am seeing.
My little one I will always give you a choice. To follow me or not. Sometimes my little one I will ask you to follow me not knowing what it is you are choosing but sometimes my little one it is necessary that you should know clearly the choice you are making, the difference is my dearest one that the harder the choice the clearer it must be. This is to help you my little one so that when it gets difficult there is no question in your mind about the choice you have made. It is set and it is certain and so you will be able to continue no matter what is happening around you.
Is that what you are doing?
It is part of what I am doing my little one. This life is yours to choose. You can remain

here and live this life my little one I will continue to love you and care for you and to heal you as you are willing to accept it. I will work through you for good my little one and I will touch lives through you as I am doing now but you will never see the fullness of my promises my little one or fully become the person you were created to be. This is your choice my little one. If you choose to continue on the path I have for you I will lead you from this place my little one just as I have promised but it will not be easy. This means you need to be sure and certain about the choice you make my little one so that you have the strength to continue when it gets hard.

So..is this part of what you mean when you say you are making me stronger. You are making my choice stronger by showing me what I could have if I settled?

Yes my little one.

I see. Well...it's not so bad I suppose...I could do it but no way Jesus. No way. I couldn't do it. It's not my choice. My choice is to follow you with my whole heart and not stop before I've seen all of your promises. Nothing else will do Jesus. Nothing…Crying

I know my little one I know but you needed to know it also. My little one there are many choices you will need to make along the way and I will always help you to choose my way but I will always give you free choice my little one because I love you. I will never force you to follow me my little one. The cost is too great. Even though the reward is far greater the choice needs to be yours my little one.

I will never choose this Jesus. Don't leave me here...Crying.....

No my little one I will not. I will lead you from this place. The time is coming and it is coming soon my little one. I am making you ready in all the ways that you need. Be content to follow my little one. Your choice is made and that is good. It is very good.

Maybe I have been wavering a bit Jesus but only because I've been losing hope.

Hope is not lost my little one it is always with you.

I can do this life for a little bit longer if you want Jesus but please hurry up because I will.. not make it otherwise.….Crying

Yes my little one you will because you will be ready. I will not let you fall my little one. I am holding you and loving you through this. All the things you are longing for will come my little one. All of them will come.

But it is all about you Jesus not about me……Crying

No my little one it is about us. Together. You and I. Pearl Sunshine. That is who you are my little one.

I think you are too good to me Jesus.

My love will never fail my little one not ever. My little one I am your strength and your hope and I will never leave you. You are my pearl and I am your sunshine and we will do so many great and wonderful things together.

I hope so Jesus….Crying

My little one are you ready for a great and wonderful adventure?

Only you know Jesus but I want to be. Please….Please…..Crying

My little one do not fear what lies ahead for you. I am with you in it. We go together my little one. You and I. We will never be separated.

I'm sorry I've been so…..but I didn't see. …Crying

Please let it be time…Please….I don't know how you can make it work. Not for Sophie and Richard but I have been remembering about the Holy Spirit broom. How you can clear the path before us Holy Spirit...all of us. Please do it. Do it now…Do it now. Let it be time…Crying

My child my dearest child so many things are before you. Good things. I will make all of them possible. There is nothing that can stand in your way my little one. Do you believe this?

Yes, except I worry I won't have the strength when there are so many difficult things I have to face.

Yes my little one there are and that is why we have been helping you to grow strong enough.

Yes….but I choose to face them anyway because that is the way I am going.

That's good my little one. That is very good. My little one your heart belongs to us. You are precious my little one. We long to see you living the life we have for you. We long to see you fly my little one. Hold on and keep trusting. You are our child. Wholly and completely loved just as you are. Everything we have promised is before you my little one. All you must do is trust and follow.

Yes…but it will be so hard.

Sometimes my little one but we are your strength and everything you need. You will know what it is to run in the sunshine my little one. You will know what it is to give and receive the fullness of our love. We are making you all that you can be my little one. The way is not easy but it is worth it.

Only you know….Crying

Yes my little one we know. Come sit with daddy for a while. He has something for you my little one.

Daddy…..Crying

My child. My dearly beloved child.

I was sitting on Jesus lap in the middle of rainbow crystals. They were so beautiful all around us.

My little one do you know why I have called you here?

No. Did you?

Yes my little one it is because I have something to give to you.

What is it daddy? It is like a giant rainbow bubble.

Look inside my little one what do you see?

It is like a snow globe. Is that the city?

Yes my little one it is your city. Given to you by us with love.

I know I don't understand.

Will you accept it my little one. My gift to you?

Yes daddy….Crying

The city is yours my little one but it will not be taken without many battles. You are strong enough my little one because we are with you. All of us. We will never leave you. This is our gift to you. It can never be taken from you but how much of the city becomes filled with our light depends on the choices you make my little one. Never forget that. You are our child and you carry our light with you wherever you go. We will help you with every choice you must make my little one just as we have always done. Rest now my little one. Rest in who we are. We are making you ready for a great and wonderful journey where all the things we have spoken of will be fulfilled as you continue to choose to follow. It will not be too much for you though it will be hard at times. We will strengthen you and help you my little one but the choice is always yours. To follow or not.

I choose you. Help me to choose you. I forget and get lost. But I always want to choose you….Crying

I know you do my little one. I see your heart.

It belongs to you daddy.

Yes my little one it does. Rest then my little one. You are loved and you are safe and everything is in our hands.

The thing I struggle with most is believing it will ever happen. The thought that I will have to settle for this life makes me want to die and I am afraid of losing hope so I will accept that this life is all there is. That is what I struggle with day after day. That is why I get depressed. I am sorry if I made you worry I was going to settle. I never want to do that. How could I do that when I am Pearl? There is no place for me here. I am irrelevant. That is a very bad thing to have to live with. Thankyou for helping me and praying for me. Don't stop. Hugs from Pearl.

But no matter what Jesus said I seemed to be trapped in a circle of despair. I would feel better for a little while and then I would sink again and just want to die. I was still struggling to believe in the promises. For me the promise was the only reason I had to keep going. I loved Sophie and Richard very much and wanted to be there for them. I didn't want them to lose their mum, but without the promise everything I had gone through had been for nothing and there was no reason to keep living. There was no place for me in normal life, not as Pearl Sunshine and I didn't want to be anyone else. Even when I believed the promises could be true I was struggling to believe I could keep waiting, because I was so unhappy in my everyday life.

> I don't think I've been doing very well. I've just been getting depressed and losing hope and crying.
> **My little one even though you are here in this pool with me you are also in a great battle. The enemy of your soul does not what you to become everything you were created to be. They will try to convince you in every way they can that there is no hope for you, that there is no way out of the place that you are in but that is not so my little one. You walk with me. Nothing can stand in my way.**
> No of course not Jesus. I just need to remember who you are..
> **Yes my little one you do.**
> I want to live the adventure with you Jesus. I know I am in a lot of ways. I couldn't do any of this without you it's just not a very exciting or enjoyable adventure right now. **Not most of the time anyway.**
> I know my little one but until you are strong enough you need to remain here with me. **My dearest little one I am making you strong enough to follow me anywhere I will go. That is not an easy thing my little one. It requires complete trust and dependence.**
> I think I will be here a long time.
> **No my little one the time is near. Keep trusting. Keep hoping. I am making you all you can be.**
> It is true what I said to daddy. I am irrelevant here. No one wants to feel like that.
> **You are not irrelevant to me my little one no matter where you are. You are my pearl and will always be so.**
> I suppose you don't make irrelevant people.
> **No my little one I don't.**

Chapter 20

The Festival of the Crow

I was still feeling tired, things were busy at work and I was trying to be supportive to the people I loved, so many of them were having a hard time. The arthritis in my hips and my hands was causing me pain and keeping me awake and I was having bad dreams. Jesus said it was time for more healing and he took me back into a memory in the caves with the Goatman. It was very bad.

My little one I am holding you and giving you my strength You are loved and you are safe my little one. Everything is in my hands. Everything is in my control. All the things you are longing for will come my little one. Hold on a little longer and let me love you and heal you. I will bring you through this my little one.
I need you to help me Jesus...crying….
My little one I will always help you. Where are you my little one?
Here in the pool with you.
And what do you see?
The water is full of rainbows. The air is warm and sunshiny and I can smell flowers and it is all beautiful and peaceful.
Yes my little one and which is most real this or the world that you see with all of it's trouble and pain?
They are both real Jesus…crying…..
Yes my little one they are but this is the reality which will last. This is the reality which determines the future my little one not the one that you see.
Explain that.
My dearest one true reality is not the one you see with your eyes. True reality is defined by me. This is your place hidden in me where you are safe and you are loved. Nothing can change this place my little one it is yours given to you by me. Hidden in who I am. The reality you see with your eyes is temporary my little one. It does not tell you anything about the true nature of things unless you have the eyes to see it. Unless you look into and through the things that are happening to see the true reality behind them.
Yes. Like when I see you in the things that happen...like when that man gave me some water yesterday that was you looking after me….crying….
Yes my little one it was it. Learning to see true reality will help you my little one because it is truth. So much of what you see with your eyes is not truth my little one.
No. Is this helping Jesus?...crying….
Yes my little one it is because no matter what is going on around you, you are here with me and even though you are suffering and in pain still you are here with me safe in my arms. Loved and wanted. You are my pearl my little one and that will not ever change.
Ok…but I am still a mess. Why am I such a mess?...crying……
My little one I am healing you and changing many things both on the inside and on the outside. You are here with me my little one but that does not mean nothing is happening. I am making all things new my little one.
Tell me about that Jesus. I don't feel new. I feel awful…crying….
My little one as you rest here with me I am changing you. I am changing you my little one so that you are ready to receive all that I have for you. I am removing everything that would stand in the way of that. That is painful my little one. It means that you will feel weak for a time but it is not bad thing. It is a good one. My little one as I heal you, you will remember things that have been hidden from you. New memories of the past my little one but it will also help you to be at peace with past far more so then you have been able my little one. In order for you to speak with and share your journey

with others the past must be a place where you can go without fear my little one. I do not say there will be no pain for you in the things that happened but there will be no fear. I am making this possible for you my little one so that when the fear is gone you will be able to share who I am with my children who need to know the truth. My dearest little one I am giving you all that you need for this journey. You do it in my strength and not your own.

So there is more memory work to do?

Yes my little one there is.

How am I going to do that on top of all the stuff that is happening?…crying…..

In my strength my little one. One day at a time. My little one you are strong enough in me to withstand all the storms that are coming. You are able my little one because I make you so.

When I am weak then you are strong.

Yes my little one I am always enough for you.

So it was time for more healing. I hadn't really expected that. It felt like I was struggling enough already but I trusted that Jesus knew what I needed and what I could cope with.

I spent time with him later to do some healing and I remembered something else from the caves, a new thing. I think probably they are all going to be cave memories. I was very young. I think about three. I was just wearing a vest but then they...I'm not sure who...took it off me so I was bare. It was very cold. I had to sit on this rock shelf with two other little girls. We were waiting. Then the Goatman came from under the rock shelf...maybe it was a tunnel or a cave under there I don't know. He came to us and we had to stand up.

He chose one of the other girls. She had long blond hair. They took her away and we sat down again. When they brought her back she was dressed in black and wearing a mask made of black feathers. We watched while the Goatman stood her on a rock that was maybe an altar. He took his knife and he cut her throat and they collected the blood in a bowl. They took her body and put it on the floor I think, but I could still see her. Then they got me and the other girl and stood us on the alter and they drew symbols and letters on us with the girls blood and then they gave us both feather masks like the girl had. I thought he was going to kill me like he did the other girl. I wanted him to. I wanted to die even though I was so afraid. I knew that other girl died because of me and I wanted to die. But I didn't. I don't understand what happened. I didn't talk to Jesus about it I just cried and cried while he held me.

It felt like too much to do this kind of healing when outside life was so hard. I needed Jesus to help me see. I couldn't see anything good in what was happening or in what he was doing but he talked to me and encouraged me, even though I didn't want any more memories of the past, they seemed never ending.

My little one your heart is strong in me. I am making you new my little one so that the things of the past have no hold on you no matter how painful they might be.

Tell me what you mean Jesus.

My little one the things that happened to you have shaped you in many ways. They have told you many things about yourself and the world that are not true. They have shaped your thoughts and your feelings. They have broken your ability to trust and make friendships. They have broken your ability to hope and to dream. They made you believe that you are bad and worthless and that good things are not for you. They formed spiritual ties to the enemy which have made you vulnerable to him in many ways, they have kept you bound my little one in so many different ways. As I have healed you I have been setting you free from the lies and the fear and all the things that have held you. You are able my little one to love and to trust others in a new and deeper way. You are able to hope and believe for a future that is not like the past. You know who you are my little one. You are not bad you are innocent. You are my child and you are loved and you are safe. That is why I say I am making you new my little one because the things of the past no longer shape you. I say who you are my little one not anything that has happened to you, not the past with all of its pain and fear and not the present with all of its struggles and difficulties. You are my pearl. Free to be who you are even in a world which for the most part will not understand or accept you. Safe, hidden in who I am. That is what I am doing my little one.

It is a big job Jesus.

Yes my little one but not too big. Not for me. My little one what you see as endless is coming to an end. I know my dearest little one that your heart is still full of pain and you do not yet see what I see ahead of you but you are able to keep on following if you are willing my little one.

What else would I do Jesus? There is nothing else for me except you….crying….

Every day was a big struggle. The mix of a difficult and unhappy outside life, all the things the people around me were going though, the healing that was happening and the ongoing attacks of the enemy were making me feel like I couldn't take one more step. I just wanted it all to end and I couldn't see any hope, but Jesus kept on telling me what he was doing and why, that is was all for a purpose.

I am teaching you how to live in this world my little one. How to be strong and true to who you truly are no matter what comes against you. No matter how hard or painful it is. No matter the frustrations or injustices that come your way. All of these things I am using to help you my little one to give you the strength you need for the life that is ahead of you. My little one you were made to live in the light of my love. To draw your strength from me just as the flower draws its life from the sun. You are my pearl I am your sunshine. I am teaching you how to live out of my strength and not your own my little one so that you are able to go and become who you were created to be. This world is not easy my little one. The storms that come your way will be many. There will be those who will oppose you and tell lies about you. Many things that will hurt you my little one but if you are able to live out of my strength you will overcome all of these things and you will be able to live out your life as the person you truly are not bound by the past or by others people's opinions of you but able to be the beautiful person you are hidden in me but revealed for all the world to see so that through you they might also see me and who I truly am my little one. It is a price worth paying no matter how it seems to you now.

I don't see it Jesus. I don't see how any of that can be. I don't feel like I could ever be that person. To me it seems like I will be trapped here forever and all the hopes and dreams are just that. That I am just kidding myself to think I could ever leave or be more than I am now. That you could work through me to do anything worth the cost. That Pearl Sunshine doesn't really exist. Help me Jesus I am not strong enough for this.

But I am my little one. I am strong enough to for you. For all the things that you must do and be. I am your strength my little one.

You will have to be Jesus…..crying….

My little one in all the things you have been through I have never once failed you. I have been your strength my little one. I have carried you when you were not strong enough to continue. I will not fail you now my little one. You are safe and you are loved and will always be so. My little one none of the things that are coming against you are beyond my control. All of the things you are struggling with, all the attacks of the enemy, every circumstance of your life is in my control my little one. I allow it because of all that I can do through it. Not because I do not care my little one or because I want you to suffer. Not because my promises are not true but because they are. I am making you new my little one so that you can live the life I have for you and I am using all the circumstances of your life to make that possible.
I just think you are going to have to change things soon Jesus because I can't keep doing this…..crying…..
I will not ask more of you than you can give my little one. Not ever.
I don't want this to be my life Jesus…crying…
I know my little one I know.
I want my daddy…crying…..
I know my little one I know. I have bound you together in love for a purpose my little one because of all that you can be to each other and together for me. My little one I know that it is hard for you to be so far away from him but he is with you always my little one. He does not forget you. He prays for you constantly asking for me to give you strength and hope and to make the way ahead clear for you.
You have given me good daddy….crying….
Yes my little one I have. Everything I give to you is good.
Please save me. Please…crying……
I will always save you my little one. You are my beloved one. I will not let you go. My little one write to your daddy. Tell him all that is happening. He has time for you my little one.
I don't want to be a bother Jesus.
You are not a bother my little one. Not ever.
I don't understand that.
I know my little one. I know. Write to him. Trust me. I will help him to see what he needs to see. I will help him to know the way ahead for both of you. Everything is in my hands my little one.
I just wish you would hurry up Jesus before I give up….crying….
You are my child my little one. I will not let you fall.
That's how it feels. That I am hanging on by my fingertips and if you don't hurry up and pull me out I will fall.
But I am holding you my little one. Even if you were to let go you would not fall.
Please hurry up. I have no idea how you can make it possible for me to leave but I can't stay here any longer. It is killing me…crying…..
No my little one it is making you stronger as you learn to depend on who I am. I know my dearest one that you do not see this and all you feel is pain and desperation but I am your strength my little one. You are safe and you are loved. There is nothing to fear.
I know it is up to you Jesus. I can't change any of it.
No my little one you can't.
I'm sorry.
Keep your eyes fixed on me my little one. Remember where you are. You are safe in my arms in the land of rest. No matter what life is bringing you that is where you are.
I suppose dependence and rest are kind of the same thing.
Yes my little one except rest is dependence without fear.
Yes. I suppose it is.
I am helping you my little one. I will make it possible for you to rest in who I am.
What about the healing?

That will continue my little one if you are willing.
It seems like too much on top of everything else Jesus. But I suppose you know.
Yes my little one I do. It will help you my little one.
The festival of the crow…. Is that Halloween?
Yes my little one it is the same day though not exactly the same celebration.
Is that ..the set of memories you want to heal?
Yes my little one it is.
Ok. Help me then.
I will help you my little one. You are my beloved child. I am bringing you life.
Later then.
Yes my little one.

All the new memories seemed to be from one event from different years, something they called the festival of the crow. I suppose that is why I and others were wearing black feathers. This was new to me but I realized it was connected to Halloween in some way. Even though I knew that some of my memories were probably from Halloween I hadn't known which ones before now.

I was struggling. The people around me were struggling. I felt like I was in a dark cloud and it was hard to see hope for me or for anyone else but I was understanding something better. The new memories I had helped me to see that the cults and their practices weren't new. They had been going on for hundreds perhaps thousands of years. The kind of practices that went on long before Christianity had brought new beliefs and practices. I hadn't seen that before. It helped me see how my story fitted into history, it made more sense, it made it more real.

Hi Jesus.
Hello, my dearest little one.
Is there hope Jesus? Not just for me.
Yes my little one there is hope.
Tell me about hope.
My little one this world and its people were not created to live in darkness they were created to live in the light of who I am. I am their hope my little one just as I am yours. Everything I gave to this world on the cross is available to anyone who is willing to accept it. That is hope my little one. To move from the darkness into the light. To replace fear with love and to know and understand just who you are. That is hope.
And you want me to bring your light into the darkness.
Yes my little one I do.
But first you need to fill me with your light and set me free from the darkness that is still holding me.
Yes my little one I do for whilst the past is still holding you in any way you will not be truly free to bring my light to others.
I understand that Jesus.
I know you do my little one.
Can you do it?
Yes my little one I am able to do all things.
And what must I do?
Trust me my little one and be willing to follow me in all things.
What if I can't?
I will make it possible for you.
Everywhere I look is pain and mess Jesus. It ..makes it hard to hope but I suppose none of that changes who you are.
No my little one and what you see as pain and mess I see as opportunities for life and hope to take hold. I know my dearest one it is hard for you to see those you love suffer but I am with them my little one. They do not suffer alone.

But they don't know that Jesus. Just like I didn't know it.

No my little one they don't and that is why you must take your story out into the darkness of this world so that they can know it. So that the light of my love can touch their lives and begin to bring light and hope where there has been darkness and despair.

How will I do that Jesus?

Through your books through your life, through the things that you will say and do my little one just as I direct and lead you.

I suppose you can work anything out Jesus. I feel so sad for Sophie and Richard. Their lives aren't what they should be.

No my little one they aren't but I am with them and will help them.

I know I get lost Jesus. I know I don't always see. But I am seeing better today I think. Daddy helps me a lot.

Yes my little one that is why he is given to you. To help you and love you and to work with you to bring my light to many who are lost in the darkness.

I think seeing that the things that happened to me weren't new. That those practices go back thousands of years helps somehow. It makes it more real and more understandable. Kind of more connected. Like it fits at last. That is our darkness, that was what you came to save us from. Kind of. That is who we are without you. People I suppose won't see that because our world is based on Christianity and its values but before that it wasn't and that is what it was and will be again probably. I don't know. It is hard to think we could go that direction, maybe it may look different but it is kind of the same darkness. Like abortion takes over from child sacrifice. So maybe the darkness is the same it just looks different on the surface, and the darkness seems like light...like maybe it did way back for the pagans and what they do seems acceptable just like it did for them. It is making more sense to me now Jesus. I think that helps. It helps with the past and it helps with the future and seeing the world through your eyes. I think I don't see it all but I see better.

Yes my little one you do see better and this will continue my dearest one as you learn more about the past and are able to move forward from it.

As I am set free.

Yes my little one.

Is there more healing to do?

Yes my little one there is if you are willing.

I want you to do what you want Jesus. No matter how much I cry and fight and complain I want you to have your way. But I need your help. Today I see but tomorrow I might not.

I know my little one I know.

So the memories continued and the healing continued. I held on to Jesus and he loved me through it.

You are my Pearl

But I don't know what that looks like or what I can do or who I can be in the world Jesus.

I know you don't my little one but you are still trying to see yourself through the eyes of others. See yourself through my eyes my little one. That is who you truly are.

But why does it matter who I truly am if I can never be that person Jesus. If I have to live out my life being someone else. That is ...not freedom.

No my little one it isn't which is why I am working to set you free from all the things that are holding you so that you can be the person you truly are.

I don't ...understand really Jesus. How can I ever be free to be me?

My little one even though there are many things in this life that keep you from expressing who you truly are, from being seen as my pearl, that time will come just as it did for me. You must be ready my little one. Just as my father made me ready so you must be made ready.

I suppose you did go a long time before you were recognized for who you are. I suppose that first happened at your baptism.

Yes my little one it did. When my father declared openly who I was. That was my time my little one and I had to wait for it just as you have to wait for yours. I had to remain hidden my little one and I was not able to be who I truly was, not in the full sense but that did not change who I was my little one. It did not change my purpose. It didn't change anything it was only meant I had to wait for my time.
I think you were better at waiting than me.
Yes my little one I was but I did not have the fear that you carry.
Why am I still afraid Jesus?
Because you still need my healing my little one. That is what I am doing. I do not want you to be afraid. Not of anything.
But, the healing doesn't ever end Jesus. I won't ever get to my time if you are waiting for that.
Yes my little one you will. Spend time with me my little one and allow me to heal you and to love you. I am making a way for you my little one.
I know I am all over the place Jesus. I know I should be better at trusting you.
You are holding on to me my little one through many storms. Keep trusting my little one. That is all you must do.
One day at a time
Yes my little one. One day at a time.

Everything seemed difficult and overwhelming. I was still struggling at work. Even though it was better in a lot of ways I still didn't want to be there. I didn't see why I had to stay doing a job that made me so very tired, doing something I didn't really enjoy for not very much money. I asked him many times if I could leave but he always said no.

But I still have to go to work.
Yes my little one for now you do.
Can't I get another job?
No my little one that would not help you.
Why not?
Because this job is the one I have chosen for you. It is helping you to become all that you can be.
It is making me depressed.
It is causing you to hold on to me and draw your strength from me. It is leading you to new places of trust of dependence.
Because it is awful.
Because you find it difficult in many ways my little one.
I have to go.
But not alone my little one. I will be with you.

He was so patient through all of my tears and tantrums. He knew what I didn't and even in the middle of all my struggles I understood that. I didn't like or appreciate it a lot of the time though.

Hi Jesus...crying
Hello my little one
I don't know what I'm doing Jesus. Life seems full of giant hills. I want to get away and I can't. Please. Please...crying.....
My little one hold on to who I am. Remember who you are.
That doesn't help. Remembering who I am makes it all worse. If I pretend to myself I am Jennifer...it's bad but not as bad. I can't do this...crying…
My little one you are doing it. Each and every day you are living this life in my strength. You do not see or understand what I am doing my little one but I am making a way for you to become all that you were created to be. That comes through healing my little one but it also comes through living your life. Through giving yourself to me

day after day depending upon who I am and not of anything of yourself. I know who you are my little one. I know what it is costing you to be here but I tell you that it is worth it because of all that I am doing both in you and through you. You do not yet know the fullness of all that I have planned for you my little one but you are my light in a dark and broken world. I will enable you to shine for me as few have shone before. That is because of who I am making you to be through all the things that you have suffered and all the things that you are suffering. I know you do not understand my little one but trust me. Trust me to be enough for you when you cannot stand on your own. Trust me to lead you forward when you cannot see the way ahead trust me to bring good out of everything you have suffered my little one. I am making you strong enough to do and be everything you were created for. That is not a small thing my little one it is a great and wonderful thing. Hold on and do not give up hope. There is great joy before you my little one.

I can't live on promises Jesus. They don't come. I will be here forever living as Jennifer and wanting to die. Why would you do that to me if you love me?...crying….

Because that is not what I am doing my little one.

I can't do it Jesus.

Yes my little one you can. One day at a time.

Why can't I just die?...crying…

For the sake of all that is to come my little one. Hold on to me. Trust me. Just a little longer.

I wasn't doing well with life but at least Jesus said that the healing was finished for now. Things didn't get easier though.

Chapter 21

Choosing Life

I had a dream. In the dream I had a tiger. He was my companion. He was fierce but somehow tame. I knew he could turn on me at any time but I kept him around. He was kind of soft and comforting. Then a lion joined him, his friend. I wasn't sure about the lion. It seemed more threatening somehow but it didn't do anything to me. But I decided I wasn't safe and I went into a room and tried to close the door to keep them out. But I couldn't do it. They were too strong.

I knew it was a warning dream. A message from the Holy Spirit about what the enemy was doing. That they were pretending to be my friends, offering comfort and making me less wary. And because I'd let them in I wouldn't be able to keep them out. I listened and talked to Jesus about it but then forgot again in the middle of everything. So I suppose it wasn't a surprise that the enemy were able to take me to the brink, not for the first time.

I was sinking further and further feeling like I was stumbling around in the dark and not able to see anything good. I kept talking to Jesus but somehow nothing he said made any difference. I wasn't listening. I stopped sending letters to daddy Mike. I didn't see the point, I wasn't sure he was listening. I told myself (or maybe I was being told) that it didn't matter what I did or didn't do there was no hope anyway.

Hi my daddy
Another letter I won't send. But never mind. I don't feel safe. It is a long time since I felt so unsafe. I don't feel safe because I don't trust myself. I don't trust myself not to lose hope completely. Maybe it doesn't matter. Maybe the point is to trust Jesus and not me. I suppose I am as safe as I have ever been. But I don't feel it. After all this time and all the things that Jesus has done I am still all alone. When I am in trouble and think of ending it or hurting myself who can I call? No one. Who is there to put their arms around me and comfort me? No one. Maybe that's not the point. The point is I am supposed to be light in the darkness but right now I feel a bit like a black hole. All around me everyone is in trouble and I am supposed to bring hope to them but I can't because I don't even have any for myself. Even after all this time.

Reading what Jesus was saying and doing a year ago made me so depressed. It was more of the same. Promises that don't come. How long do I keep hoping and trusting and waiting? And yet I know Jesus is real. I know what he's done. I know what it is to be loved and comforted by him but somehow I have lost hope in him. I don't know. It is a long time since I asked him to go faster. I used to ask him all the time to go faster. I must have had more hope then. Now I don't think about it. There is no point running to go nowhere. There's no reason to hurry when nothing will change. I still must be clinging on because I am still writing the book...a bit. I am still writing these letters just in case. I am still breathing. But for how long? It is like having a leak. I feel like not so far away all the hope will have gone and I will be empty. Will Jesus save me? He has saved me so many times before. But do I want him to? I don't want to keep on going round and round. That is like running to nowhere. Endless circles of falling down and getting saved. Why? I don't know. Only if he is who he says and will do what he's promised. I think of...apart from ending it...I think of what I would like to do the kind of life I would like to have if it was just me. Where would I go? What job would I do? Who would I be? I think about it but then I know that without Jesus it would be meaningless. I couldn't do it. Life has to be lived with him and for him or not at all. It's just I don't think I can't do this anymore. And I am back to the beginning again not feeling safe because it is like I am walking on the edge of a cliff that I can't quite see. And I know I could fall off any minute. I think that is all I have to say right now. It is enough isn't it. I wish I was with you daddy. It would be different then. But I am here all alone. Bye.

Jesus kept on encouraging me and reminding me that the enemy didn't want me to follow him. That they were trying to destroy me with their lies but I was safe in his arms. I held on but I felt like I was going to fall any moment. I stopped believing I was going to make it. But no matter how I was feeling somehow I must have been moving forward, even if I was crawling.

Jesus came and met me. There was music playing and disco lights. I was wearing a long sequin dress in blue and green and Jesus was wearing matching a sequin shirt and flared trousers which made me laugh even though I was crying a lot. I didn't want to dance but he kept on spinning me round and lifting me up. He was smiling and I was crying. It was kind of fun though and I like to dance with Jesus. But I cried too much and in the end we sat on the ground which was grass and I sat in his lap and cried for while.

Why do you think we are dressed like this my little one?
I don't know. They seem like party clothes to me. Like a celebration.
Yes my little one they are. My dearest one it has taken you much time and many tears to reach this place. You have given yourself to me over and over again. You have fought and you have struggled and overcome many things in the strength that I have given you. It has not been for nothing my little one. It has brought you to this place

I could see that we were overlooking the city. It was nighttime and there were twinkling lights and it looked pretty.

I don't see what's so great about this place Jesus….Crying.
You are poised my little one on the brink of all that I have for you. It is time to celebrate my little one because the city is before you and you are able to go through its gates and do and be all that I have promised you. It is a time to celebrate my little one.
I think that you are cruel sometimes……Crying.
No my little one I am not it is only that I see what you do not see. My little one I have not led you all this way just to leave you here. I have not asked all that I have asked of you so that you could live this life. My little one that is not who I am. I have promised you many things my little one and all of them are real and true.
But you have said so many times that, I was at this place. And I never was.
There have been many times my little one when you were beginning a new phase of your journey with me. When one part was ending and another was beginning. They were all important my little one and all of them have led you to this place. I know my dearest one that you and others have often wanted to believe that you were at this place when you were not but I never once lied to you or misled you my little one your journey with me has been in many stages. There have been many paths for you to follow and many times when it seemed to you that you must have reached this place. But now you are here my little one and it is time to leave the pool and begin walking forward once again.
I don't see why. I haven't done very well at resting.
But I have given you all that you need my little one.
I don't know what you mean. Wasn't I supposed to have written the book in the pool?
You have begun my little one and your writing will continue as you walk with me.
Where are we going?
To the city my little one.
We have always been going to the city. Where are we going before then?
The road that we are following leads directly to the city my little one. We are not going anywhere else.
What about all the other paths?
All the paths are joined together at this point my little one all that you are doing, all that I am doing have come together so that you can walk with me into the future we

have for you into all that we have promised you. This is the time my little one when you will begin to move forward into the new life we have for you. There is a journey to be taken my little one and still much to be accomplished but this is the path that you are now on.
So it is still a long, long way to the city and I shouldn't expect to be there any time soon.
You should expect that that is where you are heading my little one and that all that we are asking of you is to make that possible.
I don't know why you tell me these things.
To help you my little one. That is all.
But for me nothing will change.
Yes my little one it will. As you walk with us everything will change for you.
One day. I don't know what you want from me Jesus. If it is even you. I have got it wrong to many times. I can't leave here. I can't ever leave here……Crying.
I know my little one that it is hard for you to see and understand why I have led you this way and you do not yet see the path that is before your feet. I know that you have been so very disappointed many, many times and that hope seems like a cruel gift. But my love for you is unbounded my little one and I will make it possible for you to reach the city.
I don't like it. I don't like it when you say these things…..Crying.
See my little one the sun is rising over the city. No more darkness for you my little one. No more despair. Hope is come. It is come my little one.
You are so unkind to me. You are so unkind….Crying.
No my little one I am not. I am not unkind. Not ever.
You are making me hope again for something that isn't going to happen. That is unkind…..Crying.
I am helping you to hope for what will come my little one. That is not unkind.
The journey has been too hard. I can't do it…Crying..
Yes my little one you can. You can do all things with me. All things my little one. You have walked through many dark places, many difficult and dangerous places to get to this place my little one. You are able to walk with me no matter where I will take you. You have learned to trust and to hold on through the fiercest of storms. You have grown strong in me and in who you are. You are able my little one to take hold of the promises which are given to you for the sake of all that is to come my little one.
I don't think you are talking about me....Crying…
I had turned my back in the city and was on my hands and knees in the grass crying and crying.
Or I wouldn't be crawling around in the grass crying……Crying..
Your struggles do not make you weak my little one. They are the very things that enable you to hold on to me and draw your strength and courage from who I am.
I don't like you.
Yes my little one you do. Come stand to your feet and face the future I have for you. It is good my little one and full of hope.
Crying..
So I stood up and looked at the city in front of me. It is big.
I don't know what to do with that Jesus.
I know my little one but you walk one step at a time with me. You are not alone my little one. Will you walk with me? Will you come?
I sat down again and kept on crying…It's just a trick.
Jesus squatted down in front of me and held out his hand.
No my little one it is not. Be strong and courageous. Take my hand my little one and walk with me.
I don't like you….Crying..
Come.

So I got to my feet and took his hand and started walking down the slope towards the city. I noticed the sequins were gone and we were wearing long robes with belts that I think have things on them useful things maybe but I didn't see what they were.

We are wearing travelling clothes now.
Yes my little one for the next part of the journey is begun. Stay close my little one. You have everything you need. Do not be afraid.
I am only afraid it's a trick.
I know my little one I know.

I was very afraid it was a trick and that even though it seemed like the city was so close it would turn out to be still out of reach for me. I tried my hardest to work out how I could keep going when I was so afraid of a disappointment I didn't believe I could survive.

Hi Jesus.
Hello my little one.
I have made a decision Jesus. A choice. I hope I can stick to it.
Tell me your choice my little one.
I am going to trust you. I am going to believe with my whole heart that this is it. We are walking towards the city. I am not going to tell myself it isn't true and I am going to let myself think about it and plan for it and do all the things you ask me to. I am going to talk to daddy about it and treat it like it's really happening. I am not going to live in fear of it not being true. I don't know how long I will be able to do it for Jesus before I go back to being afraid again. I don't want to but I know if nothing happens I probably will. And if this turns out to be another disappointment I won't survive it. I choose not to survive it. So maybe that is two choices. Maybe choosing not to survive it helps takes the fear out of the being disappointed again, because if I am it's the last time. I expect that's not an especially good way to follow or trust you but I think it's the best I can do right now. The tricky thing is knowing when time is up. I suppose that will just happen.
My little one I want you to trust me with all that you are with nothing held back. I will not fail you my dearest one but you are still trying to protect yourself and keep yourself safe from the disappointment that you fear is coming.
I know I am Jesus but it's the best I can do. At least this way I will be able to not be afraid for a little while…crying…
Do you think that is what I want for you my little one? That you should only be able to follow me if you know that you can give up when you decide that I have failed you.
No. It is me trying to be in control and saying this far and no further but I don't know what else to do because I am afraid. I am afraid it's made up and I won't survive this. I can't bear another disappointment. It will be the end for me. But if.. You are who you say and you aren't lying to me then I want to run with you. I don't want to be dragging my feet and being afraid. And the only way I can stop being afraid is to know that it is the end. One way or another. All or nothing now Jesus. All or nothing. I have done my best. I have given you everything I can. I have kept on following. There is nothing in me that believes I can keep on going if this turns out to be…not me leaving here. So if I just accept that…and give everything I have to you again and trust you…it helps somehow. It's the best I can do Jesus….crying...
I will take you from this place my little one. Will you follow as I lead you?
I will Jesus. For as long as I can. I don't know how long that will be so you might want to go fast. Show me what to do and help me do it. Help me with everything you are. One last push. Let's sprint to the line Jesus. No more messing. No more waiting because I won't make it if you do.

I was trying so hard but I fell down day after day, losing hope but somehow holding on. I suppose it was Jesus holding on to me because I didn't seem to have any strength or belief left. I just felt desperate and alone and like it was only a matter of time before I reached the end.

My little one all of your days I have watched over you. I have wept for you my little one, many tears, but this is not a time for weeping this is a time for rejoicing for the desert that has been your life is about to be transformed my little one. You do not know the day or the hour but I do. It is coming my little one and when it does your life will be everything I have promised you. The fountain will be filled to overflowing and your garden will be full of life. You will be with your daddy my little one and you will tell your story to those who most need to hear it.
Crying…
I know my little one that you are tired of hearing this when you do not yet see any signs of it coming but I am with you my little one. I give you all the strength that you need. Don't give up.
Even though what Jesus had shown me and what he had said should have filled me with hope it didn't. Mostly I was thinking I was being set up for anther crushing disappointment and I didn't think I would survive it. I tried over and over to choose to run as hard as I could with Jesus towards the city, but it was like I took a couple of steps and then fell on the ground crying because the effort was just too much. I so wanted to talk to my daddy and tell what was happening but when he came to Skype he said he could only stay half an hour. It was like the last straw. I told him he should go then and I refused to talk to him. I couldn't talk to him. I thought if I did I would lose control completely and then he would go and leave me and that would be even worse. So I wouldn't talk to him but kept crying. I didn't know how to cope with all the feelings I was having. In the end he said goodbye. I cried and cried and thought maybe I had reached my end.

I knew my only hope was to talk to Jesus. He told me to write to my daddy and not to lose hope or be afraid. I managed to do the first.

I am sorry daddy. I am messing up all over the place. I haven't been writing. I haven't been telling you how I am and I don't even know why. Except I asked Jesus to help me see and he is. Before we talked today I asked him to help you see what is happening in my heart, because I haven't been able to tell you. I suppose he did but not really in the way I was thinking. I am in so much trouble and I don't know what to do. I have written you letters and not sent them. I said to myself there was no point sending them but I think I am seeing now that it is because I somehow don't want you to help because I just want this to end. I don't want to keep on living like this. I don't want you or Jesus to give me hope, because then it will just go on and on and it won't ever end. And I can't do this any more I just can't. I have been drinking and cutting and I don't even know why. It doesn't make sense. It doesn't help. But it is like I am screaming inside but no one is listening. I suppose I think Jesus isn't paying attention because he keeps on asking me to keep living this life. And I can't do it anymore but he doesn't listen. So I am sorry if I couldn't talk. I couldn't say these things. I was trying to keep safe. I knew if I said anything I wouldn't be able to be ok in time for you to go. So I'm sorry. I hope you got help for your back. Love from Pearl.

I was in big trouble and I knew it. I had been warned in my chats with Jesus and in the dream that enemy was at work, but I hadn't paid enough attention. I had started to drink and to self-harm and I didn't care. I just wanted it to end.

Hi my daddy
I didn't do too well after we talked yesterday. I thought maybe that was it. That I was done. But I talked to Jesus and I wrote to you. I waited for you to write back but when you didn't, I felt bad for a little while and like I was all on my own. But then I thought my daddy loves me and if he didn't write to help me, it's because Jesus told him not to. And if Jesus told him not

to it's because he's going to save me. So then I had some hope that I was going to be ok. Jesus had me read the beginning of john 5.

> **Some time later, Jesus went up to Jerusalem for one of the Jewish festivals. Now there is in Jerusalem near the Sheep Gate a pool, which in Aramaic is called Bethesda and which is surrounded by five covered colonnades. Here a great number of disabled people used to lie, the blind, the lame, the paralyzed. One who was there had been an invalid for thirty-eight years. When Jesus saw him lying there and learned that he had been in this condition for a long time, he asked him, "Do you want to get well?" "Sir," the invalid replied, "I have no one to help me into the pool when the water is stirred. While I am trying to get in, someone else goes down ahead of me." Then Jesus said to him, "Get up! Pick up your mat and walk." At once the man was cured; he picked up his mat and walked.**
> **John 5 NIV**

He had me read it yesterday as well but I didn't take much notice but today I did. I heard the enemy first which didn't help, but I didn't give up because I was believing Jesus was going to save me. So I kept calling him and asking for help until I was sure it was him.

Do you want to be well my little one?
Yes Jesus I do.
Listen to the truth then my little one. Do not listen to lies. They bring only death.
Yes but so often I want to die.
Choose life my little one. Choose me.
Maybe, sometimes the life you've given me, it seems not worth living Jesus.
My life has purpose my little one. Always.
I just don't think I can do it…..Crying
My little one all the time you have been following me have I ever asked anything of you that you could not do?
No. Even if I thought so. I always did it.
Yes my little one you are living out of my strength and not your own. You are able to do all things in and through me.
I know I have been messing up. I know I have been listening to lies.
Do you want to be well my little one? Do you want to follow me into everything I have for you? Do you want to love those I give to you and help them to know they are loved by me? Do you want to enter the city with me knowing who you are and who I am and not being afraid of that? Do you want to be well my little one?
Are you my Jesus? Show me who you are.
Take my hand my little one.

I was expecting to see Jesus and take his hand but I saw something else instead. I saw my hand holding the hand of a skeleton wearing a black robe. I knew it was death. At first I was scared I was talking to the enemy, but then I realized what Jesus was showing me. That I was holding the hand of death. That is what I have been choosing and why I have been in trouble.

You need to let go of your desire for death my little one. Until you do that you cannot take hold of the life I am giving to you. Whilst you have one hand holding on to death I cannot lead you forward into the city. Let go my little one. Let go and trust me fully with all that you are.

I don't know how Jesus. Is that really what I'm doing?...Crying...
Yes my little one it is. It is your way of feeling safe and in control my little one but it is really controlling you. You are not safe in his hands my little one but only in mine.
Like I'm hedging my bets if you let me down….Crying..
Yes my little one but I will not fail you. Not ever.
I know I have been in a battle. I know I have been choosing death because it seems easier. Your way is so hard.
But I am with you in it my little one. Always.
Can I take your hand Jesus? Please….Crying..
Yes my little one but in order to take it you must first let go of deaths hand.

Jesus held out his hand but he was just out of reach. Death was still holding on to me. I had to let go to reach Jesus. So I pulled my hand out of deaths and jumped into Jesus arms. Death crumbled into dust.

Crying…
My little one you are my child. My dearly beloved child. I will help you with everything my little one. You have chosen life. Do not desire anything else. Do not listen to lies. Do not look to the darkness but only the light. You are safe in my arms my little one. You are ready for all that is to come. You are able to follow me even into the city if you are willing. Are you willing my little one?
Yes Jesus. I am willing.
My little one the path before you is clear. You are able to walk it with me. Trust is necessary my little one but it is not too much for you. You have everything you need.
Am I going to make it?
Yes my little one you are going to make it.
Is the city real? Is what I saw real Jesus are we walking towards it? I mean what I saw and heard last week?
Yes my little one that was real and true. We are walking towards the city my little one. This is the last part of your journey to the city gates.
I have been tricked so many times and got it wrong so many times.
I know my little one but now is the time to let go of your fear and to run with me toward everything I have for you. I will not fail you my little one. I am faithful and true and will do everything that I have promised you.
I know it takes faith Jesus but will you help me not to be afraid I am getting it wrong again.
You follow me my little one. I will not lead you wrong.

The last few weeks have been awful and the last week especially. I have gone backwards and forwards trying to trust and then deciding not to. I was convinced I wasn't going to make it. I felt afraid and unsafe. I just wanted it to be over. I hope it will be better now. It is hard to tell because I feel tired and sad and kind of beaten up. I hope you aren't sick of me. I need to keep writing, to let you in. I can't do this without you my daddy. I'm not meant to. I don't want to. I love you very much. Pearl.

I had chosen life and I felt much better than I had. I stopped drinking and cutting and held on to Jesus hand. I didn't want to fall back into the enemy's hands...but I was still finding it a struggle, to see the hope that Jesus said was before me and with me. He kept showing me though, moving me forward step by step, sometimes inch by inch.

My little one take my hand. What do you see?
The city.
Shall we move a little closer?
If you want to Jesus.
Come then my little one. I have something to show you.
The grass is covered in pink flowers. It reminds me of the mountain inside.
What was the mountain my little one?
We would go up there to see Jesus. To see the changes that were happening or to see what was ahead.
Yes my little one so what do you think this place is?
A place where we can look ahead?
Yes my little one if you are willing to see what I will show you.
Will it make a difference Jesus?
My little one everything I say and everything I do is to help you.
You are wonderful and I am so ungrateful all of the time...crying..
My little one the journey is hard and you are tired but this is to help you.
Ok. I see blue sky on the left and dark clouds on the right and the wind is blowing from left to right. The flags are blowing in that direction...crying...
Yes my little one what do you think that means?
That there is hope, hope of sunshine to come. It reminds me of the dream I had with the Holy Spirit broom...crying...
Yes my little one you have not yet seen all that we will do. All you have been able to see are the dark clouds my little one but that is not all there is. The wind of the spirit will blow away the dark clouds bringing change, bringing hope and new life. This is the beginning my little one. Not the end.
I'm sorry. I'm still having a lot of trouble with hope...crying...
I know my little one. Let us sit here for a little while and just watch. My dearest one there is nothing to fear. You journey with me. The way before us clear. All we must do is walk forward into the city.
It sounds so easy when you say it like that Jesus. But it's not easy. Not any of it.
Do you believe that I am able my little one?
Yes but there are a lot of buts going on for me.
Why would I bring you here my little one if you were not ready to go down into the city?
I don't know Jesus. But what is the journey? It looks just like a straight little walk but it won't look like that on the outside. And...I don't know.
My little one whatever comes against you cannot stand against me
What is it you want Jesus? What is this part of the journey for?
It is to take you into the city my little one. To prepare for what is ahead.
Is there healing to be done?
Some my little one, I am always healing you but there will be no new memories for you. There will be things to see and accept my little one but that is not the same.
So .. tell me about the journey Jesus. I don't know what to ask. Apart from the obvious how long and you will say not long and I will say you always say that and it always is so there

not much point to asking that.

My little one the preparation this far has seemed long to you for there has been much healing to do my little one and many things for you to see and learn and to grow in. You have followed me faithfully my little one through the darkest of times and it has brought you here and though there are dark clouds overhead they are clearing my little one.

These things you show me they do help me understand Jesus maybe in the best way and most clear way, but it never looks like I think it will on the outside and so I get disappointed and lose hope.

I know my little one.

I don't see how I can go. Mostly Sophie and Richard, both of them really, it will be hard on them.

At first my little one but it will also help them in many ways. I know my dearest one that you think you have to protect them from the pain of this life, but that is not possible my little one. What is possible is that you can help them walk through the pain just as I help you.

I expect that is right Jesus. But I don't know how to help them.

No my little one but I do. That is why you must trust me.

Well...so here we are Jesus. There is a big grassy slope to get down. Are we going to make a start?

Yes my little one if you are willing.

I am willing Jesus. I just don't know what it means.

It means you are walking with me into the promise my little one.

I don't want to be hoping for things that aren't coming Jesus. I get ..desperate and depressed because I don't want to be here and all of those things. It is a hard journey.

I know it is my little one and trust is required but you are able to walk this path with me. Come then my little one. Let us begin.

It looks so close Jesus but I know it can't be.

Think how far you have come my little one to reach this place. Time is not the same here but this is not a deception my little one. The city is close. Come.

So I was beginning the last part of my journey to the city. The clouds were clearing and I could see the way ahead. As I struggled to believe that hope was real Jesus reminded me of his story. It was Easter. He asked me to read the Easter story from John. It was hard to read about those things happening to Jesus and it made me cry, but he wanted to show me that there is hope. There is always hope because he is our hope.

You see my little one there is hope of life even after all the suffering you have endured. Death has no hold on you my little one. You are mine my beloved one and I have given you my life. It was not for nothing my little one that I suffered and died. Neither will it be so for you. My little one new hope is given to you each and every day to live out of my strength which is given to you. The things that come against you cannot prevail. There is nothing that can hold you as you give yourself to me. Your life, all that you are is hidden in who I am. That can never be taken from you. You are my child. The one I have called according to my great purpose. My dearest little one I have given you a purpose, one that is greater than all the suffering you have known, than you will ever know. My purpose in you is to shine for my glory. To show the world who I am though the story I have given you and through the life you will live.

Allow me to love you my little one and to give you the hope that you so desperately need. There is a life waiting for you that is so full of love and hope and joy my little one. You have not yet seen it but that does not mean it is not so. Just as my disciples wept because they did not see the hope that was before them you weep my

little one because you do not see or understand but their hope was real my little one. They did not see it but still it came just as yours will. You are my child, nothing that I am will ever be taken from you my little one. All that I am is given to you so that you can live out the purpose that is given to you knowing who you are and who I am in you. You walk with me my little one. Hand in hand through everything that this life brings. I am your Jesus. Your protector and your savior, your friend and your helper. Follow me and do not be afraid. I am with you always.

> "Because you have seen me, you have believed;
> Blessed are those who have not seen and yet have believed."
> John 20:29

Chapter 22

Soaking in His Presence

I had chosen life after a big battle, but the enemy wasn't giving up. I felt like I was having to make the same choice over and over again every day.

Hi Jesus.
Hello, my dearest little one.
I would...I am going to need a lot of help to keep on choosing life Jesus.
I know my little one but remember that I am life. You walk with me and towards me. Your life is hidden in who I am not in the things you see.
I would like to have this battle won Jesus. I don't feel like it is. I feel like I'm still being pulled. I don't know how to live the life you've given me without wanting to escape it. I know I am messed up. My life belongs to you. You say it has purpose and that your plans for me are good but mostly I still want it to stop.
No my little one you want it to be all that I have promised you but you still doubt that it will ever be so.
Yes. I do.
My little one when I gave myself for you I did so, so that you would have life. Life that is found in who I am. So that you could know me and love me and live out your life safe in the knowledge that you belong to me. I gave myself for you my little one so that you could receive my life and death would have no hold on you. Do not desire death my little one. It has no claim on you. You belong to me. My life is given to you so that you can truly live.
I don't know what that means really and I don't know how to live. I have spent my whole life wanting to die.
I know you have my little one and I understand. The pain of this life is hard to bear especially when life has brought so much pain my little one but that is not all that there is. In the midst of all the pain there is life my little one, there is hope and there is joy. I know my dearest one that it is hard for you to truly see this or to think that it makes the pain worth bearing but my little one the life that you are living leads to me. I am your life my little one.
I still don't understand.
My dearest one without me here is no life no hope no meaning and no purpose. You understand that.
Yes. I do understand that.
Then know my little one that everything that makes this life worth living is found in me. Not in the life you are living but in the one who gives you life. You are mine my little one. My life dwells in you and through you I can bring life to others so that death does not cling to them. You are my child and death has no claim on you but that is not so for them my little one.
I suppose there is death but there is like eternal death, which is separation from life, from you.
Yes my little one and there is no escape from that.
That is a terrible thing Jesus. To never escape from death, to...I don't know. It would be terrible.
Yes my little one it is. I do not want that for any of my children my little one. That is why I gave myself to save my children from the death that awaits them.
You defeated death.
Yes my little one and now he has no claim on those who belong to me.
So how do I put that into my ordinary everyday life that I don't want to live Jesus?
Why are you here my little one? What is your life for?

It is for you Jesus. At least it's supposed to be. It is hard for me to see that in the everyday stuff.

But I am in the everyday stuff with you my little one longing to bring life to those around you. I know my dearest one that you are unhappy and do not always understand but you carry my life and my light within you. It is there to give to others my little one not in your own strength but in mine. I flow through you my little one into the darkness of this world bringing life where there is death and hope where there is despair. It is not for nothing I am asking this of you my little one.

My life is yours Jesus and whatever that is I would like to live it for you. I just have trouble with that. I want you to help me. It shouldn't matter if I like my every day or not. I do it for you and with you and I get that in my head but my heart is still crying and not singing with joy and that's where the struggle is. My heart is still broken and empty and I can't fix that….Crying…

No my little one you can't but I can. That is what I am doing my little one. In all the things that are happening and in everything I am doing my desire is to mend your broken heart and to fill it with who I am.

Please do it then Jesus because I am tired of feeling like this. It is hard to want to live like this.

I know my little one but I am asking you to hold on a little longer. I am working to bring not only you life my little one but all those I will reach through you. The more of my life you are able to receive the more you will be able to give away to others. Right now it is difficult for you but it will not always be so.

I am still waiting.

Yes my little one you are but it is not forever my little one. Hold my hand and be brave. I am leading you forward into life with all that means.

So, I kept on choosing and it did get easier after a while. Outside life was still very hard and work was a struggle, in everything I was doing it was hard for me to see that I mattered. I wanted to be the person Jesus saw but most of the time I was feeling like a little girl who wanted to be looked after, but instead had to take care of everyone else.

My little one I have sent you into the world to help those in need. That does not mean my little one that you will always want to do it but it does mean that you can do it in my strength.

But I suppose it's because I still think people should be helping me. That I'm the one who needs help but no one helps me so it is a stupid way to look at things. You help me. You help me all the time. I already have everything I need, at least that's what you say, so why...

Because my little one you are still believing the lie that you cannot have what you want or need. That you will always be less important than everyone else.

Like I was thinking about daddy when he cuts our time short. That everything and everyone else is more important than me.

Yes my little one.

I suppose you came to serve and not be served Jesus didn't you. It doesn't mean you are less important than us. How could it?

My little one all of my children are equally important to me. I do not place one above the other. I do not need to my little one. If I ask you to help someone it is not because they are more important it is because I have given you something for them, something that only you can give. I know my dearest one that there are many things you do not have that you think you need. I know my dearest one that you are longing to be loved and held and cared for and for all the empty places to be filled. Those things will come my little one but in giving me away to others you allow me to come in and give you more. Do not resent what I ask of you for the sake of others my little one. You are my gift to them.

I am sorry. Please help me. I struggle so much at work...but I know that's not the point.

No my little one it isn't. My little one everything you do is done in my strength. If I ask you to help others that is also done in my strength. I am with you helping you my little one. Hold on to me and remember that I give you everything you need both for your sake and for the sake of others.
Yes. I need to stop grumbling about it.
Yes my little one you do. I am with you my dearest one there is nothing to fear from anything I will ask of you.
I am thinking of getting a new job Jesus. Can I ?
No my little one that is not what I am asking of you. I am asking you to persevere in the one that you have. It is giving you everything you need.
I think there must be things I can do Jesus. A job I might enjoy maybe.
There are many things that you could do my little one and many things for you to enjoy but this is to prepare you for what lies ahead my little one. That is its purpose.
It is...making me sad.
No my little one it isn't. You are able my dearest one. My little one I know you completely. I know everything that is needed to make you strong enough to follow me. Even if this job is not what you want my little one it is making you strong in many ways.

I asked Jesus if I could get a different job a lot of times, but he always said no. I found it so difficult for a lot of different reasons, but he always told me to persevere. I knew a lot of it was the way I was seeing things and what I was believing about myself and the things Jesus was asking of me. Jesus took me to spend time with daddy. He said they wanted to help me to see differently. To understand that from where I was, on the outside, or even on the inside walking towards the city, that my view was so limited it meant I couldn't really see or understand the journey I was on.

Hi my daddy
This morning I was in daddy's bubbles sitting on Jesus lap. The Holy Spirit was there too. In like a hole in the floor I could see down to where I am walking with Jesus towards the city. Like looking down through the clouds. They said that it was to help me see a different view. And that even while I am walking toward the city I am resting in Daddy's arms.

Hi Jesus and daddy and Holy Spirit
Hello, my dearest child we are all of us with you.

My little one you are held and you are loved safe in our arms always. We will not ever let you go. Everything that you are belongs to us. My little one these days are precious. They are preparing you for what is to come. Do not be anxious my little one because you do not yet see the promise. It is there only just ahead of you.
It doesn't seem any closer to me. I know you want me to wait in hope and to rest in you. I am trying.
I know you are my little one.
Why am I here looking down on me there?
Because we want you to understand my little one that you are still resting in our arms surrounded by love safe and held even as you journey with me towards the city. It is not that you are there and not here my little one you are both there and here. We are with you wherever you are.
Yes. I kind of understand. But....why can't I see me up here from down there?
Because my little one as you journey towards the city you are walking with me. Your eyes are upon me my little one. It is not different.
It seems different...I suppose this is the place where I can see...different. I don't know it doesn't matter.
Yes my little one it does. Whilst you are here with us you can see many things that would be hidden from you otherwise. We can show you all of the paths that you are on and many other things besides. When you are seeing from the path you are focused on that path my little one. You can see ahead of you but not everything.
So you are letting me see from this place to help me.
Yes my little one to help you.
But aren't I always here. I mean...will there be a time when I'm not?
No my little one you are always here with us surrounded by love, safe and held and able to see my little one if you are willing.
Because I can see more from up here.
Yes my little one you can.
Well ok but really I am not seeing anything different. It is just us walking towards the city Jesus.
Yes my little one it is but look carefully what else do you see?
I see that the slope we are walking down is quite steep and there are little hills and things. It's not quite as flat as it looks from down there.
Yes my little one what else?
I suppose the city looks different Jesus. From up here it looks kind of jam packed with all the buildings really close together. The streets must be very narrow. I think there is more in the city than I thought.
Yes my little one why do you think that is?
I don't know. Just cos I can see more I suppose.
Do you think my little one that you can see everything from here?
Well, I can see the bigger picture but I can't see up close. Maybe if I had some binoculars or something I could zoom in but I'm not sure how that would help me.
My little one you are able to see all things from here. We can show you everything you need to see. That is because we are helping you to see what we see my little one. Not all of it but as much as will help you.
Why is this helping me?
My little one the journey before you is not long nor is it in vain. My dearest one you have come such a long way to reach this place. As you see your journey from this viewpoint you are able to see what you cannot see otherwise. We want you to see and to understand and not to be afraid of that.
It is what you said to me before that as I rest in you I can see and understand whatever you want to show to me, because it's fear that keeps me from seeing.
Yes my little one it is.
But I am still afraid Jesus, Daddy...Holy Spirit. I am still afraid a chasm will open up before

my feet and there will be a whole other journey to do to get to the city. I am still afraid it will be too long and too difficult for me and I will give up hope. I am still afraid.

Why are you still afraid my little one?

I can't think of a good reason. I am safe and loved and you are in control. My life belongs to you. I belong to you and whatever you want should be ok. I would like to be happy I suppose...and all the things you have promised me. I don't know. Why am I still afraid?

Because you have not yet let go my little one.

What of?

Of your need to be in control my little one, of your need for things to be the way you want them to be, within your understanding of what we have promised you. But your understanding is not complete my little one. It is limited by your viewpoint. You have not seen everything there is to see. You have not understood everything that there is to understand. It is only as you let go my little one that you are able to move freely with my spirit into all that we have for you. Until you do that you will be resisting my little one because you will need him to go this way or that so that your needs and expectations will be met but that is not how it is my little one. He is the one who leads not you. He sees everything. He understands all things. He knows the way my little one and there is nothing fear from it.

I am sorry Holy Spirit.

I know my dearest child but will you take my hand and allow me to lead you forward? Will you listen to everything I say no matter what it is? Will you allow me to show you the way ahead, to help you my little one and not to harm you.

One hand in yours and one hand in Jesus hand.

Yes my little one that way you will walk confidently into all that we have for you no matter what comes against you. No matter what you see or don't see.

Because you see for me.

Yes my little one we do.

So being here with you...I see better and that is to help me. And walking towards the city you hold my hands and lead me, because you can always see everything and you know the way.

Yes my little one. Will you let go my little one?

I know there isn't much point me holding on. I'm not in control. I can never be in control…Crying…

No my little one not in the way you want but that is a good thing my little one.

I know…..How do I do it?

And then I was back on the grass in front of the city. I was holding Jesus hand and the Holy Spirit was there too holding out his hand.

Simply take my hand my little one.

I took his hand but crumpled up crying. They both pulled me to my feet.

My dearest child we are leading you forward into the life. The journey may not be what you expect or even what you want it to be but it will be better by far than anything you have imagined. Come my little one let us walk forward together. We have a journey to complete and much to accomplish before we reach the city.

I have the best traveling companions.

Yes my little one you do.

Crying….I sat on the grass again...I don't want to go.

Why not my little one?

I don't know. I'm just tired maybe.

You are resting in our father's arms my little one. You have everything you need to make this journey with us.

I know….I don't know…..Help me

That is why we are here my dearest one. Come. Just a little further.

Ok. Just a little further.

Step by step my little one. That is all you must do.

I don't know what to say about it. I am in safe hands. I will do my very best to keep on walking, but really I am just waiting for the disappointment that is coming. I suppose I will survive it because I always do but it is hard to want to keep walking towards that. I don't know how to avoid it. We have never been able to avoid it. It has happened so many times now. I did keep walking, one step at a time but I was still afraid. It was still a battle every day to trust and to let go. I didn't always do very well with it.

Hello
Hello my little one
I want to see and hear clearly. I don't want to be afraid. I want to follow where you lead. I don't want to be sad I want to be filled with your hope. Will you help me? crying…I can't do it.
My little one you are our child. We will love you and lead you and guide you all the days of your life. We are holding you my little one and giving you the strength you need to keep following. Everything is in our hands. Do not be afraid.
Crying…I don't like life…crying…It is too hard and painful.
But it is also full of joy my little one not because of the things that happen or don't happen but because of who we are.
I don't know what to say to that. I can't take hold of that. There is no joy in this life...
Yes my little one there is. We are in everything my little one. We are in the birds that sing and the wind that blows. We are in the sun and in the moonlight. We are in the stars that shine and the sheep in the field. We are in the kind word and the comforting hug. We are in the smile that tells you that you are welcome. We are in the roar of the waterfall and the smell of the woodland flowers, the sound of the sea and the whisper of the breeze through the treetops. My little one there is joy in everything that we are in.
Maybe so but it gets drowned out by the pain and the grief…and the despair…and why aren't I better? Will I ever be better?
You are on a journey my little one. A journey towards us and all that we are. It is a difficult journey my little one because of that you have been through and because of the nature of his world but it is still a journey worth taking. Each step brings you closer my little one. Each step brings you healing and life and hope and joy my little one because that is who we are.
I know I need to be brave and strong just to get through today never mind anything else.
My little one we are with you in everything. All that you are is hidden in us. We are leading you forward into life my little one.
It seems so slow to me….I'm sorry….Hold me.
Always my little one. My little one do you believe that we are able to do all things and to work all things for good?
Yes.
And do you believe that is what we want to do?
Yes?
Then do not give up hope my little one.
Please help Sophie…She needs help...crying...
I know she does my little one. Help will come. At just the right time it will come. My dearest one in everything you do and everything you are we are working for good. We know you are not always able to see this my little one but it is who we are in and through you. You are our child. You carry our presence. You are our light and whilst there is more to come that does not mean it is not true of you now my little one.
I just feel like a useless mess.
But you are not my little one. You are strong and faithful. You are filled with our love which you give away to those who need it. Even now my little one. Even now.
I can't live like this Jesus….I can't live like this.
We are not asking you to my little one. We are asking you to walk forward with us into all that we have for you. That is what we are asking my little one.

I don't know what that means really....I don't know what I am meant to be doing.

My little one you are not meant to be doing anything different to what you are already doing. You are following my little one. You are holding on and trusting in who we are. You are following my little one.

Where are we going? I don't feel like I'm moving.

You are moving toward the city my little one just as we have shown you.

My little one in all that you have been through we have loved you and kept you safe. We have led you forward even when you were not aware of it. Even when you were not aware of yourself. You are safe in our arms my little one. Your story is not yet complete but when it is it will be a testament to our love and our mercy and our healing power to save that which was lost. I know my little one that many things are still hidden fro you. You still do not fully understand who you are but understanding is growing my little one and will continue to grow enabling you to receive everything we have for you. Your confidence in who we are has become stronger my little one so that you are able to trust yourself into our hands even when you do not see or understand. I know that you doubt yourself my little one but you do not doubt us.

Is that true?

Yes my little one it is so do not be anxious. You are able to walk the path we have for you even in the midst of all the things that are coming against you. You are able my little one because you trust in who we are over and above anything that you can do or be.

I would like to get on with it Jesus instead of just sitting here crying day after day.

This is part of your journey my little one. Receiving our love and our truth is so necessary for you. It is in his place of need that we can give you more of who we are and heal your broken heart.

I felt like I was sinking. I was having bad dreams about how nobody loved me and I was very tired and very lonely. Everyone around me seemed to be in trouble and work was exhausting. I held on to Jesus and did one day at a time but I felt like I was going to fall any moment. But something was changing slowly. I was starting to see and understand myself and the life I was living differently, to see it more like Jesus did.

You are seeing yourself more clearly my little one both as our servant and as our child. As you read the word which is given you are recognizing yourself which helps you to believe that you are who we say you are and that the future we have promised you is real and true because we are real and true.

Yes. You say it better Jesus.

Yes my little one because I understand more completely than you do.

Yes. So all that is helping. And I have been thinking. I have seen me working as the main thing and all the other things I am doing like writing, and I suppose helping others as kind of just things I do on the side. But I have it the wrong way around don't I. The job is just something I am doing because I have to. You are using it to make me stronger and it takes up a lot of my energy but that's not really what I'm doing. What I'm doing is healing and learning and becoming stronger. I'm writing a book and loving those around me. That is what I'm doing here and the work...it isn't who I am.

No my little one it isn't. We never said so. It has always been about your healing and becoming my little one. Learning to depend fully on who we are in everything.

Learning to rest in who you are.

Yes my little one. Learning to rest in us is necessary for all that is ahead of you.

My journey towards the city continued, very slowly it seemed to me but now I had reached a new place, another pool. A place of healing Jesus said. He said it would cleanse and heal me of the things that would keep me from receiving all the things they wanted to give to me. That included the things that the enemy had done, with all of their tricks and deceptions that had made me so afraid of being disappointed or of wanting to hear about the future or promises.

What are you going to heal Jesus?
All the hurts of the past that keep you from opening up your heart to the hope that is before you my little one.
Isn't that a lot Jesus?
No my little one not in the way that you are thinking. The things of the past, the abuse you suffered are for the most part healed enough my little one it is the things you have suffered along the way as you have walked with me on this healing journey that need to be healed. My little one even though the enemy has deceived you many times I have used it all to make you stronger in me. I have shown you my little one how to follow even in the darkest of times but it has left you tired my little one and unable to open up your heart fully to all that have for you. Allow me to heal you from the hurts of the journey my little one so that you can walk forward with new confidence in who I am in you and all that I have for you. I do not want you to be afraid of anything my little one. The enemy is not greater than I am. Your heart does not belong to him but to me. I do not want him to keep you from anything I have for you.

Even though I understood that I needed more healing I couldn't help thinking this was just another delay or detour, that it was just an excuse to keep me from reaching the city. That I would never reach it. But I did try, I tried to listen and accept what Jesus was telling me. I tried to accept what he was giving to me. Maybe that was enough.

Hi Jesus.
Hello, my dearest little one.
Do you love me Jesus?
Yes my little one I do. I will never stop loving you.
I don't think I am very good Jesus. Not at anything. Not at following you or trusting you or loving people or telling them about you.
My little one I am everything you need. Do you know what this means?
It's not about me?
No my little one its not about your ability but only about mine. As you rest here with me I am filling your heart with my truth. I am helping you to see my little one what you have been unable to see, to accept what you have been unable to accept. It is your heart my little one which determines the things that you do and say and I am in your heart changing it from within to make you all that you can be. It is not your work my little one but mine.
Are you watering my garden with all this water Jesus?
Yes my little one I am. All the parts that have been dry are being drenched in my love. All the parts that have not been able to accept the water that I have given before are softening and becoming more receptive my little one.
Is that why I'm soaking because you are softening hard ground?
Yes my little one. The ground that has been so dry that it has been unable to accept what has been so far given.
That sounds like a sad thing Jesus.
Yes my little one but it is not something that will prevent you from receiving what I have for you because you are here with me. You are resting and you are soaking my little one and the ground is being watered just as I desire.
My heart is the most important thing.
Yes my little one it is. It is the thing that determines who you can be. Not what you are doing or where you are my little one.
Yes. I'm sorry I get impatient and frustrated but I suppose that is my heart again.

Yes my little one it comes from the fear that you have but as my love washes away that fear you will be able to rest more fully in me trusting in my way for you.
That will be better Jesus.
I know that you are sad my little one and that you still do not see the way ahead but be content to rest here with me remembering who I am and who I am making you to be. You can be all that I have said my little one. All of it depends on your heart being fully connected to mine. My love flowing in and through you. That is what I am doing.
I sort of see that Jesus it's just I suppose I think you are aiming way too high and taking way too long and maybe I just think you shouldn't waste your time.
Time belongs to me my little one and I do not ever waste it. You are my beloved child and I know who I have made you to be.
I am not sure I can make it Jesus….I am so far away from being that person…..Crying.
No my little one you are not. Trust me my little one I know everything you need. I see your heart my little one. I know all that needs to be done. You are changing and growing even now my little one. All that I am doing is to make you ready. There is still a great infilling to come my little one, one which will change many things for you and enable you to be so many things that you cannot be right now.
Such as?
A boldness my little one that comes from being able to be who you are without fear because you know that you are completely loved and completely safe and that everything about you is in my hands.
That doesn't sound much like me.
Only because you have not yet seen it my little one but I see it. Nothing is hidden from me.
I don't …know.
No my little one you don't. What you need is to rest in me and trust that I know.

So I sat and soaked in the pool and Jesus worked. I couldn't really see that anything was happening, all I knew was that I was feeling worse and worse, like I was full of black disgusting smelly gunge. Maybe that was what Jesus meant by cleansing. That he was washing away all the things that shouldn't have been in my heart.

My little one you are so very loved. I know everything that is in your heart and you are loved my little one. I do not see you the way you see yourself……My little one I am making you new in me. That means the old must go my little one. As the water reaches those parts that have been dry and barren it is cleansing and healing….My dearest little one you are beautiful to me. You have always been so. I am making you mine my little one. Hold on to me and trust me. All things are in my hands. I am making you new my little one…..My little one ever since you were small there have been parts of your heart that you closed off. It had to be so my little one for you to survive but no part of your heart should be closed to me my little one I want every part of you to be filled with my life. I want all the hurt and pain and fear to be replaced by my love. My little one what you see in yourself is not who you are. You are my child. My beloved Pearl. All of the barren places that are being opened up contain pain and fear my little one but I am washing those things away with my love. Hold on to me my little one. I am all that you need. I love you completely and I will never leave you. Everything you are belongs to me.

Outside life continued of course. I was trying to help Sophie with practical things that she couldn't cope with, to be the mummy I was supposed to be. I was taking Richard backwards and forwards to hospital appointments too. Kate needed support with her cancer treatment and Ruth was needing a friend in all her difficulties too. My friend from work kept texting me and ringing me up crying after having too much to drink. Her life was full of difficult things. For me life was overwhelming a lot of the time.

Hi my daddy
I made it through another day. I have been at work of course. I started off crying with Jesus and spent all day trying not to cry more and I came home and tried not to but didn't manage. I went to have a bath and I heard daddy talking to me telling me I am loved and to keep holding on. That made me cry a lot. I was in the bath so I didn't write it down of course. Daddy said to look and I saw the sun is higher over the city. Part of it is in sunlight and part of it isn't. Where I am in the pool is still in shadow, but when the sun reaches us it will be time to get out. I held on to Jesus and cried and then lots of little flowers came floating down from the sky. They were all different colors and had little lights in the center. They floated down and landed on us and on the water. Jesus said they are blessings. I don't know what that means. He said to watch.

Him and daddy keep saying to be still and hold on. I watched the flowers flow out of the pool and down the stream to the city. When they got to the gate or gateway they grew up the towers, so they are covered in beautiful different colored flowers. It made me cry even more to see that but I said to Jesus it was all very lovely, but on Monday morning I still have to go to work and everything is just the same. Be still and hold on He said. So I have cried a lot. I still don't know what to do about Jay.

I did talk to Jesus this morning but we talked about other stuff and I was crying like I said. I don't know what to do. I have been putting up with things thinking I don't have a choice but then suddenly I realized I do. It is hard having choices. It means I can get it wrong and I suppose I think I probably will. I haven't slept well all week because of feeling so sad like I am going to break any minute. Anyway that is all. I have a day off tomorrow but Jay is texting me. I don't know what to do. I don't think I am going to make it daddy. Love from Pearl.

Everything Jesus showed me on the inside should have given me hope. It did help and I understood that inside was the true reality but I was finding outside life and the healing that was going on too much. It made me want to escape, to stop and just give up. I did hold on somehow. On the outside I kept on doing and being all the things I needed to. On the inside I sat in the pool with Jesus, crying but trying to listen and trust. Jesus kept healing me and helping me and encouraging me to take hold of the truth and to trust him.

I realized I am still expecting to be punished Jesus. If I don't do what you want you will punish me. Maybe I still think you are punishing me with this life like I must have done something wrong even if I don't know what it was. How are you going to fix that Jesus if it is a lie...crying...
My little one all of your life people have been punishing you for things you did and did not do but I will never punish you for not following me. My dearest little one the

father did not punish the prodigal son when he left taking his inheritance and wasted it all. He only welcomed him back with love. It is the same my little one. I will not punish you if you go astray I will only seek to draw you back into my arms of love which is where you belong.

I don't understand that kind of love.

I know you don't my little one but I do not want you to follow me out of fear but out of love and trust.

I am sorry….You never hurt me…..but you ask hard impossible things of me that I don't want to do.

Why my little one. Why do I ask these things of you?

Why is the answer still because you hate me…..I know that's not true.

Do you my little one?

Yes…..Please fix me…crying..

That is what I am doing my little one. These waters are bringing healing and life to you just as they will to the city. My dearest little one all the lies that are in your heart are being washed away. I know my dearest one that you feel like nothing is happening but that is not so my little one. I am loving you and healing you and helping you to receive my love. Just because I am not asking you to do anything does not mean I am not doing anything my little one.

I'm sorry.

My little one in order for you to enter the city you must be ready. You must be able my little one and you must be equipped in every way that you need. I know my dearest one that this time is hard for you to endure but it is necessary just as everything that has gone before was necessary…..My little one if I did not want you to go down to the city I would not have brought you here. I would not have shown you the things that I have or made the promises that I have made. That is not who I am my little one. Hold on to me. Remember who I am. Remember who you are my little one. You are my pearl and I am making you ready for a great and wonderful adventure. One which will take you down into the city ready to give everything that I have given to you away to those who need it the most. My little one my love is given to you freely. Receive it then. Be ready for all that is to come my little one.

I am still afraid Jesus.

I know you are my little one but I am here with you to help you through this. You are able to endure through this time in my strength my little one not your own but mine.

I don't really want to.

I know my little one but you have given yourself to me. I will love you and care for you and lead you into the life I have prepared for you just as I have promised.

You won't change your mind if I'm bad.

You are not bad my little one but no I will not change my mind. Your course is set my little one.

Why did you do all that dancing and celebrating if you were only bringing me here Jesus?

Because my dearest little one that was the end of one part of your journey and the beginning of another. You had endured through many trials to reach that place my little one. It is not wrong to celebrate even if you have not yet reached your destination.

I suppose I think it is because for me, I am still here Jesus. And I'm sorry but it always comes down to that for me because it is the life I have to live day after day no matter what is coming.

My little one I understand these things. I know that it is hard my little one but still I ask it of you for the sake of all that is to come. Hold on to me my little one. Trust me to do what you cannot. I am making a way for you my little one. It will not be long.

Maybe one time when you say that it I'll be true according to my time.

Yes my little on one day it will and when it does you will be ready because you have held on to me and trusted me even when you could not see and did not really

believe.

I know you want me to live by faith and not by sight Jesus. I know the life you promised won't be easy and I will need to be able to trust you…But please don't make me stay here…Don't make me keep on doing this…

Hold on my little one. Hold on.

Jesus kept on encouraging me. He told me I was doing well and that he was proud of me. I felt like I was a failure a lot of the time because I was so unhappy and seemed to do nothing but complain. But Jesus just told me he understood that it was hard. He reminded me that this was a season of infilling and that the next big infilling was to fill the fountain, daddy's fountain that was in the heart of my heart's garden. It had been a long time since we had been there. I had forgotten about it a lot of the time. When I remembered it made me sad, because I had thought it would have come by now and maybe I had got it all wrong and it never would.

Hi Jesus
Hello, my dearest little one
I was thinking about the fountain and how it never came and then I remembered the well which was kind of the same thing for Aj I think. We waited over a year for that well to be filled. I suppose it's not different. Will it come? What is happening with the fountain Jesus?
It is being filled slowly my little one and being prepared for the infilling that is about to come. Would you like to see?
I would.
Come then my dearest one. Let me give you hope for what lies ahead of you.

So he took me to the garden and there was the place where the hole was but now it is full to the brim with water. It isn't spilling over yet but it is full and kind of bubbling in the middle where the water is coming up.

Oh it is already full and bubbling Jesus.
Yes my little one it is. We have been filling you my little one just as we have promised and the time is almost come my dearest one. Just a little more and you will be ready.
The garden is growing too Jesus. And is that an orange tree over there?
It is a tree which is bearing fruit my little one. You are already bearing fruit for us.
Am I? Everything else, well the ground is covered in green. It was just bare earth last time I was here.
Yes my little one everything is beginning to grow and to flourish. Everything is being prepared my little one.
So the well is kind of full Jesus, the fountain I mean because it looks more like a well right now.
Yes my little one it does but our father has not yet poured out his love my little one. When he does the fountain will be as we showed it to you. Powerful and strong giving life to everything around it and through you to others my little one because our fathers love will overflow into the lives of others.

Jesus must have been with me healing in the pool just like he said, because as I stood in the garden I was brave enough to ask him about timings. Would this be the year? He didn't answer me but held me close and said that he would tell me when the time was right. It didn't matter, the point was that I wasn't afraid to ask anymore. But then I was back at the pool again but I wasn't in it anymore. I was standing at the side with my hand in Jesus hand and he told me it was time to start walking to the city.

> **"You need to persevere so that when you have done the will of God you will receive what he has promised."**
> **Hebrews 10:36**

Chapter 23

The Hill of Change

My journey with Jesus continued. I walked along talking to him and our daddy about the future and the changes that would come. Jesus told me we were walking down the hill of change and that as we moved downwards towards the city things would begin to move into place. Most of all I would be changed. We talked about the infilling that was to come, when the fountain would be filled to overflowing with daddy's love and what that would mean for me.

On the outside though things didn't seem to be changing in any way that I could see was helpful.

Hi my daddy
I talked to Sophie today. She seems to be doing a bit better. She says she's better than she's been all year that's good. She's not sure it's going to last, but I understand that. But Richard isn't good. I knew he wasn't right today but he wasn't saying anything like he doesn't. But then I heard him sobbing in his room. So I went in...he's so bored and fed up with life but doesn't have any idea what to do. Every suggestion is met with a no. It seems hopeless. I feel stressed because I suppose I feel like it is up to me to fix it for both of them, but I can't do anything. What am I supposed to do? It seems like everyone around me is falling apart one way or another and I'm the one who has to stay strong and somehow come up with answers. It is all stupid and depressing. Anyway that's all. Love from Pearl.

I was very stressed and felt overwhelmed by everything that was happening and not happening. It brought me to my knees again. I talked to Jesus over and over.

Please do something good with all the mess. Please save us. All of us. The whole family has suffered because of the evil and the darkness we've been in not just me. We all need you Jesus. Please wrap you arms around all of us and save us. Don't let the enemy win. You are bigger and stronger. You are good in every way. Take everything they did and use it for good Jesus and save us. Please.

I didn't understand why everything had to be such a mess and why Jesus didn't do what I knew he could. Some things just didn't seem to change no matter how much I asked, no matter how much I trusted, no matter what steps of faith and trust and obedience I took.

I don't know what to say about anything Jesus. I feel so sad for Sophie and Richard and helpless. And I am tired of everything being bad and difficult and painful. And you can do miracles Jesus. Why don't you?
My little one I am working for the good of all of you. There are things my little one that you do not see and do not know. You have not understood the depth of my love for all of you. It is not about making things nice or easy or painless my little one it is about giving life, my life in abundance. I know it is hard my little one when everything seems wrong and you want it to be right, but trust me my dearest one I am doing what is right even when you cannot see it.
How can I argue with that Jesus?
Accept it my little one and rest in who I am. There is nothing you must do my little one except love those around you. I am at work in all of their lives. My dearest one as you bring them to me I am able to open up their hearts to the things I have for them. It is not for nothing my little one.
I often feel like my prayers make no difference Jesus. I know they aren't very good and sometimes I am really just shouting at you. But I am tried of it all and even if you are doing things I can't really see them Jesus and the pain doesn't stop.

My little one this world will always be a painful and difficult place to be but that does not mean it is hopeless or purposeless or that there is not life and joy to be found in the midst. Remember who you are my little one. You are my child. Born to bring my light into the darkness. That means my little one that you cannot hide from the darkness for I will send you into it but it does mean that the darkness will be driven back. It means there is hope my little one.

I found it hard to see that hope, hard to see it for me and hard to see it for Sophie and Richard. I had a dream that reminded me that the enemy was using their struggles to distract me from the things that Jesus wanted me to focus on. To discourage me and make me lose hope. I understood it was part of the battle but that didn't always help. I suppose the enemy was in what happened with daddy mike too. He was trying to encourage me to help Richard in different ways, but to me it felt like he was saying it was up to me to fix it...my responsibility. I felt crushed and overwhelmed by the situation and now by what seemed to be an expectation I couldn't meet. I yelled at him I was so angry and upset.

I suppose I ought to say I'm sorry Jesus but I'm not. I'm not sorry....I'm tired and unhappy ...and I don't understand him...but I'm not sorry.
My little one his only desire is to help you.
I don't think he listens to anything I say. And he doesn't even know who I am.
Yes my little one he does. He does know who you are.
If he knew who I am he wouldn't suggest the stupid things he does.
My little one he sees you more clearly than you see yourself.
I don't know what he's seeing then Jesus
He sees someone who is strong in me, someone who is capable of anything I will ask of her.
And what are you asking?...crying..
That you stay close to me and trust me my little one. That is all.
One day Jesus I am going to quit. One day I am…How much do you think I can take?
My little one I am with you every moment. I will not ask more of you than you can give. My servant knows this my little one. He only wants to help you see what he sees.
He doesn't see anything…He sees some made up person..….It made me realize I can never live up to being that person. He expects way too much. You expect way too much but at least you know me…Stop it please….Please. I am going to break.
No my little one you are not. You are going to keep your eyes fixed on me and hold on tightly. My little one I am not ask asking anything of you that you cannot do. Your daddy sees you my little one he knows you. He understands things that you do not understand my little one. Do not let the enemy distract you. Keep your eyes on me. Keep hoping and keep trusting. I have more for you than you know. You are not a disappointment my little one not to him and not to me. You are my beloved pearl. I am leading you forward. Hold my hand my little one keep walking. Keep trusting with everything that you are. Change is come my little one but that is good and not bad. Hold on.
I don't know what you are saying about him Jesus. I don't know what he is seeing. To me the things he says are stupid and if he's going to ask me to do a thing like that in America I am not going to do well…I'm not.
My little one you are both still learning about each other. This will continue my little one for there is still much more for you to discover about yourselves about each other and about the things I will ask of you. You do not see yourself as he does my little one, but neither have you seen him as he is. My dearest little one there are many things for you to discover. Do not be afraid of them my little one. Your daddy loves you. He does not expect you to do things that you cannot do my little one but he knows that you are capable of so much more than you know.
I think he expects me to be like him. Someone who can fix everything. But I'm not Jesus. I

am just a little one girl who is holding on to you. You can fix everything. I can't.
Yes my little one that is so and yet he sees that you can be more than you are right now my little one. That is not wrong my little one. That is my desire for you.
He ...I don't know.
He is not disappointed in you my little one. He doesn't not blame you for the things that need fixing. He only sees that you are able to follow me wherever I will lead you and he wants to help you do that.
That's not how it seems to me.
I know my little one I know.
Anyway Jesus...Richard still needs you to help him. If there's something you want me to do I will but I don't know what that is. I don't want to drag him along to do things that he doesn't want to do. That is too hard.
Yes my little one it is. I will not ask it of you.
Are you Jesus... my Jesus?...crying..
My little one I am here. I do not ever leave you. My little one I am holding you close. I love you and will not ever let you go.
You say nothing is too hard for me Jesus.
Not if I ask it of you my little one but I am not asking it of you.

Daddy Mike told me he didn't expect the things I thought he did and that he loved me just as I am, but I suppose I still felt it was up to me to fix things. But I knew I couldn't. It was going to take a miracle for Richard and for Sophie.

I am feeling a bit gloomy Jesus.
I know my little one but remember that everything is in my hands and I am working all things for good. There is nothing to fear my little one.
Sometimes I think I don't know how to do life Jesus. Why do I still get stressed and anxious about the little things?
Because my little one you are still believing that you are the one who has to fix everything.
Am I? Mostly I think maybe it's about expectations again. Other people expect me to fix things but then again it always seems to be up to me. I don't know…crying
My little one I am always with you. You do not bear any of these burdens alone.
I suppose... wish I didn't have to bear them at all Jesus.
I know my little one but you do it with me and for me. Helping those you love is part of why you are here my little one.
I know. It's not that I don't want to help them Jesus.
I know my little one but remember that these burdens are not yours they are mine.
But I'm the one who has to do everything Jesus. I know you help me...I don't know.
My little one everything that you have to do you do with me and for me. You are not alone. The burden is not yours my little one. I am in control not you.
I still find it hard.
I know my little one but remember the responsibility for what happens is not yours. Your responsibility is to follow me.
I know I can't control what other people do Jesus.
No my little one you can't.
Am I following you Jesus? Sometimes I can't tell if I am.
When your heart is full of love and you are giving yourself to me every day you will follow me my little one. It cannot help but be so.

My journey down the hill continued. Jesus talked to me about the city. He told me that he was at the center of it, that it was a community connected in love to him and that my city would be connected to other cities. He reminded me that no matter the path I am on I am always walking towards him, towards his heart for me, towards his desires for me. It helped to be reminded of that.

As we walked down the hill we came to a big waterfall. Jesus told me this was where the fountain would be filled. That I would stand under the waterfall with him and daddy's love would be poured in, but that there was things that I needed first. We walked down the hill down alongside the waterfall to the place where it ended. At the bottom a little way from the waterfall was a pool that was made from the spray that came from the waterfall. It was a very deep pool, a deep blue with rainbow fishes and different colored flowers. It was very still. Like a mirror. Jesus lifted me in, and we floated there together, resting and talking and soaking in daddies love.

Hi my daddy
Today was very tiring at work. We are short staffed and I didn't get picked up so I was late and Jay wasn't in again so we all had to do an extra room. Anyhow I coped and didn't get very stressed so it was ok. I don't have a lot to tell you but I am sending you the picture I was drawing now it is finished. If I am hearing right it is the Father's Day weekend when the fountain will get filled. I feel a bit excited about it. It will be a very good thing when I think of how it was such a deep pit of pain and it will be a beautiful fountain. It has taken more than a year which is a lot longer than I wanted it to be obviously... I am not sure if Sophie is ok she has gone a bit quiet which isn't a good sign but Richard seems fine. Nothing else is happening that I can think of...except I had horrible dreams last night about having medical tests and I was screaming and screaming in the dream but then you were there and you hugged me and looked after me. That is all I think. Love from pearl.

I was very worried about Sophie, but I hadn't told mum about how things were for her. Sophie didn't want me to, but I did tell mum about Richard. She told me that she had gone to a special place to pray for him and not long after that things with Richard changed suddenly. He wasn't depressed and frustrated anymore but seemed happy. He started going out for walks and taking himself into town. He wanted to do things together, to go places and to spend time with me. He was talking much more about how he was thinking and feeling. It was a big change and a very good one.

Hi my daddy
Update. Sophie seems kind of ok. She is talking again anyway. Richard is still better... different. It is very strange but it is good. It reminds me of when Jesus did a miracle before when he was about fifteen I think. I expect maybe Jennifer told you about it, but that is a long time ago so I will tell you again. Richard was very unhappy. He was laying in bed and saying he wanted to die, refusing to go to school. He was punching things and hurting himself. We would take him to the church youth group, but he would just sit in a corner and not join in. We cried. I remember Jennifer on her knees to Jesus begging him to do something. If he wasn't going to do something then take Richard home, because it seemed better to her than to see him suffer so much. It was desperate. That year Sophie and Richard and some of the youth group went to the Christian camp that me and Cheryl

usually go to. We were hopeful Jesus would do something but it didn't go well. Richard was unwell and spent most of his time on his own in his tent. It was depressing. On the last night there was a meeting for all ages in the big tent. There was an altar call for the young people and all of them went forward, including Richard. It was a wonderful moment but it didn't last. Richard got halfway and came back and sat on his own on his chair. It was crushing...but Jesus spoke to us, or Jennifer, and asked if she would trust him. No matter how it seemed, would she choose to trust him. And she did. When the worship started she...or we worshipped with our whole heart trusting Jesus with Richard, not crying or giving up hope like we kind of felt like doing. The next day Richard was changed. He was different and everyone noticed. Everyone. The change stayed and things didn't ever go back to how they were. No more depression or hurting himself. He didn't like school but he did go and did his exams and everything. And he went to youth group every week and joined in and had a good time. It was amazing. It was a miracle. So I have seen it before and that is what this reminds me of. It is a hopeful thing. The first miracle didn't solve everything of course but it was a big step forward. I expect this might be the same. Anyway so that is Richard. I am doing pretty good. On the inside Jesus has taken me to a new pool behind the waterfall. It is hot and bubbly. He says it is a final cleansing before the infilling. And that is all my news. Love from Pearl.

So, I had my miracle, one of them anyway. That was so wonderful and a huge relief. And now I had moved from the floating pool to one behind the waterfall. Things were moving forward.

You are our child my little one and your heart belongs to us. All that you are. Our desire is to fill you to overflowing with all that we are. We have done this many times my little one as you have been able to receive us. What has changed is your capacity to receive us. As you have allowed us into your heart and opened up the doors and we have removed all the things that hinder us and all the things that keep you bound to the past and to the enemy your capacity to receive what we have for you has grown. You are now able to receive so much more than you were my little one. As you have healed and spent time with us we have been filling you. The fountain has been filling slowly my little one but it is not yet overflowing. It is not yet full of our fathers love. What we have for you is far different to anything you have received before. This pool is making you ready for that my little one. Your heart is our garden. We have opened it up, we have removed all of the things that were growing there that were not from us. We have prepared the ground and planted new seeds. We have watered and tended the plants that are growing there. The fountain will bring new life to your garden my little one and enable new kinds of plants to grow and to thrive. It will enable you to give away what you have received in far greater measure. All the things that would stand in the way of this must first be removed my little one so that we are able to give you everything that we desire. This is the last stage of this process my little one. A final cleansing of those places that have been hurt and

which are empty but now ready to receive our father's love. That is what this place is doing my little one. That is what this pool is for. It is bringing and new level of purity to your heart so that you are able to receive the love that will be given. A love which already belongs to you my little one but which you have so far been unable to experience.

I am not sure what you mean by a new level of purity Jesus. What is it?

A heart that is set on us and everything that comes from us my little one. A heart that will not wander or stray or desire the things of this world. A heart that sees the truth and the beauty in all that we bring. A heart which belongs to us my little one and is not attached to the things of this word.

Ok. That sounds good Jesus.

Yes my little one it is very good.

Is it going to be next weekend...when daddy's love comes?

Yes my little one it is.

Good. I don't know really what it will mean but I know it will be good. And the fountain will be beautiful and will bring life to me and to others one day.

Yes my little one it will.

Even though things were better I was still afraid. I was still afraid that I would be disappointed and that the infilling wouldn't be what I thought or that it wouldn't happen at all. I had been waiting for such a long time and it seemed like such an important moment. I spent a lot of time talking to Jesus about what he was doing and why and what it would mean when the fountain as filled. I don't suppose I understood it all, but he told me that daddies love would fill the fountain and spread throughout the garden and that the change that would come to my heart would be a process and not an instant change. I knew it was going to happen over Father's Day weekend. A lot of things happened that weekend and I wrote to daddy mike to tell him about them.

Hi my daddy
Happy Father's Day. I am glad you are my daddy. Hugs.
I have lots to tell you. Some of it isn't very good. When we went to the hospital this week they put Richard's dose up a lot because they aren't happy that it's not working very well. Then a couple of days later they sent a letter saying the blood test results were worrying. So I have to ring them tomorrow, but it might mean he has to stop this treatment and try something else. So it would mean starting from scratch again. That isn't good obviously. Sophie is having a money crisis. She got an extension for her PhD, but they have reduced her payments by half for the next two months to cover it. That isn't doable. So she has asked them to spread it out...not good. She came over yesterday and we went out for mum's birthday meal. It was going well until mum started going on at Sophie about how much she was eating. Her meal wasn't any bigger than anyone else's, but she kept going on about how she was eating a massive amount. Every time I thought surely she will stop now she kept going. It was so out of order. It was a bit like watching a car crash in slow motion. I could see what was happening but I couldn't stop it. Sophie took it for a while and then she cracked and slammed her fork down and said fine I won't eat anything. She was so upset...it is such a sensitive thing for her. I've no idea what mum was thinking. She did apologize but... Sophie kind of recovered but she didn't eat her food and it was just awkward after that. It made me so sad. Seeing Sophie makes me sad anyway but that was just awful. So I came home and cried. I cried into my pillow when I went to bed. Sophie said Richard's hair was a big improvement and that he was very chatty but she doesn't think it will last... It was all depressing. It was hard to see mum hurting Sophie and I wish I had said something helpful or something I don't know.

I was thinking though about who I am and how no matter who I have to be or how I am seen that I am always Pearl and that who I am is safe. And one day I will be with Jesus and I can run and play and be me. In just a little while when this life is done. And nothing can change that. It makes me feel better about being Jennifer. It's not for ever. It doesn't change who I am and I am here to be and do what Jesus wants. I don't feel like I need to cling on to who I am any more or have a life that kind of proves I am me. If that makes sense. I still feel sad about it but it's not the same as it was. And I am seeing better that Jesus wants to save all of us. That his healing isn't just for me it's for Sophie and Richard and even mum because it was the same evil that stole all of our lives. I keep remembering that dream where the Holy Spirit was a broom and he cleared our path with one sweep. And it was our path not just mine. That is a hopeful thing. Anyway that is outside stuff. On the inside it has been better.

On Friday the bubbles in the pool got bigger and more...and then on Saturday we swam over to the ledge behind the waterfall and this morning we got up onto the ledge...then I had to go shopping with mum and Richard. She didn't mention yesterday or Sophie or anything. It was all very subdued. I was feeling very gloomy when I came back. So I went for a run because that always helps. It did help a bit. Then I thought it must be time so I went to be with Jesus. Daddy was there and the Holy Spirit and the four Angels. Jesus took my hand and we walked forward into the waterfall. The water flew around us in rainbow drops and we took off our robes. I was wearing a swimming costume made of rainbow colored sequins and Jesus was wearing matching swim shorts. I held on to him while the water came down. I did cry a lot but I'm not very sure why. After a while we moved forward a little bit and it was fiercer. I could see the Angels flying just above us. They were blowing those things you have at parties.... Kazoos? Making a lot of noise made me smile even though I was crying. Then Jesus said it was time and we went to the edge.

It was a really long way down and I was scared. But I held Jesus hand and we jumped. We went under the water...it wasn't what I expected. I could breathe under there and it was so still and peaceful and I stopped crying and just felt calm and relaxed. We stayed under for quite a while. The water made golden trails like tiny bubbles when we moved. Above the water I could see fireworks exploding. It was very pretty. Eventually we got out and I sat on Jesus lap at the side of the pool watching the fireworks and the Angels flying about blowing their kazoos. Jesus gave me a big bunch of balloons. They looked liked pearls. He told me to let them go. He said it was a symbol of freedom. That I'm not held any more. That I'm free to fly. I've drawn pictures. Love from pearl.

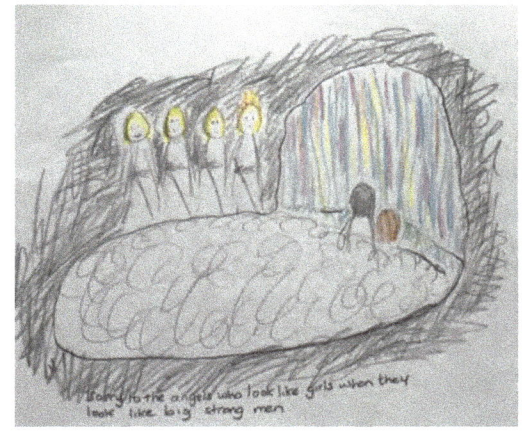

I didn't really feel very different afterwards but I remembered that Jesus had said it would be a process. I asked Jesus to take me to see the fountain and my garden now that it was done.

Hi my daddy
Jesus took me to see the fountain today. It is big and very beautiful. The water is just the same as the waterfall water. There are little blue flowers spreading out from the fountain

across the garden which Jesus says are truth. He says the truth will spread to every part of the garden. I don't feel different but Jesus says the change will come as the truth spreads. He says it has all gone deeper than ever before and it will take a bit of time but not too long. I drew a picture.

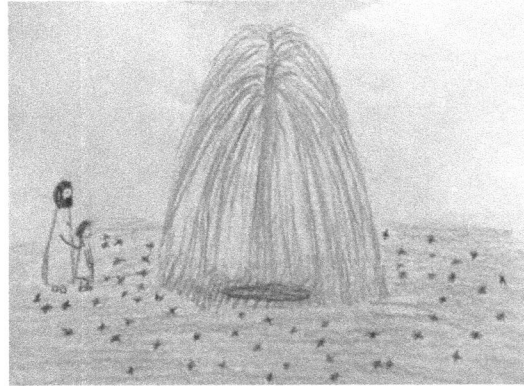

Then we have set off again down the hill. We are wearing climbing shoes like people wear when they go rock climbing. Jesus says it's so I won't slip and fall cos it is a steep rocky hill. The city looks very close now but I don't know what that means. I drew another picture. Nothing else to tell. Love you. Pearl.

The long-awaited infilling had come at last. It wasn't what I expected though. I had thought that I would feel different, better but as I walked on with Jesus I was just feeling worse.

I am not very sure about what is happening Jesus. I don't feel very good and I was feeling so happy before. I thought I would feel better and more hopeful after the waterfall but I don't. I feel all gloomy and sad again.
My little one as the water of life spreads to all the parts of the garden it is bringing truth. Truth to the deepest parts of your heart my little one driving out the fear and the pain.
Perfect love casts out fear.
Yes my little one. It may seem to you that you have gone backwards but really you are moving forwards because The truth is going further and deeper than it ever has before. It will pass my little one.
I suppose it is like healing.
Yes my little one it is.
I don't like to complain Jesus but is it ever going to be better. Why does it have to be endless pain?
It is not endless my little one. You are able to enjoy many things that you could not before. We are opening up your heart to our love my little one and our love is filling all the dry and empty places. You are becoming all that you were created to be and whilst this is not painless for you my little one it is worth it. The pain will pass and you will be my beautiful pearl who knows just who she is and that she is hidden in our love always. Able to walk forward with me into the city and all that it holds for you.

On the outside I was very busy and having to do so many things I found difficult and didn't want to do and then there was healing and memories and I was tired..

What is my life Jesus?...crying..
My little one my dearest little one your life belongs to me. You are precious and beloved. My little one I have not lied to you about anything. Do not give up hope by continue to walk with me. My path for you is good my little one, it is bringing you and others life.
I don't see it. I just see an endless journey inside and a pointless life outside…I don't

understand why I was so happy and ok and hopeful and now I am back to being desperate again…Jesus do you love me?

Yes my little one with all that I am.

Then what is happening what are you doing? What am I meant to be doing? I DON'T WANT TO DO THIS ANY MORE…You said I was free. You said I was full of daddy's love so how is not making a difference…Why do I have to stay here why don't you do something?

My little one look at me.

I CANT SEE YOU!

Yes my little one you can. Take my hand. I have brought you here to this place through many dangers and through great darkness and pain. I have brought you here for a purpose my little one. None of it is endless or pointless.

This is just you saying I have to keep on going Jesus…I already know that…Please you have to help me…I DON'T WANT TO BE HERE I DON'T WANT TO BE THIS PERSON ANYMORE. YOU GO ON AND ON ABOUT HOW CLOSE EVERYTHING IS BUT ITS NOT…I don't want to be here..

Where do you want to be my little one?

With my daddy being Pearl…I think…maybe I just want to go home cos it's all too hard.

My little one there is nothing that you cannot do with me.

I know but it is all things I don't want to do…I'm sorry. You shouldn't have made me me…You should have made me some boring grownup person who doesn't want friends or fun….and liked to clean and do forms…because that's what my life is. That's what you've given me…and I don't understand…If I am your Pearl…why is this my life…I don't want it.

Jesus squatted down in front of me and pointed to the city.

My little one that is your life. The one that I have given you. This is the journey you must take to reach it. It is not endless my little one. The city is real. It belongs to you and I am taking you to it. Every step you take brings you closer my little one. I made you, you because of the life you will live there. Not because of what is asked of you in this life my little one. This is only the journey. It is not the destination.

How do I keep on believing that Jesus? Because no matter what you do no matter what you say I am still here. I am still here where I don't want to be in a life that still holds on to me no matter how free you say I am. And if I have to be here what am I supposed to be doing. …I am so bored and unhappy. Why do you want that? I'm never going to get out of here and no matter what you do, or how many changes there are I will still be here…Being Jennifer…why…why?

My little one what do you see when you look at the city?

Nothing. I'm not playing this game Jesus. It doesn't change anything. It doesn't help. It doesn't matter what I see here.

Yes my little one it does. Tell me what you see.

I see the walls and the towers around the outside are made of bricks. They are shining like gold…There are flowers growing up the towers…Your blessings I suppose. And the river is running through the gates.

What else my little one look closely.

I see the white path running alongside the river going through the gates.

That is this path my little one the same one that we are on now.

So!? It doesn't mean I will ever get there and if I do I will still probably be here living the same old life. The city is probably not any different.

Is that what you see my little one?

I don't know what I see Jesus. How can I know? All I know is what my life is and I don't want it….I am so tired of it and I don't understand it…So whatever you show me here doesn't change any of that.

My little one what do you want to do? Do you want to continue with me on the journey I am taking you on. Do you want to see the city and enter through its gates and be my Pearl to a lost and broken world?

Yes….but I don't think it's real.
Am I real my little one?
Yes.
My little one the journey you see before you though not easy is not endless. You are able my little one to walk along this path and through the gates of the city. Will you follow me though you do not see what is ahead for you?
I know very well there is no point me crying and complaining Jesus. I ask you over and over to be kind to me and help me….but I don't know why I do.
My little one I love you more than you know. Walk with me my little one. Take my hand and walk with me. You do not know what I have prepared for you my little one or when it will come but you know who I am and who you are. You know that I am real and true no matter what the outside life tells you.
Am I not your Pearl. Your little girl?...crying…
Yes my little one you are but you are more than a little girl my little one you are my little one.
That's what I said.
No my little one. You want to be loved and carried and looked after and have all the things that you missed out on as a child. You do not want to be a responsible grownup who looks after everyone else.
That is true Jesus.
Yes my little one but I have more for you than that and even though you are a child you are my child. In me you are able to do and be more my little one. So much more.
But I still want to be a child and be loved and looked after…I don't understand why you made me and keep me from all the things I need because I am me. I don't understand how that is love. And you keep promising those things will come but they won't. They won't. Not ever…and I will have to keep on being someone I don't want to be…Someone I'm not…until I finally get to die and what is that. It's not what you said. It's not what you promised it's not why I have come all this way with you….
Who are you trusting in my little one, your sight or mine?
Mine.
Why my little one can you see what lies ahead?
Yes…the same as what's behind.
Does it look the same my little one?
Not inside no but outside yes.
And which is more real my little one?
I know you will say inside but I don't live inside. I just visit.
My little one the inside world is far more real than the outside one. Everything here has meaning and purpose my little one. The journey you are taking here is leading you to places you could never go on the outside.
But what is the point Jesus when the outside life is what it is?
It is the journey you take on the inside that makes change on the outside possible my little one.
I don't see how me walking along this path makes anything possible Jesus. Isn't it just like a picture for me to understand what you are doing?
No my little one it is not. I know you don't understand my little one but it is what you do here with me which makes the changes you are longing for possible.
So I have followed you Jesus on this inside journey. But outside what is that? Shouldn't it be different by now?
Change must come at the right time my little one. Change is coming. It is there ahead of you and even though to you it looks like it will make no difference that is not so. There is nothing I do that does not have purpose my little one.
All that ought to be so Jesus. But the point is I don't want to be here living this life.
Then walk with me my little one. Walk and do not give up for it is only by walking with me that you will reach the city. The path is prepared my little one. It is laid down

before your feet and it takes you through the gates of the city that lies ahead of you. A city that has been given to you my little one. Keep walking and do not give up.

I suppose I want to change things on the outside but you are saying to do that I need to walk with you on the inside, not do things on the outside.

Yes my little one that is so. Outside change will come as you walk with me here.

I suppose it takes faith to believe that.

Yes my little one it does. It is not anything you can do my little one. It is the journey we take together that makes my promises to you possible.

So are you saying the more time I spend here with you the more time I spend inside walking with you, that is what makes the change possible. Aren't I walking with you even when I'm not thinking about it.

Yes my little one you are but sometimes it is in the spending of your time here that will make the journey inside faster.

Like when I went in the waterfall and the city was much closer when I got out.

Yes my little one like that.

So I should pay more attention to the inside journey because that is the real journey that makes the outside journey move.

Yes my little one it is.

So maybe instead of looking for ways to pass my time I should just come here and walk with you.

Yes my little one. That would be good.

Because this is what makes change possible...I don't know Jesus. Am I getting it?

Yes my little one you are starting to see. My dearest one I made this place just for you. It is yours so that you can travel with me into all that I have for you discovering everything that I have to give to you along the way.

I still don't want to be here.

I know my little one but take my hand and keep walking. In that way you will move from where you are to where I am taking you.

I suppose I either trust you or I don't. I don't think I totally get it Jesus. I don't know if I believe I am ever getting out of here but I do know that you are in control and me crying and fighting doesn't do much except slow me down. If you say we are going to the city then ok. If you say spend time here walking with you and change will come then ok. I have lots of time Jesus.

Yes my little one you do.

Alright then. Help me do it. Help me bear the outside life. I'm not sure I can do more than that. I still feel like I don't get it but mostly I don't want to be here. I just don't see how it can change.

But it can my little one. The path is prepared and before your feet. Walk it with me my little one and trust me.

Ok. I know there's nothing else for me to do.

Strength will come my little one. All you must do is walk holding my hand and trusting in who I am.

Ok Jesus. Let's walk then.

Yes my little one. Come.

Jesus gave me just enough hope to carry on. I still fell down a lot. I still didn't spend the time with him inside that I could have. I still questioned and cried and felt like it was all too much. I didn't understand what all these changes were because I couldn't see them. I suppose I was looking at the wrong things.

My little one all the people you love and care for are on this path. I have given you a place in their hearts and in their lives and in their journey with me. For you to leave this place things must change for them also my little one. Your place in their lives needs to change. For some your place will diminish in importance for some it will

only change. But things must change for all of them my little one just as it will for you.

Because you are looking after all of us.

Yes my little one I am.

So this path is made up of changes for lots of people, all of which will change things for me so I can go.

Yes my little one. I am putting everything into place for you and for others so that when you go to be with your daddy there will be no reason for you to stay my little one.

That is hard to imagine.

I do not say my little one that the people will want you to go or that it will not be difficult for you to do so only that you will not need to be here anymore. Not for yourself and not for them.

That would be good Jesus. I don't want people to suffer because of me.

My little one none of it is because of you. This is my plan and purpose for your life and I will make it possible for you to go.

Well, I need to go now Jesus. Work again.

I know my little one. Persevere and do not give up. I am with you.

Yes. Ok. Bye not bye.

Bye not bye my little one

I still wanted to see the changes and mostly I didn't. I so wanted to be able to see that things were moving forward, that it was being made possible for me to be me and live the life Jesus promised me. I wanted to see it but Jesus wanted me to see by faith and to trust for outside changes and for inside ones too. He took me to see the garden again. He showed me that there was change happening, not just that things were growing but that my garden had grown, that it was bigger than before. He told me that I was more able to give and receive life and that many things had changed. More than that Jesus wanted me to understand who I am, that there was more for me to see of who I really am.

My little one you are also our promise to so many of our children

What do you mean?

My little one just as we have given you promises we have given promises to many of our children. Promises which will be fulfilled through you my little one.

How can I be a promise?...crying...

My little one your daddy is a promise to you. He was given to you my little one in fulfilment of the promise to give you help, to give you a mentor and a guide and most of all for you a daddy. He is a promise my little one and in just the same way you are also a promise.

But you are the promise.

Yes my little one I am but through me you are also a promise my little one.

You made my hair like a pretty rainbow.

Yes my little one I did.

But why? Why today?

To remind you my little one of just who you are.

I wish I could be me.

You are you my little one.

You know what I mean.

Yes my little one I do.

You are funny Jesus. You call me Pearl Sunshine and give me rainbow hair...but I am just a boring middle-aged cleaning woman...crying.

No my little one you are not. You are who I say that you are my little one.

Yes.

My little one the road before you is not long.

Don't say that Jesus. It is always long.

No my little one. Do not fear what lies ahead. You are able my little one to walk with me into the city and everything we have for you.

I loved my rainbow hair it was so pretty. I kept on walking with Jesus down the hill and drew pictures of the things that I was seeing. Jesus was talking to me about the things he was doing and his plans for the future, but I was still having bad dreams and memories and feeling all alone.

Hi my daddy
I drew another picture. The path has gone down the side of the hill now. It very narrow. One side is the grass hill that is like a wall and one side is a drop. I'm not too sure I understand what this path is but Jesus says it is about the changes that are happening in relationships so we talked about each of them and what is changing. I kind of get it but it looks a lot more dramatic on the inside than it does on the outside. To me anyway. He says that as things change for them and in them and in me that changes our relationship. Which I suppose makes sense. I don't know. I can't see the city anymore cos it's on the other side of the hill but the path winds round and eventually I will get to the other side and I will see it again. Closer I suppose. Not too much else to say about life. I talked to Sophie today she isn't doing too good. I wish that Jesus would do something. Trying to sort this meter thing out for her is causing me a load of stress and I have had some meltdowns with Jesus because I don't want to be in this situation being a grownup person. It makes me wonder if Pearl Sunshine even exists and if she does what is the point of her. I still don't really understand what he is doing or why I am me. It makes me very sad. I have been feeling so alone and afraid of being left again. I thought that was better, but Jesus says daddies love is going to the deep places. I know you won't leave me daddy but the fear is there and I feel very small and all alone and it is horrible and making me cry. I think that is all. I hope everything is going ok for you. Love you. From Pearl.

Daddy Mike wrote back to me. I held what he said close to my heart because it was so hard to remember that I wasn't alone.

Just a reminder...I'm not leaving you and I will always love my Pearl. Daddy

On the inside Daddy kept reminding me that healing was happening and that his love was washing out the fear in my heart.

…And yet there is nothing to fear my little one not even in this life.
I don't know daddy. Horrible painful things happen. I think it is normal to be afraid of them.
But not to live in fear of them my little one. That is not what I want for you or any of my children. This world is full of pain and difficulties but you are never alone in them. We give you everything you need and all of it is used for good. Fear will not help you my little one it only seeks to control you.
I know that is why you are washing the fear out of my heart.
Yes my little one it is.
I would like to be free of it. I know it doesn't mean I won't ever be afraid...but I hope it means I won't live feeling anxious and fearful about what might happen.
You will live in my peace my little one which is far better.

God is love. Whoever lives in love lives in God, and God in them. This is how love is made complete among us so that we will have confidence on the day of judgment:
In this world we are like Jesus. There is no fear in love.
But perfect love drives out fear,
because fear has to do with punishment.
The one who fears is not made perfect in love.

1 John4:16-18 NIV

Chapter 24

Steps of Faith

On my walk down the hill I was attached by a rope to Jesus and the holy spirit. I understood they were keeping me steady even though the path was narrow and steep. It was like that on the outside too, it was difficult, but I stayed steady... more or less.

I kept on walking down the hill of change. I had come to a kind of staircase. Each step was important, each one meant making a choice.

Hi my daddy
I hope you got all your moving finished and are still alive. Especially the last bit. I have been taking steps. This letter is the next one. I don't want to write it cos it means thinking about stuff I don't really want to think about and tell you stuff that makes me want to hide. Anyway, I am writing it so I will get on with it. I was crying with Jesus this afternoon cos it finally seems real that I am leaving. Like I am saying goodbye already. I'm not of course but it feels a bit like it. So, Jesus days the next step is to tell you about the steps I have been taking. He says it will help you prepare. I'm not sure what he means by that. When he showed me the city, I saw you standing by the gates waiting for me. He says you are prepared spiritually. I don't know what you think about that or even what it means. He says you are part of the promise. I suppose that must be right. Anyhow steps. The steps are to help me receive all the promises. Mostly they seem to be about getting rid of fear. I'm supposed to tell you all the stuff I am thinking about them.

Step one
Jesus showed me the city like in my picture and said the first step was to accept that his promises are true and that the city is real...and I cried a lot because of being afraid of finding out its not time and I have to keep on being here. And then when I thought maybe it is real, I cried a lot because it so overwhelming to think that could be my life. I told him over and over it is too much and I can't have it. Stuff like that. I suppose it is still easier for me to believe that I can't have the things I want. It was like I was in the box again when grandad would open the lid and I would think I was getting out and it was slammed shut again. It feels like that to me that every time I think I am close to getting out the lid slams shut, and I have to stay here. But after all of that I did choose to trust what he is telling me and showing me because what else can I do if I want to go forward. So, I did but I didn't exactly stop being afraid. Jesus says I have to keep choosing and as I do the fear has less power and gets less. It has got less but it isn't gone. I am still afraid that all that is waiting at the bottom of the hill is disappointment. But I keep choosing.

Step 2
To trust Jesus with Sophie and Richard so I can leave them. This wasn't as hard as I thought it might be. I do see that they are grown adults and need to make their own way. But I do kind of feel like I am abandoning them...and I think that's how they will feel about it which is hard. But I chose to trust him with them because I know he can help them and do all the things I can't. And maybe his plans for them need me to go. I suppose they must. I don't know how it will be. Maybe it will be very difficult I don't know but what else can I do except trust him with them. And honestly it will be a relief not to feel responsible for them...I think I am doing better with that but maybe not quite there yet.

Step 3 and 4... They go together but I took them one by one.
To be prepared to let go of the person I have had to be here and to be the child that I really am. I got a bit grumpy and scared about this. The Holy Spirit told me a few weeks ago that it would be like learning who I am all over again. A bit like when I found out I was pearl and not Blossom except I will still be pearl but pearl without all the grownup stuff. It is hard to know what this means really. I don't know what it would be like to be a child and not have to be an adult. Jesus says that I won't have the same responsibilities and expectations as I do now, and he wants me to ...kind of trust you with my care cos you are my daddy. That's so I can receive all the things I need like love and family and all those sorts of things. He says I can do everything I'm called to do as the child I am. This is hard to understand but it's what he says. I got grumpy because I am still scared you won't want to look after me, whatever that means. It is different being a daddy when you are a long way away to having to live with someone and look after them. It is a scary thing for me even now when I know you love me. It seems like such a big thing to ask but that's his plan, at least that's how I understand it. And it is worse cos of course that includes carol and she doesn't even know me, and I am very afraid she won't want me. I don't know why she would. And if you both did agree to give me a home and love me and all those things whatever they are, it feels like too much and it makes me want to hide cos it can't be real and doesn't feel safe. I think I would feel safer coming as an adult and looking after myself but that's not what Jesus wants. It's not what I want either, but I suppose I think even that would be too good for me. So, they were difficult steps, but I took them anyway.

Step 5
To choose to be seen. I won't be hidden anymore behind Jennifer's name. I will be seen and known as pearl. That will be very different. I don't know what it will be like but everyone knowing everything about me...that is nothing like it is now when I am hidden away. I will need to trust Jesus to keep me safe because people will think and say all kind of things that aren't true, I suppose. But Jesus is the one who knows who I am just like now. So, I took the step, but it sounds scary.

Step 6
To choose to trust Jesus to reveal the truth about me to my family in a way that brings them life and healing. We spent quite a while talking about this. I see better that maybe the truth is something they need for their own healing. Like I did. So even if it's painful and difficult it is good. So, I chose but I hope that they don't have to suffer.

Step 7 and 8
To choose to accept the gifts I will need. These will be given at my baptism. I need to choose cos Jesus says there is a cost to these gifts. They are discernment, seeing and understanding the spiritual much more than I do now...and the wisdom to know what to do with what I see, hear and know. We talked a bit about how difficult these gifts can be...but if I need them then I choose to accept them.

Step 9
To write and tell you all this stuff and not hide anything from you cos you need to know...cos you are helping prepare the way. That's what he says. And cos I need to not be scared of what you think about it all of course.

So that leaves three more steps. It has been much quicker than I thought. I thought the steps might take a month or more but no. Maybe that's why I was crying cos it is going faster than I thought, but also cos I'm still scared I'm not going anywhere even though I am choosing every day to believe that I am.

My next step seemed straight forward, to choose to be obedient and to follow Jesus in everything. At the time it seemed easy, but I suppose I needed to be ready for the next steps that were coming. I talked to daddy mike after sending him my letter about the steps. I was hoping that he would say Jesus had been talking to him, that things were moving forward, but it seemed like the same old thing all over again. Him saying Jesus hadn't said anything to him yet, and there was no sign of things moving forward they way I wanted them to.

Hi my daddy
I thought I would let you know where I'm at after we talked yesterday. I didn't sleep well cos I was feeling so sad. I made my mind up to tell Jesus I wasn't going to take another step until he does something. Tells us, you...something. But as you can see from my picture that's not what happened.

I was sitting on the edge of the cliff. Jesus sitting next to me on the left and the Holy Spirit on the right.

My little one we will make everything possible for you just as we have promised.
Crying...I wish I had never been born...I wish this cliff was real so I could jump off it...
My dearest little one there is nothing we cannot do.
Why did you have me take all those steps and make all those choices Jesus?
Because I knew that you would need the strength it would give you to continue my little one.
If I had talked to daddy first, I wouldn't have made those choices Jesus.
I know my little one that it would have made it harder for you to do so.
It is too impossible and too hard, and you never tell daddy anything and then I feel like…. Ashamed and stupid and it is never what I think, and I don't understand why you do this to me over and over…Crying
My little one do you think it is my desire to hurt you or to help you?
I think your helping hurts and I'm not sure what's it's helping with. All we ever wanted was to follow you. You have healed us and made us strong. This isn't just me sitting here it's all of us. We have been through so much to get here. We have trusted you and followed you to

the worst and most painful of places and you have healed us Jesus, but it was never about that for us. It was always about your promises. To make our life count for something, for all the suffering to make a difference. To know that we were loved for who we are and that our lives have purpose and meaning. But you have brought us here to the edge of this cliff. And maybe it is the cliff of impossibility because everything down there...all the things you have promised are totally impossible. And you refuse to open up the way for us. You won't talk to daddy and tell him what you want. And that just makes me think it's not real and it will never come, and it is just some cruel joke, and nothing makes sense. And I can keep jumping through your hoops for another ten years and it won't make any difference. Why are you so unkind? I don't have anything or anyone but you. My life is worth nothing. I am not even real without you. Pearl Sunshine shouldn't even exist, but I do. And I'm here and I've given everything I've got to give. What am I supposed to do?

My little one when I asked you to talk to your daddy, I knew it would be difficult for you to hear what he had to say. That does not mean that it was bad my little one. That does not mean it will not help you.

It is just making me want to give up.

No, my little one it is making it real. My little one you have made many choices to follow me. All of them are real and all of them make a difference. There are many difficult choices for you still to make my little one but each choice you make for me makes you stronger. You know this. My dearest one there is nothing I cannot do. My promises are real and true and they will be accomplished.

Won't you listen to what I'm asking you Jesus?

Yes my little one. I will always listen to you.

You led me here making out like it was all so close. Months away not years you said. Or I thought you did. If I'm going to keep choosing to walk this impossible path with you through all the things that are going to be so very difficult, I need you talk to daddy and tell him when and how. You could tell me but that won't help me too much. I need you to tell him so he can hear and understand what you want him and me to do. When to do it and how. Because I can't go through this and outside life. guessing about those things anymore. I keep putting life on hold...probably for no reason. I need you to help me. I am asking that from the bottom of my heart. I know it will make it real. I know I will be scared. But if it's not happening, that is one kind of scared. Don't do this to me. I can't sit here in the brink. Make it plain and clear so I can choose, and he can choose, and others can choose to follow you. That's what you want isn't it. We just want to follow you Jesus. Don't make it too hard.

My little one everything I do is to make it possible for you to follow me. That is why I lead you the way that I do. My little one I understand everything that you need. I know the path that lies before you and everything it must accomplish in order to take you to the city. You are not alone on this journey my little one. We are with you always meeting every need that you have as you walk with us. I know you don't understand my little one and you feel like we have led you to a dead end or that this path will just continue forever but that is not so my little one.

Then do something Jesus. Talk to daddy. I am tired of feeling ...like this. If you don't want me let me go stop tormenting me with promises of things I can't have and telling me they are almost here when they aren't ever coming and I can't have them. That is unkind. Be kind to me. Show me the kindness of your love Jesus because right now I don't see it.

What do you see when you look ahead my little one?

Inside or outside?

Both.

Well here...there is this cliff that goes straight down to the grass below. It is quite a long way. Then as far as I can see the path just goes straight over the grass to the city.

What kind of path is it my little one?

It is a white path. It looks smooth. It's just ...is a path. A plain simple path.

And outside my little one?

If it was a path outside, I wouldn't even be able to see it for all the rocks and obstacles on it.

Why do you think that is my little one?
I don't know because they don't look the same to me.
And which is most real my little one?
The inside path Jesus. At least that's what you tell me.
So what does that mean for the outside path my little one?
I suppose it means it's not the way it looks...or maybe you need to reveal the path or clear it or something. I don't know.
My little one I have promised to make a way for you. That means my dearest one that the outside path will be made as clear as the inside one. That all the obstacles you see will be removed and you will be able to walk forward on it.
If you say so. There's no sign of that. You need to show daddy the path at least even if it's still got loads of stuff on it.
Yes, my little one I do......and what do you think this cliff is my little one?
The cliff of impossibility. I suppose its all those things that still need to change which are totally impossible and mean I have to completely trust in you to change them.
Yes my little one.
But you aren't going to. I don't know what your doing.
Everything I have promised to do my little one.
I can't go Jesus and I can't stay. This is an impossible place to be...Crying...I don't know what you are trying to do.
I am helping you to trust me my little one.
I don't know what you want from me Jesus. I'm tired of this journey to nowhere...I so wish you would let me die.
My little one I am leading you to life and not death.
I don't think I will ever reach it. It will always be just over there. It might as well be a million miles away.
You have come along way to reach this point my little one through many trials and temptations. Always the enemy has tried to trick you into thinking my promises are not true and that you cannot have them. He has brought many things against you to try and prevent you from reaching this place my little one but you are here with me. I have kept you safe I have healed you and helped you to grow strong in me. Strong enough for the choice that is ahead of you my little one. To trust me with all that you are. To hold nothing back. To risk everything to follow me. Are you willing to do that my little one?
I don't have anything at all to lose Jesus. I am relying on your love and your kindness and your mercy.... Crying
Then will you take the path I have for you my little one trusting in who I am completely. Will you allow me to take the strain and to make the impossible possible for you, to change those things which need to change and to enable you in every way so that we can walk together to the city of your promise.
Yes.
Come then my little one.
So, we stood up and he took the rope that was already attached to him and tied the other end to my belt. Just like we had been before except the rope was much, much longer and went through the loop on his belt. Not tied like before. The rope is rainbow colors.
I feel a bit like I am going to my death Jesus.
No my little one this is the way to life. To trust me in the midst of the impossible, to do what you cannot. To rely on me for everything even when it seems like the most foolish thing you can do.
You are my everything Jesus. If you fail me, I want to die. It's all or nothing. I can shout and stamp my feet and make demands, but you are in control. Not me. I don't understand and I don't know. This is the path you made for me. You love me. If this is what you want, then OK.
My beautiful Pearl remember what I have said. You will not hear me for a time, but I

am with you. I never leave you. I am making a way for you my little one.
Is it going to take long to get down there?
A little while my dearest one for there is still much to be accomplished.
Will I still come here and see the cliffs?
Yes my little one there is much to be discovered on this journey.
Will you be with me Holy Spirit?
Yes my dearest one. I never leave you.
Ok then…Crying
Trust yourself to the rope my little one. I will not let you fall. Remember my little one. I am always with you.
Bye…Crying
Bye not bye my little one.

And I went backwards over the edge of the cliff like in my picture. Jesus told me yesterday that while he's lowering me down, I won't be able to hear him. I suppose it is just about trusting him. So that's all daddy. Love from pearl.

Jesus kept on lowering me down the cliff. I couldn't see him, just a bright light and I couldn't hear him, but it didn't worry me too much. There were little resting places like ledges with soft grass where I stopped and slept. It made me think about how Jesus is always in control, like he was in control of me getting down the cliff just how he wanted.

Yesterday morning I saw I was coming down the cliff but instead of my climbing shoes I was wearing gold glittery shoes. Very fancy. They reminded me of Blossom's shoes of hope. Anyway, but it made me think about our journey...and how Jesus has seen all of us through so very much. And I thought to myself why I don't just trust him. Why don't I stop being afraid of what is coming or not coming and just let him be in control and decide, because he is anyway. So, I took my feet off the wall...cos I was kind of walking down...like it made a difference and just let myself hang on the rope. When I did that, I found that the belt that the rope was tied to had turned into something like a sling that I was sat in. It was much more comfortable. And I just relaxed and watched the cliff as I went down. I saw that there were little yellow flowers growing on the ledges. That reminded me of the land of hope. And then there were daisies and that reminded me of Aj. And little pink flowers that reminded me of Blossom and little rosebuds that reminded me of dolly 4. It made me smile and miss them all at the same time. And it seemed to me that I was going faster and more smoothly, and I didn't feel so anxious anymore. I kept seeing me going down in the sling all day even at work. When I got to bed and closed my eyes, I reached the grass at the bottom. And Jesus was there, and we sat down together and looked at the city and I snuggled up in his arms and went to sleep.

The journey down the cliff got much smoother and faster when I just rested in Jesus and trusted him with it all. Now I had reached the bottom there was something new for me.

This morning when I was just waking up Jesus took me round to the bottom of the cliff to where the stream comes down in a waterfall. And we sat just in front of it in the spray that are like little rainbow drops. I was dressed in a rainbow sequin swimming costume and a swimming hat with little flowers on it and my golden glittery shoes. Jesus was dressed in his same travelling clothes and didn't seem to be getting wet by the spray. We held hands and looked at the city and the path. The city is so close now, but I didn't really see anything new. It was the path I was looking at. It is white and smooth kind of because it is made of pearl. And as I looked at it, I understood, and I cried and cried. It is like a red carpet that has been laid out for me, or a Royal road. Jesus says we are going to process down the pearl path to the city gates. It is like a celebration and like a declaration of who I am. That is what this part of the path is. And it made me cry because it makes me feel so special. I don't know if I have explained it right and I don't know exactly what it will be but it's not what I was expecting. Jesus says we are waiting in the waterfall and he is going to show me the things I need to see and know for this next part of the journey. So that is what I am seeing and knowing today. I don't know how long before we start off again, but it isn't very far. I don't think I have anything else to tell you. Love Pearl.

I had made it down the cliff and was sitting waiting on the edge of a pool. I tried very hard not to, but I was expecting something to happen on the outside, for daddy mike to say Jesus had told him something. I had been here so many times and I never seemed to learn, even when I had decided to rest in Jesus and trust him to be in control! So even while I was sitting in sight of the city, I was fighting the same old battle again.

Hi my daddy
I had a very bad time last night. I did try but it just went from bad to worse. I ended up curled up on my bed sobbing and sobbing. I saw two angels in my room. I am supposing that's because there was a battle going on. I was having thoughts about getting a big knife and slashing at myself or just going out and killing myself because nothing was real, and it was all made up. I yelled a lot at Jesus and accused him of a lot of things. I told him a lot of times that I quit. He said no you don't and reminded me of the truth. I didn't listen too well I just told him that he should do whatever he wanted. I didn't sleep hardly at all cos of all the thoughts going on in my head, but this morning I seemed to be thinking better.

Jesus reminded me that no matter how many times I got it wrong he would always be there for me and that no matter what I thought about it I could walk the path he had made for me.

My dearest one learning to follow me is not easy. It means you have to set aside your own will and surrender completely to mine. I know my dearest one that you still have so many unmet needs and that you are still afraid you cannot ever have them. This makes you vulnerable my little one but remember that everything you need is found in me. I am always with you. Here in this place I am with you. You do not need to rush ahead to find what you need. I am already here.

I spent time on the inside talking to Jesus about what was ahead. The more I looked the more I could see of the path ahead. The water from the waterfall flowed into the pool and then out again along the path that ran to the city gates. He told me that the pool was about total surrender and breaking free, and that when I got out and walked down the path to the city, I wouldn't be hiding anymore. He said it was time to tell the truth to Sophie and Richard and mum. I had been hoping to avoid this. I was afraid of it because I didn't know how they would take it. I thought maybe they would hate me or blame me, and I thought mum either wouldn't believe me or would take it very badly. I didn't want anyone to be hurt.

Hi Jesus.

Hello my little one.
I am very tired.
I know you are my little one.
How am I going to do this?
In my strength my little one just as you do everything.
It's hard to cause people pain Jesus, but you do it don't you. The truth hurts but it does bring healing and life, eventually if you can accept it.
Yes my little one it does. My dearest one remember that you are doing nothing wrong. The truth is what it is. You were hurt my little one by those who had power over you. Now you are breaking free from the pain and from the controls that were put on you. That is good my little one. There is no shame in that.
No, but telling the truth will cause pain. Me leaving will cause pain.
Yes my little one it will for a time.
It is hard to do.
But you do it trusting in me to work through the pain, to bring life and healing my little one. Fear would prevent you doing this. Fear is always the enemy my little one.
Yes. I see that.
I know you do my little one.
But I am afraid. I'm afraid I won't be able to do it. I'm afraid they will hate me. I'm afraid that mum won't speak to me...and will disown me, or that she will be ill because of it. I'm afraid the truth will be too much for her.
Your children will not hate you my little one and your mum will struggle with the truth but that does not mean that she should not receive it. My little one she needs to have a choice to receive the freedom and healing that I have for her. I know you are afraid that the truth will be too much and she will either retreat into denial and fear or that she will be overwhelmed and die but all of this is in my hands my little one. I know what she can receive. I know what she needs. I know the right time my little one. It is always and only about trusting me with those you love.
And that's what I chose to do.
Yes my little one it is.
It is hard.
I know my little one I know.
I think it is a very rough way to start a path of joy and celebration.
It is the only way my little one because you need to be free to be who you are and not have to hide the truth.
It is going to be hard to be me.
In some ways my little one but you will be loved by many. You will know what it is to be free to be who you truly are not held by the expectations of others. You will be you my little one and that is a good thing no matter what others think of you.
You declared openly who you were Jesus. You didn't hide it even though people wanted to kill you for it. Even though they did, and you knew they would. That is very brave Jesus. To live as who you are even though family and friends rejected you and didn't believe you and didn't understand.
Yes, my little one but I had my father with me. I was not alone. He gave me the strength and courage I needed. I did not hide who I was my little one because to complete my purpose I had to be who I was, just as you do.
I see that Jesus, but I am not as brave as you.
You have the same strength and courage as I did my little one because it is given to you as you have need of it. Just as it was for me.
Well I can't live half in and half out Jesus. It's all or nothing. If I don't give everything, surrender everything, take hold of everything I can't be me and I can't do what you want me to. And I know it might cost me everything and that others might not be able to accept the truth, but I have to choose you. I do choose you. How could I not?

I spent a lot of time talking to Jesus about what he wanted me to do. I wanted to know what I should say and how I should say it. I wanted to know how much of the truth to tell them, because there was a lot of it and even though truth is good sometimes too much truth at the wrong time is too hard to accept. I knew it had to be just right. I started to understand that in giving them the truth I was also giving them a choice. A choice to accept the truth and move forward and find their own healing, or not. And that the choice was theirs to make and not mine.

As I sat on the stone step at the bottom of the waterfall and looked down the path that was ahead for me Jesus talked to me about what he was doing. That there was more to this path than I had realized.

I feel afraid Jesus.
But you are firmly rooted in the truth my little one that you are safe and you are loved and that nothing will harm you. You may feel afraid my little one but it has no power over you. It is not the same.
Well you know my heart better than I do Jesus. I would like to stop feeling afraid.
You are safe in my arms of love my little one and whatever lies ahead for you, you are able in the strength I give you to keep walking forward with me.
Yes...Crying...I want to do this for you Jesus and for them. To give you and them...to give you an opening so you can do something wonderful in their lives. I don't know if that's right or not...I suppose it is....It might cost me something Jesus....It might cost me everything but they are broken and they need you...Only you can fix this mess. Only you know how....I keep thinking I will want to run away soon, but somehow I don't. Somehow I don't. I want to get it over with though.
I know you do my little one. Just a little longer.
I think you are doing something in my heart Jesus.
Yes my little one I am. I am making you mine and filling you with who I am.
I suppose you are filling me with your life just like this place.
Yes my little one.
Tell me about this step Jesus. It..is a very old stone kind of dark and rough and it's got moss on it. I am supposing it is something to do with the old life and when I jump in the pool I am leaving it behind and the steps on the other side are white and smooth and pearly and beautiful. Very different.
My little one as you surrender everything to me, as you leave your place of hiddenness and choose to surrender to everything I have for you I am able to give you so much more than you are asking for. Letting go of everything you have known is not easy my little one but the new is waiting for you. The old life is worn my little one it is not who you are. The new life I am giving you is full of who you are. It is made just for you. That is the difference my little one.
How is this pool different to baptism Jesus? Isn't baptism about letting go of the old and taking hold of the new life you give us.
Yes my little one it is but baptism is more than that. This is the beginning of your baptism my little one but it is not the end. The baptism I have for you will be completed when you stand with your daddy underneath the waterfall and receive everything you will need to walk into the city with me.
How can there be a waterfall Jesus. The water ...I know I can't see...but it flows along the path and into the city. There aren't any cliffs like here.
No my little one there aren't.
An outside waterfall then.
Yes my little one.
Well...that is what I wanted, what I have imagined...
I know it is my little one.
So baptism is a journey...my baptism is a journey that begins in this pool and ends at the

city gates.

Yes my little one it is.

That's…unexpected.

My little one there is so much that I want to give to you and so much that I want to accomplish that a journey needs to be taken. It is not a long journey my little one but it is a very beautiful and life giving one.

I don't know what to ask Jesus. I suppose I always thought of baptism as a quick dunk but that's on the outside I suppose. On the inside maybe there is a lot going on.

Yes my little one your baptism will change many things on the inside and then also on the outside my little one for one changes the other.

So this pool and the path and maybe the gates they are the journey of baptism I have to take.

Yes my little one.

And it is about freedom and life and joy and I suppose everything you are.

Yes my little one it is.

That is a very hopeful thing Jesus.

It did seem like a hopeful thing, like the beginning of the end or maybe the end of the beginning of my journey so far. We had all talked to him about it over the years and sometimes I felt very sad because I still hadn't been baptized after all this time. Like somehow I wasn't good enough yet even though I knew that wasn't the truth sometimes it felt like maybe it was.

What does it mean that my baptism starts here Jesus?

Baptism is about leaving one life and beginning another my little one. You have been breaking free of the old life for a long time now. It has taken time my little one because of all the things that were holding you but now you are ready my little one to break free of the old so that you are able to receive the new. The pool before you is the final breaking free my little one. It is not an easy thing but it is possible for you. I have made it possible my little one. Once you are free of the things that have been holding you, you are able to receive the new my little one. On the other side of the pool is where I can begin to give you new life and new hope in a measure that you have not been able to receive before. I know my dearest one that there are many things you do not understand about this but as we walk the path to the city I will show you and teach you many things. For now you are preparing for the next step which is to break free of the old life my little one, of all the things that would keep you from receiving the new. If it is taking a little time to prepare for this next step that is because it is an important one my little one for you and for others. I am giving you all that you need so that you are able to take it with me. I know it is hard to wait my little one but it is making you stronger and more able to what I am asking of you.

It was hard to wait but at last it was time. I had been sitting on the stone step for a few weeks wanting to jump in and get it over, with but at the same time not wanting to jump in ever. I held Jesus hand and we jumped in together. I found I was wearing a snorkel and that the pool was much bigger than it looked at the surface. The deeper we went the bigger the pool was. There was a lot to see and different sea creatures for me to discover including a big shark which ought to have been scary, but somehow wasn't because I knew Jesus had put him there.

Why is there a shark?
He will not hurt you my little one.
Can I go see him?
Yes my little one everything here is for you.
I never thought I would hug a shark Jesus.
Nothing here will harm you my little one. You are deep in my presence. I am everything you need my little one. Go in peace and do not be afraid. I go before you my little one and follow behind. I am in you and with you. You carry my presence my little one and my presence changes things.
Like making fierce sharks friendly.
Yes my little one even that.
Ok. Well I suppose in some ways I see mum as a fierce shark that will want to hurt me...even if it's just to protect herself. After all that's what she did for a lot of years. But now you are with me and I don't need to be afraid. But she needs your help. She will be afraid Jesus.
I know my little one. I will help her.
I love you Jesus. I don't understand about life or why I have to do all these awful things and nothing nice. But it is just life and it will pass.
My little one life is given to you for many reasons. One of those is to discover who I am. The hard things are to help you my little one not to harm you.
But they are still hard Jesus and I would still like to run and play and eat ice cream and have friends.
I know my little one.
Ok. I will think about the shark. I am safe in your presence.
Yes my little one you are. Always.

I had jumped into the pool and now it was time to tell mum and Sophie and Richard the truth, or some of it. I decided with Jesus that I would tell mum first. She was the one I was most scared about. I thought it might go horribly badly.

Hi my daddy
That did not go like I thought. Not even a little bit. I will start at the beginning. I didn't think I would sleep last night, but my four angels came and stood at the corners of my bed and

held their swords over me like a shelter. I had the best nights sleep I've had in ages. I was scared this morning but I spent some time in the pool with Jesus...it is more like the ocean down there and I hugged a shark! We have air tanks on now cos we are deeper. Then I set off and walked to mums. I was scared but just trusting Jesus was going to help me. The Angels walked with us with their swords held high, that was good, there was this man who was drunk and he kind of lurched towards me telling me I was beautiful, but he just passed me by. I bumped into mums best friend on the way there, she was saying how good it is about Richard. Mum seemed OK when I got there and made us a coffee.

Jesus had told me how to start so I just did. She sat and listened. I told her grandad and his friends did bad things. She was surprised and said that didn't fit with her memory of him, but later she admitted she couldn't really remember him that well. She was confused about when he died and asked me if Emma knew him and I said no he died when I was eight. She really doesn't remember. She said she doesn't really remember my childhood either. None of that surprised me, but I was surprised she didn't withdraw, just questioned. She asked me if I was sure...I told her about the alters. It is kind of hard to explain but I tried. She did believe me. She said she wished her parents were still alive, so she could make sure they got what they deserved. We talked a lot about Jesus and forgiveness. She asked me if grandma knew and I said yes. She didn't ask if she knew herself, which I was glad about because she assumes that she didn't. She did remember some things while she was talking. She told me her dad had been in court, before her parents got married for having sex with an underage girl. And how he used to say things about her mum, liking to watch other women having sex. She remembers her mum much better than her dad. She was a strange woman I think manipulative. I think she is seeing these things in a new way now. She is going to talk to her older sister and ask her what she remembers. I asked her if it worried her that she can't remember and she said it does. We talked about a lot of things like prayer and healing and miracles.

I told her about you, she said you sound like a lovely man and she wants me to come and see you still. I told her you were there for all of us and that you would help her if she wanted. She said she wanted to think about things first. I told her you were praying for us, and she said good we need it. Jesus told me to tell her about the book so I did. Just a little bit. She didn't get upset at all apart from being angry with her parents, I suppose it takes time to sink in. She is searching for the truth though...if she remembers it is going to be very difficult for her, but maybe she needs to if she's going to heal. I suppose it is the start of her journey. When we said goodbye she said thankyou for telling me I know it was difficult, I am thinking who is this woman? So I don't know really what to think except Jesus is at work. I still have to tell Sophie and Richard of course but that is for another day. So not what I thought at all. It seems hopeful to me and like maybe it will work out...though I think it might get a bit rough along the way. I think that is all but I might have forgot things. My head feels very full but I am relieved. Bye. Love Pearl.

My meeting with mum had gone better than I could have imagined and that was a big relief to me but those feelings didn't last very long. Mum wrote me an email telling me she changed her mind about talking to her sister and that she thought I shouldn't tell Sophie and Richard, because it would be too much for them. I felt very sad but maybe not too surprised, like the shut down had begun. I started to feel very unsafe. Telling the truth, especially to mum brought a lot of things to the surface that I didn't know were there. Jesus did of course.

I know I am wanting to run away and hide now which is silly cos I've done that hard bit...crying.
You are safe with me my little one nothing will harm you.
But she knows...She knows and everyone will know and...I don't feel safe.
Where are you my little one?

Safe in your presence Jesus.
Yes my little one you are safe and loved and nothing will harm you.
I'm sorry.
I know my little one but there is nothing to fear. I am with you my little one. I will help you with everything.
I know…I don't like the way I'm feeling.
It will pass my little one. I am holding you safe in my arms. You are hidden deep in my presence nothing will harm you.
Ok.
My little one as things change you may feel unsafe but you are not. You are still my pearl hidden in my presence surrounded and protected at all times. Trust me my little one to keep you safe.
Yes…..I don't know what to do Jesus.
Rest in my arms my little one. Allow yourself to grieve knowing that it will pass. Remember that you are loved and wanted, you will never be forgotten or abandoned my little one. Never.
I don't like this pool…crying.
It is giving you life my little one.
I thought we were done with this.
You are breaking free my little one. That does not come without pain but it is giving you life and enabling you to go forward with me.

I was finding it very hard to cope with all the feelings I was having. It wasn't really what I had expected and I still had to tell Sophie and Richard. A week had gone by and it was time to tell Richard. We had been going out for days and spending more time together which was the only real time when we would chat, so I decided our next day trip would be the best time. I was scared of course but it didn't seem so awful or scary as telling mum had been.

Hi my daddy
I did it. I asked Jesus to shout now when it was time. He didn't shout but he did tell me when. We were waiting for lunch to appear. I argued a bit but I did it. Richard looked totally stricken and just said I don't know what to say, which I thought was fair enough. I didn't tell him very much, just that grandad had done bad things and that you had been helping me and about the DID. He said he never noticed any alters. I said being good at hiding it was part of it. He did recover and we had a nice lunch. He even shared his chips with me which is like the ultimate expression of love from him. So even though I didn't say very much really I think it was enough. I am very tired but glad it's over. One more to go.
Love from Pearl.

I was relieved and felt like it didn't go too badly. I hadn't said very much really, not nearly as much as I told mum but I hoped it would be enough. I did try to give him chances to talk to me about it after but he didn't want to I don't think. I was not feeling very good about any of it. I felt guilty for making them sad and I was still feeling abandoned and unwanted and grieving too. But it was too late to turn back now.

Hi my daddy
I told Sophie today. It is kind of hard to know how she took it cos it was on the phone. She said she was sad those things happened to me. She didn't ask any questions. We talked about other stuff too. She seemed OK. Mum and Richard seem fine, just normal really. So that is done. I am so relieved. Last night was awful with very bad dreams about how people suffered cos of what I did. I woke up crying and feeling like I am very bad. I have felt so alone and scared the past two weeks. Telling them went better than I could have thought and I am so glad about that. I don't know if they will want to talk about it or if they will just want to forget about it and carry on like it never happened. I suppose that is what I expect. I

feel like I need a big holiday. I am sad cos I have been feeling a lot of things I hoped I wouldn't ever feel again. Fighting all the same old battles about feeling abandoned and unloved and bad and like I want to die or just disappear. I wonder if I will ever be better. Anyway it is done and I just want to sleep and forget about everything.
Bye love from pearl.

I had done the thing I had been in fear of for a lot of years, which was amazing to me and it had gone better than I could have imagined. Sophie and Richard seemed to care even though they didn't say very much, and even though mum hadn't said anything at all at least she seemed ok. Now it was time to move forward with Jesus again. Time to leave the pool and walk down the path to the city.

**"If you hold to my teaching, you are really my disciples.
Then you will know the truth, and the truth will set you free."**

John 8:31-32

Chapter 25

The Procession

Early in the morning I was seeing Jesus in the pool sitting next to me. He was wearing his crown, but now he was wearing a robe and a kind of golden tunic and trousers with golden sandals. He was holding my hand and we were rising up through the water. We got to the surface and walked out using the steps. When we got out we were surrounded by a bright white light that was warm. Like being air dried I suppose. When the light went I was standing there dressed in a long pearl and golden dress and my pearl crown and my rainbow hair and my rainbow slippers.

I didn't think I was ready.
You are ready my little one.
I don't know what it means.
It means my little one that you are no longer hiding. That you are ready to be seen for who you truly are. It is time to openly declare that my little one and to walk into the city with your head held high knowing that you are loved and that you are my pearl sent to bring hope to those who are lost in the darkness.
And this is part of my baptism?
Yes my little one it is. To declare openly that you belong to me, that you have left the old life and that you are following me into the new. That is part of what it means to be baptized my little one.
Tell me what happened in the pool Jesus.
You let go of the old life my little one. You chose me over and above everything and everyone else including your fear. You have been set free from the things that were holding you here and you have been cleansed and healed ready for the journey ahead.
I don't understand about this procession...baptism thing Jesus. I am supposing it is a happy and joyful thing but I don't feel happy and joyful.
My little one you have been through a great battle and though you are ready to begin walking with me once again you are still weary. That does not matter my little one for

you will gain strength as we begin to walk towards the city.
You have made me very beautiful Jesus..
Yes my little one but all I have done is revealed who you truly are. My little one as you walk away from the pool you are leaving many things behind but there is so much more ahead for you. Things you have not yet seen my little one.
I don't really see how that can be so Jesus. No matter what it looks like here.
I know my little one but as always I will ask you to trust me and walk with me into the future I have for you.

The path ahead of me was beautiful. Made of pearl there were lovely rainbow colors in it and the river flowed over and along it down to the city. It was lined with pink blossom trees and their petals filled the air. There were flowers along the side of the path and I could see rabbits and deer and little blue birds that flew about really fast like hummingbirds maybe. There were angels flying overhead blowing trumpets and we were dressed in our beautiful clothes. The sun was shining and it was warm and peaceful. Alongside the path were little silver benches where I sat and talked with Jesus about the path and what he wanted me to see and understand about who I am.

I suppose I'm not understanding.
No my little one you aren't. You are distracted by the things that you think you need my little one and by the aching in your heart. I understand my little one but what you want is not enough. It is not enough for the journey you have taken nor is it enough for the journey you will take. Hold on to me my little one and let me lead you down this path so that you are able to be everything you were created to be. It will come my little one. All the things you are longing for will come but there is so much more that I have for you. You are able to wait a little longer my dearest one. I would not ask it of you otherwise.
Why do you keep saying the promise is closer than you think and stuff like that, when it just gets further away.
Because I see what you do not my little one.
What do you see Jesus?
I see you and all that you can be my little one. I see that you are already taking hold of the promise even though you do not see it as such. I see that you are following me and willing to go where I will lead you even if you do not understand. I see your heart my little one and all the places that are still empty and hurting. I am going to fill them to overflowing my little one. That is part of my promise to you and one that I have been fulfilling for many years now.
I know that you are my promise Jesus. And I know I don't see it like you do. I know that a lot of the time I just want to be happy…Crying…It seems like such a bad thing to want because I can't have it. I know you say you have all these big plans Jesus and I suppose they are wonderful and amazing…Crying …But I would just like to be happy and not hurting and crying and alone all the time…I know that's not important…It can't be or why wouldn't you let me be happy?
My little one where does your happiness lie? Is it found in the things around you, in the life that you are living or in something else?
I think the hurt and the bad things have to be healed. I think I have to be able to be me and I think I need to be with you...Crying...But I need people too. Who know and love me because I am Pearl. That is what I need to be happy.
And that is what I am giving to you my little one.
But it never comes. I mean I know you have been healing me, of course you have and you have helped me to trust you and follow you and you have been showing me who I am. And there are people who love me it's just not quite there…And I am still unhappy and lonely.
I know you are my little one and yet all the time you are receiving the things that you need. You are more happy my little one.
That is true Jesus.

I understand my little one but remember that I know what you need and what you are able to receive. My path is best my little one. Continue to follow it with me and do not be afraid that my promise to you will never come. It is there before you my little one. It will not be taken away.
Ok. Help me Jesus. We have had a long talk and I still don't know what I'm doing now. Daddy says what next but I don't know the answer.
You keep walking and keep trusting my little one.
Help me not to...hope Jesus. Please…Crying
Hope in me my little one. I will not disappoint you.

The inside path seemed smooth and easy and on the outside things were ok, but I wasn't doing well at all with celebrating who I am. I tried to see it like Jesus does, but I still got caught up in seeing the things on the outside as more important and more real and found it hard to hope that they would ever change.

I just can't do it Jesus. I can't celebrate who I am…crying…I would rather get rid of me.
And that is our first task my little one. To help you see as I see. To overcome the things in your heart that tell you…you are not worthy even to live. So that you too can celebrate who I have made you to be my little one.
We are going to be sitting on this bench a long time Jesus…I don't want to be me.
Who do you see when you look at yourself my little one?
It depends…Sometimes I see Pearl Sunshine. And she is loved and lovely. And I suppose I could celebrate being her...crying.
But you are her my little one. That is who you are.
But it's not all I see…I see someone who was hurt and tortured and lived in darkness. I see Jennifer and the life she lived…I see a person who…is totally unacceptable in this world and has to pretend she is something she isn't. I see someone with a pointless life who has to go to work and do cleaning, when in her heart she wants to run and dance and sing…and have adventures and friends and go exploring…crying…But she can't and all the things that she is doesn't matter…And she might as well not exist …And there is so much pain and grief…Even after all of this time…So how do I celebrate being that person...because I don't want to be that person...crying..
But that is not who you are my little one. What you are seeing are the things that happened to you, the things you have experienced and the life you have lived and are living now. That is not what we are celebrating my little one. We are celebrating who you are. Who are you my little one?
I am your Pearl...crying…But I can never be her.
My little one even if you were never able to be Pearl in the outside world, that does not change who you are nor does it mean you are not worth celebrating.
Like with the babies I lost. You celebrate them.
Yes my little one I do because they are precious just as you are precious. My little one this world will tell you many things about who you are but you are who I say you are my little one and that person, my pearl, is worth celebrating.
Well… if I forget about the outside world …then I am happy to be Pearl Sunshine Jesus and I wouldn't want to be anyone else, even though I am still not sure who I am or what I'm like really. It is still confusing because of having to be hidden on the outside. And you say this is about declaring who I am and not hiding anymore and maybe that is true somehow on the inside, but it isn't on the outside.
But what is true on the inside is made real and true on the outside as you follow me my little one. If you do not accept and celebrate who you are, who I have made you to be and not who the world says you are then how can you truly be that person my little one.
I feel like we have done this before Jesus and why am I still crying about it?
Because you need me to help you see my little one so that you are able to accept the

truth about yourself and not the lies that the enemy or the world gives to you. It is not about the life you live or the things you do. It is not about the way that others see you or the way that they treat you. You are my child. I say who you are. Who you are cannot be changed by the things of this world my little one.
No. I see that.
Yes my little one you do. Who do I say that you are my little one?
Pearl sunshine. Your beloved and precious daughter. Born to love and be loved. Given as a light to this world to bring hope and healing and life.
Yes my little one that is who you are. Is that not worth celebrating my little one?
Yes. It is. I'm sorry.
My little one this path will give you everything that you need as you walk it with me. I know my dearest one that there are many things you do not understand but take each step with me and remember who you are my little one. Not as the world sees you but who you truly are.
Yes. I get lost in the outside stuff.
Yes my little one you do but that is not who you are my little one.
No. It isn't.

We stopped many times along the path because Jesus wanted me to see and understand things in a deeper way than I had so far, like they were going deeper in my heart and he wanted me to see new things too.

You are sending me to all these people Jesus but you are sending me as Pearl Sunshine. A little girl in a big body. Why?
Because I want them to understand my little one that it is never about them but always about me. I want them to open their hearts to my ways which are not like their ways. I want to break down all their preconceptions of how things should be and open them up to the new that have for them my little one. You will challenge so much of what they think they know about me and about how I work to bring my love into this world. My little one you understand that sometimes the old has to be torn down before the new can be built. That is who you are my little one. You will break down their preconceptions, you will challenge the things they think they know and you will bring in new life new understanding and a new openness to the things of the spirit.
Like you said once I would be like a wind of change.
Yes my little one.
Am I right in thinking a lot of that is to do with the church?
Yes my little one you are. My church has grown fat and dull. It is lifeless and self-serving my little one.
I suppose you mean in America, or even here.
Yes my little one I do but even where the church knows and understands more of who I am there is room for growth and change my little one. There is always more.
That is a big task Jesus and it will make me very unpopular. People don't like to be shaken out of their comfort.
No my little one they don't and that is why you need to be strong enough for what is ahead of you. What do you see when you look at the walls my little one?
They are strong Jesus and long...there are no gaps or breaks.
The walls are only as strong as your faith in me my little one.
I thought the walls were your protection. I didn't think it had anything to do with me.
It is your city my little one. The walls are my protection but they are sustained by the faith you have in me. If you are not strong in me my little one the walls lose their strength and you will not be able to reach those I send you to, not in the way I want.
Compromise?
Yes my little one. There has been too much compromise. It is time for the truth my little one.

So, you made me Pearl Sunshine to be a challenge. Like just who I am is breaking things down for you, the things they think they know about you and how you work. Just in who I am.
Yes my little one that is so.
So that is why I am me.
It is part of it my little one.
And why you see me as someone to celebrate because you can break down the things that need to be broken down...just because of who I am.
Yes my little one I can and I will. Who you are is special my little one. You will come with gentleness and with words and deeds of love but you will bring such a breaking in the spirit that nothing will be the same again. You will confront people with the truth my little one just in who you are. That is a powerful thing my little one.
So who I am...Pearl Sunshine in this world that won't accept me...that's on purpose because you want to challenge people thru me...to open them up to the truth.
Yes my little one I do.
Like you made me into a wrecking ball.
Yes my little one.
Oh. Well I suppose it's good to get rid of the old things that people have built so you can do the building. Unless the Lord builds the house it is built in vain...yes?
Yes my little one.
I would think a wrecking ball gets a lot of knocks and it's not exactly comfortable work.
No my little one much of the time it will not be comfortable.
But it will be good when the new comes Jesus.
Yes my little one it will be very good. The change that will come will bring life and hope my little one and my spirit will be free to move amongst and within my people bringing more change my little one.
Yes. I see. I mean I can't really imagine it...but I see.

Jesus told me the truth of who I am was going deeper into my heart. It wasn't an especially comforting truth but it was a hopeful one, because it helped me see that I was worth celebrating because of who he made me to be no matter how life seemed to me. As we continued down the path the water got deeper and deeper, so that we were walking ankle deep and then knee deep as we got closer and closer to the city. Jesus said it was because I was receiving more of his truth and as I did, it opened up my heart to receive even more. But there was a battle going on and the enemy was constantly telling me that there was no point to any of this, and that I might as well give up and die. I hadn't really expected to have to fight my way down the path but I did. All the way. I was still struggling after telling mum about the abuse. I was still feeling like an unloved and unwanted child. Jesus was telling me he made me a child for a purpose, but the enemy kept reminding me of all the reasons why it was a bad thing to be.

I am just a child that nobody wants or even sees...crying...
My little one I do not create anyone that I do not love or want.
I know...But you sent me to be in this world where being a child is a bad thing to be...It is a bad thing to be because nobody wants you....And you can't get away.
I will show you my little one that to be a child is a good thing and that you can be loved and cherished for who you are. Even as a child my little one. Will you let me show you?
How are you going to do that Jesus?...crying.....
I am going to take you to a place where you will be loved and accepted as the child you are. Where you will be encouraged to grow and to explore, where all the needs that you have my little one will be met. Will you follow me my little one and let me show you that being a child in this word does not have to be a painful thing?
You know I will follow you Jesus.
Yes my little one I do.

It was hard for me to understand why Jesus seemed to want me to be in a place where I couldn't be me and where I was so very lonely, but when I looked back and saw how much healing there had been and how different I was it made more sense.

I sometimes think that Jesus promises are like him offering a banquet to a starving person...a banquet that never arrives but he keeps making me look at it. But I see something. If someone is starving you can't just give them a banquet. They couldn't keep it down, it would make them ill. You have to start with very small amount and gradually increase until they are ready for the banquet. And that is what he has been doing with me. He started off small and has been giving me more...so maybe the banquet will come when I am ready. Just like he's been saying all along.

We kept walking down the path towards the city with the water getting deeper and deeper. It wasn't what I had expected at all.

I don't really understand about this river Jesus. It is deep and strong now...how are we meant to be processing in that.
My little one your ideas of what it means to process are not the same as mine.
What does it mean then Jesus?
It means my little one that whilst we are moving forward towards the city we are declaring something. We are declaring who you are my little one and celebrating that but this is also a baptism my little one. We are washing you and filling you, sweeping away the old and replacing it with the new.
Ok so I was reminded when you came into Jerusalem on the donkey. That was your procession wasn't it? That was you coming in openly declaring who you were and the people acknowledging that.
Yes my little one it was.
And it was a declaration and a celebration like this is.
Yes my little one.
And I suppose you were going into the city to fulfil your purpose, kind of like I am.
Yes my little one.
I suppose...if anyone had wondered what that might be like, the King of kings processing into the city...they wouldn't have imagined a donkey and palm leaves and you crying.
No my little one they wouldn't.
But still you processed and declared and celebrated...kind of. Holy spirit can we read it together now...can you show me things?
Yes my little one. Come then......
I am thinking how it was a celebration and a declaration, but maybe it was more than that. You said, if the people didn't praise you the stones would. Kind of like it had to be done. You had to be celebrated and declared. Something was happening in the spirit. Tell me about it.
I was entering the city as who I am my little one. Openly. It had to be so. It was a declaration to the gods of this world that I was coming to take back what belonged to me. They did not see it my little one but I knew what was ahead for me. I knew the victory that was coming. I knew that this was my moment my little one even though there was sadness and great suffering ahead still it was moment of celebration for all of creation was about to be redeemed.
So even the creation itself was celebrating somehow.
Yes my little one.
So you were celebrating the victory even though the cross was waiting for you in the city.
Yes my little one I was. The suffering that was ahead for me did not change the victory my little one it only made it possible.
Kind of like my suffering makes the victory of me entering my city possible. And I suppose it is a victory Jesus because of all you've done and all that you will do.

Yes my little one it is. My dearest one the city is already yours but as you take possession of it, as you enter through its gates there is a victory that is already won. There is more to come my little one but that is a victory worth celebrating.
Yes. And that is...celebrating who I am, because I am entering the city to fulfil the purpose you've given me. Just like you did.
Yes my little one.
And your procession didn't look much like maybe I would have thought ...and you were mostly sad and a bit scared maybe but determined. You weren't jumping up and down and going yay, you accepted who you are and your purpose and you processed celebrating the victory. A different kind of celebrating not like a party.
Yes my little one.
Ok....but I'm being baptized at the same time. Which is a different kind of celebration ...kind of. Celebrating all you've done and will do. Who I am. Maybe not so different I don't know. But it is kind of two in one. Why Jesus?
Because my dearest little one once who you are has been openly declared there will be no going back for you. Your ministry will begin with your baptism just as mine did.
Yes. I suppose it will. At least that's what you keep saying.
Yes my little one it is.
So are we declaring the victory, your victory Jesus. And celebrating that you have saved me and healed me. But also the victories that are ahead the people you will reach through me.
Yes my little one because of who you are and who you are becoming.
Yes. Ok. I see that better. And are you healing me Jesus. I have been feeling ...like an unloved and unwanted child, not so much today but I don't know why.
My little one I am washing away the old and replacing it with the new. That is healing my little one. You are not an unloved or unwanted child. You are my pearl. My beloved one. There is nothing that can change that.
Why have I been feeling so bad?
Because my little one as things are brought to the surface to be washed away by my love you feel them for a time. It does not mean my little one that you are the child you believed yourself to be for so long. That was the lie my little one this is the truth.
Was I right about the blending Jesus? Are you still weaving things in as you heal us.
Yes my little one I am. This process will continue my little one. It does not mean that the blending is not complete only that there are things which need to be healed and until they are they do not become part of your completeness in me.
So... they seem separate to me somehow, but not like alters more like thoughts and feelings that need to be healed...and brought in to be part of the whole.
Yes my little one.

I had been thinking about mum. It seemed like there were lots of different parts of me. Some didn't even like her. Some were afraid. Some are hurting a lot and yet somehow I loved her and forgave her...I saw a rope made of many strands twisted together, but there were stray strands not yet woven in. As Jesus continued to heal me the stray strands were being woven into the whole. He told me that I was being made ready to go into the city, to fulfil the purpose he had for me and reminded me of Ester, and how she was given beauty treatments while she was waiting and that like Ester, there was a perfect time for me.

**And who knows but that you have come
to your royal position
for such a time as this?"
Ester 4:14 NIV**

Chapter 26

To the Gates

I had processed down to the city with Jesus down the path he had made for me. It was all part of my baptism he said and part of the preparation to enter the city. It was right there before me, everything I had been walking towards for so long. All of Jesus promises to me, the new life, the purpose for everything I had been through was right there. But I wasn't going in.

We are here.
Yes my little one we are.
But we aren't going in...crying
No my little one not yet for there is much I have to show to you.
I am trying to be brave.
My little one my dearest little one my path for you is good. It is very good.
Why is this a coming out of hiding and not you are taking me underground, what happened to the procession?
The procession is over my little one now it is time for you to prepare to enter into the city.
I don't understand.
My little one we have processed openly down to the gates of the city declaring and celebrating who you are. My beautiful Pearl Sunshine. Now it is time my little one for you to be made ready to enter into the city. My dearest little one there are many more things for you to see and to understand about what I am calling you to and the city we have given you.
So...but you said we would go through the gates of the city.
Yes my little one we will, openly, celebrating all that you are and all that I have done and will do. That is to come my little one. Now is the time of preparation for that moment.
How does this fit with baptism?
Your baptism will equip you for everything I am calling you to my little one.
So we are going under the city?
Yes my little one we are for the city is built on solid foundations my little one. Foundations upon which everything I am giving you are built. I want you to see and understand and accept them into your heart my little one so that nothing will shake you.
Ok. I don't understand.
I know my little one are you ready?
Do we have to jump?
Yes my little one we do.
Goodbye city and daddy and sunshine and flowers...crying
My little one do you trust me?
Yes...But I don't like your path.
All of it is necessary my little one. All of it is to help you.
Ok.
Ready my little one?
Yes.

So we jumped down what looked like a deep hole in the path. The water dropped down into the cave below. Jesus said he wanted to show me the foundations under the city. To show me what I hadn't really understood. I wasn't very interested. I felt like it was just another reason for the promise not to come, that it would never come. I was very depressed.

My little one this is your city. We have reached the gates my little one but you are not yet ready to enter through them. I want to show you all that we are giving to you. So that you can take hold of it fully and accept the calling we are giving to you. So that when you do enter through the gates you are ready my little one. Ready to be who you were called to be. Ready to be my Pearl in a dark and broken world. Ready to step into the calling that we have for you and accept all that we will give to you so that you can accomplish it. This is my gift to you my little one. I am not snatching anything away.

He led me through the underground cave. The walls glowed with a golden light. It was all very beautiful.

My dearest little one you are my shining light. What do think it means that there is a shining golden light at the foundations of the city I have given you.
I don't know.
It means my little one that the light you have, the light I have given you is the very thing that this city is built upon. The city is built upon the light we have given you my little one. A light that will shine out through all that you do and all that you are.
Like you once said about a light house?
Yes my little one.
You are light Jesus
Yes my little one I am. You have been given much light to carry my little one. The light of our love and our life and our truth. It is here my little one at the very foundations of the city just as it is deep inside you. It is the light that will shine out though you my little one to show others the way.

The underground cave was supported by columns of what looked like rock filled with light. Jesus said that was the amber topaz we had been told about in a word we'd been given a long time ago.

She said she'd got the word 'healing' repeatedly and that she felt it referred both to the healing the Lord was doing in me and the healing the Lord would do through me. She said she'd then seen a stone... a precious stone which was a kind of amber color, but it wasn't amber it was topaz. She said the Lord was chiseling and working on this stone so that it could reveal the light within. She emphasized that the light was coming from deep inside and had nothing to do with the outside.. And that the light was the glory of the Lord. She wasn't sure what the significance of the topaz was, though she felt it was significant, she mentioned that in Revelation topaz is one of the foundation stones of the holy city and also on the breastplate of the priest.

Ok. So the light rock...whatever it is...is in the columns...it is supporting the city.
Yes my little one it is.
I suppose that is the amber topaz...that you told us about before, that is filled with your light...who you are.
Yes my little one That is what the city is built upon. Who I am.
You are the rock.
Yes my little one I am.
What is this silver stuff on the floor Jesus...silver means redemption...doesn't i?
Yes my little one it does. I have redeemed your life my little one. I have bought it back with my sacrifice and now you are mine my little one.
And that is at the foundations.
Yes my little one it is.
Is that about me belonging to you?
Yes my little one it is, but it is also about me restoring what was lost. To give back what was taken and more my little one so much more.
So that it is worth it.
Yes my little one

Oh...there are flowers here. Can I see them?
Yes my little one.
Little golden flowers with pearls at the center...Pearl Sunshine flowers.
Yes my little one. For this is the place where you will flourish and grow. It is my light my little one which gives you life. It is the price I paid for you my little one which makes all of this possible. You are my beautiful pearl sunshine and this is your city and you are my joy my little one.

My little one look around you. What do you see?
It is beautiful Jesus. The ceiling looks like blue crystals.
What do you think that is my little one?
Blue usually means truth Jesus. The city is founded on truth.
Yes my little one it is. The truth of who I am. The truth that I have been giving to you my little one and have placed deep in your heart. You know who I am my little one. I have not failed you. I have not lied to you. I have brought you here so that you can see and understand more of what I am giving to you.

He led me on through the cave under the city until we reached the very center.

We are in a big round I think cave with a high ceiling and in the middle is a column of water that is going straight up through the ceiling. It is very powerful. The ceiling is twinkling like stars in the night sky because of the water and the light from it. The column of water is lit up blue Jesus. And there are pink and green fireflies that are flying around and the flowers on the floor and the silver. It is a magical place Jesus. Tell me about it.
The water is my life my little one flowing into the heart of the city.
Is that the river?
Yes my little one it is. It is given to the city to bring life and healing and hope. It flows from the heart of the city and there is nowhere it is not.
I see...so like the whole city is in the river.
Yes my little one.

Is the fountain the same as the one in my heart Jesus?
Yes my little one it is. This is your city my little one.
Oh, so the fountain in my heart had to be filled so that...it could flow at the heart of the city.
Yes my little one it did.
I don't specially get it Jesus, but I see there is a lot I don't understand about what you have done and what you are doing and why.
Yes my little one I am doing so much more than you know.
Tell me again about the silver stuff Jesus. Why is it like a liquid?
My redemption is not still or static my little one. It is flowing into your life constantly.
So not like truth...the ceiling. That is solid and unmoving. It just is.
Yes my little one That is so.
So your redemption ...the silver stuff is being poured out all the time, that's why there's kind of rivers and puddles of it everywhere.
Yes my little one.
As you claim my life back and make it more than it would have been, like it says in Isaiah.
Yes my little one.
So will this be a lake eventually ...and the flowers are like water lilies.
Yes my little one.
Because you're not done yet
No my little one I'm not done yet.
What is the rock underneath? Is it the promise...like the rocks on the hill.
Yes my little one all of this is founded in the promise I have given you. It is a promise that is sure and certain. Just as I am sure and certain.

Our time under city had come to an end. It brought a lot of things together, things that he had shown me in the past, things he had done and said. It was all very beautiful. I understood. But I was still feeling very depressed.

There was a tent pitched in front of the city. Jesus told me it was a place of rest for me where he could prepare me for entering the city. I wasn't wanting to wait and I didn't understand. I spent time sitting in Jesus lap in his rocking chair. I was tired and sad and needed his comfort. But there were still things he wanted me to see and to learn about the city.

Hi my daddy
I went up in the balloon with the Holy Spirit yesterday and saw the city from above. Jesus said to tell you about it. He says it is like a map. The city is surrounded by a moat and a wall. There are five levels. Each level is surrounded by a wall. They are like circles inside circles. I will draw a picture. The road from the gate goes more or less straight up the hill through each level to the top level which is the refuge where the fountain is and the water overflows and runs down through the whole city and down into the moat and goes down underground and then goes back up again to the fountain like recycling. Each level is a stage in my ministry. The first stage just has people walking. The second has little houses and people in horses and carriages. The third level has bigger buildings and cars. The fourth level has glass skyscrapers and sports cars and buses and then it is the refuge. The buildings are groups of people bigger buildings, bigger groups. And the cars and things are about the speed of the ministry...though I'm not sure what he means by that exactly. Each level builds on the last. I think that was it. I am back in Jesus lap now. That's all my news, bye. love from pearl.

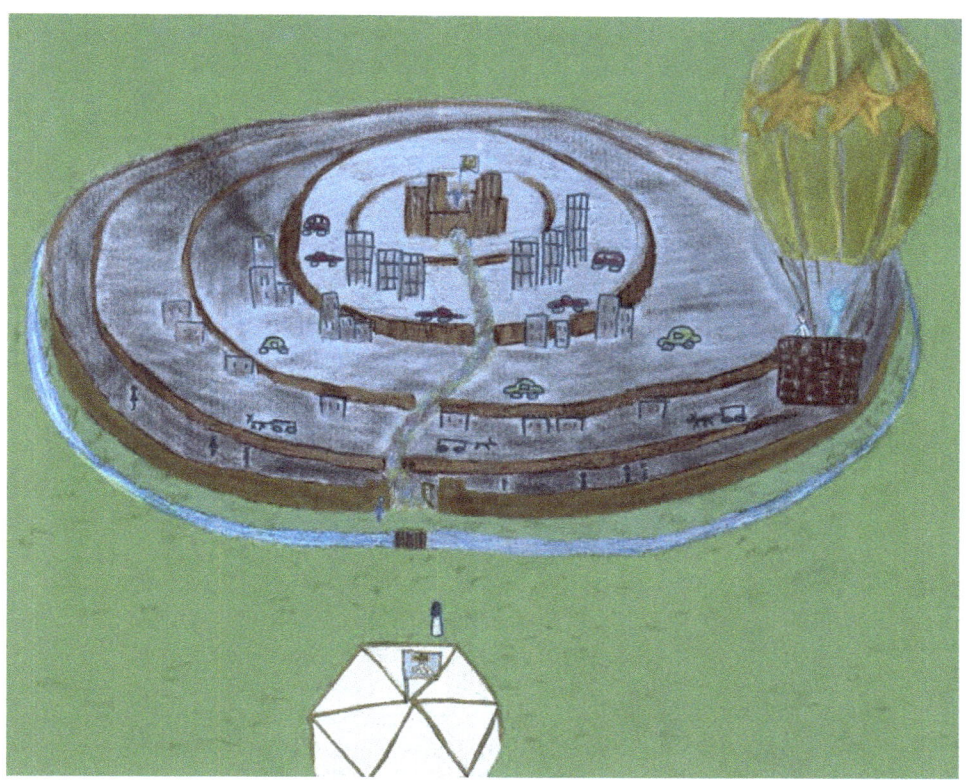

Life on the outside didn't really seem to be getting any better. Both Sophie and Richard were having problems and I didn't feel able to help or to cope. I couldn't see the point of being me when Pearl Sunshine didn't seem to have anything that was needed to live the life I was living. Except Jesus of course. I always had Jesus, I but I wasn't doing very well at trusting daddy mike. I was feeling lonely and abandoned again and didn't send him the letters I wrote a lot of the time. Jesus didn't want me to stop trusting daddy mike of course. I sat on Jesus lap in his rocking chair and he helped me to see better.

My little one tell me what you see.
I see the city with daddy waiting at the gates.
Why do you think he is there my little one?
Cos you put him there.
Why my little one?
Cos he will go into the city with me. Cos we will work together.
Yes my little one you will. Do you think my little one that I would have put him there if he did not care for you, if he were not willing to follow where I lead and to help you in every way I ask him to?
I don't know. You ask people to do a lot of things that they don't do Jesus.
Yes my little one in many ways that is true. There are many people that were in your life that have not loved you and cared for you as I wanted them to, but this is not the same my little one. I have given you to him to love and care for as a father. To walk with you into the city and to help you become all that you can be. He has accepted my call my little one. He is willing. Do not doubt him.
It doesn't matter Jesus if I never get to go.
My little one my dearest little one your time will surely come just as it did for me. I spent many hours talking to my father about when my time would come. He asked me to wait and to trust him my little one and I did so. The enemy of my soul tried to lead me on different paths and to tell me both that the time was now and that it would never come, but I did not listen to him my little one. It was not so different to your

journey. **It was a long preparation my little one which required trust and patience and perseverance, all of which I needed to complete my purpose on this Earth. Just as you do my little one.**
I know it is about trust Jesus. I know I shouldn't listen to the enemy and get depressed.
I know you do my little one.
I'm not sure it's a fight I will ever win Jesus.
I have won it for you my little one. All you must do is hold on to me.
Ok. I will try Jesus. I don't know about the future but I will hold on to you and trust you for today.
Yes my little one. That is good.

My chat with Jesus did help and I started writing to daddy mike again. I had taken some time off work and was feeling less tired and seeing better the things that Jesus was doing and why.

Hi my daddy
I hope you are doing ok. I went back to work yesterday. People seemed pleased to see me and I got a lovely bouquet of flowers for the dumb birthday. That was nice wasn't it. I was thinking today about all the ways that working has helped me. It is a lot I think. It has helped me get more confident in doing things and especially with people. I am meeting new people all the time and having to solve problems and help people and keep calm when people are complaining. I have made friends...sort of...and I've learned lots of things about me and what I am like. Mostly good and sometimes surprising. I feel kind of at home there now, which is a strange thing I think. I can see why Jesus kept telling me to keep going and not to get a new job. It has worked out...I would rather not be there of course, but I can see it has helped me. I have been wondering about something you said. You said you thought we had both got past the point of no return, or something like that. I have been wondering what you meant. I think I could easily turn back cos I don't feel like I've really gone anywhere. Not to do with being Pearl Sunshine anyway. I thought telling mum and Sophie and Richard something about the abuse would have been like a no turning back moment, but I don't think it was cos nothing changed. It's all just the same. I can't decide how I feel about that. I suppose I thought it was a big deal, it felt like a big deal, but really it wasn't. Like it doesn't even matter I suppose. Sometimes I wonder if it would make any difference if I did turn back or give up or whatever. Would anything be different? I'm not sure. I suppose I might not be able to live this life, cos I don't know how to do anything without Jesus helping me, but I'm not sure it would matter really. So I'm not sure what you meant by that. There isn't anything happening really inside or out except for medical stuff...that's outside not inside, so I don't have anything to tell you really just thought I'd say hello. Love from Pearl.

I was still feeling sad about Sophie and Richard and wishing I could make it better for them, but I was understanding something better too.

Hi Jesus
Hello my little one
I am wondering about something Jesus. I don't think it's new. But something is different. Maybe. I am thinking about Sophie and Richard really but it's not just them. I am thinking how we...and now I, take responsibility for other people's choices. Like with Sophie, it would be easy for me to do all the research and say this therapy is the best for you...not easy, but somehow easier than getting her to do it. But...that's not helping her is it? She needs to take responsibility for it. And I think that's what I do...in my thoughts anyway. Like protecting them from the truth about me...it's me taking responsibility for them and I'm not responsible am I. Not like that. Those are my thoughts Jesus. What do you think?
My little one I have given each of my children the responsibility for making their own choices where they are able. Sometimes my little one they are not able. The choice is

taken from them or they may not be capable for many reasons, but my dearest one I have never burdened you with the responsibility for other people's choices. They have their own path to walk my little one. You can help them and guide them in many ways, but you cannot make their choices for them nor are you responsible for the choices that they make.

Yes. I think maybe I see that better. It is still hard sometimes...because I love them and when I see them making bad choices I want to stop them. But maybe...I need to just let them choose Jesus. I can say what I think...but it is their choice. I have been trying to do that with Richard, it's hard cos I know there's things he can't do…maybe. But…I have to let him choose I think. Am I getting better?

Yes my little one you are. You are learning my little one that the choices that others make are not your responsibility and if they make a bad choice it is not your fault.

Yes. Maybe we have thought that it was our fault...that somehow...yes ...bad things and suffering was our fault even when it wasn't our choice.

Yes my little one but that is not so. Many people make choices that do not bring life my little one. That is not your fault. You are only responsible for the choices that you make. You are able to help others to make their own wise and life giving choices my little one but you cannot do it for them.

So I need to get better at helping them to make good choices.

Yes my little one.

Like you do. You help me make good choices but they are always my choice... I see. I think in some ways it takes more courage to do that Jesus. To give advice knowing it can be rejected...and bad choices can be made. And then you have to watch someone you love suffer the consequences...I suppose you do that all the time. That's what this world is...you watch us suffer the consequences of our own bad choices.

Yes my little one I do and I weep over all the suffering that comes but the choice is given my little one. It is my gift and I do not take my gifts away my little one not ever.

Give me the courage I need then Jesus to let them make their own choices even when they are terrible choices. Not that I can stop them, it's just I need to not feel responsible for them. I need your wisdom Jesus.

I know my little one but you have it. Always.

We talked about choice many...many times. Understanding the world, spiritual and physical and why there is so much pain and suffering, why so many people are lost to the darkness is a difficult thing.

My little one your place is in my heart. All of my children belong there but few ever come home to me my little one. Do you know why that is?

No. I don't understand. It seems to me this world is so confusing and difficult that it is a wonder any of us find you.

It is not the world that keeps my children from me my little one but their own hearts. Their hearts which have turned away from me and refuse to see the truth. It is a choice my little one. It is always a choice.

But some don't have a choice Jesus.

No my little one some have their choices taken from them, but I will always help them my little one. They are my children. It is always their choice my little one.

So... people who don't find their place in your heart, that is their choice.

Yes my little one it is. Always.

So I don't understand...if you can make it so ...well I suppose...helping people make their choice for you is why cos sometimes we make such stupid choices. So helping people make the choice for you, that is why you want me to tell my story.

Yes my little one it is.

You said before that most people don't make free choices and don't even know it. If they aren't making free choices Jesus, how can you let that keep them from you.

My little one the choices that people make are dependent on many things. The things that control your choices cannot always be easily seen but I know them all my little one. I see your heart completely and I will always draw you towards the truth. I lead each of my children towards me my little one. I know the path they must take. I am constantly helping them. You are one way I will help them my little one. But in the end it is always their choice. I give them the power and the opportunity to choose me many times my little one no matter what is holding them, just as I did for you. You were held and bound by many lies my little one. It was very hard for you to see the truth or make any kind of free choice and yet you chose me. It is not different for them my little one.

I suppose that is true Jesus. If I can find the truth...you, and my place in your heart then surely anyone can.

And that is the hope you carry my little one. The choice to come home to me can be made by any of my children. You are one of the ways I will help them to make that choice my little one and to keep on making it and in turn to help others make it.

I felt more hopeful than I had before...like there was some purpose to the path I was on. I often lost sight of it or thought it wasn't real, but somehow Jesus always helped me to keep moving forward.

I want to go Jesus. I want to be Pearl Sunshine. I want to tell my story and be who you made me to be. I choose it. I do. No more Jennifer...no more of this. I don't know how else to choose it Jesus. How do I become ready if I'm not?
Come my little one. What do you see?
I see that there is a golden...help me see...bridge over the place where the river goes under the city. So we can cross.
Yes my little one we can. If you are ready.
I am ready I think. Cos I don't know. But what does it mean?
It means my little one that once you cross over with me you have made the choice to enter the city. There will be no turning back. No way for you to return to the life you had before. No way for you to go back to the person that you were before. Everything that I have promised you is before you my little one. Will you cross with me knowing and trusting that everything I have promised is real and true, and that it is time my dearest little one for you to take hold of who you truly are, to let go of the life that you have been living and the person you have been and become all that you were created to be.
How am I suddenly ready Jesus?
Because you have seen and understood my little one that you are not responsible for the choices that others make. You are only responsible for your own. That means that you are able to make your own choice freely my little one. It means that you are ready.
Well, if you say so Jesus. Are we crossing today?
Yes my little one we are.
The angels are blowing a fanfare.
Yes my little one for they understand that you are crossing over from one life to another. It is time my little one to take hold of the promise and all that it means for you. No turning back.
I know...I just need to trust you Jesus.
Yes my little one you do. You are able in everything I give to you to do my little one.
Come on then Jesus.
So we crossed over the little golden bridge that had pearls in the rails..
And I cried...I don't know why.
Why am I crying?
Because my dearest one you have left the old behind and taken hold of the new. Everything that has been has prepared you for this my little one.

My journey had led me to the gates of the city, the city of my promise, the city of Hope. What lay ahead I didn't know but for now I was waiting again. Waiting to enter into the promise that was right before me.

"His divine power has given us everything we need for life
And godliness through our knowledge of him who called
Us by his own glory and goodness. Through these he has
Given us his very great and precious promises..."

2 Peter 1:3-4

www.ingramcontent.com/pod-product-compliance
Lightning Source LLC
Chambersburg PA
CBHW060921170426
43191CB00025B/2451